Latino/a Theology and the Bible

Latino/a Theology and the Bible

Ethnic-Racial Reflections on Interpretation

Edited by

Francisco Lozada, Jr.
and Fernando F. Segovia

LEXINGTON BOOKS/FORTRESS ACADEMIC
Lanham • Boulder • New York • London

Published by Lexington Books/Fortress Academic
Lexington Books is an imprint of The Rowman & Littlefield Publishing Group, Inc.
4501 Forbes Boulevard, Suite 200, Lanham, Maryland 20706
www.rowman.com

6 Tinworth Street, London SE11 5AL, United Kingdom

Copyright © 2021 by The Rowman & Littlefield Publishing Group, Inc.

All rights reserved. No part of this book may be reproduced in any form or by any electronic or mechanical means, including information storage and retrieval systems, without written permission from the publisher, except by a reviewer who may quote passages in a review.

British Library Cataloguing in Publication Information Available

Library of Congress Cataloging-in-Publication Data

Library of Congress Control Number: 2021933226

ISBN 978-1-9787-0549-4 (cloth)
ISBN 978-1-9787-0551-7 (pbk)
ISBN 978-1-9787-0550-0 (electronic)

Contents

Acknowledgments	vii
Latino/a Theology and Studies: A Note	ix
About the Contributors	xi

PART I: INTRODUCTION — 1

1 Approaching the Bible in Latino/a Theology: Doing Theological Construction and Biblical Criticism in an Ethnic-Racial Key — 3
Fernando F. Segovia

PART II: LATINO/A THEOLOGY: APPROACHING THE BIBLE — 27

2 Reading and Hearing Scripture in the Latina/o Pentecostal Community — 29
Sammy Alfaro

3 "She orders all things *suavemente*": A Lascasian Interpretation — 47
Edgardo Colón-Emeric

4 Biblical Silence: Where is the Bible in Latino/a Theology? — 73
Michelle A. Gonzalez Maldonado

5 Is It Truly a "Good" Book? The Bible, Empowerment, and Liberation — 89
Nora O. Lozano

6	Reading against the Grain: Scripture and Constructive Evangélica Theology *Loida I. Martell*	103
7	Darkening the Image: An*other* Allegory of the Beauty of the Shulamite *Elaine Padilla*	127
8	La Guadalupe, The Bible, Pentecost *Nancy Pineda-Madrid*	151
9	Liberation Hermeneutics in Jewish, Christian, and Muslim Exegesis: A Latino/a Perspective *Rubén Rosario Rodríguez*	169
10	Popular Ritual as Liberating Pedagogy *Christopher D. Tirres*	189

PART III: CONCLUSIONS — 207

11	How Do Latino/a Theologians Employ Scripture? *Francisco Lozada, Jr.*	209
12	Approaching Latino/a Theology and the Bible: Doing Cultural Analysis on an Ethnic-Racial Key *Fernando F. Segovia*	235

Names Index — 289

Subjects Index — 295

Acknowledgments

This volume has been made possible due to the assistance and support of a good number of people, to whom we are deeply indebted and most thankful. First and foremost, to all those who took part in the project, for their gracious acceptance of our invitation and fine contributions. Second, to Dr. Neil Elliott, Senior Acquisitions Editor at Lexington Books/Fortress Academic for his full support of this project, and to Jayanthi Chander, Project Manager, for her kind and keen assistance throughout the editorial process. Third, to Ludwig Noya (Research Assistant at Vanderbilt University) and John Kirts (Student Assistant at Brite Divinity School). Finally, to the entire publications staff of Lexington Books for their assistance throughout the process of publication.

Latino/a Theology and Studies: A Note

The term "Latino/a" is the nomenclature most often used in this volume for both the field of studies in general, Latino/a Studies, and the religious-theological movement and discourse, Latino/a Theology. Its use is by no means unproblematic, given the gendered character of the Spanish language, the gender binary created by the use of the slash, and the primacy conferred on the masculine gender by its position before the slash. At the same time, as the conclusion on the juncture between Latino/a Theology and Latino/a Studies will set forth, with reference to the recent volume by Ronald L. Mize, *Latina/o Studies* (Short Introductions; Cambridge, UK–Malden, MA: Polity Press, 2019), no term is ultimately unproblematic. The list of appellations has shifted over the years: from Latino Studies at the beginning; through Latino/a, Latina/o, Latin@; to Latinx more recently—always in search of greater inclusivity in the use of linguistic conventions. The volume has followed the use of Latino/a not because it is viewed as the most correct appellation for the group. It has done so rather because it is the one adopted by the contributors themselves, the one most often used in the field of studies over time, and the one that marks the explosion of this religious-theological movement discourse in the 2000s and 2010s. This is a difficulty that, alas, our minoritized ethnic-racial counterparts in the United States do not face, given the use of English—African, Asian, Native Americans. In conclusion, the title is problematic, but there is no substitute that would not be, not even Latinx. Were the project to be launched at this time, a rigorous discussion on nomenclature would certainly be in order.

About the Contributors

Sammy Alfaro, Associate Professor of Christian Studies, Grand Canyon University, Phoenix, Arizona

Edgardo Colón-Emeric, Irene and William McCutcheon Associate Professor of Reconciliation and Theology, The Divinity School, Duke University, Durham, North Carolina

Michelle A. Gonzalez Maldonado, Dean, College of Arts and Science, and Professor of Theology/Religious Studies, University of Scranton, Scranton, Pennsylvania

Francisco Lozada Jr., Charles Fischer Catholic Associate Professor of New Testament and Latina/o Studies, Brite Divinity School, Fort Worth, Texas

Nora O. Lozano, Associate Professor of Theological Studies and Director of Latina Leadership Institute, Baptist University of the Américas, Houston, Texas

Loida I. Martell, Vice President of Academic Affairs and Dean, Professor of Constructive Theology, Lexington Theological Seminary, Lexington, Kentucky

Elaine Padilla, Associate Professor of Philosophy and Religion, and Latin American/Latinx Studies, University of La Verne, La Verne, California

Nancy Pineda-Madrid, Associate Professor and T. Marie Chilton Chair of Catholic Theology, Loyola Marymount University, Los Angeles, California

Rubén Rosario Rodríguez, Professor of Systematic Theology and Director of the Mev Puleo Scholarship Program, St. Louis University, St. Louis, Missouri

Fernando F. Segovia, Oberlin Graduate Professor of New Testament and Early Christianity, School of Divinity, Vanderbilt University, Nashville, Tennessee

Christopher D. Tirres, Associate Professor of Religious Studies and Grace School of Applied Diplomacy, De Paul University, Chicago, Illinois

Part I

INTRODUCTION

Chapter 1

Approaching the Bible in Latino/a Theology

Doing Theological Construction and Biblical Criticism in an Ethnic-Racial Key

Fernando F. Segovia

Any analysis of the relationship between biblical texts and theological visions—or, to put it otherwise, the views and uses of the Bible at work in the field of theological studies—constitutes an exercise in interpretation. This it does, moreover, at various levels of critical inquiry. Three such angles of vision come readily to the fore: the trajectory of biblical criticism, the tradition of theological construction, and the realm of cultural analysis. In effect, any such analysis represents, at once, an exercise in biblical hermeneutics, an exercise in theological reflection, and an exercise in cultural expression. Any such analysis may thus be examined from any one of these critical perspectives. Given its focus on Latino/a Theology as an area of studies within theological studies and on the ways in which this movement and discourse invoke and deploy the writings of Scripture, the present project on the conjunction between Latino/a Theology and the Bible constitutes a variation on such an exercise.

What is the nature of this variation? As the title for the area of studies indicates, Latino/a Theology, this is a project that is motivated, shaped, and guided by the problematic of ethnic-racial identity in interpretation. As such, this ethnic-racial dimension is active in, and may be examined from, all three levels of inquiry—the biblical, the theological, and the cultural. I should like here to show how this project does so in all three angles of vision. This task I shall undertake by tracing the path of the academic-scholarly discussion in each perspective and situating the project within such a mapping. I shall do so in two steps. In this introductory essay, I address the first two levels of inquiry, biblical criticism and theological construction, while taking up the third level of cultural analysis in the concluding essay. I opt for this division on two grounds.

The first reason is pragmatic in nature: the division is warranted by the question of length. A proper mapping of cultural analysis, to be undertaken by way of Latino/a studies, demands considerably more exposition and is thus best pursued on its own terms. This is especially the case because, by and large, the project of Latino/a Theology has not been in close and sustained critical dialogue with the field of Latino/a studies. The second reason is academic in character: the division is warranted in terms of affinity. The relation of the project to the religious-theological fields of biblical studies and theological studies, within the realm of Christian studies, is quite pointed and explicit, whereas its relation to Latino/a studies within cultural studies is more subtle and implicit. A preliminary word on these two levels of inquiry is in order.

To begin with, the project represents an exercise within the field of biblical studies. Contemporary biblical criticism may be construed as encompassing a variety of grand models of interpretation, among which lies the religious-theological paradigm. It is within this model that this project should be situated. All participants reflect on the biblical texts—in one way or another, to one extent or another—in terms of their relevance for and impact upon their work of theologizing. This they do, moreover, in response to an invitation extended by biblical critics who have themselves appropriated, problematized, and pursued the question of identity in their work—both ethnic-racial, as Latino/a American critics in the United States, and spatial-geographical, as Latin American critics in the diaspora. The invitation for such reflection on the Bible constitutes, therefore, an expansion of their own similar and ongoing reflection as biblical critics.

In addition, the study signifies an exercise in the field of theological studies. Contemporary theological construction may be approached as involving a variety of movements and formations, overall orientations and grand models of inquiry, among which stands the political turn and its set of global formations, which includes minoritized ethnic-racial theological traditions. It is within this turn in general and this set in particular that the present project should be located. All participants would define themselves, and would be so perceived from the outside, as—in one way or another, to one extent or another—theologians rather than critics, by training, profession, and orientation. All would further regard themselves, and would be so viewed from the outside as well, as belonging—in one way or another, to one extent or another—to a set within this field studies configured by racial-ethnic identity and thus as Latino/a theologians. It was in the light of such personal self-understanding and external recognition that the invitation to ponder on the relevance and reach of the Bible in their task of theologizing was issued.

In what follows, I shall expand on these two angles of vision, advancing a critical overview of such lines of inquiry and situating the project within each critical mapping. I shall address, first of all, the trajectory of biblical criticism, highlighting the model of religious-theological criticism. I shall then turn to the tradition of theological construction, foregrounding the movement of political engagement. Subsequently, I shall proceed to show how the project fits within each framework: on the one hand, within religious-theological criticism, as an example of the reception of the Bible in other fields of Christian studies, specifically that of theological studies; on the other hand, within the political orientation, as an example of a global ethnic-racial formation. I shall conclude with a word about the future of this type of undertaking.

THE TRAJECTORY OF BIBLICAL STUDIES

For many years now, since my initial formulation of such a proposal in 1992, I have argued for a number of grand models of interpretation at work in biblical criticism, from the final quarter of the twentieth century into the first decades of the twenty-first century.[1] This proposal, I should clarify, has always been advanced from within the ambit of the field of studies; as such, the models represent academic-intellectual frameworks or discourses for approaching the interpretation of biblical texts. Over the course of time, as my thinking on the matter has progressed and matured, the number of umbrella models in question has witnessed an increase: from an original set of four; through expansion, first to five and then to six; to a present vision of seven such paradigms, which I outlined in my presidential address to the Society of Biblical Literature in 2014.[2] Synchronically, I would identify these as follows: historical criticism; literary criticism; sociocultural criticism; ideological criticism; religious-theological criticism; social-cultural criticism, and global-systemic criticism. Diachronically, I would highlight certain key features marking the development of this multipolar configuration: a swift, prolific, and consequential process of formation.

First, in terms of pace, this development has taken place in a remarkably brief period of time: a span of four decades in all, from the mid-1970s to the mid-2010s. For this demarcation, I take a point of departure and a point of stock-taking that are both highly symbolic. For the former, I have in mind the launching of the journal *Semeia* by the Society of Biblical Literature in 1974, which was introduced as an "experimental" journal in contradistinction to the established ways of the *Journal of Biblical Literature*. For the latter, I opt for my presidential address to the Society in 2014, for it is here that I first advanced the need for a global-systemic paradigm of interpretation. Second, in terms of production, this development has also proved remarkably fertile:

from one to seven umbrella models in the course of these four decades. Prior to 1974, there was but a single paradigm, historical criticism, in place since the first half of the nineteenth century; by 2014, six other paradigms beside the historical had emerged, actual or proposed. Third, in terms of effects, this development has had weighty ramifications: a remarkable shift in the conceptualization and exercise of biblical criticism, from a traditional "discipline" to a convoluted "field of studies." This change has entailed a move away from a relative sense of unity—fairly distinct object of study, fairly unified mode of analysis, fairly coherent body of knowledge or trajectory of scholarship, and fairly stable set of objectives—toward a marked sense of diversity in all respects.

In times past, I have outlined in detail the historical trajectory of this development in both discursive and materialist terms: laying out the dynamics and mechanics of theoretical frameworks and methodological approaches as well as the turns and twists in scholarly demographics in the Global North and scholarly involvement from the Global South. For my purposes here, I limit myself to various features of this process that I view as relevant for a proper situating of this study. The first such feature has to do with the realm of the texts—a significant broadening of the object of study. The second involves the context of the academy—a marked rise in interdisciplinary work. The third feature deals with the realm of readers—a sharp awakening in concientization regarding the context and agenda of interpretation.

First, then, a move can be detected from sole consideration of the production of texts (composition; interaction; target) toward incorporation of their reception (interpretation; evaluation; interchange). Thus, the first three paradigms—historical criticism along with literary and sociocultural criticisms—focus intensely on analysis of the texts in the context of antiquity. When attention is given to reception, it is along the lines of the concept of original audience (what I have designated as "target" above) and/or the element of the state of the question (recovery of meaning and history). By way of contrast, the remaining paradigms—from ideological criticism, through social-cultural and religious-theological criticisms, to global-systemic criticism—allow for, if not prioritize, the analysis of reception, in principle throughout but primarily in the worlds of modernity and postmodernity.

Second, an impulse can also be traced toward ever greater critical engagement with other fields of study in the world of the academy. Thus, from the initial interaction with historical studies in historical criticism, a turn toward literary studies and social studies takes place in literary criticism and sociocultural criticism, respectively. Then, as ideological criticism appears on the scene, the question of unequal formations and relations of power along the various axes of human identity demands engagement with the corresponding fields of study in question: gender and economics; sexuality and race-ethnicity; geopolitics; disability; and climate. Subsequently, as the dimension of reception in the social-cultural and religious-theological realms at large beckons, dialogue with cultural studies, on the one hand, and religious/theological studies, on the other, emerges as imperative. Lastly, the appeal to texts and interpretations as resources in addressing the global crises in the world and the crisis of the world-system demands conversation with such fields as climate studies and migration studies, alongside global studies.

Third, a turn toward ever greater awareness regarding the agency of the interpreter in interpretation can be discerned as well. The first three paradigms—historical criticism, largely followed by literary and sociocultural criticisms—place great emphasis on objectivity, on reconstruction, on analyzing the reality and experience of the ancient world as conveyed by the texts. With the advent of ideological criticism, the role of the interpreter as agent in the representation of antiquity, whether textual meaning or contextual framework, plays an ever more prominent role. Great emphasis now begins to be placed, therefore, on subjectivity and construction instead. In the process, a further development takes place: just as the world of antiquity is viewed as crisscrossed by the dynamics and mechanics of differential power along the lines of identity, so are the world of modernity and postmodernity. Consequently, any study of interpretation is perforce regarded as irretrievably contextual and perspectival, as is the case with the remaining three paradigms.

Assessing the State of Affairs

The proposed configuration of biblical criticism in terms of a variety of grand models of interpretation might come across, at first sight, as utterly atomized, tightly disciplined, and intensely separatist. Such might indeed be the case in some quarters; however, it need not be the case at all. The different umbrella models, while distinctive and competitive, need not be seen as mutually exclusive, not altogether so anyway. A different vision of this state of affairs is possible. Three observations are helpful here.

To begin with, the models are by no means monolithic. They encompass, rather, a variety of approaches within their respective boundaries. Certain features in common allow these approaches to be brought together under the same formation, but each approach also possesses its own theoretical orientation and methodological repertoire. Within the grand models, therefore, one finds much fluidity. Second, the models present no strict walls of separation. They reveal, instead, borders that are porous and transgressible, making it possible for movement across and interaction with other models. Consequently, there is much fluidity also among and between the grand models. Third, the fields of studies with which the models have entered into critical dialogue are certainly not immutable. They have all undergone, rather, not dissimilar processes of transformation during this same period of time, emerging in the process as quite diverse, quite porous, and quite intersectional as well. There is much fluidity as well, therefore, in other fields of study across the academic-intellectual spectrum.

Thus, instead of envisioning the multipolar configuration of the field as atomized, disciplined, and separatist, it would be more appropriate to see it as decidedly complex, highly open-ended, and thoroughly interrelated. The conclusion is clear: in any task of interpretation, a high degree of sophistication and a sharp measure of clarity are of the essence.

Religious-Theological Mode of Interpretation

In light of this mapping of the field, the question of the religious-theological dimension in interpretation can be more securely addressed and this volume itself more pointedly situated. Toward this end, the exposition stands in need of greater precision, for there are various lines of inquiry that must be surfaced and differentiated, all of which are in need of sustained pursuit. These would be as follows: the underlying religious-theological frameworks of biblical critics; the role of the Bible in ecclesial formations; the approach to the Bible in religious studies; and the approach to the Bible in Christian studies. In the first line of inquiry, the question leads to a further variation within a paradigm, ideological criticism. In the other three lines, the question turns into a paradigm in its own right, religious-theological criticism. Its focus is on the reception of the biblical texts in religious-theological circles. Three concentrations come to the fore, depending on the various contexts of reception: the realm of ecclesial institutions and formations; the field of religious studies; and the field of Christian studies.

Biblical Criticism

For the first line of inquiry, the task would be to examine the differential relations of power revolving around the axis of religious-theological identity, alongside all other axes of identity, such as gender and geopolitics, and thus involving analysis of dominant and subordinate positions and agendas. Such analysis applies in principle to the texts and contexts of antiquity as well as the interpreters and interpretations of modernity and postmodernity. However, the emphasis would lie not so much on the former aspect, since matters of religious-theological discussions and conflicts have been examined throughout the trajectory of the field. It would fall, rather, on the latter aspect, an area of study that has remained, even in the context of ideological criticism, largely unexplored. The main reason for such silence is, to my mind, a result of the deep-rooted tradition of objectivity and impartiality that dates back to the scientific ideal of criticism developed in the pre-1970s period—a stance formulated in reaction to ecclesial control of interpretation of the Bible. The pursuit of this task would entail, consequently, critical analysis of the religious-theological visions, implicit or explicit, operative among biblical critics.

The Ecclesial Realm

In the second line of inquiry, a first concentration within the religious-theological paradigm, attention would center on the interpretation of the Bible on the part of ecclesial formations, institutional or popular. In the case of institutional bodies, the concern would be with the use of the Bible in declarations issued by the various ecclesial communities that make up the world of Christianity. Most pointedly, this would apply to official pronouncements on the ways and means of interpreting the Scriptures, and the trajectory of such pronouncements. It would apply, however, to statements of any sort having to do with matters of church life, belief as well as behavior, in which the Bible is invoked. In the case of popular groupings, the concern would take up the use of the Bible by the church at large in movements and endeavors, large or small, beyond the pale of the institution. The pursuit of this task would involve, therefore, critical analysis of the readings of the Bible advanced in such circles.

Religious Studies

In the third line of inquiry, the second orientation within the religious-theological paradigm, attention would concentrate on the field of religious studies. Two possibilities come to mind. On the one hand, a view of the Bible as a set of holy scriptures, one among various such sets to be found in the religions of the world—a document providing insight into the dynamics and mechanics of religion from an interreligious perspective. On the other hand, a view of the Bible as a work of human literature, one among many such works forthcoming from the religions of the world—a document offering insight into the ways and means of life from a humanist perspective. Both approaches would share a sense of formal distance from any acceptance of or adherence to Christianity as a religious-theological tradition—or, for that matter, any other such tradition. The pursuit of this task would demand critical analysis of how the Bible fares in such interreligious or humanist undertakings.

Christian Studies

For the final line of inquiry, the third orientation within the religious-theological paradigm, attention would be directed at the field of Christian studies. Traditionally, this field has encompassed a number of areas of study, all of which possess extensive and complex scholarly trajectories of their own.

The number of such subfields vary, depending on the ecclesial formation in question and its particular view of Christian studies and its order of studies. Whatever the case, these areas of study are regarded as related to one another in one way or the other, again depending how the particular conceptualization of Christian studies at play. A basic such set might include, for example, the following divisions: biblical studies, historical studies, theological studies, ethical studies, practical studies, liturgical studies. The pursuit of this task would call for critical analysis of the appeal to and use of the Bible in the subfields outside biblical studies.

THE TRADITION OF THEOLOGICAL STUDIES

In his magisterial panoramic view of Christian theological studies through the course of the twentieth century, a work published in 1992,[3] Rosino Gibellini describes the overall path of Christian thought as a discourse—clear, rigorous, responsible—"in honor of God."[4] Such a discourse, he points out, unfolds within the decidedly secular context of the century, and hence in the face of challenges and attacks from the realm of scientific thought. This is a framework, therefore, in which this distinguishing phrase, along with the underlying disposition and driving objective that underlie it, has lost not only all credibility but also all respectability. As the century transpires, this discourse, he notes, increasingly takes on the task—in line with the most shining moments of the Christian tradition—of defending and favoring what is human, the "Humanum." In so doing, Gibellini explains, drawing on the words of Johann Baptist Metz, theological discourse retrieves the "memory of God . . . from the biblical-Christian tradition," a recalling that allows it to speak on matters of "humanity and solidarity, oppression and liberation" and to protest against the presence of "injustice that cries to high heaven."[5] At the time of writing, then, theological discourse, he notes, finds itself in the process of rediscovery as legitimate and necessary within the highly complex context of the end-of-the-century world. This is a framework, consequently, in which its credibility and respectability find themselves on the ascendancy.

This view of the history of Christian thought in the twentieth century, it should be noted, is distinctly global in scope, extending well beyond the usual Western confines of the discourse. Such range should not be at all surprising, given the interest of Gibellini on theological developments outside the West throughout his entire life and career.[6] Indeed, it should further be noted in this regard, that the work is (partly) dedicated, "in a spirit of communion and solidarity," to the members of the Ecumenical Association of Third World Theologians (EATWOT), an organization founded in 1976 with the aim of bringing together voices from throughout the Third World of yesteryear

(Africa, Asia, and Latin America) as well as from minoritized groups in the First World.[7] Such voices are prominently represented and analyzed toward the end of the proposed trajectory and hence during the last four decades of the century.

This trajectory is drawn in terms of a series of four major movements, encompassing among them a total of sixteen formations in all.[8] While the movements refer to the primary object of inquiry, the main orientation of the theological task, the formations stand for the leading lines of approach, the grand models of theological inquiry. They are all presented, Gibellini explains, as perspectives "on the incommensurate and co-enveloping object (Barth) of Mystery and Revelation (the proper theme of theology) in the experiential, social, and cultural context within which the theological reflection of our century is successively articulated."[9] They are also as viewed as logically connected as well as sequential. The overall flow reflects the intensifying concern for and commitment to humanity on the part of theological discourse through the century: from the realm of God; through the world of human beings and the reality of political contexts; to the realm of the church. This flow is worth unpacking in detail.

First, the century begins with a focus on the Word of God, what has traditionally been considered as the proper object of theology. It starts with the emergence of Dialectical Theology, which is said to find a formal parallel in other areas of thought, and leads directly to the Theology of the Word, with reference to Karl Barth. In this first phase of the trajectory, Gibellini argues, theological discourse keeps its eyes fixed on the realm of God, the mystery and revelation of God, in sharp contradistinction and reaction to the ways and means of Liberal Theology. Although two theological lines of approach are mentioned, both are placed within the same formation and hence receive one and the same designation, Dialectical Theology (formation #1).

Second, the century witnesses an anthropological turn, with attention to the historicity of the subject. Here four formations are mentioned, three in Protestant theology and one in Catholic theology. The former include: the Existential Theology of Rudolf Bultmann (formation #2); the Hermeneutical Theology of Gerhard Ebeling and Ernst Fuchs (formation #3); and the Theology of Culture of Paul Tillich (formation #4). The latter is the Transcendental Theology of Karl Rahner (formation #7, actually designated as "The Way of Catholic Theology from the Modernist Controversy to the Anthropological Turn"). In this second phase, Gibellini addresses the turn in Protestant Theology by way of Bultmann as point of departure and the turn in Catholic Theology by way of Rahner as point of arrival. With Bultmann, on the one hand, theology is said to take up the hearer of the Word and its historicity: existential questions; cultural contexts of expression; *a priori* structures of spirit-in-the-world. With Rahner, on the other hand, theology is said to undergo the anthropological turn on the shoulders of the *Nouvelle Théologie* and its move away from the stranglehold of scholasticism, toward the novel methods of historical criticism and dialogue with culture and philosophy.

Third, the century reveals, with the advent of the 1960s, a deepening or sharpening of the anthropological turn, with a turn to political consciousness. A threefold historical distinction is introduced; these stages one may characterize as preparation, outbreak, and expansion. Ten formations in all are mentioned.

- To begin with, three formations are viewed as setting the stage for the emergence of the political: the Theology of History (formation #8), represented by Oscar Cullmann and Wolfgang Pannenberg; the debate regarding Theology and Modernity (formation #5), signified by Dietrich Bonhoeffer; and the Theology of Secularization (formation #6), symbolized by Friedrich Gogarten.
- Then, two formations are identified—actually three—as embodying the flowering of the political, by way of Europe: the Theology of Hope (formation #9) and Political Theology (formation #10), represented by Jürgen Moltmann and Johann Baptist Metz, respectively. Here too, it would appear, another formation is to be placed, although it is not highlighted as such: the Theology of Experience (formation #11), with reference to Edward Schillebeeckx.
- Lastly, a variety of formations are presented as taking the political beyond Europe, to the world at large: Liberation Theology (formation #12), followed by a set of variations—Black Theology (formation #13), Feminist Theology (formation #14), and Third World Theology (formation #15).

In this third phase, Gibellini points out, theological discourse undergoes a fundamental shift in its description of faith: no longer by way of intellectual, existential, and individual categories; now rather in terms of praxis in history and society.

Fourth, the century concludes with an ecclesial turn, with attention to the church and its transformation into a global reality, given the expansion of political consciousness throughout the world. It is marked by the rise of Ecumenical Theology, which then leads to the Theology of Religions, both with Hans Küng as primary agent. In this fourth phase of the trajectory, Gibellini argues, theological discourse veers toward a Christian church that has become planetary, not only ecumenical, moving away from confessionalism, but also polycentric, moving beyond its Western heritage. Here too, as at the beginning of the century, two theological lines of approach are mentioned, but both are brought under the same designation and assigned to the same formation, Ecumenical Theology (formation #16).

In this remarkable overview of the trajectory, described as an "arduous path along the course of a dramatic century,"[10] Gibellini identifies the decade of the 1960s as the most creative period of the century, theologically as well as ecclesially—in effect, the beginning of the third movement, with its impulse toward consciousness and analysis of the political in the task of theologizing. Beyond its initial stirrings in Europe, this move toward praxis in society and culture reaches into ever-broader circles and regions: starting in Latin America and among African Americans in the United States, subsequently extending into Africa and Asia, and accompanied throughout by Feminist Theology. Out of such planetary migrations comes an ever-greater sense of a church global—spread throughout a multitude of cultures and standing alongside a multitude of religions.

On this path from Dialectical Theology to Planetary Theology, through the shift brought about by historicity and the revolution wrought by the political, Gibellini casts a theological reading as well. What theological discourse has done through the course of the twentieth century, assuming as it does in ever greater fashion the defense and promulgation of what is human, has been, no more and no less, than to demonstrate the "logic of the Incarnation and the Redemption."[11]

LATINO/A THEOLOGY AND THE BIBLE: SITUATING THE PROJECT

The Trajectory of Biblical Criticism

The mapping of biblical criticism through the twentieth century into present times has identified a critical spectrum of seven grand models of interpretation in the field in place at this point, among which lies that of religious-theological criticism. Within this paradigm, a series of four lines of inquiry were delineated, depending on the context within which such interpretation was carried out. In the light of this mapping, the present project on the invocation and deployment of the Bible in Latino/a Theology can be more properly situated and described.

This project belongs not in the first option—the participants are not approaching the Bible in the role of professional biblical critics, shaped and guided by the trajectory of biblical criticism. It does not belong either in the second option—they are not speaking with regard to the Bible as official representatives of ecclesial institutions or as spokespersons for popular movements or circles of reading. It also does not belong in the third option—they do not present themselves or function as practitioners in the realm of religious studies, whether in its interreligious or humanist varieties. The project belongs, rather, in the fourth option—the participants speak as constructive theologians in the realm of Christian studies. They hail from different branches of this tradition, and they are at work in articulating, in conscious and creative fashion, a theological vision of their own. It is in such capacity and from such a point of view that they address the significance and impact of the Bible upon their work.

In sum, the project signifies an exercise in biblical criticism in which the reception of the Bible in the area of theological studies, within the field of Christian studies, is analyzed. Such an exercise can be carried out with any set of voices and faces as well as from any number of ideological perspectives and agendas. In the present project, both components are circumscribed by the focus on ethnic-racial identity, in general, and Latino/a American identity, in particular. The interest lies, therefore, in ascertaining the status and role of the Bible in Latino/a Theology as the production of a minoritized formation, both religious-theological and social-cultural, within the U.S. scene.

As such, a driving interest of the project is on foregrounding what has been and continues to be erased or marginalized in the religious-theological circles of the dominant society and culture. Such foregrounding should lead to expansion as well as comparison. For this purpose, then, a set of faces and voices from the group in question is activated, coming from different traditions and displaying different visions in theologizing. The task was posed in various ways: as a historical exercise, in which the use of the Bible in the tradition of Latino/a Theology is analyzed; as a constructive exercise, whereby the use of the Bible in their own theological endeavors is examined, whether as a given or as an ideal; and/or as a comparative exercise, in which the use of the Bible in Latino/a Theology is compared with such usage among other marginalized traditions, whether in the United States or in the Global South.

The Tradition of Theological Studies

The mapping of theological construction through the twentieth century has presented a critical spectrum of sixteen grand models or formations of reflection, reflecting in turn a fourfold shift of orientation, among which lies, within the third shift toward the political, a set of four formations comprising the global expression of such a turn. Within this set, one ethnic-racial formation is traced, Black theology, forged in the United States. Following this mapping, the present project on the appeal to and use of the Bible in Latino/a Theology can be appropriately placed and explained. Latino/a Theology would constitute, in effect, a further example of ethnic-racial theological reflection emerging in the United States, and hence another formation that would have to be incorporated into this third set within the global political turn. In fact, it is not the only addition in order. This set stands in need of significant reconfiguration, not only in terms of minoritized formations within the United States but also on account of minoritized formations throughout the world.

Gibellini himself makes no reference to the Latino/a theological movement and discourse in his account of the spread of political consciousness in theological thought throughout the world, in regions that had remained theologically voiceless and among groups that had not functioned as theological subjects in their own right. What he calls Black Theology is amply highlighted and pursued, but the faces and voices of other minoritized formations in the United States are not, including those that make up the complex experience and reality of Latino/a Americans, the Latin American diaspora and presence in the country. This omission is largely understandable, if one takes into account the publication of the volume in 1992. At the time, Latino/a Theology was still very much in its period of formation. Indeed, the previous year, in what would be my first engagement with this movement, I authored a review essay for *Religious Studies Review* in which I set forth the contours of this nascent movement, encompassing a total of eight volumes by seven authors in all.[12]

I say "largely" understandable, however, because the movement can actually be traced back to 1983, the date of publication for the first volume in question, and because by 1990, the date of publication for the last one, all volumes reviewed had already seen the light of day. Thus, from my perspective then, this initial stage of the movement had begun with Virgilio Elizondo's *Galilean Journey: The Mexican American Promise* (1983) and closed with Justo L. González's *Mañana: Christian Theology from An Hispanic Perspective* (1990).[13] These first contributions came from a variety of national and ecclesial backgrounds; they also represented a number of different areas and approaches in Christian Studies. All had Liberation Theology—as forged in Latin America since the late 1960s and the early 1970s and thus for about fifteen to twenty years by then—as their social matrix, cultural horizon, and intellectual élan.

Recalling Liberation Hermeneutics. As such, the place and role of the Bible within the movement of Liberation are worth recalling. To be sure, the Bible was always central to the movement, indeed pivotal. Yet, a distinction is necessary: its use in the theological circles of liberation preceded its analysis in the critical circles of liberation. Thus, if one thinks of the emergence of liberation in terms of a foundational series of events taking place over a number of years, as I do, one can see that the formulation of a hermeneutical approach from the realm of biblical criticism begins to take place only at the end of such a process of formation, after various, reinforcing, efforts had already been taken toward the development and solidification of a constructive approach from the realm of theological thought. Such a process of emergence I see as a septennium, extending from the year 1967 through the year 1973.

The process began with the issuance of "A Letter to the Peoples of the Third World" in 1967.[14] This was a document drafted by a group of bishops from the Third World, eighteen in all, addressing the question of poverty in the undeveloped world. In this open letter, the bishops presented poverty as the result of exploitation by the developed nations and called for a world of dignity and justice in keeping with the mandate of the Bible and the Gospels. The process would end with the publication of the volume *Liberación y libertad: Pautas hermenéuticas* by José Severino Croatto in 1973.[15] This was the first attempt by a biblical scholar to formulate an approach to interpretation from the materialist perspective of the poor and the oppressed. In this work, Croatto's express goal was to supplement the theological project already underway, with which he was fully acquainted, by providing a proper hermeneutical support that he obviously viewed as both lacking and imperative.[16]

The developing theological approach was quite ambitious: a critical overview of present realities, past frameworks, and future possibilities. Toward this end, a threefold critical mediation was posited, with a focus on poverty and oppression throughout. Such reflections encompassed: (1) a critical analysis of society and culture, examining the dimensions of and reasons for poverty and oppression in the world—borrowing methods from the social sciences; (2) a critical analysis of the biblical texts and the ecclesial traditions, with emphasis on the testimony of Scripture, searching for the views on poverty and oppression in the Christian tradition—calling upon the established tools of scientific historical criticism; and (3) a critical analysis of goals and strategies with transformation in mind, devising a program of action and a set of strategies designed to change the given conditions of poverty and oppression—drawing on models from practical experience and social theory.

In this critical overview, the second mediation emerges as key. On the one hand, the Bible is viewed as constituting the criterion for the evaluation of the social-cultural context, *as analyzed*. On the other hand, the Bible is seen as offering the blueprint for the transformation of this social-cultural context, *as analyzed*. Thus, the role of the Bible in the movement, as stated above, is pivotal. What the hermeneutical approach would set out to do in time, beginning with this early contribution of Croatto, was to fashion a solid and sophisticated foundation, theoretical as well as methodological, for the envisioned materialist analysis of the biblical texts and the ecclesial traditions. Such a foundation Croatto himself would develop by way of structuralism and semiotics in the field of literary criticism.

Latino/a Theology and Liberation. It is this theological-critical tradition of Liberation that had been in existence for some time already under which Latino/a Theology begins to be forged and to which it is deeply indebted.

When Elizondo wrote *A Galilean Journey* in 1983, seventeen years had elapsed since the start of the septennium in 1967, marked by the open letter of bishops from the Third World, and ten years since its close, signified by the hermeneutical endeavor of Croatto. As such, the early exponents of Latino/a Theology wrote in a liberationist key, adopting the movement and project of liberation as reference and framework. In so doing, they also appropriated the central role assigned to the Bible in liberation, placing it at the heart of their own theological projects, while attending to its status and role within such constructions. At the foundations of Latino/a theological discourse, therefore, the interpretation of the Bible was not only present but also decisive.

In the formative stage of Latino/a Theology, furthermore, the same discursive sequence identified at work in Latin America can be observed: the constructive use of the Bible in theological circles, broadly writ, precedes the hermeneutical analysis of the Bible in critical circles. Such appeal to and deployment of the biblical texts I examined in another early study of mine, where I traced the use of the Bible at the beginning of the movement through the works of four major figures: Ada María Isasi Díaz and Mujerista Theology; Harold Recinos and Barrio Theology; Virgilio Elizondo and Mestijaze Theology; and Justo L. González and Mañana Theology.[17] In all instances, I argued, the Bible emerged—with a variety of nuances, ranging from unquestioned acceptance to critical evaluation—as an "effective weapon" and "faithful ally" in the struggles of the Latin American diaspora in the United States. It was a weapon "in the struggle against marginalization and discrimination" and an ally "in the struggle for liberation."[18] It would not be until a couple of years later, in 1995, that the first hermeneutical contribution from biblical criticism would be advanced, and that came from my own pen and as a result of my interest in contextual criticism.[19]

Project on Latino/a Theology and the Bible. The present volume, therefore, represents a return to and resumption of that early stage in Latino/a Theology, when the movement pursues the problematic of a constructive approach to the Bible in the realm of theological studies, again broadly defined. It is a way of gauging what has happened since then with regard to the status and role of the Bible in the theological circles of Latino/a Theology. Regrettably, to the best of my knowledge, no such inquiry has been conducted. By way of contrast, what has happened in the critical circles of Latino/a Theology has been, and continues to be, explored in thorough and sustained fashion.[20] Thus, while the impact of the transformation of biblical criticism on ethnic-racial criticism, in general, and Latino/a criticism, in particular, can be readily observed, it is impossible to say how such developments have fared in Latino/a religious-theological studies. The present volume is meant to begin to fill a gap in this regard.

A CONCLUDING WORD: LOOKING AHEAD

In this study, I have explored the background for and position of this project on the views and uses of the Bible in Latino/a Theology from the perspective of two fields of study that form part of this movement and discourse, biblical criticism and theological construction. In so doing, I have highlighted the ethnic-racial focus that lies at the core of this exercise in interpretation, as the product of a minoritized ethnic group in the United States. In both fields of studies, I have set forth the rationale for the emergence of such a focus as well as its significance. This is a development that, as I shall describe in the piece on cultural analysis, can be traced to the ethnic-racial awakening that came to the fore, in the country and throughout the world, in the decades of the 1960s and 1970s. Such conscientization had a profound effect across the entire disciplinary spectrum of the academic-scholarly world. Christian studies was no exception. The repercussions of this racial-ethnic heightening were felt across its full range of constitutive fields, including biblical studies and theological studies. Now, by way of conclusion, I should like to offer various reflections on the path marked by this project with the future in mind.

I do so first from the perspective of biblical criticism. Two comments are worth making with regard to the grand model of religious-theological interpretation, and here I leave aside, as not directly relevant, two of its applications as outlined above, the use of the Bible in ecclesial communities and in religious studies. First, it is fair to say that biblical scholars have not addressed, by and large, the problematic of religious-theological frameworks in the execution of this task. This focus would involve two areas of concern. One has to do with the religious-theological beliefs and practices—or lack thereof—held and followed, respectively, by critics. The other concerns the relation between such frameworks and their critical standpoints, their principles and procedures in matters of method and theory. Second, it is fair to say that theological scholars have failed to address, by and large, the problematic of methodological-theoretical frameworks in approaching the biblical texts. This focus would also involve two areas of interest. One concerns the reason or the *why* for doing what they do. The other has to do with the mode or the *how* for doing what they do in the way that they do it. In both regards, Latino/a critics and theologians have followed suit.

I should like to expand on both of these reflections. On the one hand, critics have pursued the ideological dimensions of texts and interpretations along any number of directions—from gender and economics to disability and ecology. They have refrained from doing so, however, with respect to the religious-theological axis of identity and its corresponding set of differential relations of power. An exception is in order: Critics from more traditional ecclesial circles who have dealt with the issues of revelation, inspiration, and normativity regarding Scripture and who view such concerns as indispensable to their craft as interpreters. This exception does call for nuance: such issues have been pursued on an integrative rather than ideological key. On the other hand, theologians have made use of the biblical texts in a wide variety of ways. They have done so, however, without reflection on the dynamics and mechanics of such engagement, let alone in conversation with the methods and theories of criticism. Again, an exception is in order: theologians in the tradition of liberation have expounded on the why and how of their approach to Scripture. This exception does require qualification as well: such exposition has been carried out on a similarly integrative rather than ideological mode.

A key objective of this project has been to rupture and move past this state of affairs. To this end, it has raised the question of interpretation on the part of Latino/a theological scholars through a call for formal reflection on its why and how. Much work remains to be done along these lines. Such work should include, not only as a desideratum but also as an imperative, engagement with methodological and theoretical models in criticism. At the same time, while not pursued in this project, similar reflection on the part of Latino/a biblical scholars is imperative regarding the religious-theological frameworks that underlie their critical commitments and practices. Indeed, this would make for a pointed follow-up to this project.

Such reflection, by way of anticipation, would call for attention along various lines of inquiry. First, it would address the traditional issues of revelation, inspiration, and normativity revolving around the notion of Scripture as Word of God. This move would provide a keen sense of where critics stand in such matters. Second, it would demand engagement with the movements and discourses of theological construction. This measure would lead to informed formulation of visions and commitments on the part of critics. Third, it would require ideological analysis of underlying religious-theological frameworks. This step would yield a thorough critique by critics of unequal relations of power at play in all such frameworks.

I turn now turn to the perspective of theological construction. A further comment is worth making regarding the particular approach to the Bible adopted by the tradition of Liberation Theology, given not only the pivotal position that the Bible occupies in its process of theologizing but also the extensive influence of this tradition in the theologies of the Global South and the minoritized theologies of the Global North. Both Bible and interpretation occupy the central stage in the threefold process of critical mediations. This conjunction may be described as follows: Interpretation brings to the Bible the findings of social-cultural analysis for enlightenment and evaluation, and interpretation derives from the Bible the blueprints and signposts for social-cultural action. The position thus accorded to the Bible in the process is an exalted one. With respect to status, it is endowed with utmost authority as the revelatory and inspired Word of God; with regard to role, it is viewed as a foundational charter for both discernment and praxis in the world. Similarly, the function accorded thereby to interpretation is a crucial one. Criticism emerges as an extractive undertaking, validating and steering at once—laying bare what is and should not be in the present and laying forth what should be in the future. In this respect, Latino/a theologians have also followed suit, certainly at first and overwhelmingly so. Subsequently, however, it would be fair to say that Bible and interpretation have lost presence in the movement.[21]

I should like to expand on this reflection as well. Given the lofty status and role ascribed to it as the Word of God, the Bible becomes an entity to be consulted and followed, not to be questioned or challenged. Given its key extractive function, interpretation adopts a combination of historicist reading, involving securing and judging, and mimeticist reading, involving appropriating and applying. Consequently, the ideological critique that is readily accorded to and demanded of the first and third critical mediations of the process is out of the question. While it is imperative to carry out an ideological analysis of society and culture in the present as well as an ideological analysis of visions and strategies for the future, an ideological analysis of the past, the biblical texts and contexts, is simply not to be had.

A key objective of this project has been to problematize and move past this state of affairs. With this mind, it has brought before Latino/a theological scholars the question regarding the significance of the Bible through a call for formal consideration of its status and role. First, given the high stance taken by traditional Liberation Theology, theologians have been asked to ponder what status and role are, or should be, assigned to the Bible? Does it continue to stand as the Word of God? If such be the case: What would such a claim mean and entail? Would ideological critique remain out of bounds? If not: What would the Bible signify and convey? Furthermore, given the subsequent distantiation from the Bible in theological construction, theologians have been asked to consider what role the Bible plays, or should play, in theologizing? Can it be disregarded altogether? If such be the case: What would be the rationale for so doing? If not: What would be the grounds for inclusion and relevance? Here, too, much work remains to be done.

This project, needless to say, represents but a first step along these various lines of development. All such work would help to strengthen and advance the movement and discourse of Latino/a Theology.

Such work would bring closer together the areas of biblical criticism and theological construction. While theologians would formulate their approach to biblical interpretation by way of the models of criticism, critics would express their position on religious-theological interpretation in terms of the formations of theologizing. To know and use the concepts and terms of other areas of study within the same general field constitutes a mutually beneficial and creative cross-disciplinary move.

Such work would display the breadth of thought and activity regarding the Bible at work in the religious-theological production of this minoritized ethnic-racial group in the United States, at present and over time. It would establish the range of critical positions taken by biblical scholars as well as the spectrum of theological approaches adopted by theological scholars. Bringing such parameters to the surface would, in turn, make it easier to establish dialogue within each area of study: we would all have a much keener sense of where we and our fellow scholars stand and move.

Such work would provide a solid point of entry for work along transnational lines between the movement and discourse of Latino/a Theology in the United States and the tradition and variations of Liberation Theology in Latin America and the Caribbean. It is from this historical movement that Latino/a Theology emerges, and it is in Latino/a Theology that Liberation Theology finds one of its many historical variations. In so doing, transnational links, trajectories, and alliances would be furthered for the benefit of all.

Such work, lastly, would provide a foundation for work within the United States along two lines. One such development would be informed and sophisticated conversation with the religious-theological production of other ethnic-racial minoritized groups in the country. The other would entail pointed and confident conversation with the religious-theological production of dominant religious-theological circles both in the past and present. Minoritization remains very much a fact of life in religious-theological circles in the academy and scholarship.

All such work, to conclude, stands as more necessary and urgent than ever, as the country has entered what might be described as the age of Trumpism. It is an age in which radical nationalist groups have claimed, loudly and even violently so, an exclusivist hold on the United States. It is an age in which ethnic-racial minoritized groups have been singled out as the culprits behind the perceived decline of the country. It is an age in which the Latino/a population stands as a salient target of such demonization, especially in terms of Mexico and Central America. In such an age, all fields must rally and devise visions of and strategies for resistance and justice. This applies to Christian studies, and this project in Latino/a Theology represents, I would submit, one such modest endeavor.

NOTES

1. Fernando F. Segovia, "'And They Began to Speak in Their Own Tongues': Competing Modes of Discourse in Contemporary Biblical Interpretation," in *Reading*

from This Place. Volume 1: *Social Location and Biblical Interpretation in the United States*, ed., Fernando F. Segovia and Mary Ann Tolbert (Minneapolis: Fortress Press, 1995), 1–32; and "Cultural Studies and Contemporary Biblical Criticism: Ideological Criticism as Mode of Discourse," in *Reading from This Place. Volume Two: Social Location and Biblical Interpretation in the Global Scene*, ed., Fernando F. Segovia and Mary Ann Tolbert (Minneapolis: Fortress Press, 1995), 1–17.

2. Fernando F. Segovia, "Criticism in Critical Times: Reflections on Vision and Task," *Journal of Biblical Literature* 134 (2015): 6–29.

3. Gilberto Gibellini, *La teologia del XX secolo*, Biblioteca di teologia contemporanea 69 (Brescia: Editrice Queriniana, 1992). Here it is the translation in Spanish by Rufino Velasco that I reference: *La teología del siglo XX*, Presencia teológica 94 (Santander: Sal Terrae, 1998). All citations from this work rendered in English are my own translations.

4. Gibellini, *La teología del siglo XX*, 13-14 ("Preámbulo").

5. Gibellini, *La teología del siglo XX*, 14. The reference to Metz is not by way of bibliographical entry but rather by way of historical recollection—a presentation given at a conference on "The Future of the Enlightenment" in 1987 in Germany, held in celebration of the fortieth anniversary of the publication of Gabriel Adorno and Max Horkheimer's *The Dialectic of Enlightenment* in 1947 (revised version)—*Dialektik der Aufklärung: Philosophische Fragmente* (Amsterdam: Querido, 1947). The proceedings of the conference were subsequently published, including the essay by Metz: "Wider die zweite Unmündigkeit: Zum Verhältnis von Aufklärung und des Christentums," in *Die Zukunft der Aufklärung*, ed., Jörn Rüsen, Eberhard Lämmert und Peter Glotz (Frankfurt am Main: Suhrkamp, 1988), 81–90.

6. See, e.g., the two collections of essays edited by him: *Frontiers of Theology in Latin America* (Maryknoll: Orbis Books, 1979 [Italian original 1977]); *Paths of African Theology* (Maryknoll: Orbis Books, 1994 [Italian original 1994]); with Michael Amaladoss as coeditor, *Teologia in Asia*, Collana: Giornale di Teologia 322 (Brescia: Editrice Queriniana, 2006). See also: *The Liberation Theology Debate* (Maryknoll: Orbis Books, 1988 [Italian original 1986]).

7. The work is also dedicated, it would appear, to his mother, Mamma Clementina. The dedication includes two comments: her life paralleled the century (1905–1991), and so, in fact, she has recently passed away; and she lived through the century with great strength of spirit.

8. Gibellini, *La teología del siglo XX*, 553–554 ("By Way of Conclusion: Four Theological Movements"). The sixteen formations in question appear in the Table of Contents.

9. Gibellini, *La teología del siglo XX*, 13–14.

10. Gibellini, *La teología del siglo XX*, 554.

11. Gibellini, *La teología del siglo XX*, 554.

12. Fernando F. Segovia, "A New Manifest Destiny: The Emerging Theological Voice of Hispanic Americans," *Religious Studies Review* 17 (1991): 103–109. The eight volumes came from seven authors: two authors had produced two volumes each; two others had coauthored one volume; and the other three authors had each authored a volume.

13. Virgilio Elizondo, *Galilean Journey: The Mexican-American Promise* (Maryknoll: Orbis Books, 1983), followed by *The Future is Mestizo: Life Where Cultures Meet* (Bloomington, IN: Meyer Stone Books, 1988). Justo L. González, *Mañana: Christian Theology from a Hispanic Perspective* (Nashville: Abingdon Press, 1990), preceded by *The Theological Education of Hispanics* (New York: The Fund for Theological Education, 1988).

14. Dom Hélder Pessoa Câmara et al., "A Letter to the Peoples of the Third World," in *Between Honesty and Hope: Documents from and about the Church in Latin America*, The Bishops' Commission for Social Action (Lima, Perú), trans. John Drury, Maryknoll Documentation Series (Maryknoll: Orbis Publications, 1970), 3–12.

15. José Severino Croatto, *Liberación y libertad. Pautas hermenéuticas* (Buenos Aires, Mundo Nuevo, 1973).

16. Croatto, *Liberación y libertad*, 9: "Varios son los motivos que inspiran este estudio.... Un segundo motivo fue sugerido por la lectura de diversos trabajos sobre "liberación" (Gustavo Gutiérrez, Hugo Assmann, Enrique Dussel, etc.). Su riqueza es inmensa, y nuestro propio futuro dirá cuanto habrán aportado a la formación de una 'conciencia crítica' latinoamericana desde el ángulo de la fe o de la filosofía cristiana. Pero suscitan también un deseo de completarlas con algunas pautas hermenéuticas que les sirvan de apoyo, más que de crítica."

17. Fernando F. Segovia, "Hispanic American Theology and the Bible: Effective Weapon and Faithful Ally," in *We Are A People! Initiatives in Hispanic American Theology*, ed. Roberto S. Goizueta (Minneapolis: Fortress Press, 1992), 21–49.

18. Segovia, "Hispanic American Theology and the Bible," 49.

19. Fernando F. Segovia, "Toward a Hermeneutics of the Diaspora: A Hermeneutics of Otherness and Engagement," in *Reading from this Place*. Volume 1: *Social Location and Biblical Interpretation in the United States*, ed. Fernando F. Segovia and Mary Ann Tolbert (Minneapolis: Fortress Press, 1995), 57–74.

20. See Francisco J. Lozada and Fernando F. Segovia, eds., *Latino/a Biblical Hermeneutics: Problematics, Objectives, Strategies*, Semeia Studies 68 (Atlanta: SBL Press, 2014). See especially Fernando F. Segovia, "Approaching Latino/a Biblical Criticism: A Trajectory of Visions and Mission," in *Latino/a Biblical Hermeneutics*, 1–39.

21. This is a trend that was confirmed for me in private correspondence by Benjamín Valentín of the School of Theology and Ministry at Boston College, a prominent Latino theologian in the Protestant tradition, both a constructive voice in and a historical observer of the movement.

BIBLIOGRAPHY

Amaladoss, Michael and Gilberto Gibellini, eds. *Teologia in Asia*. Collana: Giornale di Teologia 322. Brescia: Editrice Queriniana, 2006.

Croatto, José Severino. *Liberación y libertad. Pautas hermenéuticas*. Buenos Aires, Mundo Nuevo, 1973.

Elizondo, Virgilio. *The Future is Mestizo: Life Where Cultures Meet*. Bloomington, IN: Meyer Stone Books, 1988.

———. *Galilean Journey: The Mexican-American Promise*. Maryknoll: Orbis Books, 1983.

Gibellini, Gilberto, ed. *Frontiers of Theology in Latin America*. Maryknoll: Orbis Books, 1979 [Italian original 1977].

———. ed. *Paths of African Theology*. Maryknoll: Orbis Books, 1994 [Italian original 1994].

———. *La teología del siglo XX*. Translated by Rufino Velasco. Presencia teológica 94. Santander: Sal Terrae, 1998.

———. *La teologia del XX secolo*. Biblioteca di teologia contemporanea 69. Brescia: Editrice Queriniana, 1992.

———. *La teología del siglo XX*. Translated by Rufino Velasco. Presencia teológica 94. Santander: Sal Terrae, 1998.

———. *The Liberation Theology Debate*. Maryknoll: Orbis Books, 1988 [Italian original 1986].

González, Justo L. *Mañana: Christian Theology from a Hispanic Perspective*. Nashville: Abingdon Press. 1990.

———. *The Theological Education of Hispanics*. New York: The Fund for Theological Education, 1988.

Lozada, Francisco J. and Fernando F. Segovia, eds. *Latino/a Biblical Hermeneutics: Problematics, Objectives, Strategies*. Semeia Studies 68. Atlanta: SBL Press, 2014.

Metz, Johann Baptist. "Wider die zweite Unmündigkeit: Zum Verhältnis von Aufklärung und des Christentums." In *Die Zukunft der Aufklärung*, edited by Jörn Rüsen, Eberhard Lämmert and Peter Glotz, 81–90. Frankfurt am Main: Suhrkamp, 1988.

Pessoa Câmara, Dom Hélder et al. "A Letter to the Peoples of the Third World." In *Between Honesty and Hope: Documents from and about the Church in Latin America*, 3–12. The Bishops' Commission for Social Action, Lima, Perú. Translated by John Drury. Maryknoll Documentation Series. Maryknoll: Orbis Publications, 1970.

Segovia, Fernando F. "'And They Began to Speak in Their Own Tongues': Competing Modes of Discourse in Contemporary Biblical Interpretation." In *Reading from This Place*. Volume 1: *Social Location and Biblical Interpretation in the United States*, edited by Fernando F. Segovia and Mary Ann Tolbert, 1–32. Minneapolis: Fortress Press, 1995.

———. "Approaching Latino/a Biblical Criticism: A Trajectory of Visions and Mission." In *Latino/a Biblical Hermeneutics: Problematics, Objectives, Strategies*, edited by Francisco J. Lozada and Fernando F. Segovia, 1–39. Semeia Studies 68. Atlanta: SBL Press, 2014.

———. "Criticism in Critical Times: Reflections on Vision and Task." *Journal of Biblical Literature* 134 (2015): 6–29.

———. "Cultural Studies and Contemporary Biblical Criticism: Ideological Criticism as Mode of Discourse." In *Reading from This Place*. Volume Two: *Social Location and Biblical Interpretation in the Global Scene*, edited by Fernando F. Segovia and Mary Ann Tolbert, 1–17. Minneapolis: Fortress Press, 1995.

———. "Hispanic American Theology and the Bible: Effective Weapon and Faithful Ally." In *We Are A People! Initiatives in Hispanic American Theology*, edited by Roberto S. Goizueta, 21–49. Minneapolis: Fortress Press, 1992.

———. "A New Manifest Destiny: The Emerging Theological Voice of Hispanic Americans." *Religious Studies Review* 17 (1991): 103–109.

———. "Toward a Hermeneutics of the Diaspora: A Hermeneutics of Otherness and Engagement." In *Reading from this Place*. Volume 1: *Social Location and Biblical Interpretation in the United States*, edited by Fernando F. Segovia and Mary Ann Tolbert, 57–74. Minneapolis: Fortress Press, 1995.

Part II

LATINO/A THEOLOGY

APPROACHING THE BIBLE

Chapter 2

Reading and Hearing Scripture in the Latina/o Pentecostal Community

Sammy Alfaro

An analysis of the main components of the Latina/o Pentecostal service reveals the central place of Scripture within the community. From beginning to end, Latina/o Pentecostals reimagine the biblical text as it is being read, heard, sang, proclaimed, and even performed. It is through their appropriation of the biblical narrative, as a living text that informs their everyday experience of God through the Spirit, that they are enabled to cope with the difficulties of life in diaspora. Eldin Villafañe recently put it like this:

> To speak of the Scriptures in Latino Pentecostal circles is to speak of the "book of the Spirit".... Latino Pentecostals tend to read the Scripture in a way that I would call "existential[ly]-spiritual" In essence, this means that the believer approaches the text in a manner which is almost sacramental. There is an expectation that the Spirit will speak to him or her in the present. Every part and all of Scripture, from Genesis to Revelation, may equally speak as the word of the Spirit.[1]

For this reason, throughout the Latina/o Pentecostal gathering, whether it is the main Sunday service or a home Bible study, great emphasis is placed on reading and hearing Scripture through the witness of the Spirit. It is the text of the Bible, read and activated by the Spirit, that becomes a living text for the Pentecostal community and, as such, serves to guide—on an individual basis—and to direct the congregation in everyday decision-making.

This study aims to describe the role and use of Scripture in the Latina/o Pentecostal community and to discern strategies for interpreting the Bible from this perspective. First, an overview of the Pentecostal way of engaging Scripture will be given in order to present the main elements of Pentecostal theological hermeneutics in general. Second, an analysis of the components of the traditional service will be given as a window into the use of the Bible in local congregations. Lastly, a reading of Acts 6:1-7 will be offered in order to exemplify the use of Scripture by Latina/o Pentecostals.

READING AND HEARING SCRIPTURE IN PENTECOSTAL COMMUNITIES: THEN AND NOW

Given the oral and narrative nature of Pentecostal theology in general, it is best to begin by analyzing the relationship between hermeneutics and theology in Pentecostal communities.[2] For example, take the account of a Bible study that took place at Bethel Bible College in Topeka, Kansas, which gave birth to the doctrine of Baptism in the Holy Spirit. This event also helps to exemplify the sort of theological hermeneutics that pervaded within early Pentecostalism.

> In December of 1900 we had our examination upon the subject of repentance, conversion, consecration, sanctification, healing and the soon coming of the Lord. We had reached in our studies a problem. What about the second chapter of Acts? . . . . I set the students at work studying out diligently what was Bible evidence of the baptism of the Holy Ghost.[3]

The Pentecostal pioneer Charles Parham's request for his students to search the Scriptures for conclusive biblical evidence with regard to the baptism of the Holy Ghost yielded an irrefutable answer: speaking in other tongues under the guidance of the Spirit as evidenced in Acts 2. Here the reciprocal relationship between Spirit, Scripture, and Community can be highlighted.

In describing this event, Frank J. Ewart states that "their adopted method was to select a subject, find all the references on it, and present to the class a scriptural summary of what the Bible had to say about the theme."[4] However, the study was done in a prayerful and communal approach to the biblical text and also resulted in turning their hearts to await the confirmation of Scripture through the reception of the gift of the Spirit. This early account of Pentecostal theologizing, therefore, reveals a hermeneutical model that, though perhaps simplistic in nature, reflects the type of interpretive method discussed more thoroughly by Kenneth Archer, among others.[5] In what follows, I will briefly tease out the main elements of Pentecostal theological hermeneutics.

First, it might be said that Pentecostals' appeal to experience decisively frees their hermeneutical method from the modernist quest for a purely objective retrieval of the meaning of the original text of the Bible. Whereas the historical-grammatical method applies its tools to the biblical text in order to establish what it meant to the original readers, Pentecostals opt for a more nuanced "postmodern"[6] hermeneutic by recognizing that the act of interpretation necessarily includes their preconceived ideas and experience. In short, Pentecostal hermeneutics understand that every act of interpretation is informed by their particular view of the Spirit's moving in the events of the text itself as well as in and through the interpreting community.

Second, in view of the appeal to experience by Pentecostals, one must say that their approach to the biblical text is not simply a primitive or irrational method. Instead, since the early days of the movement, Pentecostalism has had a very dynamic view of Scripture, in that the text was considered a "living text" capable of speaking to the community in ways that perhaps the original authors had not envisioned. In order words, from a Pentecostal perspective, the Bible does not simply provide ancient stories and words spoken by God; it is the Word of God and, as such, it speaks to the believer in ways that guide and transform everyday life. Veli-Matti Kärkkäinen summarizes early Pentecostals' use of the Bible as follows:

1. Scripture is the inspired Word of God, authoritative and wholly reliable.
2. [They] have not recognized a historical distance between themselves and the text.
3. Little or no significance was placed upon the historical context, and the Bible was understood at face value.
4. [Their] interpretation was theologically colored by the christological "full gospel" pre-understanding, where Jesus stood at the center of charismatic life.
5. The prime interpreter and preacher was the local pastor, most of whom were uneducated, ordinary folk.[7]

What strikes the critical mind is that in some ways the reading of the biblical text resembles the approach taken by Fundamentalists, because Pentecostals place great stress on the authority of the Bible; it is, in its entirety, the Word of God. However, if one were to attend a "classical" Pentecostal service (i.e., a church meeting where spontaneous worship, testimony, and prayer precede a very personal and emotive exposition of a Scripture text),[8] one would soon realize that their approach to Scripture is not a rigid, objective, and rational-making sense of the text. Instead, for example, a woman gets up, reads a certain passage from Scripture, and says that the Scripture was fulfilled in her life through a supernatural intervention by God through the Spirit. Upon such affirmation, any biblical scholar that values the historical context of Scripture might cringe at the thought of such a naive attempt to bridge across Lessing's historical ditch. And, yet, this is precisely what Pentecostals unwittingly claimed to be able to do in their use of the Bible as they preached, taught, or gave testimony of God's power in their lives.

Take, for example, this explanation concerning the evidence of the reception of the Baptism of the Holy Spirit by an early Pentecostal leader, Joseph H. King:

> The Book of Acts is the only one in the Bible that presents to us the Pentecostal baptism from an historic standpoint; and it gives the standard by which to determine the reality and fullness of the Spirit's outpouring, since in every instance where the Spirit was poured out for the first time this miraculous utterance accompanied the same, so we infer that its connection with the baptism is to be regarded as an evidence of its reception.[9]

The thought that as a result of the narrative structure of Acts one could not infer doctrines from its text would have made no sense in the mind of King as well as any early Pentecostal thinker. Furthermore, this line of interpretation was considered best because of its exegetical woodenness. For early Pentecostals, what the text said was taken as is, and it was what we should believe today; there simply was no other way about it.

Third, significantly then for Pentecostals, the biblical text may contain different levels of meaning that can be recovered through the medieval approach of *lectio divina* or "spiritual reading." Simon Chan highlights the significance of the "spiritual reading" but warns about not tilting the pendulum completely in this direction:

> All this is not to say that we should abandon the historical-critical study of the Bible in order to be spiritual. Our God is the God of history. At the same time we must not suppose that the only meaning of Scripture is the one deriving from the literal interpretation of the texts. There is still something to be said for the medieval concept of the *sensus plenior* [fuller meaning] of Scripture so long as it does not lead to an unrestrained kind of allegorization which ignores the literal sense.[10]

This "fuller meaning" is essentially referred to in Pentecostal sermons and testimonies as a "word from the Lord"—a prophetic or anointed utterance spoken through the messenger by the Holy Spirit. In contrast, a sermon, testimony, or song that is lacking in this spiritual orientation is said to be lacking "inspiration."[11]

Fourth, given the availability of "inspired" utterances within the Pentecostal community, what is the role of Scripture and its authority? Unlike Fundamentalists or some Conservative Evangelicals who give priority to the doctrine of inerrancy in order to establish the veracity of the written Word, Pentecostals ground the authority of Scripture in what Kärkkäinen calls "a dynamic interaction between the written text and the Holy Spirit."[12] What is more, Kärkkäinen suggests that "Land boldly places the authority of the Spirit ahead of the authority of Scripture," when he writes that,

> The Spirit who inspired and preserved the Scriptures illuminates, teaches, guides, convicts and transforms through that Word today. The Word is alive, quick and powerful, because of the Holy Spirit's ministry. The relation of the Spirit to Scripture is based on that of the Spirit to Christ. Even as the Spirit formed Christ in Mary, so the Spirit uses Scripture to form Christ in believers and vice-versa. Anointed preaching, teaching and witnessing evidence this wholeness, this fusion of the Spirit and Word, Spirit and Christ.[13]

A couple of pages ahead, Land goes on to say that within early Pentecostalism "the order of authority was Spirit, Scripture, church."[14] Thus, it is the Spirit who gives authority to the Scriptures. This emphasis on the role of the Spirit in relation to the authority of the Bible serves to accentuate the need for engaging the biblical text not simply through a historically oriented methodology but also under the guidance of the Spirit who breathed forth the Scriptures.

John Christopher Thomas helps us to understand the role of the Spirit in the task of theological hermeneutics.[15] Thomas demonstrates that Acts 15 serves to exemplify Pentecostals' theological use of Scripture. In this passage, the Council of Jerusalem meets to discuss the inclusion of the Gentiles into the church. The main question is over the issue of whether to impose regulations on the Gentiles that would require them to keep the Mosaic Law as a prerequisite for becoming partakers in the community of God. Central to Thomas' proposal is the testimony of the community, the activity of the Holy Spirit, and the community's use of Scripture in accordance with the Spirit. When the council convened, they sought to arrive at a theological conclusion regarding a real problem in the church. As they sought to find an answer, they first appealed to the experience of the community. Peter reminded them how they had witnessed God's outpouring of the Spirit over the Gentiles. Then, Barnabas and Paul testified of the move of the Spirit among Gentiles as evidenced in their missionary trip. Lastly, in order to pen down a statement to take back to the Gentile congregations, James appealed to Scripture in a very creative fashion.

Significantly, Thomas goes on to apply this paradigm to the contemporary divisive issue of women in ministry in order to affirm the participation of women in the church and the Pentecostal academy. The result is a liberating reading that understands the qualifications for a preaching and teaching ministry in the church are not based on gender identification but rather on the Spirit of God who moves freely to empower men and women alike for such task.

EL CULTO: READING AND HEARING SCRIPTURE IN THE TRADITIONAL LATINA/O PENTECOSTAL SERVICE

Considering the above-mentioned general approach to reading and hearing Scripture within Pentecostal communities, it is significant to point out the importance of the community context in which the Bible is interpreted. For this reason, locating the interpretative strategies of Latina/o Pentecostal communities requires examining how local congregations approach and use Scripture. Thus, an examination of the use of the Bible in the traditional Latina/o Pentecostal *culto* (service) will allow the reader to understand the role and use of Scripture at the grassroots level.

Growing up Pentecostal, I became accustomed to church meetings where the move of the Spirit was a regular part of our worship time. The Spirit-filled services I experienced in my childhood typically could be described in a way that is not foreign to many Pentecostals despite our ethnic, cultural, and language differences. Samuel Solivån provides a helpful description of the main components of the typical Latino Pentecostal *culto* in a manner that is characteristic across denominational lines.[16] Seeking to identify the main contours of Pentecostal worship, Solivån finds three theological presuppositions to explain the orientation of Pentecostal liturgy.[17] First, Solivån establishes that Pentecostal liturgy takes seriously the priesthood of all believers because in theory everyone is welcome to participate in the service of the worshipping community. Second, Pentecostal worship has a noncreedal stance, which "frees worship style to be defined by the context and culture of the community."[18] Third, Solivån describes Pentecostal worship as following an "open" or "free" liturgy, which is not restricted by a written liturgical code that restricts and prefabricates ritual order. Moreover, this "nonliturgical" liturgy is fully open to the leading of the Spirit and the cultural traditions of the community. What follows are my own recollections from being an active participant within Latino Pentecostal services.

Most *cultos* would typically begin with a reading of Scripture followed by a short reflection inviting the presence and direction of the Spirit over the service. The selected opening biblical text would be used as an opening exhortation, and thus provided the one leading (female or male) an opportunity to speak prophetically to the church. Notwithstanding the lack of formal biblical or ministerial training, the speaker would interpret the selected text and provide encouragement, correction, direction, or whatever the Spirit placed in his or her heart for the edification of the church.

Then, the person leading the service would hand it over to a more musically inclined man or woman to select the hymns under the guidance of the Spirit and in relation to special days and celebrations. Two or sometimes three hymns would be sung from our traditional hymnbook, *Rayos de Esperanza*.[19] The hymns of course contained biblical allusions and imagery that continued to speak to the congregation as they sang. Depending on who was in charge of the *culto*—whether it was being led by the youth, women, men, or children—the hymns and songs would have a distinct style and fervor. Significantly, though, leading the singing became a Scriptural activity, in that the selection of songs and transition between songs yielded the person leading them an occasion to speak to the congregation about what he or she sensed God was doing or needed to do in the midst of them. The hymns might focus on gratitude, healing, trust, or even be prophetic reminders of the times in which we live. However, through the explanation of why the song would be sung and the singing itself, the congregation was invited to discern and respond to the voice of God.

After the hymns, when most of the congregation had finally arrived, we would be asked to share any special prayer requests. After a number of prayer requests were placed, the person leading would pray or ask another spiritually mature member to come to the pulpit and lead the congregation in a corporate prayer. This time of prayer would be a powerful moment in the service, where almost everyone would lift their voices to cry out to God asking him to intervene in the problems and situations presented. The sick who were present or others in representation of them would be asked to come to the altar to be anointed with oil and prayed over by the pastor and other church leaders. The prayers would invoke God's promises in the Bible regarding healing, deliverance, provision, and other needs, and many times the lay person praying would cite Scripture verbatim and apply it to the situation related to the prayer. What is notable with regard to this time of prayer was the desire for those things being prayed for to be in the will of God, and Scripture became the ultimate litmus test for determining if what was being asked for was a legitimate request.

Following the time of prayer and a transitional *corito* ("a short and repetitive spiritual song . . . [revealing] an indigenous Hispanic Pentecostal singing style"),[20] we would enter a time of testimonial thanksgiving upon which anyone in the congregation could stand to give thanks or take the pulpit to sing a special song. This was a period of great liberty for all, but at times also a comical time in the service where our musical and spiritual sensitivities were challenged by very "anointed" singers who could not carry a tune. More importantly, though, it was a time for literally anyone, whether young or old, male or female, to participate in the service and read a selection of Scripture and apply it to his or her life. These participations could become mini sermonettes that spoke to the rest of the congregation about what God was doing in a family or individual. As Soliván puts it:

> This time of testimony is also the place where one gains insight into the common and daily struggles of the community and the concrete ways God has answered

their prayers. Testimony time is a public witness to the ongoing ministry of the Holy Spirit in the life of the community. It engenders faith, thanksgiving, and hope. It also serves to keep the community abreast of the needs, concerns, and celebrations of its members.[21]

Typically, these testimonies followed a non-written formula: a Scripture reading; a narrative of the problem; and an explanation of how God resolved the problem, which served as confirmation of the biblical portion read and the work of the Spirit in the life of the church. Though a biblical exegete might find the selection and explanation of the text wanting, even the somewhat "eisegetical" reading of a text would produce loud "amens" on account of how the Spirit of God was shown to be at work in the life of the individual speaking. Darío López Rodríguez describes the Pentecostal testimony in this manner:

> Consequently, when a Pentecostal gives a testimony of his/her faith, it is not the narration of an unknown story nor are they retelling an unfamiliar experience, but rather they are speaking of their continued relation with God recounting what is currently happening in their spiritual pilgrimage because there is a fresh story or testimony to tell. This is so because for them God is not a datum from the past or a simple doctrinal formulation, but a God who is near and accompanies during all circumstances and who is by their side at all times. God is not a stranger, nor is he someone unknown, absent, distant or uninterested of the situation they live. In a certain way, the Pentecostal testimony narrates a life story in which the central character is the God of life, the God who journeys together with his people in every step of the way.[22]

For example, an individual whose life was drastically changed by the power of the Spirit, who freed him of alcohol abuse, might opt to read 2 Cor. 5:17: "Therefore, if anyone is in Christ, he is a new creation. The old has passed away; behold, the new has come."[23] This could be a verse recited verbatim, paraphrased somewhat loosely, or read directly from the Bible. Either way, the purpose of reading the text would be to frame the testimony as a fulfillment of the passage and the experience of the individual as evidence of the activity of the Spirit. The person testifying would then go on to narrate his or her experience of how God delivered them, at times even providing very telling details of the transformation. In addition, a heartfelt rendition of a hymn such as "Una llaga podrida era mi vida" (My life was like a festering sore) could be sung. This popular hymn would serve not only to illustratively retell the story of the one singing but also serve as a reminder to many in the congregation of the place out of which God had brought them. Indicative of this, a line of the hymn states: "Estoy a medio camino de mi jornada / Para llegar a Canaán, donde será mi morada" (I'm halfway in my journey / To get to Canaan, where my home will be). The biblical allusion to Canaán as heaven, the final spiritual destination, contrasts with Egypt, the place of sin and perdition from which they have been delivered. Moreover, another line of the hymn depicts God's transformation of an individual as having been found thrown away in the garbage but having been restored when God himself lovingly extended his hand to deliver and heal.

After the time of testimony, the service coordinator would pray for the tithes and offering, usually after reading a passage of Scripture that focused on the joy of giving and the promises to those who are faithful in their contributions. Then, as the ushers collected it, a *corito* like "Dios bendice al dador alegre" (God blesses the cheerful giver) would be sung to motivate the giving. Again, in typical Pentecostal fashion, the short emotive song would allow the congregation to intone Scripture accompanied by cheerful musical beat.

Following the offering, the service would shift to the main element: the preaching of the Word. The pastor, a respected leader of the local congregation, or an invited visitor would preach an anointed Word from the Lord addressing what the Spirit had to communicate for the daily lives of those present. Last, but certainly not least, the preaching of the Word would be followed by an altar call, which could in turn lead to another prolonged time of worship where *corito* after *corito* would be sung as believers tarried at the altar seeking to experience the presence of the Spirit.

Concerning the place of the sermon in the *culto*, Samuel Solivan comments: "Probably the most important part of the [Hispanic Pentecostal] service is the preaching of the Word."[24] Though it might be said that some Hispanic Pentecostal sermons lack the academic rigor of a homily to be presented in a seminary classroom, it is less likely they lack Pentecostal passion or fervency. In fact, López Rodríguez sees "passion or fervency" as one of the most distinctive characteristics of preaching within the Pentecostal tradition.[25] Thus, what a Pentecostal preacher might lack in eloquence or academic training she or he certainly makes up for it in passion. Significantly, though, for López Rodríguez passion or fervency should not be understood as pertaining to emotional manipulation. Instead, it relates to the message that burns in the Pentecostal preachers heart: "A liberating message that has transformed their lives, and a missionary burden that cannot be postponed or bartered at any moment."[26]

In this sense, the passion that accompanies Pentecostal sermons is the burning desire for God to communicate a fresh Word to his people. Solivan highlights it like this: "The preacher in the Hispanic Pentecostal tradition sees himself or herself as a messenger from God with a word for the people of God. Preaching is to be understood to be in the tradition of the Old Testament prophets who, inspired by an encounter with God, brought the Word of the Lord to the people."[27]

Moreover, it is not an exclusive activity that only ordained and/or credentialed ministers can participate in, for even children, youth, and women are featured as preachers in the Pentecostal service. As Solivan notes, what qualifies someone for preaching is spiritual gifting: "In most Hispanic Pentecostal churches, the preaching of the gospel is open to men and women, lay and ordained. What is required is the community's affirmation that one should possess a preaching gift and preach with anointing –that is, with clear signs one is led by the Holy Spirit."[28]

Thus, it is not enough to interpret the biblical text. What matters most is the spiritual reading given of the text through the illumination of the Spirit. In this way, the text of the Bible takes on a new life as it speaks directly to a situation the congregation is experiencing.

SPIRIT-FILLED SERVANT LEADERSHIP: A LATINA/O PENTECOSTAL READING OF ACTS 6:1-6

Daniel A. Rodríguez's metaphorical application of Acts 6:1-6, where Greek-speaking widows in the primitive Christian community are being overlooked, assists us in reading the text from a Latina/o perspective and pinpoints the broader cultural problems facing the Latina/o church. He states:

> With the rapid growth of the Hispanic evangelical church during the past three decades, problems have arisen. One of the most significant is that US-born English-dominant Latinas/os are unintentionally being overlooked in the distribution of the church's attention and resources. To take the metaphor from the book of Acts, US-born English-dominant Latinas/os, the modern-day Greek-speaking Jews, are grumbling against foreign-born Spanish-dominant Latinas/os, the modern-day Aramaic-speaking Jews. The complaint of the former is that many Spanish-dominant Latinas/os still equate "Hispanic ministry" with ministry conducted almost exclusively in Spanish. Under this perspective and historic paradigm, generations of US-born English-dominant Latinas/os are subsequently "being overlooked in the daily distribution" of spiritual care.[29]

Rodríguez goes on to unpack the multigenerational problem that Latina/o Pentecostal congregations are experiencing because of the language barriers with second- and third-generation children and youth.[30] In many regional conventions and conferences, a text like this would definitely be read with prophetic insight, calling the church to adapt to the changing cultural context of Pentecostal immigrant communities in the United States.

As Latina/o Pentecostal churches have continued to grow in the United States, so have the problems, and dealing with them has led to the ever-growing need to send laborers to the harvest. As the biblical text reminds us, the issue was more than just figuring out how to distribute food justly among widows who were apparently being discriminated on the basis of their cultural identity. Rodríguez rightly points out that the solution to the problems facing the Latina/o Pentecostal church has everything to do with leadership. The apostles in the primitive church quickly recognized they were overwhelmed with the task of taking care of both the spiritual and material needs of the growing community. If they continued to try to do both, similar problems would continue to emerge, so the solution was simple: elect new leaders to help with the burdens of ministry. This is an area where the Latina/o Pentecostal church has exceled, and at times suffered, because of an overemphasis on the priesthood of all believers. Indeed, what is one of its greatest assets can, from time to time, become a problematic issue due to a lack of preparation and total reliance in the assumed anointing of the Spirit.

In many of today's Latina/o Pentecostal congregations, similar problems can be experienced due to the failure, or resistance, of pastors to train and equip new leaders who will share in the ministry responsibilities of the church. Instead of developing leaders, many pastors make the mistake of attempting to become everything and anything in the congregation. A surprise visit to a typical Latina/o Pentecostal congregation might shed light on the multiple hats pastors often wear when seeking to attend to all the needs of their congregations. In short, the pastor could be occupied in anything from being the church bus driver to being the drama director. For this reason, Acts 6:1-6 contains three very important lessons in leadership for both pastors and lay persons in the congregation.

First, as can be gleaned from the inclusive participation of women and men, young and old, lay or ordained alike in the *culto*, a prescriptive reading of Acts 6:1-7 informs the Latina/o Pentecostal congregation of the importance of understanding we have all been chosen to serve in the church. Leaning heavily on the biblical text for direction, a passage like this provides clear guidelines for the selection of volunteers who will help in menial tasks in service of the congregation. In the text, the apostles order the rest of the disciples in the church "select from among yourselves seven men of good standing, full of Spirit and of wisdom" (Acts 6:3c–d, NRSV). As in the primitive church, job opportunities for volunteers in the church are open to those who give good testimony before the congregation, walk in the fullness of the Spirit, and have wisdom to handle situations that might arise.

Second, although the narrative in Acts betrays a patriarchal preference for men to be chosen, this has never stopped Pentecostal churches from appointing women to participate in the ministry of the church. In fact, Pentecostal churches grow and thrive due to the efforts of faithful women who outwork the men in the church. The reason for this is simple: the text prioritizes being "full of the Spirit" as the most important qualification for those chosen to serve. What is highly significant about this in the Latina/o Pentecostal context is the fact that it does not matter if one is going to preach or setup chairs in the service because both activities require the anointing of the Spirit. This alone serves to inspire and empower everyone in the congregation to become an active participant in the ministry of the church. Concerning this, the biblical text is clear that those who are chosen to serve tables needed the fullness of the Spirit just as the apostles required it to serve the word.

Third, as evidenced in the rest of Acts 6, Stephen, who was one of the seven chosen, was not limited by his community service assignment. When the church gathered, he knew perfectly well he had a task for which he was responsible. However, during the rest of the week, Stephen was an anointed preacher who, full of the Spirit, "did great wonders and signs among the people" (Acts 6:8). Likewise, for many Latina/o Pentecostal church members, their Sunday assignment or mid-week serving opportunity in congregational gatherings are assumed as positions of service, but they are also empowered to preach the word and pray for those in need in the workplace and neighborhoods. This understanding and openness to the move of the Spirit inside and outside the walls of the church is what continues to attract Latinas/os who want to be involved in the ministry of the church through body and spirit.

CONCLUDING COMMENTS

Having briefly looked at Pentecostal interpretative approaches to the Bible past and present, let me, by way of conclusion, make some final reflections regarding Latina/o Pentecostal hermeneutical strategies. As a community whose gatherings are centered on the biblical text from beginning to end, it comes as no surprise that the collective and individual imagining of the biblical text is a priority, but not the exclusive task of pastors and church leaders. As a result, the congregant is not a mere spectator during the church service but has the opportunity to preach the word through a testimony or song. With or without formal guidelines for engaging in the interpretative task, Latina/o Pentecostals rely on the inner witness of the Spirit to guide them into all truth as they read and hear God speak through Scripture as a community practice.

This active role in the interpretation of Scriptures creates an environment where everyone in the congregation can leave at the end of the service having heard God speak to them. This ongoing reading and hearing of the biblical text is what characterizes the Latina/o Pentecostal traditional *culto* as an engaging and dynamic worship experience. Moreover, since the interpretative focus shifts from person to person throughout the order of the service, at times a specific song or testimony could be the Word of the day for someone in the congregation. It is not unlikely for someone in the congregation to break into tears as they experience God's presence powerfully due to the moving words spoken or sung by another person. The thought of being used by God to speak to someone else is a humbling experience that empowers congregants to aspire for greater spiritual gifts and to live a sanctified life. One does not just attend service. We gather to minister to one another through the gifts the Spirit has given to many in the congregation.

In short, the Latina/o Pentecostal community seeks to embody what Paul describes as the Spirit-filled congregational life when he says in Eph. 5:18-20 (NRSV): "Do not get drunk with wine, for that is debauchery; but be filled with the Spirit, as you sing psalms and hymns and spiritual songs among yourselves, singing and making melody to the Lord in your hearts, giving thanks to God the Father at all times and for everything in the name of our Lord Jesus Christ."

This is done through the testimony of Scripture as Paul states in a parallel passage in Col. 3:16, "Let the word of Christ dwell in you richly; teach and admonish one another in all wisdom; and with gratitude in your hearts sing psalms, hymns, and spiritual songs to God."

Thus, during the week and in preparation for church gatherings, Latina/o Pentecostals live with a constant outlook for how God could be speaking to their lives each day in order to then come together to minister to others from what they themselves have received. At times it might be a word of comfort, a song of joy, or even a tearful testimony or prayer request that speaks to an individual so powerfully that it made the time at church worth it. Overflowing then with the witness of the Word through an experiential hermeneutic of the Spirit, the Latina/o Pentecostal believer heads out of the church building with a renewed sense of calling and a commitment to share the gospel with others: this is the secret of the continued growth of global Pentecostalism.

NOTES

1. Eldin Villafañe, *Introducción al Pentecostalismo: Manda Fuego Señor* (Nashville: Abingdon, 2012), 129.

2. Harvey Cox describes the Pentecostal way of doing theology like this:

The difference is that while the beliefs of the fundamentalists, and of many other religious groups, are enshrined in formal theological systems, those of pentecostalism are imbedded in testimonies, ecstatic speech, and bodily movement. But it is a theology, a full-blown religious cosmos, an intricate system of symbols that respond to the perennial questions of human meaning and value. The difference is that, historically, pentecostals have felt more at home singing their theology, or putting it in pamphlets for distribution on streets corners. Only recently have they begun writing books about it. Harvey Cox, *Fire from Heaven: The Rise of Pentecostal Spirituality and the Reshaping of Religion in the Twenty-first Century* (Reading, MA: Addison-Wesley, 1995), 15.

3. Sarah E. Parham, *The Life of Charles F. Parham, Founder of the Apostolic Faith Movement* (Joplin, MO: TriState, 1930), 51–52.

4. Frank J. Ewart, *The Phenomenon of Pentecost* (Hazelwood, MO: Word Aflame, 1975), 60.

5. Kenneth J. Archer, *A Pentecostal Hermeneutic for the Twenty-First Century: Spirit, Scripture and Community* (*Journal of Pentecostal Theology Supplement* Series 28; London: T & T Clark, 2004). Other similar, yet distinctive, approaches that discuss the role of theological hermeneutics in the making of meaning within Pentecostal traditions are: Amos Yong, *Spirit–Word–Community: Theological Hermeneutics in Trinitarian Perspective* (Burlington, VT: Ashgate, 2002); and John Christopher Thomas, "Women, Pentecostals and the Bible: An Experiment in Pentecostal Hermeneutics," *Journal of Pentecostal Theology* 5 (1994): 41–56.

6. Here I simply like to mention that some Pentecostal scholars would be hesitant to label Pentecostal hermeneutics as "postmodern" and would opt for perhaps the designation of "paramodern" to indicate the reappropriation of modernistic hermeneutical tools that move away from a purely objective method. On the other hand, some Pentecostal thinkers would advise the community to "jump off the postmodern bandwagon." Thus, it would be important to remember the old adage, "Don't throw the baby out with the bath water" and apply it to both modern and postmodern hermeneutics. See Archer, *A Pentecostal Hermeneutic*, 29–33, 148–54. See also: Timothy Cargal, "Beyond the Fundamentalist-Modernist Controversy: Pentecostals and Hermeneutics in a Postmodern Age," *PNEUMA* 15:2 (Fall 1993): 163–87; and Robert P. Menzies, "Jumping Off the Postmodern Bandwagon," *Pneuma* 16:1 (Spring 1994): 115-20.

7. Veli-Matti Kärkkäinen, "Hermeneutics: From Fundamentalism to Modernism," in *Toward a Pneumatological Theology: Pentecostal and Ecumenical Perspectives on Ecclesiology, Soteriology, and Theology of Mission*, ed. Amos Yong (New York: University Press of America, 2002), 5–6.

8. In his introduction to Pentecostalism, Allan H. Anderson provides a descriptive global account of the Pentecostal/Charismatic service. See Anderson, *An Introduction to Pentecostalism: Global Charismatic Theology*, 2nd ed. Introduction to Religion (Cambridge-New York: Cambridge University Press, 2009), 1–9. For "classical" accounts of the Pentecostal church service one can turn to a very accessible resource that preserves selected excerpts from *The Apostolic Faith*, the official publication of the Azusa Street Revival. See Eddie Hyatt, *Fire on the Earth: Eyewitnesses Reports from the Azusa Street Revival* (Lake Mary, FL: Creation House, 2006).

9. Joseph King, *From Passover to Pentecost* (Franklin Springs: Advocate, 1911), 183, cited in Gary B. McGee, *Initial Evidence: Historical and Biblical Perspectives on the Doctrine of Spirit Baptism* (Peabody, MA: Hendrickson, 1991), 109.

10. Simon Chan, *Pentecostal Theology and the Christian Spiritual Tradition*, *Journal of Pentecostal Theology Supplement* Series 21 (Sheffield, UK: Sheffield Academic, 2000), 27–28.

11. Although some Pentecostals would go so far as to say that the Spirit may give a new "inspired" message, most would say that what they mean by "inspiration" in the sense mentioned above is perhaps better designated as "illumination." For a very careful analysis of the meaning of "inspiration" and "illumination" from a Pentecostal perspective, see French L. Arrington, *Christian Doctrine: A Pentecostal Perspective*, vol. 1 (Cleveland, TN: Pathway, 1997), 71-80.

12. Kärkkäinen, "Hermeneutics," 9.

13. Steven Jack Land, *Pentecostal Spirituality: A Passion for the Kingdom*, *Journal of Pentecostal Theology Supplement* Series 1 (Sheffield, UK: Sheffield Academic, 1993), 100.

14. Land, *Pentecostal Spirituality*, 106.

15. Thomas, "Women, Pentecostals and the Bible," 41–56.

16. Samuel Soliván, "Hispanic Pentecostal Worship," in *¡Alabadle! Hispanic Christian Worship*, ed. Justo L. González (Nashville: Abingdon, 1996), 52–54. See also, Pedrito U. Maynard-Reid, "In the Spirit of Fiesta," in *Diverse Worship: African-American, Caribbean & Hispanic Perspectives* (Downers Grove, IL: IVP Academic, 2000), 161–86, esp. 173–77; and Darío López Rodríguez, *La Fiesta del Espíritu: espiritualidad y celebración Pentecostal* (Lima, Peru: Ediciones Puma, 2006), 47–55.

17. Soliván, "Hispanic Pentecostal Worship," 49.

18. Soliván, "Hispanic Pentecostal Worship," 50.

19. *Rayos de Ezperanza* (Rays of Hope) continues to be the official hymnbook of Latino congregations within the Spanish-speaking Church of God (Cleveland, TN). Among the Spanish-speaking Assemblies of God congregations, *Himnos de Inspiración y Alabanza* is used, while the Church of God of Prophecy uses *Himnos de Gloria y Triunfo*. Yet, despite the change of hymnbook, the traditional order and use of hymns for the most part remains the same across denominational lines.

20. Soliván, "Hispanic Pentecostal Worship," 52–53.

21. Soliván, "Hispanic Pentecostal Worship," 53.

22. López Rodríguez, *La Fiesta del Espíritu*, 52.

23. Here the English Standard Version (ESV) is used because it most resembles the text of the Spanish language Reina-Valera Version, which is the most common Bible version used in Latina/o Pentecostal churches. The Spanish text reads: "De modo que si alguno está en Cristo, nueva criatura es; las cosas viejas pasaron; he aquí todas son hechas nuevas."

24. Samuel Soliván, "Hispanic Pentecostal Worship," 53. For a brief but interesting description of preaching in the Hispanic Pentecostal service, see also Maynard-Reid, *Diverse Worship*, 195-196.

25. López Rodríguez, *La Fiesta del Espíritu*, 52.

26. Ibid., 54.

27. Soliván, "Hispanic Pentecostal Worship," 54.

28. Soliván, "Hispanic Pentecostal Worship," 54.

29. Daniel A. Rodríguez, "Between Two Worlds: Hispanic Youth in the United States," in *Pentecostals and Charismatics in Latin America and Latino Communities*, ed. Néstor Medina and Sammy Alfaro (New York: Palgrave Macmillan, 2015), 127.

30. Jeremías Torres provides an insightful and prophetic charge of the generational problems within the Latina/o Pentecostal church. As a bishop and president of the Movimiento Iglesia Cristiana Pentecostal, he analyses the situation by offering an analogous reading of the biblical story of Joseph as an example of someone of the third generation who empowers those of the fourth generation. Jeremías Torres, *La bendición de la cuarta generación: Como vivir y disfrutar plenamente tu generación y preparar el camino para la proxima* (Lake Mary, FL: Casa Creación, 2011).

BIBLIOGRAPHY

Anderson, Allan H. *An Introduction to Pentecostalism: Global Charismatic Theology*. 2nd ed. Introduction to Religion. Cambridge-New York: Cambridge University Press, 2009.

Archer, Kenneth J. *A Pentecostal Hermeneutic for the Twenty-First Century: Spirit, Scripture and Community. Journal of Pentecostal Theology* Supplement Series 28. London: T & T Clark, 2004.

Arrington, French L. *Christian Doctrine: A Pentecostal Perspective*, Vol. 1 (Cleveland, TN: Pathway, 1997).

Assemblies of God. *Himnos de Gloria y Triunfo*. Miami: Editorial Vida: 1985.

―――. *Himnos de Inspiración y Alabanza*. Miami: Editorial Vida, 1961.

Cargal, Timothy. "Beyond the Fundamentalist-Modernist Controversy: Pentecostals and Hermeneutics in a Postmodern Age." *PNEUMA* 15:2 (Fall 1993): 163–87.

Chan, Simon. *Pentecostal Theology and the Christian Spiritual Tradition, Journal of Pentecostal Theology Supplement* Series 21. Sheffield, UK: Sheffield Academic, 2000.

Church of God. *Rayos de Esperanza*. San Antonio: Editorial Evangélica, 1952.

Cox, Harvey. *Fire from Heaven: The Rise of Pentecostal Spirituality and the Reshaping of Religion in the Twenty-first Century*. Reading, MA: Addison-Wesley, 1995.

Ewart, Frank J. *The Phenomenon of Pentecost*. Hazelwood, MO: Word Aflame, 1975.

Hyatt, Eddie. *Fire on the Earth: Eyewitnesses Reports from the Azusa Street Revival*. Lake Mary, FL: Creation House, 2006.

Kärkkäinen, Veli-Matti. "Hermeneutics: From Fundamentalism to Modernism." In *Toward a Pneumatological Theology: Pentecostal and Ecumenical Perspectives on Ecclesiology, Soteriology, and Theology of Mission*, edited by Amos Yong, 3–21. New York: University Press of America, 2002.

King, Joseph. *From Passover to Pentecost*. Franklin Springs: Advocate, 1911.

Land, Steven Jack. *Pentecostal Spirituality: A Passion for the Kingdom. Journal of Pentecostal Theology Supplement* Series 1. Sheffield, UK: Sheffield Academic, 1993.

López Rodríguez, Darío. *La Fiesta del Espíritu: espiritualidad y celebración Pentecostal*. Lima: Ediciones Puma, 2006.
Maynard-Reid, Pedrito U. "In the Spirit of Fiesta." In *Diverse Worship: African-American, Caribbean & Hispanic Perspectives*, 161–186. Downers Grove, IL: IVP Academic, 2000.
McGee, Gary B. *Initial Evidence: Historical and Biblical Perspectives on the Doctrine of Spirit Baptism*. Peabody, MA: Hendrickson, 1991.
Menzies, Robert P. "Jumping Off the Postmodern Bandwagon." *PNEUMA* 16:1 (Spring 1994): 115–20.
Parham, Sarah E. *The Life of Charles F. Parham, Founder of the Apostolic Faith Movement*. Joplin, MO: Tri–State, 1930.
Rodríguez, Daniel A. "Between Two Worlds: Hispanic Youth in the United States." In *Pentecostals and Charismatics in Latin America and Latino Communities*, edited by Néstor Medina and Sammy Alfaro, 127–39. New York: Palgrave Macmillan, 2015.
Soliván, Samuel. "Hispanic Pentecostal Worship." In *¡Alabadle! Hispanic Christian Worship*, edited by Justo L. González, 43–56. Nashville: Abingdon, 1996.
Thomas, John Christopher. "Women, Pentecostals and the Bible: An Experiment in Pentecostal Hermeneutics." *Journal of Pentecostal Theology* 5 (1994): 41–56.
Torres, Jeremías. *La bendición de la cuarta generación: Como vivir y disfrutar plenamente tu generación y preparar el camino para la próxima*. Lake Mary, FL: Casa Creación, 2011.
Villafañe, Eldin. *Introducción al Pentecostalismo: Manda Fuego Señor*. Nashville: Abingdon, 2012.
Yong, Amos. *Spirit–Word–Community: Theological Hermeneutics in Trinitarian Perspective*. Burlington, VT: Ashgate, 2002.

Chapter 3

"She orders all things *suavemente*"
A Lascasian Interpretation

Edgardo Colón-Emeric

When I think of reading the Bible in Spanish, the picture that comes to my head is of a small living room in East Durham, overcrowded with women, children, and a few men (like me) reading the Bible in unison and taking turns to talk about what we read in light of our daily struggles. When I think of Latino/a biblico-theological hermeneutics, the picture that comes to my mind is a beautiful office at Duke Divinity School, overcrowded with books in many languages, read in silence by me. What is it that joins these two pictures? What is it that makes the Bible study in East Durham theological and the theological work in my study Hispanic? What has Duke to do with Durham? For answers to these questions, I turn to Bartolomé de Las Casas, whose life and work built bridges between the university and the barrio, between Salamanca and Cumaná.

The turn to Las Casas requires explanation. Tradition is an ambiguous source for Latino/a theology.[1] The tortured development, transmission, and reception of Christian doctrines and practices makes retrieving figures from the Western tradition like Las Casas a complex task requiring "rigorous command of historical theology and Church history" and "a full command and appreciation of the Hispanic theologian's own culture."[2] The binocular vision demanded by this task is crucial and daunting. In this chapter, I focus on the first aspect of this task, an analysis of Las Casas, while trying to keep Latino/a culture within the field of vision.

Reading Las Casas denotes a return to the wellsprings of Latino/a theology. It is an exercise in *ressourcement latinamente*. In a programmatic essay underscoring the Iberian roots of Hispanic theology, Gary Macy outlines the steps in this exercise.³ *Ressourcement* involves truthful remembrance, recognition, and critical pause.

Ressourcement begins with truthful remembrance. "The first step in this process of remembering," Macy argues, "is to point out that there has been, and continues to be, an unbroken succession of distinguished and influential Christian theologians in this theological tradition, stretching from the fourth to the twenty-first centuries. This long line of theologians were creatively engaged with the important issues of their day and offered new and creative answers to those issues."⁴

Remembrance is followed by recognition. There is irreducible plurality of traditions within the Iberian heritage but also common features that can be recognized. For instance, the Iberian heritage is marked by an intercultural approach to theology, "Iberian Christian theology emerged from a continuous dialogue with other peoples and faiths."⁵ One need only recall the eight centuries of the Christian, Jewish, Muslim *convivencia* in the Iberian peninsula and the fruitful if fraught nature of those encounters. The Iberian heritage also displays concern for social justice as evidenced in its conflicted history of throne and altar collaborations. Consider Hosius of Córdoba, advisor to Constantine, "immersing himself in the complexities of the Arian controversy and calling the bishops together in the name of the emperor at Nicea."⁶ Finally, the Iberian heritage is incarnational. There is a widely held conviction among the heirs of this tradition that the material, the fleshly, and the institutional can serve as instruments of the divine will.

The Iberian streams of tradition that Macy traces can be discerned in the work of Las Casas. In turning to Las Casas, Latino/a theologians are drinking from their own wells.⁷ His approach to theology like "Hispanic theology, and hence US Latino/a theology, is intercultural by heritage, history, and almost by instinct."⁸ From figures like Las Casas, "Latino/a theologians inherit, then, a legacy of political and social involvement."⁹ Las Casas, too, believed that institutions like the Spanish monarchy could carry out God's will, but as Las Casas grew to recognize the presence of the crucified Jesus in the suffering of the Amerindians, his incarnational theology burst the seams of its Spanish institutional expressions.

The third step in a Latino/a *ressourcement* of the Iberian heritage, represented by figures like Las Casas, is a critical pause. Historical appropriation is a risky exercise. On the one hand, there is the risk of projection, "Today's political/national divisions in the Iberian peninsula and in Latin America cannot be projected back to the medieval or colonial past."¹⁰ On the other hand, there is the risk of romanticism. Macy pleads for a non-innocent *ressourcement* which acknowledges that "part of the heritage of Latino/a theology is intimately bound to the dominant theological paradigm that has in turn marginalized it."¹¹ The present study will attempt to guard against these pitfalls while acknowledging that the only way to completely avoid these risks is to abandon a *ressourcement* of Las Casas in the first place.[12]

PORTRAYING LAS CASAS

There are many portraits of Las Casas. In the United States, there are empty canvases, blank portraits. Las Casas is largely unknown. Most of the students who sign up for the class that I teach on Las Casas first search Wikipedia to find out what the class is about. (I actually had a student sign up for the course thinking that the class would be about the theology of the Christian home.) More colorful portraits are found among the works of scholars.

There are positive, flattering portraits of Las Casas. Las Casas, the historian of the Indies, whose three volume *Historia de las Indias* is an invaluable witness to the early period of the discovery and conquest. It is here that one finds the sole witness to Antón de Montesino's sermon, concerning which I will have more to say below. Las Casas, the protector of the Indians, who dedicated his intellectual and physical energies in the defense of the humanity of the indigenous. Las Casas, the bishop who wrote a *Confesionario* instructing priests to demand manumission of Amerindian slaves prior to granting absolution. Las Casas, the Dominican missiologist and tractarian. Las Casas, the prophetic author of the *Short Account of the Destruction of the Indies*. The Las Casas in these portraits strikes a powerful pose. Even his foes conceded the power of his words, describing the Dominican as "most subtle, most vigilant, most fluent, compared to whom the Ulysses of Homer was dumb stammering!"[13]

There are also negative portraits of Las Casas. Las Casas, the poor scholar, who is scolded for the inaccuracies in his citations. Las Casas, the bad Thomist, who dishonored his theological father by passing a doctrine of subjective natural rights under the banner of Aquinas. Las Casas, the self-promoting propagandist, dismissed by his contemporaries as a "frivolous person, of little authority and credit, who spoke of things he had not known or seen and made himself the talebearer of every rumor."[14] Other negative portraits include: Las Casas, the naïve evangelist, who thought that the Spanish colonists could be bearer of good news to the indigenous of Cumaná; Las Casas, the author of the black legend;[15] Las Casas, the inventor of African slavery;[16] and Las Casas, another face of empire.[17]

Some of these portraits are more faithful than others. Some say more about the author of the portrait than of the one being portrayed. In this chapter, I want to propose another portrait, Las Casas the scriptural interpreter. I present this portrait in the hope that it might shed light on another side of the Bishop of Chiapas and also serve as a guide for how to read the Bible theologically in a Latino/a context.

LAS CASAS, SCRIPTURAL INTERPRETER

The life of Las Casas could be narrated as a long struggle to read and be read by Scripture. The first stirrings of Las Casas' conscience occurred in 1511 while listening to a sermon by Antón de Montesinos on John 1:23—"I am the voice crying in the wilderness" (*Ego vox clamantis in deserto*). This voice questioned Las Casas:

> By what right and justice do you hold these Indians in such horrible and cruel bondage? By what authority have you waged such detestable wars on these people who dwelt in their peaceful gentle lands, whose infinite number you have consumed with untold deaths and violations? Are these not human beings? Do they not have rational souls? Are you not required to love them as you love yourself? Do you not understand? Do you not feel? How is it that you are so soundly asleep?[18]

Las Casas ignored that particular wakeup call, but the voice of Christ cried out again three years later. In 1514, while preparing a Pentecost sermon, Las Casas came across a text from Ecclesiasticus 34, which states, "Like one who kills a son before his father's eyes is the person who offers a sacrifice from the property of the poor" (NRSV).[19] The Vulgate version is even sharper: *Qui offert sacrificium ex substantia pauperum* ("The substance of the poor, their very existence, is at stake"). As Rivera Pagán avers, "What has been stolen is decisive for the being and existence of the dispossessed poor; their dispossession leads to the death of the oppressed."[20] Las Casas could no longer feign ignorance. He preached the sermon, sold his slaves, and committed his life to freeing the Amerindians from bondage. From then on, Las Casas' exegesis of Scripture would always be on behalf of the indigenous.

To study and illustrate Las Casas' *pro indigenas* exegetical practice, I consider his interpretation of two biblical passages, Wisdom 8:1 and Luke 14:15-24. The first of these speaks of how God's wisdom is active in creation. It is the cornerstone text in the missiological treatise known as *The Only Way*. The second is the parable of the wedding banquet. This passage was one of the arrows in the textual quiver of the foes of the indigenous. The detailed, rambling, and powerful Lascasian apology *In Defense of the Indians* offers a counter interpretation.

THE ONLY WAY TO CALL—WISDOM 8:1

The treatise *De unico vocationis modo* (*The Only Way to Call*) was written during Las Casas' "retreat" in Hispaniola soon after his entry into the

Dominican order in 1531. In this treatise, Las Casas offers theological justification for a practice of non-violent evangelism irrevocably set against that common among Spanish conquistadors and missionaries. The argument in *De unico* proceeds in a scholastic fashion. Las Casas offers a conclusion, which he then proves by presenting a series of arguments. The chief conclusion that he sets out to prove is the following:

> There is only one way, identical in all the world and for all times that was established by divine providence for teaching the true religion to all humans, namely, that way that is persuasive of the intellect with reasons (*intellectus rationibus persuasivus*) and gently attractive and exhortative of the will (*voluntatits suaviter allectivus vel exhortativus*). This way should be universally in common for all the humans of the world, without any regard to distinction of sect, errors, or corrupt customs.[21]

In proof of this conclusion, Las Casas weaves a string of "reasons, examples from the ancient fathers, the command and manner established for preaching throughout the whole life of Jesus, the manner in which this way of preaching was carried out and demanded by the apostles, citations from the holy teachers, the most ancient customs of the church, and also, its numerous decrees on the subject."[22] This catalogue of arguments falls into two broad categories: arguments from reasons (*rationibus*) and arguments from authorities (*auctoritatibus*).[23]

Evidently, Las Casas considers that arguments from reason, while necessary, are by themselves insufficient. Anthropologically, we need commands, trustworthy examples (which is part of what of what Las Casas means by arguments *auctoritatibus*), if a person is going to commit fully to a particular course of action. Significantly, Las Casas considers Scripture as a source for both kinds of arguments. The Bible is able to excite the will with its examples and also stimulate the intellect with its deep wisdom.

The Way of Divine Wisdom

The first reason that Las Casas offers in proof of his "novel" conclusion is that "one and one alone is the way proper to Divine Wisdom to provide for and move all created things to their natural acts and ends, namely, that way which is smooth (*blande*), sweet (*dulciter*), and gentle (*suaviter*)."[24] The reference to "Divine Wisdom" is noteworthy. For Las Casas, "Divine Wisdom" is an attribute of God. Throughout the treatise, Las Casas speaks of "Divine Wisdom" to name God's relation to creation. God creates, cares for, and directs creatures in accordance to his eternal wisdom. Attributing to Divine Wisdom the way of leading people to the gospel proposed by Las Casas sets up a rhetorical tension which Las Casas resolves later in the treatise. If the way of gentle intellectual and volitional persuasion is the way of wisdom, then the way of forceful pacification is the way of fools.

Las Casas anchors this first argument *rationibus* in Wisdom 8:1. Las Casas' Bible was the Vulgate. His interpretive work does not give evidence of familiarity with Greek or Hebrew versions of the biblical text. Since he is working with the Vulgate and in the Western tradition, Las Casas presupposes the canonical status of books like *Wisdom* and *Ecclesiasticus*, both of which play important roles in his life and scholarship. The Vulgate version of Wisdom 8:1 reads that wisdom *attingit ergo a fine usque ad finem fortiter, et disponit omnia suaviter*.[25] The NRSV reads this text as, "Indeed, she spans the world from end to end mightily and governs all things well."

In interpreting this text, Las Casas appeals to the *glosa ordinaria*, which states that "from the beginning of the world throughout the Old Testament until the coming of Christ he accomplished with might wondrous deeds and manifest proofs, while since the incarnation of the Word until the end of the world, he develops the suavity (*suavitatem*) of the gospel."[26] God's wisdom extends over all creaturely needs and provides for their sustenance and fulfillment. Not only does God's wisdom direct *what* God gives to his creatures but also *how*. He governs and disposes all things *suaviter*, delicately, gently, like a lover. The use of the adverb *suaviter* forms a textual link between Wisdom 8:1 and the theological refrain of the text. For Las Casas, the universe is in vibrant motion. All things come from God and return to God, and this circular movement is gently guided by God's wisdom.[27]

Las Casas' interpretation of this Wisdom 8:1 is indebted to Thomas Aquinas. As mentioned earlier, the time of composition of *De unico* coincided with Las Casas' entry into the Dominican order on the island of Hispaniola. This was a season of intensive study of the writings of Aquinas. Given the importance of Thomas for Las Casas' engagement with the biblical text, a few observations regarding the Angelic Doctor's understanding of Scripture are in order.

For Thomas, revelation is an event in the mind whereby God's light elevates the intellect to attain knowledge of things beyond its capacity. God can use anything as a means of revelation (a burning bush, a talking donkey). The means is not to be confused with the thing itself. Scripture is not revelation. However, revelation cannot be separated from Scripture, because the Bible is the best witness to the revelation received by the patriarchs, the prophets, and the apostles. The writings of these human authors are the *causae instrumentales* of Scriptural revelation, but God is the true author of Scripture.

From the divine authorship of Scripture follows the multiplicity of senses of the biblical text. Humans signify things with words, but God can signify things by words and by other things. As Brevard Child observes, for Thomas, "the spiritual senses are derived not from the words, in the Augustinian sense, but from the things signified by the words, they can themselves be signs of other things."[28] The multiplicity of senses in Scripture is ordered and Aquinas asserted the priority of the literal sense over the spiritual senses when it came to interpreting Scripture for matters of faith and morals. Having said this, it is important to clarify that by literal sense, Thomas meant that which is intended by the author, namely, God. For this reason, "nothing false can ever underlie the literal sense of Holy Writ."[29] When a tension arises, that is to say, when the letter of Scripture posits something that is patently false or morally reprehensible, the interpretive task is to find the meaning which is intended by the divine author.

Following Thomas' Exegetical Footsteps

Las Casas follows Thomas' exegetical footsteps. This will be more evident when we consider the debate regarding the right interpretation of the parable of the wedding banquet. For now, let us stay with *De unico* and the reading of Wisdom 8:1. Las Casas references three passages from the *Summa Theologiae*.

The first of these is Question 110, Article 2 of the *Prima Secundae*, which deals with the question of how grace affects the human soul.

> Now He so provides for natural creatures, that not merely does He move them to their natural acts, but He bestows upon them certain forms and powers, which are the principles of acts, in order that they may of themselves be inclined to these movements, and thus the movements whereby they are moved by God become natural and easy to creatures, according to Wisdom 8:1: "she . . . ordereth all things sweetly (*disponit omnia suaviter*)."

The second passage Las Casas references is Question 23, Article 2 of the *Secunda Secundae*, which considers the effects of charity on the soul.

> Now no act is perfectly produced by an active power, unless it be connatural to that power of reason of some form which is the principle of that action. Wherefore God, Who moves all things to their due ends, bestowed on each thing the form whereby it is inclined to the end appointed to it by Him; and in this way He "ordereth all things sweetly." (Wisdom 8:1)

The final passage Las Casas references in the first proof from reason for his non-violent vision of evangelism is Question 165, Article 2 of the *Secunda Secundae*, in which Thomas considers the fittingness of the role played by angels and demons in God's providential direction of humans beings.

God's wisdom "orders all things sweetly" (Wisdom 8:1), inasmuch as His providence appoints to each one that which is befitting it according to its nature. For as Dionysius says (Div. Nom. iv), "it belongs to providence not to destroy, but to maintain, nature."

Clearly, Wisdom 8:1 is the running thread that weaves these passages together. Las Casas does not exegete theses texts from the *Summa* but rather relies on them as authoritative guides to understanding what is at stake in Wisdom's sweet ordering of the world. He draws three inferences.[30]

First, Divine Wisdom moves rational creatures to their end in a gentle manner. After all, since God has provided creatures with the abilities that they need in order to attain their natural end, how much more will God grant humans the graces that they need in order to attain their supernatural end? Furthermore, although the human's true end is supernatural, the way in which God moves humans to this end is not unnatural. Humans are not dragged to God; they move themselves toward the vision of God by means of the theological virtues that God infuses into them.

Second, the way of leading human beings to Christianity must be gentle. The norms for guiding people to faith are set down in Matthew 28:19-20 (the "Great Commission") and Romans 10:17 ("faith comes from what is heard"). The manner in which Divine Wisdom leads humans to communion with God is analogous to the practices of teaching and preaching, or, rather, the practices of teaching and preaching are to participate in God's sweet, gentle care of creatures. Were it to be otherwise, that is to say, were the gospel to be announced in a violent way, the divine order would be overturned and the dignity of the human being would be annulled. At this point, Las Casas references the passage from Dionysius mentioned by Aquinas. In leading creatures to himself, God does not commit violence against human nature but perfects it.

Third, "the one and only way to instruct human beings in the true religion was instituted by divine providence for all the world and for all times."[31] There is one way because there is one human nature, one law of Christ, one Christian faith. Divine Wisdom (or Divine Providence, Las Casas uses the two interchangeably) is not surprised by temporal events in such a way that it has to react with violence to the vicissitudes of history. It instituted the various theological times of history (before the law, under the law, under grace) and orders all things sweetly from beginning to end.

Programmatic Significance

Having presented Wisdom 8:1 as the biblical anchor for the first argument from reason in demonstrating his thesis of non-violent evangelism, Las Casas does not quote the passage again in *De unico*. However, the location of the passage and its utilization establishes its programmatic significance for the rest of the argument. As we have seen, the language of the Vulgate version of this passage is wedded to the theological refrain of the treatise—the only way is *suaviter*. And the reality signified by the words of Wisdom 8:1 was discerned by philosophers, proclaimed by patriarchs and prophets, and embodied by Jesus Christ.

In *De unico*, wisdom's call is heard by all humans. Its suaveness can be known by human reason. Las Casas appeals to Aristotle, who taught that everything has a tendency to move in conformity to its natural capacity (*aptum natum*).[32] Las Casas associates this teaching of the Stagyrite with the words of Ecclesiasticus 6:5: *Verbum dulce multiplicat amicos et mitigat inimicos*—rendered by the NRSV as: "pleasant speech multiplies friends, and a gracious tongue multiplies courtesies." Moving someone to understanding is accomplished with sweet words rather than threats or shouts. The way of Wisdom was recognized and followed by the people of God at all stages of history: before the law (*ante legem*), under the law (*sub legem*), and under grace (*sub gratiam*).[33] The Christian faith has increased in clarity through history so that under grace the understanding of what is to be believed has grown, but the method of communicating the faith has not changed. In other words, what is taught has changed, but how it is taught has not.

By way of example, Las Casas considers the paternal mode of exhortation practiced *ante legem* by Adam, Noah, Abraham, Isaac, and Jacob. Las Casas cites various passages from Genesis in support, but when he turns his attention to the children of Jacob, Las Casas makes an interesting move. He appeals to the apocryphal *Testament of the Twelve Patriarchs* and examines in great detail how Jacob's instructions to his sons rely on a mode of paternal exhortation that persuaded the intellect and attracted the will.[34]

Las Casas appears to take the authenticity of these texts for granted. In defending his use of the Pseudepigrapha, Las Casas echoes a commonly held belief in his day that the omission of these texts from the canon was due to the perfidy of the Jews who hid them from Christians because of the clarity with which these prophecies witnessed to Christ.[35] The editors of the critical edition of *De unico* suggest that Las Casas was attracted to the universalistic outlook of the text and its message of inclusion of the Gentiles. He cited the text extensively to make up for the lack of suitable patristic material, which supported his case.[36] Perhaps. One thing is for sure. Las Casas believes that there is more to the biblical story than what is expressed within the canon of Scripture, and he also believes that the same canon provides him with a rule of faith that can serve as an interpretive lens and measure for extrabiblical texts.

Turning to the time *sub legem*, Las Casas quickly covers the time of Moses, the judges, and the kings, and only slows down his narration when considering the sapiential and prophetic literature. The conclusion of his Old Testament survey is clear: Divine Wisdom has instituted the only way to form people in the faith—*suaviter*.

The time *sub gratiam* (under grace) begins with the birth of Christ.

> Christ, as the eternal Son of God, is the Wisdom of the Father, the true and only God with the Father and the Holy Spirit. And since the essence of these three divine persons is one and the same, so, without a doubt, are wisdom and providence one . . . . The orthodox faith testifies that the works of the Trinity *ad extra* are undivided and inseparable. Thus all that Christ established or commanded, while living in the mortal flesh, was established and commanded by Divine Providence.[37]

The union of providence and wisdom in the life of Christ is the core of the argument of Las Casas' *De unico*. The Divine Wisdom that put on flesh in Jesus guides all things gently, and his disciples are commissioned in the same way. Las Casas underlines the story when Jesus sent the twelve out to proclaim the gospel to the lost sheep of Israel. Jesus instructs his disciples to travel lightly: "Take no gold, or silver, or copper in your belts, no bag for your journey, or two tunics, or sandals, or a staff" (Matt 10:9–10d).

Application to the Indies

Las Casas applies this text directly to the situation in the Indies. The only way to lead people to God is non-violently: without forceful arguments, without powerful rhetoric, without protection. Such a way of living is dangerous because there are wolves, but disciples are to put their trust in Jesus, the great shepherd of the sheep, rather than on carrying a big stick. Like the apostles, all heralds of the gospel must be wise and holy persons. If a preacher is going to stimulate the mind of the listener with reasonable arguments and credible examples for the salvific uniqueness of Christ, the preacher needs to know the subject matter well. However, technical competence is not enough. Only a person who is gentle, humble, meek, and peaceful will earn the trust that is the necessary condition for the gospel to gain a joyfully reverent listening.

In the aftermath of *De unico*, Las Casas grasps Wisdom 8:1 as the interpretive key to the events in Tuzutlán, Guatemala. Las Casas sent missionaries to this region as a test case for "The Only Way." The inhabitants of Tuzutlán had rejected Spanish priests on a number of occasions because the words of the preachers were not so much proclamations of the gospel as preludes to conquest. Yet, when the Lascasian evangelists arrived without a military escort or threats of violence, the Guatemalans willingly listened to the preaching and singing of the gospel in their own language. The land of war (Tuzutlán) became the land of true peace (Verapaz). How? "All natural things want to be directed to their end gently," Las Casas explains and adds a paraphrase of Wisdom 8:1, the Lord "orders all things to the good."[38] The way of wisdom "is absolutely contrary to that movement which our adversaries dream up with drawn swords, destructive means, and bombardments."[39] The latter is the way of fools whose interpretation of the parable of the wedding banquet as a sanction for violent evangelism does violence to Scripture and to the Amerindians. It is to a consideration of this text that I now turn.

IN DEFENSE OF THE INDIANS: THE WEDDING BANQUET (LUKE 14:15-24)

In Defense of the Indians presents Las Casas' most comprehensive refutation of the Spanish case for coercive evangelism. This case had been cogently made by the humanist scholar Juan Ginés de Sepúlveda in *Democrates Alter*. According to Sepúlveda, the Amerindians were what Aristotle called "natural slaves." These are people whose weak mental constitution needs to be ruled by other's wills for their own good. Not only were the natives *homunculi*, barely meriting the name "human," they were the most depraved of sinners whose slaughter of myriads of innocents in savage sacrificial rituals needed to be forcefully stopped.

Las Casas debated Sepúlveda at Valladolid in 1551. A significant aspect of their debate is a dispute over the proper interpretation of the parable of the wedding banquet in Luke 14:15-24. In this parable, the master commands his servant to fill his house with guests for his son's wedding even if they have to "compel them to come in."[40] This latter phrase, *compelle intrare*, became a kind of great commission for Sepúlveda, who believed that the church could gain a solid foothold in the Americas if military pacification preceded Christian evangelization. The Franciscan friar Toribio de Benavente (also known as Motolinía, the "poor one") spoke for many when he wrote to Charles V, "Since it falls to Your Majesty's office to makes haste that the holy gospel be preached throughout these lands, and since they who do not wish to hear the holy gospel of Christ of their own will should be forced, here the proverb applies, 'Better forced to be good than free to be bad.'"[41]

Biblical Hermeneutics

In refuting Sepúlveda's interpretation of the parable of the wedding banquet, Las Casas offers his richest articulation of biblical hermeneutics. Given the length, loose structure, and density of secondary sources, a detailed examination of Las Casas' rebuttal of Sepúlveda's reading is not possible here. Instead, I focus my attention on his statement regarding the interpretation of parables which contains *in nuce* his chief exegetical principles:

> Now parables may be explained in very many ways and receive very many interpretations, and the same parable can be applied to different things according to the various points of similarity. Moreover, the literal sense, upon which other meanings are based and which cannot be false, is not that which anyone may want it to be but what the author of Sacred Scripture, that is, the Holy Spirit, intends it to be. The interpretation of what or what sort that meaning may be, however, is not the function of just anybody but only of the sacred doctors, who have surpassed other men by their way of life and their teaching .... Furthermore, all theologians teach that nothing that concerns the faith or the salvation of men is proposed in sacred literature in a parable or a spiritual sense and is not clearly presented by other passages of scripture in a literal sense.[42]

Several exegetical principles are evident in Las Casas' comments on parables. First, Las Casas recognizes the plurality within Scripture. There are different kinds of texts, multiple senses to these texts, and many interpretations of these texts. Sepúlveda stands accused of misunderstanding the nature of parables. A parable is "an obscure teaching or figure of speech."[43] The "venerable doctor," as Las Casas calls him, has erred in reading an imperative nestled within a "spiritual" reading of this parable. Sepúlveda displays unbelievable "rashness" in using a parable to prove that Christ intended the church to use compulsion in order to make space for the proclamation of the gospel. "What do joyful tidings," he asks, "have to do with wounds, captivities, massacres, conflagrations, the destruction of cities, and the common evils of war?"[44]

Las Casas reads the Bible with attention to the distinction between the Old and New Testaments. Sepúlveda's interpretation of the *compelle intrare* as an imperial mandate is buttressed by numerous appeals to the Deuteronomic code and to the parallels between Israel's wars of conquest and the Spanish wars of expansion. Las Casas counters this hermeneutical move by showing how it is based on a false understanding of history.[45] The events of Scripture (and of history) are to be read in light of how Divine Wisdom guides the creaturely return to God through a diversity of theological times (*ante legem, sub legem, sub gratiam*), a diversity that is expressed in Scripture in two testaments. This theological understanding of history originates in Scripture and was codified in canon law which stated that "The Scriptures are to be understood according to the diversity of times, peoples, and places."[46] Without a Christian theology of history, a proper interpretation of the biblical text as Christian Scripture is impossible. The Sepulvedan interpretation is a completely novel reading of the parable without biblical, theological, or historical merit.

Second, Las Casas defends the priority of the literal sense of Scripture. Like Aquinas, Las Casas believes that the literal sense is that sense which the true author of Scripture, the Holy Spirit, intends for us to understand. Of course, Las Casas knew of the tradition of reading multiple senses in Scripture. He does not deny the fecundity of the text as a moral guide or as a window into the life to come. What he asserts is the primacy of the literal sense for the development of doctrine. This emphasis is hardly surprising given our friar's formation in the Dominican order. Dominicans favored the literal sense of Scripture over the spiritual interpretations for several reasons.[47] For one, the emphasis on the literal sense was a strong check against the fanciful spiritual readings found among apocalyptic groups like the Franciscan friars, whose zealous missionary activity in the Americas was strongly motivated by the belief that such work would usher in a new age of the church, the age of the Spirit when the meek friars would inherit the earth. In emphasizing the literal sense, Las Casas moves away from Franciscan Spiritualists, like Motolinía, whose apocalyptic interpretation of Scripture robbed historical events of their earthiness. At the same time, the literal sense as interpreted by Las Casas was deeply theological. Scripture must be read according to the intent of its divine author, the Holy Spirit.

Applying this principle to the parable, Las Casas states that "by the words of the parable 'Force them to come in' Christ means that, immediately by himself or through angels or men, he usually moves and attracts to himself in an intellectual fashion and, as it were, compels by a visible or invisible miracle those who do not know his truth, yet without exercising any force on their will. That is the literal sense."[48] The compulsion that the parable commends is not physical; it is the compulsion of a true, persuasive argument.

In supporting this interpretation of the literal sense, Las Casas cites many authorities and considers biblical counter-examples. Was not Paul forcibly thrown to the ground when he was called by Christ?[49] Yes. But the church considers this to be singular example and not a common pattern. Sepúlveda's appeal to Old Testament texts like the story of Sodom and Gomorra as sanction for violence stand discounted on the ground that "not all of God's judgments are examples for us."[50] Some of the actions of God in the Bible "must be admired rather than imitated."[51] In any case, when it comes to how God leads humans to himself, compulsion is excluded, even in the case of Paul, because God (and only God) can change the will without forcing it. In support of this claim, Las Casas cites yet again Wisdom 8:1, "she deploys her strength from one end of the earth to the other, ordering all things gently."[52]

The universal reach of Wisdom allows Las Casas to develop what might be called a "hermeneutic of humanity." In rejecting an interpretation of a papal decree sanctioning the use of violence to punish pagan sins against natural law, Las Casas states, "Something must not be asserted or an interpretation chosen from which could follow absurdity, inhumanity, or incongruity. And so each commentary must be interpreted in such a way that no inhumanity or absurdity follows, because absurdity must always be avoided. That is why, to avoid absurdity, a general commentary must be narrowed."[53] In other words, texts are to be interpreted charitably both with respect to their intent and to their application.

Of course, such a generous reading is not always possible, as when Aristotle states that barbarians are to be hunted down and killed like wild animals, to which Las Casas replies: "Good-bye Aristotle! From Christ, the eternal truth, we have the command 'You must love your neighbor as yourself.'"[54] Las Casas is convinced that Scripture and Christian tradition support his case. Texts that complicate the defense of the Indians are ignored rather than reinterpreted. In this regard, he is like a defense attorney who presents all the evidence in favor of his client and will not bring up opposing evidence unless it has already been introduced by the prosecution.

There is a risk here that one ends up with a tendentious reading of Scripture. Nevertheless, according to Elsa Tamez, "Intentional selectivity is one of the characteristics of a contextual biblical hermeneutic precisely because the context leads the exegete or ordinary reader to choose those texts which are a lamp unto the path and a light for the way."[55] This hermeneutical approach bears resemblance to the way in which Las Casas was taught to read texts in Salamanca, but with two additions: an explicit Christological basis and an intentional Indian perspective. The hermeneutic of humanity is ultimately vindicated by the incarnation of the Word. Divine Wisdom puts on flesh.

Third, the interpretation of Holy Scripture is best done by holy interpreters. Las Casas considers the reading of Scripture to be a spiritual task that requires abandoning self-interest in order to be sensitive to the movement of the Holy Spirit. "In explaining Scripture, shall we give greater credence to holy men, who probably had God's spirit as they interpreted the sacred writings, or to Sepúlveda and his accomplices, who in violation of Christ's law try to destroy that immense world by ruinous war?"[56] Sepúlveda is found wanting not in education but in character. "For what spirit leads a theologian, mature and well versed in human letters, to set these poisons before the world so that the far-flung Indian empires, contrary to the law of Christ, would be prey for most savage thieves?"[57]

Las Casas' denunciation of Sepúlveda bears similarity to a fallacious *ad hominen* argument, but the resemblance is a passing one. In a study of Thomas Aquinas as reader of Scripture, Eugene Rogers introduces a distinction that illuminates Las Casas' argument.[58] Hermeneutics and interpretation are not to be confused with each other. The former requires linguistic skills, knowledge of history, keenness of mind; in short, the kinds of abilities that are either innate or learned. The latter requires assistance from a different realm. The hermeneutical task is important but it leaves the interpretation underdeveloped. Only God's grace can lead to a reading of Scripture that is revelatory; this grace works within and around the interpreter.

When working within the interpreter, we speak of infused virtues. For instance, the virtue of temperance can restrain a reader from interpreting a text in a manner that is self-serving. At Valladolid, Las Casas does not question Sepúlveda's skills as a reader, which Las Casas acknowledges on many occasions, but his virtues as an interpreter. When working around the reader, we speak of providence. According to Rogers, "providence names among other things a way in which for Thomas interpretation resists human attempts to control it."[59] What prevents illicit eisegesis of Scripture is its author, God. As Roger states, "the influence that an interpreter's interpretation exerts on the way in which his or her purposes meet with success or failure stands under providence, too."[60] Ultimately, the truthfulness and goodness of an interpretation of Scripture depends not on hermeneutical skills or even personal virtues but on God's providence. Las Casas was not a better interpreter of Scripture, because he was more pious than Sepúlveda or because as a Thomist he drank from deeper wells than his opponent. Personal or methodological Donatism is to be eschewed. It was God's providence, Divine Wisdom, which *suaviter* led Las Casas to an encounter with the Indian that opened his eyes to seeing Christ and Scripture in a new way.

Much more could be said of Las Casas' refutation of Sepúlveda's interpretation of the parable of the wedding banquet. I hope that this is enough to illustrate some of his core convictions regarding biblical exegesis.

The Sketch of An Exegete

After considering how Las Casas interpreted Scripture in his theological treatises, I move to offer a sketch of Las Casas as biblical interpreter. The sketch is tentative on account of the few texts considered here, but hopefully accurate in its outlines and suggestive in its open-endedness.

First, Las Casas is a lover of Scripture. Detailed studies of his works give ample evidence of the extent of his engagement with the Bible.[61] As might be expected, he appeals numerous times to passages like Gen. 1:26 (humanity in the image of God), the prophets (Ezek. 34, which condemns the shepherds who mistreat their sheep), and the wisdom writings (especially passages like Prov. 8:15, which submit royal power to God's authority). It is risky and at times erroneous to assess the importance of biblical passages to the thought of Las Casas simply by tallying up the frequency of their use. Nonetheless, a survey of his most commonly used texts reveals a strong preference for the New Testament, in particular for the Gospel according to Matthew and Paul's Epistle to the Romans.[62] The Lascasian work with the most biblical citations is the treatise *The Only Way* (550 direct citations), followed by *In Defense of the Indians* (300 citations). In these same works, Las Casas cites Aquinas (120 and 150 times respectively) and Aristotle (55 and 75 times, respectively).[63] Las Casas was a Thomist before he was Aristotelian, but he was first and foremost a student of Scripture.

Second, Las Casas is a lover of wisdom. He searches the Scriptures for understanding into the events unfolding around him. One might say that Las Casas' attention to Scripture is simply a sign that he is a child of his age. Columbus and Sepúlveda also cherished the Bible.[64] However, as Néstor Míguez observes, these interpreters presented the Bible "as a closed book and in Latin, as a sacred image."[65] Pizarro's Bible did not speak to Atahualpa, who rightly saw it for what it was—a sign of conquest. The case of Las Casas is evidence that "Latin America was 'evangelized' with a closed Bible against an open Bible, and that when the Bible is opened its location in the history of domination changes."[66] Las Casas is not simply a child of Spain, he is a child of the wisdom that guides all things to God and that judges as unnatural, unscriptural, and blasphemous whatever is violent in the world.

David Ford has spoken extensively on the significance of wisdom as a hermeneutical category and of how at the heart of the theological task lies the responsibility of addressing the suffering present in the world.[67] Las Casas understood all too well that "Prophetic scriptural wisdom is inextricably involved with the discernment of cries."[68] The Divine Wisdom that guides all things gently (*suaviter*) cries to the exegete through the pages of Scripture, but it is not bound to this text alone. The wisdom of God is incarnate in the crucified Christ.

This is the most important interpretive principle in the Lascasian corpus. As Las Casas states: "The works of Christ, much more than his words, are law for us. For being the eternal law himself, and the art and wisdom of the Father, and the Word clothed in mortal flesh, through whom God the Father spoke to the world, all that he said corresponds to the mind and will of the Father, and thus to the Trinity most high."[69] The works of Christ in proclaiming release to the captives and his identification with the suffering of the Amerindians are also megaphones of God's wisdom and carry the weight of law for Las Casas and us. "The wisdom that is embodied here is simultaneously one that hears God's voice . . . and worships God, and that hears the cries of the suffering and brings good news to them."[70] Las Casas hears the voice of Christ in the cry of the Amerindian, and it is their cry that opens his eyes to read the biblical text and the historical context wisely.

Third, Las Casas is a lover of preaching. The only extant Lascasian interpretations of Scripture are found in treatises. Yet, it is reasonable to see

Montesino's sermon as a model for Las Casas' own preaching. A few considerations argue in favor of the significance of this sermon as a model for Las Casas preaching.

First, there is Las Casas' own testimony to the sermon. When one considers the paucity of Las Casas' records of colonial preaching (either by conquistadors or by indianophiles), the extensive citation of the Montesinos sermon is noteworthy. All indications suggest that Las Casas wrote the account of this preaching into his *Historia* after his entrance into the Dominican order during his time of study in Hispaniola. Las Casas does not seem to base his narration on a sermon manuscript but on his own recollection of an event that happened years, if not decades, before.

Second, the responses to Las Casas' preaching are similar to those experienced by Montesinos. A letter written in 1533 to the king of Spain complains that Las Casas' homilies had "sown opinions about the Indians which had given rise to scruples of conscience among his neighbors."[71] When colonists on their way to New Spain came by his church in the town of Puerto Plata, Las Casas put the fear of God into them with his sermons, telling them that "they were in mortal sin and that they could not in good conscience own Indians."[72] In a letter of explanation to the king in 1534, Las Casas admits that he is guilty of condemning "the great offenses committed against God and toward the destruction of the souls and bodies of the unhappy peoples of these previously unknown lands" but rejects the charge that these words are seditious. On the contrary, Las Casas informs the king that the preaching in Puerto Plata is an act of loyalty, because the colonists' actions place the king's conscience in "incredible danger of the strict account that he is to give before God."[73]

In sum, Las Casas reads the Bible as the book of the church, a book that becomes alive when proclaimed in a liturgical context. Las Casas reads himself and us into the text. Whatever his limitations, Las Casas represents at the time of the conquest a "reading of the Bible from the perspective of the impoverished, the exploited, and marginalized cultures."[74] He is the voice of Christ in the wilderness of the Spaniards' consciences. He is not Isaiah crying out comfort, but John the Baptist, preaching the need for repentance, the imminence of judgment, and the hope of forgiveness. He is a preaching fool on a quixotic quest to announce a wisdom that was deeply disturbing in his time and ours.[75]

CONCLUSION

In the town of Juayúa in El Salvador, there is a large cross on which hangs a very dark-skinned Christ. The statue dates to sometime in the 1600s, but its origins are unknown. Some stories say that Franciscan missionaries introduced the statue of the "Cristo negro" as a way of connecting more closely to the indigenous people of the region. More likely, the statue was made in Spain and that the skin was originally more olive in tone. What is certain is that over the centuries the chemical interaction of the Spanish wood with the smoke of burning candles has darkened its hue to its present complexion. In other words, years of the prayers of the faithful have changed the Spanish Christ into a mestizo/mulatto Christ. In the case of Las Casas, it was the cry of wisdom calling from Amerindian lips that changed his perception of Christ and opened the Bible anew.

When Latina/os open the Bible they tend to read the text in one of two ways.[76] On the one hand, there are those who look for connections between the biblical text and the reader's context. To read the Bible through Hispanic eyes entails finding and building bridges between the world of the Bible and our own, between Rome and Washington, Nazareth and Nogales, Jesus' experience of marginality and the plight of the mestizo. On the other hand, there are those who worry that such an approach can close the distance between the text and us too easily, a distance that is important for the text to critique our context, and also for our context to critique the text. The first of these approaches, the hermeneutics of correlation, is one that has been practiced and continues to be practiced, by many Latinas and Latinos in pulpits, classrooms, kitchens, and fields all over this land. The second of these, the hermeneutics of otherness, is perhaps less common in the sanctuary than in the academy and yet appears to be the waxing one.[77] If the first one draws attention to the subject who reads through Hispanic eyes, the second one draws attention to the hyphen that both joins and separates text from context.

A Lascasian interpretation looks for both correlation and otherness between the biblical text and our context in the humanity of Christ. When it comes to interpreting biblical texts, what must be avoided is not simply a logical or historical absurdity but the theological absurdity that the God who is love would promote inhumanity toward Christ and Christ's own. Las Casas invites an interpretation of Scripture that opts for the *lectio difficilior*. The harder reading which calls on us to love the neighbor as Christ loved us is the true reading. Other hermeneutical strategies, the hermeneutics of otherness and the hermeneutics of correlation, are to be approached via the hermeneutics of Christ's humanity, which is ultimately the hermeneutics of charity, the *vinculum amoris* which binds all things in perfect harmony.

In closing, I return to the opening images of the study and the living rooms as settings for a theological reading of the Bible in Spanish. From the contrast of those two settings, I asked a series of questions to which I offer now a tentative Lascasian reply. What is it that makes the Bible study in East Durham theological and the theological work in my study Hispanic? What has Duke to do with Durham?

What makes a Hispanic reading of the Bible theology? A Hispanic reading of the Bible is theology (theo-logia, God-Word) because it is chief and foremost about God, and all other things as they are related to God. Las Casas reminds us that Christ is the Divine Wisdom that guides all things gently (*suaviter*), including all things Latina/o. Christ is the norm of Scripture, history, and theology, and all dialogue with Christian and non-Christian texts and traditions is precisely through the Word (*dia-logos*).

What makes Latino/a readings of the Bible Hispanic? Las Casas might point to the apologetic intent of these readings. A Latino/a interpretation of Scripture is apologetic, in that from the truth of the Word of God (*apo-logos*) it mounts a double defense: a defense of what is good and true in Hispanic culture and history against the evils of poverty and alienation and also a defense of the Christian doctrines threatened by these very evils.

What image unites reading the Scripture in the study at Duke and the living room in the barrio? Las Casas offers the portrait of crucified wisdom for our consideration. The Latino/a reader of Scripture in the barrio and the academy are united in their common longing for wisdom, a wisdom that comes from above and cries from below, a wisdom that redraws the maps of theological education, a wisdom that denounces violence as it affirms life.

NOTES

1. See Sixto García, "Sources and Loci of Hispanic Theology," in *Mestizo Christianity: Theology from the Latino Perspective*, ed. Arturo Bañuelas (Maryknoll, NY: Orbis Books, 1995), 108–110.
2. García, "Sources and Loci of Hispanic Theology," 110.
3. Gary Macy, "The Iberian Heritage of US Latino/a Theology," in *Futuring Our Past: Explorations in the Theology of Tradition*, ed. Orlando Espín and Gary Macy (Maryknoll, NY: Orbis Books, Kindle Edition, 2014).
4. Macy, "Iberian Heritage," 1126–1129.
5. Macy, "Iberian Heritage," 1254–1259.
6. Macy, "Iberian Heritage," 1270–1271.
7. See Gustavo Gutiérrez, *We Drink from Our Own Wells: The Spiritual Journey of a People* (Maryknoll, NY: Orbis Books, 1994).
8. Macy, "Iberian Heritage," 1254–1259.
9. Macy, "Iberian Heritage," 1276–1278.
10. Macy, "Iberian Heritage," 1292–1295.
11. Ibid., 1229–1230.
12. Other examples of *ressourcement a la latina* are: Michelle González's work on Sor Juana Inés de la Cruz, *Sor Juana: Beauty and Justice in the Americas* (Maryknoll,

NY: Orbis Books, 2003); and Alex García's study on Martín de Porres, *St. Martin De Porres: The Little Stories and the Semiotics of Culture* (Maryknoll, NY: Orbis Books, 1995). The first brings the muse of the Americas into a conversation revolving around theological aesthetics, and the second fosters a dialogue between the poor mulatto of Lima and semiotics.

13. Cited in Henry Raup Wagner, *The Life and Writings of Bartolomé de las Casas* (Albuquerque: The University of New Mexico Press, 1967), 247.

14. Juan Comas, "Historical Reality and the Detractors of Father Las Casas" in *Bartolomé de las Casas in History: Toward an Understanding of the Man and His Work*, ed. Juan Friede and Benjamin Keen (DeKalb: Northern Illinois University Press, 1971), 506.

15. Comas notes that for many: "Las Casas grossly exaggerated the exploitation and unjust treatment of the Indians when he denounced such actions to the Spanish king and the Council of the Indies" ("Historical Reality," 489).

16. Comas notes that some of Las Casas detractors say: "That Las Casas was pro-slavery because he proposed to bring Negro slaves to America" ("Historical Reality," 505). However, as Las Casas himself observes:

> This advice to give a license for the bringing of black slaves to those lands was first given by the *clérigo* Casas, who was unaware of the injustice with which the Portuguese take them and make slaves of them; later, after falling into this snare, he regretted it and would not have given this advice for anything in the world, for he always believed them [sic] made slaves unjustly and tyrannically, because they have the same right to freedom as the Indians. The *clérigo* Casas soon repented of the advice he had given, judging he had been guilty of carelessness, for as he later saw and ascertained that the slavery of the blacks was as unjust as that of the Indians, he perceived how unwise was the remedy he proposed in bringing in blacks in order to make possible the freedom of the Indians. True, he had supposed that the blacks were justly made slaves, but he was uncertain whether his ignorance and good intentions would excuse him before the divine judgment.
>
> ("Historical Reality," 505)

17. Daniel Castro, *Another Face of Empire: Bartolomé de Las Casas, Indigenous Rights, and Ecclesiastical Imperialism* (Durham: Duke University Press, 2007).

18. Bartolomé de Las Casas, *Historia de las Indias*, ed. André Saint-Lu (Caracas: Biblioteca Ayacucho, 1986), 13–14.

19. The full text from Ecclesiasticus 34:21–27 reads:

> If one sacrifices ill-gotten goods, the offering is blemished; the gifts of the lawless are not acceptable. The Most High is not pleased with the offerings of the ungodly, nor for a multitude of sacrifices does he forgive sin. Like one who kills a son before his father's eyes is the person who offers a sacrifice from the property of the poor. The bread of the needy is the life of the poor; whoever deprives them of it is a murderer. To take away a neighbor's living is to commit murder; to deprive an employee of wages is to shed blood.

20. Luis Rivera Pagán, *A Violent Evangelism: The Political and Religious Conquest of the Americas* (Louisville: Westminster/John Knox Press, 1992), 238.

21. Bartolomé de Las Casas, *Obras Completas 2. De unico vocationis modo* (Madrid, Alianza Editorial, 1990), 16. All translations into English are my own.

22. Las Casas, *De unico*, 16.
23. Cf. Las Casas, *De unico*, 368.
24. Las Casas, *De unico*, 16.
25. I am using the online version of the Vulgate found at http://www.drbo.org/lvb/.
26. Las Casas, *De unico*, 22. Sap. 8:1 "*Attingit a fine.* Id est a principio mundi usque ad adventum Christi, mirifica opera et sincera testimonia per Vetus Testamentum fortiter asserit, et ab incarnatione Verbi usque ad finem mundi suavitatem Evengelii exponit. *A fine ergo usque ad finem fortiter pertingit*, quia ubique perfecte agit: finis enim perfectionem significat." J.-P. Migne, ed., *Patrologiae Cursus Completus,* Vol. 113 (Paris: Migne, 1852), 1172.
27. Cf. Las Casas, *De unico*, 19.
28. Brevard S. Childs, *The Struggle to Understand Isaiah as Christian Scripture* (Grand Rapids, MI: William B. Eerdmans Publishing Company, 2004), 152.
29. *Summa Theologiae* 1.1.10.ad3. Citations for the *Summa Theologia* are from *The Summa Theologica of St. Thomas Aquinas*, Second and Revised Edition, translated by Fathers of the English Dominican Province, accessed online at http://www.newadvent.org/summa.
30. See Las Casas, *De unico*, 16–22.
31. Las Casas, *De unico*, 16.
32. (Aristotle, *Physics* 2.8 cited in Las Casas, *De unico*, 24).
33. Las Casas, *De unico*, 107.
34. Las Casas, *De unico*, 133ff.
35. Las Casas, *De unico*, 139.
36. Las Casas, *De unico*, n. 47, 138.
37. Las Casas, *De unico*, 161.
38. Bartolomé de las Casas, *In Defense of the Indians*, trans. Stafford Poole (DeKalb: Northern Illinois University Press, 1992); *Obras Completas*, Vol. 9: *Apología*, ed. Angel Losada (Madrid: Alianza Editorial, 1988), 180.
39. Las Casas, *In Defense*, 276.
40. Luke 14:23 in the Vulgate reads: "Exi in vias, et sepes: et compelle intrare, ut impleatur domus mea."
41. Cited by Gustavo Gutiérrez, *Las Casas: In Search of the Poor of Jesus Christ* (Maryknoll, NY: Orbis Books, 1993), 137.
42. Las Casas, *In Defense*, 269.
43. *In Defense*, 269.
44. *In Defense*, 270.
45. See José Alejandro Cárdenas Bunsen, *Escritura y Derecho Canónico en la obra de Bartolomé de Las Casas* (Vervuert: Iberoamericana, 2011), 237. Cárdenas Bunsen states, "There were many references to the Deuteronomic code in respect to the holy wars between Israel and the Canaanites. The dispute between Sevúlpeda and Las Casas is centered in part on an exegesis of those wars and their relevance . . . . According to Sevúlveda, the Deuteronomic war code clarifies the transcendent meaning of the armed conquest of the Americas by Spain and justifies it. According to Las Casas, Sepúlveda "has not researched the scriptures with sufficient determination," since "in this era of grace and piety" he remains obstinate "in his unbending

application of the rigid precepts of the old Testament." This hermeneutical error has a tragic consequences: "It facilitates the way for the cruel invasion by tyrants and looters, and for the oppression, exploitation, and slavery of innocent nations."

46. Cited in Cárdenas Bunsen, *Escritura y Derecho Canónico en la obra de Bartolomé de las Casas*, 115.

47. Cf. Nicholas Healy, "Introduction," *Aquinas on Scripture: An Introduction to his Biblical Commentaries*, ed. Thomas Weinandy, Daniel Keating, and John Yocum (New York: T&T International, 2005), 8–17. Nicholas Healey offers several explanations to account for this newfound emphasis. First, the turn to the literal sense corrects the fanciful spiritual readings of mystics like Joachim of Fiore (d.1204). Second, the rise of Aristotelianism increased interest in the reality of visible things as good in themselves and not simply as shadows. Third, the Dominican insistence on conforming the form of their life to the life as codified in the counsels of perfection resisted exegetical moves that looked for meaning beyond the history described in the text. Fourth, the change in the context of theological education from monastery to university, from *lectio* to *disputatio*, gave rise to a method of "dialectical inquiry" that addressed questions and tensions that emerged from the text itself.

48. Las Casas, *In Defense*, 271.
49. *In Defense*, 275.
50. *In Defense*, 121.
51. *In Defense*, 121.
52. *In Defense*, 275.
53. *In Defense*, 123–124.
54. *In Defense*, 40. Las Casas describes an altogether different kind of hunt where the proclamation of the gospel tames the inner beasts that torment humanity before coming back to the philosopher: "This chase was different from the one Aristotle taught. Although he was a profound philosopher, he was not worthy to be captured in the chase so that he could come to God through knowledge of the true faith" (*In Defense*, 41).

55. Elsa Tamez, *Bajo un cielo sin estrellas* (San José, Costa Rica: Editorial Departamento Ecuménico de Investigaciones, 2001), 21.

56. Las Casas, *In Defense*, 278.
57. Las Casas, *In Defense*, 267.
58. Eugene F. Rogers, "How the Virtues of an Interpreter Presuppose and Perfect Hermeneutics: The Case of Thomas Aquinas," *Journal of Religion* 76.1 (1996): 64–81. Bruce Marshall, "Absorbing the World: Christianity and the Universe of Truths," in *Theology and Dialogue: Essays in Conversation with George Lindbeck*, ed. Bruce Marshall (Notre Dame: Notre Dame University Press, 1990), 69–102. Paul Blowers, "The *Regula Fidei* and the Narrative Character of Early Christian Faith," *Pro Ecclesia* 6.2 (1997): 199–228.

59. Rogers, "How the Virtues," 80.
60. Rogers, "How the Virtues," 80.
61. The most thorough study of this topic is by Eduardo Frades in *El uso de la Biblia en los escritos de Fray Bartolomé de las Casas* (Caracas: Instituto Seminario Santa Rosa de Lima, 1997).

62. Frades, *El uso de la Biblia*, 52.
63. Frades, *El uso de la Biblia*, 179.
64. Jean-Pierre Ruiz states that "Columbus was in fact employing the Bible in a radically new way. It furnished both the ideology of conquest and the rationale for his millenialistic and messianic designs." See *Reading from the Edges: The Bible and People on the Move* (Maryknoll, NY: Orbis Books, 2011), 134.
65. Néstor Míguez, "Lectura Latinoamericana de la Biblia: Experiencias y desafíos," *Cuadernos de Teología* 20 (2001): 77–99, 78. The conquest gave rise to an imperial reading of Scripture.
66. Ibid.
67. David F. Ford, *Christian Wisdom: Desiring God and Learning in Love* (Cambridge: Cambridge University Press, 2007). See also David F. Ford, *The Future of Christian Theology* (West Sussex: Wiley-Blackwell, 2011).
68. Ford, *Christian Wisdom*, 5.
69. Las Casas, *De unico*, 215.
70. Ford, *Christian Wisdom*, 19–20.
71. Cited by Alvor Huerga, the editor, in Bartolomé de Las Casas, *Obras Completas. 1: Vida y Obras,* (Madrid: Alianza Editorial, 1998), 159.
72. Huerga, *Vida y Obras*, 159.
73. Las Casas, *Obras Completas 13: Cartas y Memoriales* (Madrid: Alianza Editorial, 1995), 84.
74. Elsa Tamez, *Bajo un cielo sin estrellas*, 138. I speak of limitations because Las Casas was obviously shaped by his own context (male, Spanish, Catholic) in ways that influenced his engagement with Scripture and also because of the limitations of the history of scriptural interpretation itself. Tamez's melancholic warning is not to be easily set aside:

> La lucha por una lectura liberadora de la Biblia es buena, sin embargo, me parece que, después de echar una mirada a la historia y vernos en ella como en un espejo, debemos ir más allá de la lucha hermenéutica. Debemos revisar el discurso de nuestro canon escrito y la lógica del pensamiento cristiano; quizás existe un problema que facilita la rápida inversión de valores. Me refiero a aspectos de la concepción bíblica del tiempo, es decir, la progresión infinita hacia la victoria final . . .la idea de un Dios universalista, intolerante e igualitario, . . . el discurso sacrificial, . . . el concepto der elegidos, la guerra santa, etc." (145).

Understandably, memory of this history is what led a group of indigenous people to officially return the Bible to John Paul II. Their words are reprinted by Tamez and bear repeating: "La Biblia llegó a nosotros como parte del cambio colonial impuesto. Ella fue el arma ideológica de ese asalto colonialista. La espada española, que de día atacaba y asesinaba el cuerpo de los indios, de noche se convertía en la cruz que atacaba el alma indígena" (136).

75. For a brilliant reflection on the preacher as fool, see Charles L. Campbell and Johan H. Cilliers, *The Preaching Fools: The Gospel as a Rhetoric of Folly* (Waco, TX: Baylor University Press, 2012). The image of the fool as a quixotic, paradoxical figure is one that merits further study as an interpretive lens through which to read Las Casas.

76. Luis R. Rivera-Rodríguez, "Reading in Spanish from the Diaspora through Hispanic Eyes," *Theology Today* 54 (1998): 480–490. Rivera-Rodríguez's proposal to these two hermeneutical approaches is a hermeneutics of critical correlation. "Instead of deciding in advance that the 'text' is neither distant nor strange (hermeneutics of correlation) or that the text is distant and strange (diaspora hermeneutics), a critical correlation model would allow the reader to explore his or her first perception in reading the texts, whether it be one of initial affinity or of distancing" (489–90).

77. Jean-Pierre Ruiz decries the problems with the hermeneutics of correlation, which can be little more than prooftexting and tend toward abstraction from the particularities of the social situatedness of the text or the density of the present situation. By contrast: "A hermeneutic of otherness and engagement offers a salutary alternative, suggesting instead that mapping relationships between texts and their contexts, between readers and their contexts, and between texts and readers across contexts is a matter of complex negotiation and not linear correspondence" (*Reading from the Edges*, 8).

BIBLIOGRAPHY

Aquinas, Thomas. *The Summa Theologica of St. Thomas Aquinas*. Second and Revised Edition. Trans. Fathers of the English Dominican Province. Accessed online: http://www.newadvent.org/summa.

Blowers, Paul. "The *Regula Fidei* and the Narrative Character of Early Christian Faith." *Pro Ecclesia* 6.2 (1997): 199–228.

Campbell, Charles L., and Johan H. Cilliers. *The Preaching Fools: The Gospel as a Rhetoric of Folly*. Waco, TX: Baylor University Press, 2012.

Cárdenas Bunsen, José Alejandro. *Escritura y Derecho Canónico en la obra de Bartolomé de Las Casas*. Vervuert: Iberoamericana, 2011.

Castro, Daniel. *Another Face of Empire: Bartolomé de Las Casas, Indigenous Rights, and Ecclesiastical Imperialism*. Durham: Duke University Press, 2007.

Childs, Brevard S. *The Struggle to Understand Isaiah as Christian Scripture*. Grand Rapids, MI: William B. Eerdmans Publishing Company, 2004.

Comas, Juan. "Historical Reality and the Detractors of Father Las Casas." In *Bartolomé de las Casas in History: Toward an Understanding of the Man and His Work*, edited by Juan Friede and Benjamin Keen, 487–537. DeKalb: Northern Illinois University Press, 1971.

de Las Casas, Bartolomé. *Historia de las Indias*. Ed. André Saint-Lu. Caracas: Biblioteca Ayacucho, 1986.

———. *In Defense of the Indians*. Trans. Stafford Poole. DeKalb: Northern Illinois University Press, 1992.

———. *Obras Completas*. Vol 1: *Vida y Obras*. Ed. Alvor Huerga. Madrid: Alianza Editorial, 1998.

———. *Obras Completas*, Vol. 2: *De unico vocationis modo*. Madrid, Alianza Editorial, 1990.

———. *Obras Completas*, Vol. 9: *Apología*. Ed. Angel Losada. Madrid: Alianza Editorial, 1988.
———. *Obras Completas*, Vol. 13: *Cartas y Memoriales*. Madrid: Alianza Editorial, 1995.
Ford, David F. *Christian Wisdom: Desiring God and Learning in Love*. Cambridge: Cambridge University Press, 2007.
———. *The Future of Christian Theology*. West Sussex: Wiley-Blackwell, 2011.
Frades, Eduardo. *El uso de la Biblia en los escritos de Fray Bartolomé de las Casas*. Caracas: Instituto Seminario Santa Rosa de Lima, 1997.
García, Alejandro. *St. Martin De Porres: The Little Stories and the Semiotics of Culture*. Maryknoll, NY: Orbis Books, 1995.
García, Sixto. "Sources and Loci of Hispanic Theology." In *Mestizo Christianity: Theology from the Latino Perspective*, edited by Arturo Bañuelas, 108–110. Maryknoll, NY: Orbis Books, 1995.
González, Michelle. *Sor Juana: Beauty and Justice in the Americas*. Maryknoll, NY: Orbis Books, 2003.
Gutiérrez, Gustavo. *Las Casas: In Search of the Poor of Jesus Christ*. Maryknoll, N.Y.: Orbis Books, 1993.
———. *We Drink from Our Own Wells: The Spiritual Journey of a People*. Maryknoll, NY: Orbis Books, 1994.
Healy, Nicholas. "Introduction." In *Aquinas on Scripture: An Introduction to his Biblical Commentaries*, edited by Thomas Weinandy, Daniel Keating, and John Yocum, 8–17. New York: T&T International, 2005.
Macy, Gary. "The Iberian Heritage of US Latino/a Theology." In *Futuring Our Past: Explorations in the Theology of Tradition*, edited by Orlando Espín and Gary Macy, 43–82. Maryknoll, NY: Orbis Books, 2014.
Marshall, Bruce. "Absorbing the World: Christianity and the Universe of Truths." In *Theology and Dialogue: Essays in Conversation with George Lindbeck*, edited by Bruce Marshall, 69–102. Notre Dame: Notre Dame University Press, 1990.
Migne, J.-P., ed. *Patrologiae Cursus Completus: Series Graeca*. Vol 113. Paris: Migne, 1852.
Míguez, Néstor. "Lectura Latinoamericana de la Biblia: Experiencias y desafíos." *Cuadernos de Teología* 20 (2001): 77–99.
Raup Wagner, Henry. *The Life and Writings of Bartolomé de las Casas*. Albuquerque: The University of New Mexico Press, 1967.
Rivera Pagán, Luis. *A Violent Evangelism: The Political and Religious Conquest of the Americas*. Louisville: Westminster/John Knox Press, 1992.
Rivera-Rodríguez, Luis R. "Reading in Spanish from the Diaspora through Hispanic Eyes." *Theology Today* 54 (1998): 480–490.
Rogers, Eugene F. "How the Virtues of an Interpreter Presuppose and Perfect Hermeneutics: The Case of Thomas Aquinas." *Journal of Religion* 76.1 (1996): 64–81.
Ruiz, Jean-Pierre. *Reading from the Edges: The Bible and People on the Move*. Maryknoll, NY: Orbis Books, 2011.
Tamez, Elsa. *Bajo un cielo sin estrellas*. San José, Costa Rica: Editorial Departamento Ecuménico de Investigaciones, 2001.

Chapter 4

Biblical Silence

Where is the Bible in Latino/a Theology?

Michelle A. Gonzalez Maldonado

Like a good Catholic, I will begin with a confession: speaking about the Bible makes me nervous. Part of this is due to the fact that I am trained as a systematic theologian and much of my research has focused on constructive and liberationist theologies. Within many of these theological conversations, the Bible is one of many sources used to inform theology. Furthermore, in my own theological writings, I have not drawn heavily from the Bible. It is not a primary resource in my research. In this, I am not alone. This chapter focuses on a biblical silence within Roman Catholic Latino/a theology, where the Bible does not play a central role in theological constructions. Instead, I argue, the faith experience of the Latino/a community and the work of other academic theologians are the primary conversation partners.

    This chapter begins with a brief introduction to Latino/a theology, highlighting the primacy of the ambiguous category of Latino/a religious experience as a starting point for Latino/a theologians. The second section examines some inroads into critical biblical hermeneutics among Latino/a scholars. In the third section, I explore one example of a possible wedding of critical biblical scholarship and Latino/a popular religion. I conclude with some thoughts surrounding the role of the Bible within Latino/a theology. The primary focus of this chapter is Latino/a Roman Catholic theology. While not wanting to dismiss the contributions of Protestant Latino/a theologians, given the heterogeneous nature of Latino/a theologians, the manner in which the Bible functions in the Protestant context can vary quite dramatically. Focus on Roman Catholic theology is one manner of narrowing the broader Latino/a theological terrain.

LATINO/A POPULAR RELIGION

The lived religious practices of Latino/a Christian communities throughout the United States serve as the fundamental starting point of Latino/a theology. The emphasis is overwhelmingly ecclesial, while nodding to the fact that many Latino/a religious practices exist on the border of Christian ecclesial structures and in some cases incorporate non-Christian elements within them. Latino/a theologians struggle to negotiate their strong commitment to Latino/a theological categories that speak to the lived reality of Latino/a faith, while simultaneously remaining equally committed to the traditional categories of theological discourse as classically articulated throughout the centuries. This struggle emerges from the historical absence of Latin American and Latino/a intellectual and religious traditions within the construction of academic theology. Latino/a theologians labor to insert the lived religious lives of Latino/as into an academic language that developed without taking them into consideration. While this may seem minor, it is a core intellectual obstacle for Latino/a theologians, because language shapes the terminology of theology and the worldview behind this academic discipline.

Latino/a theologians, while not all self-proclaimed liberation theologians, share a close connection to Latin American liberation theology. Some Latino/a theologians explicitly claim a liberationist identity, while others distance themselves from this categorization, though they may utilize liberationist sources in their scholarship.[1] In addition, whether using the term liberationist or not, Latino/a theologians often privilege the poor and oppressed in a manner that mirrors the hermeneutics of liberation theologians. Whether all Latino/a theologians are properly described as liberation theologians, and thus their collective body of work as liberationist, is a matter of debate.

Latino/a theologians argue that liberation theology influenced Latino/a theology so that Latino/a theology contains various methodological elements that characterize it as liberationist. As Benjamín Valentín states: "These include a concern with oppression and the achievement of justice, an emphasis on the contextual character and accountability of theological reflection, and the desire to reach into and draw on the specific experiences and expressive cultures of a people or community."[2] Liberationist methodological patterns in Latino/a theology include: (1) a critical reading of the contemporary context of Latino/as; (2) the use of concrete voices of Latino/as in their theology; (3) the use of autobiography and critical denunciation; and (4) its utopian vision.

While there exist liberationist strands within the writings of some Latino/a theologians, Latino/a theology as a whole is not a self-proclaimed liberation theology. Does this mean that Latino/a theology offers a counterpoint to Latin American and other liberationist discourses? Far from it. However, as a theology that has always claimed to express the faith of the people, the faith of the people is not necessarily liberationist. Liberation ecclesiologies represent only a small percentage of Latino/a churches. In fact, if we look at Christianity among Latino/as, it is becoming increasingly *evangélica*, characterized by a more conservative theology that does not emphasize the social transformative action so fundamental to the work of liberation theologians. Latino/a theologians have made a significant effort to present the Latino/a community as a marginalized and oppressed community in the United States. Does writing a theology on behalf of or about an oppressed community automatically make that theology liberationist?

Latino/a theologians today face a multidisciplinary context in which theology is not the only methodology used to study Latino/a religion. The growing scholarship by anthropologists, historians, and sociologists that study Latino/a religion both challenges the primacy of theology and offers excellent opportunities for collaborative work across disciplinary boundaries. In addition, the complexity of Latino/a religious life challenges the assumption that we can talk about a homogenous Latino/a religious experience in a monolithic manner. Despite this diversity, I am in agreement with Miguel De La Torre and Gaston Espinosa when they write, "We still have a strong sense for a common *Latinidad* that, regardless of all our different ethnic, theological, generational, sexual, and disciplinary identities, still anchors our scholarship and our psyches in our respective Latino/a communities, countries of origin, religious traditions, and subcultures."[3] In other words, something unites communities that are categorized as Latino/a and the scholars who claim a Latino/a identity in the United States.

Latino/a theologians consistently engage conversation partners in academic theology in order to demonstrate the manner in which their work fits into the larger intellectual genealogy of traditional theology. We employ traditional theological categories, sometimes seasoning them with the language and flavor of Latino/a culture.

The 1999 volume in Latino/a Catholic systematic theology entitled *From the Heart of Our People* began with the question, "What would Catholic systematics look like if it were done *latinamente?*"[4] Glancing at the table of contents of *From the Heart of Our People*, one is struck by whether or not its success can be measured by its connection, or lack thereof, to Latino/a faith communities. Sure there are articles with the words "Tierra," "Pueblo," "Fiesta," and "Convivencia," in the titles. Yes, these Spanish words mask traditional Roman Catholic systematic theology. While *From the Heart of Our People* attempted to do Latino/a Catholic systematic theology, it actually reflects a European-born systematic theology flavored with the spices of Latino/a culture. While the language has changed, the theological loci covered in the book remain the normative paradigm.

A similar methodological gesture is found in the anthology *In Our Own Voices: Latino/a Renditions of Theology*. This chapter, to which I contributed, offers a constructive read of classic doctrines in Christian theology from a Latino/a perspective. In his introduction to the chapter, Editor Benjamín Valentín argues, "It is reasonable to claim that the effort to interpret, to evaluate, and to reformulate the meanings of themes or doctrines such as God, Creation, human nature, human sin, Christ, the church, and eschatology, for instance, has received sparse consideration in the works of Latino/a theologians."[5] While recognizing that Latino/a theology needs to offer its own distinctive contributions to the field, Valentín contends that theologians, as theologians, are called to interpret the symbols and religious worldviews of the Christian tradition. My question is, which tradition? The academic tradition of systematic theology? A universalist understanding of Christianity as a whole? Or Latino/a Christian tradition grounded in Latin American Christianity? These are not all the same tradition.

It is important to note that I am not being critical of these projects per se. As theologians that wish to engage the theological academy, Latino/a theologians have the difficult task of remaining relevant within their field and accountable to the communities they represent in their writings. In this conversation, the Bible plays a minor role.

The Latino/a dimension of Latino/a theology privileges the lived religious experiences of Latino/a faith communities. This is done through an emphasis on everyday life and, in Roman Catholic circles, a heavy privileging of the category of popular religion. Contrary to Latin American liberation theologians, Latino/a theologians add the element of justice, power, and marginalization into their definition of Latino/a popular religion. As Empereur and Fernández state:

> Popular religion provides a structure of meaning for those who are dominated by a social order not their own . . . . Although people who belong to the institutional church engage in popular religious practices, they, through these same practices, offer a critique of the institution. In that sense we can say that liberation theology is a form of popular religion.[6]

Popular religion becomes a means for the marginalized to express their religious faith.

Within Latino/a theology, one does not find debates regarding whether or not popular religion is liberating. This is in sharp contrast to Latin American liberation theology. Popular religion is often defined by Latino/a theologians as the religion of an oppressed or marginalized community and is linked to liberation. Popular religion is frequently presented as that which is most authentically Latino/a.[7] "The religion is 'popular' because the disenfranchised are responsible for its creation, making it a religion of the marginalized."[8]

Yet not all definitions of popular religion see it as exclusively the religion of the oppressed. Some emphasize inculturation or context versus liberation.

For Latino/a theologians, popular religion, or more narrowly defined popular Christianity or Catholicism, cannot just be reduced to religious acts, objects, or rituals. As Orlando Espín states:

> Indeed, it has been shown that popular Christianity is one of the most foundational bearers of social and cultural identity among the majority of Christians. . . . Popular Christianity is, arguably, and above all else, *an epistemology: a way of constructing and interpreting "the real" by means that are culturally-specific*, grounded in equally culturally specific experiences of God and of the Christian message.[9]

Popular Christianity reveals the religious worldview of Latino/a communities. It discloses the manner in which Latino/as experience engages the sacred in light of their concrete everyday experience.

Latino/a theologians' elaborations on popular religion emphasize its contextual nature, its location in everyday life, and the function of power, perhaps most clearly seen in the ambiguous and porous relationship between the institutional and popular church. Popular religion is "popular" as opposed to "orthodox" as a result of its marginalization by orthodoxy. The impulse behind Latino/a popular religion is not to stand in contrast to or critique orthodoxy. However, in some instances, the social location of Latino/as forced Latino/a religious practices to be marginalized. In its primary being, popular religion is not intended in any way to be subversive, yet in refusing to be silenced, rejected, and ignored, it becomes so.

However, popular religion always needs to be understood in light of broader institutional and social religion. The risk is that studies of popular religion become reduced to personal devotionalisms.

> The danger of this approach is that, in its effort to document local everyday religious practices, it may lose sight of the institutional, structural, and systematic processes in which these practices are embedded, the decontextualization of popular religion may in turn lead to a failure to recognize the multiple ways in which power and resistance shape and are shaped by religion.[10]

There needs to be a balance between the study of lived, local religion, and its role in broader religious movements and institutional histories. Similarly, studies of popular religion must also contextualize the theology behind them within both theological and biblical narratives. There is a manner in which popular religious practices both challenge and affirm dominant biblical narratives.

The claim that Latino/a theologians have a privileged access to authentic Latino/a religious life, often based on their Latino/a identity, must be problematized in light of the study of popular religion. Manuel A. Vásquez reminds us of the epistemological violence Latino/a theologians can do when we claim to speak for "our people," particularly in light of the role of *mestizaje* within Latino/a theology. As Vásquez states:

> Latino/a communities, no matter how *mestizo* they are, always carry subalternity, those others, at the margins of the margins, which we theorists and theologians cannot present as part of our communities without to some extent reducing them . . . . We need to acknowledge that in "giving voice to them" as *mestizos*, even as the God-chosen marginalized, we are re-presenting them, and thus doing symbolic violence to the multiplicity and uniqueness of their experiences.[11]

We must acknowledge that any Latino/a Christian theology contains elements of the colonial enterprise of Christianization, indentured servitude, and violence. In addition, we must be wary of theologians' ability to represent any marginalized population and the manner in which such constructs can create a homogenous "ontological Latinidad" within Latino/a theology.[12]

LATINO/A BIBLICAL SCHOLARSHIP

Latino/a theologians have much to learn from their colleagues in biblical studies, particularly in light of the role of identity in contemporary readers' encounter with historical texts. This has implications for contemporary constructions of identity. Francisco Lozada highlights the politics of erasure that function when students and scholars engage biblical texts and approach the ancient world as a monolithic culture. This monocultural view of early Christianity can lead to an oppressive universalism that seeks to erase difference under the guise of unity. This essentialist understanding of the first Christians sets the foundation for an essentialized vision of contemporary Christian identities and other identities across the board.

In contrast, Lozada promotes the celebration of diverse identities. "I am interested in highlighting cultural identities and histories, whether in the biblical text or not, and demonstrating that diverse identities do not lead to radical separateness, but to self-reflection, openness to others, and seeing more of the world's horizons."[13] This leads to diverse readings of texts that welcome diverse identities in light of the power structures that inform such readings. Lozada's scholarship offers a cautionary tale for contemporary constructions of Latino/a identity while also reminding contemporary theologians that they must not create a monolithic depiction of the biblical past. This contemporary issue is pressing given the hermeneutical stance taken by many Latino/a theologians who claim to represent the Latino/a Christian community as a whole.

While recognizing the importance of social location hermeneutics, Lozada remains well aware of the limitations of reading the Bible with one's social location as the point of departure. "Such a strategy also tends to place more attention on the biblical tradition in order to legitimate and authenticate the identity of the reader or the community."[14] This is seen, for example, in Virgilio Elizondo's approach to the New Testament in which he advocates for "sincere dialogue between our own specific sociohistorical experience of suffering, marginalization, enslavement, and struggles for liberation and the sociohistorical experience of liberation and new life brought about by the Jesus event."[15] For Elizondo, the basis of christology is this dialogue between the New Testament and the experience of liberation.

Fundamental to Elizondo's christology is the sociocultural identity of Jesus as Galilean. For Elizondo, Jesus' identity as a Galilean is not accidental; it is revelatory of his life and ministry. "Like every other man and woman, he was culturally situated and conditioned by the time and space in which he lived.... Jesus was not simply a Jew, he was a Galilean Jew, throughout his life he and his disciples were identified as Galileans."[16] Born in Galilee, Jesus was not born at the center of Jewish life and society, namely Jerusalem, but on the border. Elizondo connects this marginal, border reality to the contemporary context of Latino/as, more specifically Mexican-Americans.

Elizondo's Galilean Jesus has been a source of academic controversy among biblical scholars, particularly those that argue that his analysis at best is fueled by romanticism and at worst is anti-Semitic.[17] Without entering into the details of these critiques, what is at stake here is the manner in which theologians appropriate biblical texts within their constructive theologies. Michael Lee, in his excellent summary and response to the controversies surrounding Elizondo's Galilean Jesus, emphasizes that what is significant for Elizondo's christology, like most constructive christologies, is the "historic" Jesus and not the historical Jesus. "My point is that in *Galilean Journey* Elizondo does not seek to describe the historical Jesus, but rather focuses on the theological import for the reader of the Gospels' portrayal of Jesus as a Galilean."[18] As Lee reminds us, quests for the historical Jesus are always marred by the interpretive horizon of the researcher that precludes ever arriving at an authentic depiction of the historical Jesus. More importantly, however, this is not what Elizondo sets out to do; he is interested in the theological and symbolic import of Galilee in light of the contemporary marginalization of Latino/as.

Mujerista ethicist Ada María Isasi-Díaz's christology is inextricably linked to social justice, placing an emphasis on a praxiological and ethical understanding of *Jesucristo*, so that discipleship requires our active participation in the kin-dom of God as it is realized here and now. "All who commit themselves to proclaim with their lives and deeds the kingdom of God are mediators of the kingdom."[19] This mediation is grounded in humanity's *imago Dei* and calls followers of *Jesucristo* to realize God's kingdom concretely here on earth, though never in its fullness. The Latina faith in the Crucified Jesus cannot be found in the dogmas, official teachings, or theological treatises of academic theology but instead is situated in the concrete faith and lives of Latino/a communities. "What Latinas believe about Christ is not a matter of an applied doctrine, an application of what the churches teach."[20] *Mujerista* christology is concretely historical, emerging from the daily lives and struggles of contemporary Latinas.

The work of both Elizondo and Isasi-Díaz easily falls under the categorization of social location hermeneutics, aiming "to contextualize fully the reading process in order to construct a rereading of the biblical tradition with the objective of liberation and empowerment in mind."[21] While locating himself within this tradition, Lozada is wary that it may become stagnant. An important concern he highlights is that social location hermeneutics does not challenge the biblical tradition's authority and is used to confirm the otherness of marginalized peoples. "Rather than challenging the authority of the biblical tradition, minority readers use the biblical tradition to harmonize their otherness with the otherness represented within the biblical tradition."[22] Their otherness becomes legitimized by the biblical tradition. Can we be liberated in this paradigm? Is otherness essentialized? I share Lozada's concern that ultimately Latino/a theologians risk canonizing their marginalization by inserting contemporary Latino/a experience into the biblical narrative of otherness.

Elizondo and Isasi-Díaz's work can also be characterized as employing liberation hermeneutics, which reads the Bible from the perspective of the poor and oppressed as the only method that reveals the true God of liberation. "Reading the Bible from the margins of society is not an exercise that reveals interesting perspectives on how other cultures read and interpret biblical texts. To read the Bible from the margins is to grasp God in the midst of struggle and oppression."[23] Ethicist Miguel De La Torre argues that reading the Bible in this way challenges the dominant interpretations that use the text to legitimize power and privilege. However, it still casts Latino/as into an esssentialized category of the oppressed.

New Testament scholar Fernando F. Segovia reminds us that within liberation hermeneutics, while dominant interpretations of biblical texts undergo a substantial critique, the Bible itself remains unchallenged. "It stands above critical engagement as the unquestionable Word of God, a God whose construction in the Bible is taken for granted rather than evaluated."[24] Isasi-Díaz, however, is the exception here. In her work, the ultimate authority lies in grassroots Latinas, not the biblical text. "As such, it is not the Bible that stands over Latinas, unchallenged and unchallengeable, but rather Latinas that stand over the Bible."[25] While Isasi-Díaz places Latinas above the authority of the biblical text, the status of Latinas as marginalized remains unchallenged in her corpus. An essentialized construction of identity remains.

Linked to the essentialized construction of a community's identity is the notion of the Latino/a theologian as Latino/a. In his excellent article problematizing the construction of the Latino/a biblical critic, Segovia argues that there are two moments in the birth of a Latino/a biblical critic: the first is his/her membership through birth, the second refers to his/her consciousness raising in adopting a marginalized status and agenda. "Thus, I would readily avow, I would not qualify as a Latino/a scholar in my initial phase in the academy . . . but only in my later phase, as a result of a process of conscientization, whereby I was 'reborn' as such in 'spirit and truth.'"[26] This remains a long-standing point of debate among Latino/a theologians, particularly in Roman Catholic circles. Within the Academy of Catholic Hispanic Theologians in the United States, for example, the secondary status given to non-Catholic theologians and non-Latino/a theologians promotes a Latino/a theological birthright and a confessional requirement for admittance into this academic organization. Must all members of ACHTUS be practicing Catholics? Is baptism the rite of initiation for this academy? These questions continue to plague ACHTUS even today, raising the broader issue of what constitutes a Latino/a theologian.

As Latino/a theologians continue to negotiate these issues, the work of biblical scholars would be a helpful conversation partner. In addition, the role of biblical narratives within Latino/a popular religious practices is a much needed area of study. The historical role of these biblical narratives within Latin American Christianity and the manner in which they function in contemporary lived religion would offer a fruitful entry point in constructive theological engagement of biblical texts. In the case of Cuban and Cuban-American Catholicism, this is clearly seen in devotion to the unofficial "Saint" Lazarus.

SAN LÁZARO

The statue is of a thin man, supporting himself on crutches, dressed in tatters. His emaciated body is covered in sores, and dogs are at his feet. This is the Lazarus of Cuban and Cuban-American devotions. While they consider him a saint, he is not the official saint of the Catholic Church, the Lazarus who is sometimes associated with the man resurrected by Jesus in the Gospel of John, and other times associated with the Bishop of Marseille. This is a different Lazarus, a poor man, a beggar, who appears in one of Jesus' parables. Although a fictional character, he is one of the most significant devotions within Cuban/Cuban-American religiosity.

The parable of Lazarus and the rich man is found solely in the Gospel of Luke and is situated in the larger pericope of Luke 16:14-31. The central theme of this passage is the avoidance of the love of money. There was once a rich man who lived in a mansion and feasted every day. At the gates of the rich man's opulent home lay a poor man named Lazarus, covered in sores, who longed for merely the scraps from the rich man's table. When both men die, angels carry Lazarus to Abraham and the rich man—who remains nameless—is condemned to hell. The rich man begs for mercy for himself and his brothers, but Abraham indicates that there is a great chasm between heaven and hell and that, if the rich man and his brothers did not listen to the prophets, they would be lost causes.

A simple read of this parable would seem to condemn riches. This is not the case. The man is not judged based on his wealth. "His judgment and condemnation to hell," points out De La Torre, "were based solely on the fact that he was rich and failed to share his resources with those, like Lazarus, who lacked the basis for survival. In this case, God's judgment was not based on anything the rich man did or any belief system he confessed; rather, it was based on what he failed to do."[27] The rich and powerful man, who as a counterpoint to dominant history remains nameless in the story, while the powerless poor Lazarus is named, is condemned for what he does with his riches. Or, I should say, what he fails to do. In addition, he is condemned for his failure to see Lazarus. Even after his condemnation, he fails to see Lazarus. He only thinks of his brothers—those who are like him.

In Cuba and among Cuban-Americans in the United States, images of this incarnation of Lazarus are widespread. His presence reaches well beyond Catholicism for he is also a prominent figure in the Afro-Cuban religion of Santería. Santería has its roots in the Yoruban religious traditions that were brought to Cuba through the trans-Atlantic slave trade. While a monotheistic religion, practitioners of Santería focus their religious life on *orishas*, supernatural beings that mediate humanity's relationship with the sacred. The Cuban "Saint" Lazarus has strong Afro-Cuban roots and is associated with the *orisha* Babalú Ayé. Introduced to mainstream U.S. culture by the singing and bongo drums of Desi Arnez on *I Love Lucy*, Babalú Ayé is a significant presence within Afro-Cuban religions. He is "El Dueño de las Enfermedades" ("Owner of Illnesses").

As noted by Ada María Isasi-Díaz, "The story of San Lázaro says a great deal about the relationship between the official theology and liturgy of the Catholic Church and Cuban's popular religion. The latter is not church-based, definitely not church-sanctioned, and very much mixed with *Santería*."[28] The

Roman Catholic Church has made various efforts to replace the Afro-Cuban image of Lazarus in Cuban's hearts with the official image of the Bishop of Marseilles. At the shrine devoted to St. Lazarus in Cuba, devotees often bring images of the unofficial saint to be blessed. In the 1960s, the Cuban Church replaced images of the Afro-Cuban Lazarus with the official saint, one who was evoked during the Middle Ages in Europe as the patron of lepers and victims of the plague. This mirrors the efforts of the Catholic Church in Miami, which seeks to "correct" the image of Lazarus in Cuban-American minds and hearts on various fronts. The image of the official Lazarus in the shrine, as well as the material on the canonized saint, are all part of the church's wider efforts to evangelize the Cuban-American population and strip this Afro-Cuban devotion from the Cuban-American ethos. Another effort to redirect this Cuban-American devotion is found in literature published by the Archdiocese and distributed at the pastoral level. At San Lázaro Catholic Church in Miami, images of the non-official Lazarus are rejected and catechetical efforts focus on correcting this "confusion."

In Cuba, many visit El Rincón, Lazarus' shrine, in order to fulfill a promise to Babalú Ayé.[29] The devotion to Saint Lazarus with amulets, the Lucan Lazarus, predates Cuba. Shrines and churches dedicated to him are found in Spain, including one near Santiago de Compostela. This devotion has been linked to hospitals and leper sanctuaries. On entering El Rincón, you are greeted with a sign that reads, "1714 Hospital San Lázaro 1936." This former chapel in a hospital for lepers has become the most important pilgrimage site in Cuba. In one of the few scholarly studies of the shrine, Laciel Zamora gives five reasons for the mixture of San Lázaro with Babalú Ayé: (1) similarities in their stories (illness, skin illness, poverty, dogs, crutches); (2) the manner in which Lazarus' story captivated black Cubans; (3) petitionary prayers; (4) the location of the shrine outside yet near the city; and (5) bandage imagery in both.[30]

One must ask questions of *why* and *how* this non-sanctioned, fictional, New Testament character became associated with an African *orisha* and only in Cuba. While I can offer some theological analysis on the former, one is left wanting on the latter. There is no historical documentation of how devotion to the Lucan Lazarus began in Cuba.[31] What appears evident is that one cannot separate "Saint" Lazarus' prominence in Cuba from his association with Babalú Ayé. The Afro-Cuban roots of this figure have grounded him in the broader Cuban ethos. It is difficult to find another explanation for why a gospel figure, albeit fictional, who was a prominent character in one of Jesus' teachings would be so problematic. The Archdiocese has not really explained why this gospel figure is so threatening outside of his association with Babalú Ayé. Besides physical similarities between the Lucan Lazarus and Babalú Ayé (dogs, some sort of limp, and open sores), I would also argue that the theological vision behind this parable contributed to his appeal for Afro-Cubans. The message of the parable is God's solidarity with the poor, the marginalized, and the forgotten. The fact that the poor man, and not the rich man, triumphs must have been appealing for Afro-Cubans. Devotion to Saint Lazarus offers an interesting entry point into discussions of the manner by which popular religious practices rewrite institutional ecclesial history and privilege particular biblical narratives.

CONCLUDING COMMENTS

So where does this leave the Bible? I have spent a lot of time speaking about theology and lived religion. It is difficult for me to assess the role of the Bible in Latino/a Roman Catholic theology because I would argue it is not a normative text within this discourse. This is not to say that Latino/a theologians are anti-biblical. However, the Bible often enters into Latino/a theology through two channels: (1) the work of other academic theologians (often non-Latino/a) who employ biblical texts; and (2) the use of proof-texting regarding Latino/a faith life. Here Lozada is to the point, "A simple rereading of texts does not lead to liberation, but rather to inverting the hierarchy of privilege."[32] Latino/a theologians often use scripture to justify either Latino/a faith experience or the constructions of theological categories (such as Christology or Mariology) employed in their interpretations of those experiences.

I realize that I am setting myself up for some major critique here. Can I be accused of making abstract blanket statements regarding the work of my colleagues? Am I just imposing my own biblically weak theology on all Roman Catholic Latino/a theologians? Perhaps. Although I am not saying that the Bible is absent entirely, I only argue it is not central. It would be difficult to counter my claim that the Bible is not a central normative primary source in the discourse of Latino/a theology. Are there Latino/a biblical scholars? Of course. Do Latino/a theologians critically engage their scholarship on the Bible? Not really. The invitation to write this piece was a challenge for me because of this. It forced me to question why the Bible is so absent in our work, especially when the broader U.S. culture is moving toward a bibliolatry where the Bible is cited as proof-text to legitimize legislation and validate political currency in disturbing decontextualized manners. The Bible is a powerful text not only in theological circles but also in U.S. culture as a whole. Perhaps it is time for us Latino/a theologians to tap into it.

NOTES

1. A clear example of this is found among Latina theologians. "In its initial and formative phase of Latina theology, while some Latina theologians employed a

feminist hermeneutic, others published in the field of pastoral theology. This second group of Latinas focused their attention on making theological sense of the various ministerial needs of the Latino/a community." These pastoral Latina theologians do not outright reject the moniker of feminist or liberationist, yet they also clearly do not self-identify as liberation theologians. Similarly, much of their scholarship does not reflect a systematic engagement of liberation theologies. Nancy Pineda-Madrid, "Latina Theology," in *Liberation Theologies in the United States*, ed. Stacey M. Floyd Thomas and Anthony B. Pinn (New York: New York University Press, 2010), 69.

2. Benjamín Valentín, "Hispanic/Latino(a) Theology," in *Liberation Theologies in the United States*, 103.

3. Miguel De La Torre and Gaston Espinosa, "Introduction," in *Rethinking Latino(a) Religion and Identity*, ed. Miguel A. De La Torre and Gastón Espinosa (Cleveland: Pilgrim, 2006), 5.

4. Orlando O. Espín and Miguel H. Díaz, "Introduction," in *From the Heart of Our People: Latino/a Explorations in Systematic Theology*, ed. Orlando O. Espín and Miguel H. Díaz (Maryknoll, NY: Orbis Books, 1999), 1.

5. Benjamín Valentín, "Introduction," in *In Our Own Voices: Latino/a Renditions of Theology*, ed. Benjamín Valentín (Maryknoll, NY: Orbis Books, 2010), xii.

6. James Empereur and Eduardo S. Fernández, *La Vida Sacra: Contemporary Hispanic Sacramental Theology* (Lanham, MD: Rowman and Littlefield Publishers Inc., 2006), 5.

7. See Roberto S. Goizueta, "U.S. Hispanic Popular Catholicism as Theopoetics," in *Hispanic/Latino Theology: Challenge and Promise*, ed. Ada María Isasi-Díaz and Fernando F. Segovia (Minneapolis: Fortress Press, 1996), 268. In his discussion of Latino/a popular religion as the religion of the marginalized and as that which is most "ours," Goizueta relies heavily on the essay by Orlando Espín and Sixto García, "'Lilies of the Field': A Hispanic Theology of Providence and Human Responsibility," *Proceedings of the Catholic Theological Society of America* 44 (1989): 73.

8. Miguel De La Torre and Edwin Aponte, *Introducing Latino/a Theologies* (Mayknoll, NY: Orbis Books, 2001), 118–119.

9. Orlando O. Espín, "Traditioning: Culture, Daily Life, and Popular Religion, and Their Impact on the Christian Tradition," in *Futuring Our Past: Explorations in the Theology of Tradition*, ed. Orlando O. Espín and Gary Macy (Maryknoll, NY: Orbis Books, 2006).

10. Anna L. Peterson and Manuel A. Vázquez, "Introducing Religion in Latin America," in *Latin American Religions: Histories and Documents in Context*, ed. Anna L. Peterson and Manuel A. Vázquez (New York, NY: New York University Press, 2008), 7.

11. Manuel A. Vásquez, "Rethinking *Mestizaje*," in *Rethinking Latino(a) Religion and Identity*, 153.

12. See Victor Anderson's critique of ontological blackness in *Beyond Ontological Blackness: An Essay on African American Religious and Cultural Criticism* (New York: Continuum, 1995).

13. Francisco Lozada Jr., "Encountering the Bible in an Age of Diversity and Globalization," in *New Horizons in Hispanic/Latino(a) Theology*, ed. Benjamín Valentín (Cleveland: Pilgrim, 2003), 17.

14. Francisco Lozada Jr., "Reinventing the Biblical Tradition: An Exploration of Social Location Hermeneutics," in *Futuring Our Past*, 134.

15. Virgilio Elizondo, "Elements for a Mexican American *Mestizo* Christology," in *Jesus in the Hispanic Community: Images of Christ from Theology to Popular Religion*, ed. Harold J. Recinos and Hugo Magallanes (Louisville: Westminster John Know Press, 2009), 3.

16. Virgilio Elizondo, *Galilean Journey: The Mexican-American Promise* (Maryknoll, NY: Orbis Books, 1994), 49.

17. See Jean-Pierre Ruiz, "Good Fences and Good Neighbors? Biblical Scholars and Theologians," *Journal of Hispanic/Latino Theology* 12 (2007): 18–41; and Jeff S. Siker, "Historicizing a Racialized Jesus: Case Studies in the 'Black Christ', the 'Mestizo Christ,' and White Critique," *Biblical Interpretation* 15 (2007): 26–53.

18. Michael Lee, "The Galilean Jesus as Faithful Dissenter," in *Jesus in the Hispanic Community*, 28.

19. Ada María Isasi-Díaz, "Christ in *Mujerista* Theology," in *Thinking of Christ: Proclamation, Explanation, Meaning*, ed. Tatha Wiley (New York: Continuum, 2003), 162.

20. Isasi-Díaz, "Christ in Mujerista Theology," 158.

21. Lozada, "Reinventing the Biblical Tradition," 113.

22. Lozada, "Reinventing the Biblical Tradition," 114.

23. Miguel De La Torre, *Reading the Bible from the Margins* (Maryknoll, NY: Orbis Books, 2002), 4.

24. Fernando F. Segovia, "*Mujerista* Theology: Biblical Interpretation and Political Theology," *Feminist Theology* 20:1 (2011): 21–27.

25. Segovia, "*Mujerista* Theology," 24.

26. Fernando F. Segovia, "Toward Latino/a American Biblical Criticism: Latino(a) ness as Problematic," in *They Were All Together in One Place? Toward Minority Biblical Criticism*, ed. Randall C. Bailey, Tat-Siong Benny Liew, Fernando F. Segovia (Atlanta, GA: Society of Biblical Literature, 2009), 203.

27. De La Torre, *Reading the Bible from the Margins*, 79.

28. Ada María Isasi-Díaz, "La Habana: The City that Inhabits Me: A Multi-Site Understanding of Location," in *La Lucha Continues: Mujerista Theology*, Ada María Isasi-Díaz (Maryknoll, NY: Orbis Books, 2004), 136.

29. Babalú Ayé was a Yoruba king that due to his carnal excesses contracted a terrible disease. He was expulsed from his kingdom and was only accompanied by two dogs, given to him by Ogún. He wandered until he reached the neighboring kingdom of Dahomey. A huge storm approached as he entered a village, and too his surprise he was named king. It had been prophesized in the village that a man would come during a storm and cure the population of an epidemic.

30. Laciel Zamora, *El Culto de San Lazaro en Cuba*. Colección La Fuente Viva (Habana, Cuba: Fundación Fernando Ortiz, 2000), 102–103.

31. The origins of Lazarus and his iconography are unknown. In his excellent introduction to Afro-Cuban religion, David H. Brown documents disputes over the lineage and authentic houses of worship dedicated to San Lázaro / Babalú Ayé. However, this does not shed light on the origins of devotion to "Saint" Lazarus. David Brown, *Santería Enthroned: Art, Ritual, and Innovation in an Afro-Cuban Religion.* (Chicago: University of Chicago Press, 2003), 138-139.

32. Lozada, "Encountering the Bible in an Age of Diversity and Globalization," 32.

BIBLIOGRAPHY

Anderson, Victor. *Beyond Ontological Blackness: An Essay on African American Religious and Cultural Criticism.* New York: Continuum, 1995.

Brown, David. *Santería Enthroned: Art, Ritual, and Innovation in an Afro-Cuban Religion.* Chicago: University of Chicago Press, 2003.

De La Torre, Miguel. *Reading the Bible from the Margins.* Maryknoll, NY: Orbis Books, 2002.

De La Torre, Miguel and Edwin Aponte. *Introducing Latino/a Theologies.* Maryknoll, NY: Orbis Books, 2001.

De la Torre, Miguel and Gaston Espinosa. "Introduction." In *Rethinking Latino(a) Religion and Identity*, edited by Miguel A. De La Torre and Gastón Espinosa, 1-16. Cleveland: Pilgrim, 2006.

Elizondo, Virgilio. "Elements for a Mexican American Mestizo Christology." In *Jesus in the Hispanic Community: Images of Christ from Theology to Popular Religion*, edited by Harold J. Recinos and Hugo Magallanes, 3-15. Louisville: Westminster John Know Press, 2009.

———. *Galilean Journey: The Mexican-American Promise.* Maryknoll, NY: Orbis Books, 1994.

Empereur, James and Eduardo S. Fernández. *La Vida Sacra: Contemporary Hispanic Sacramental Theology.* Lanham, MD: Rowman and Littlefield Publishers Inc., 2006.

Espín, Orlando O. "Traditioning: Culture, Daily Life, and Popular Religion, and Their Impact on the Christian Tradition." In *Futuring Our Past: Explorations in the Theology of Tradition*, edited by Orlando O. Espín and Gary Macy, 1-22. Maryknoll, NY: Orbis Books, 2006.

Espín, Orlando O. and Miguel H. Díaz. "Introduction." In *From the Heart of Our People: Latino/a Explorations in Systematic Theology*, edited by Orlando O. Espín and Miguel H. Díaz, 1-5. Maryknoll, NY: Orbis Books, 1999.

Espín, Orlando and Sixto García. "'Lilies of the Field': A Hispanic Theology of Providence and Human Responsibility." *Proceedings of the Catholic Theological Society of America* 44 (1989): 70-90.

Goizueta, Roberto S. "U.S. Hispanic Popular Catholicism as Theopoetics." In *Hispanic/Latino Theology: Challenge and Promise*, edited by Ada María Isasi-Díaz and Fernando F. Segovia, 261-288. Minneapolis: Fortress Press, 1996.

Isasi-Díaz, Ada María. "Christ in Mujerista Theology." in *Thinking of Christ: Proclamation, Explanation, Meaning*, edited by Tatha Wiley, 157–176. New York: Continuum, 2003.

———. "La Habana: The City that Inhabits Me: A Multi-Site Understanding of Location." In Ada María Isasi-Díaz, *La Lucha Continues: Mujerista Theology*, 122–156. Maryknoll, NY: Orbis Books, 2004.

Lee, Michael. "The Galilean Jesus as Faithful Dissenter." In *Jesus in the Hispanic Community: Images of Christ from Theology to Popular Religion*, edited by Harold J. Recinos and Hugo Magallanes, 16–37. Louisville: Westminster John Knox Press, 2009.

Lozada Jr., Francisco. "Encountering the Bible in an Age of Diversity and Globalization." In *New Horizons in Hispanic/Latino(a) Theology*, edited by Benjamín Valentín, 13–34. Cleveland: Pilgrim, 2003).

———. "Reinventing the Biblical Tradition: An Exploration of Social Location Hermeneutics." In *Futuring Our Past: Explorations in the Theology of Tradition*, edited by Orlando O. Espín and Gary Macy, 113–140. Maryknoll, NY: Orbis Books, 2006.

Peterson, Anna L. and Manuel A. Vázquez. "Introducing Religion in Latin America." In *Latin American Religions: Histories and Documents in Context*, edited by Anna L. Peterson and Manuel A. Vázquez, 1–19. New York, NY: New York University Press, 2008.

Pineda-Madrid, Nancy. "Latina Theology." In *Liberation Theologies in the United States*, edited by Stacey M. Floyd Thomas and Anthony B. Pinn, 61–85. New York: New York University Press, 2010.

Ruiz, Jean-Pierre. "Good Fences and Good Neighbors? Biblical Scholars and Theologians." *Journal of Hispanic/Latino Theology* 12 (2007): 18–41.

Segovia, Fernando F. "*Mujerista* Theology: Biblical Interpretation and Political Theology." *Feminist Theology* 20:1 (2011): 21–27.

———. "Toward Latino/a American Biblical Criticism: Latino(a)ness as Problematic." In *They Were All Together in One Place? Toward Minority Biblical Criticism*, edited by Randall C. Bailey, Tat-Siong Benny Liew, Fernando F. Segovia, 193–226. Atlanta, GA: Society of Biblical Literature, 2009.

Siker, Jeffrey S. "Historicizing a Racialized Jesus: Case Studies in the 'Black Christ', the 'Mestizo Christ,' and White Critique." *Biblical Interpretation* 15 (2007): 26–53.

Valentín, Benjamín. "Hispanic/Latino(a) Theology." In *Liberation Theologies in the United States*, edited by Stacey M. Floyd Thomas and Anthony B. Pinn, 86–114. New York: New York University Press, 2010.

———. "Introduction." In *In Our Own Voices: Latino/a Renditions of Theology*, edited by Benjamín Valentín, ix-xviii. Maryknoll, NY: Orbis Books, 2010.

Vásquez, Manuel A. "Rethinking Mestizaje." In *Rethinking Latino(a) Religion and Identity*, edited by Miguel A. De La Torre and Gastón Espinosa, 129–157. Cleveland: Pilgrim, 2016.

Zamora, Laciel. *El culto de San Lázaro en Cuba*. Colección La Fuente Viva. La Habana: Fundación Fernando Ortiz, 2000.

Chapter 5

Is It Truly a "Good" Book? The Bible, Empowerment, and Liberation

Nora O. Lozano

Since theological studies and biblical studies are not done in a vacuum, I want to identify myself as a Baptist woman who looks at life and theology from a bridge. By looking from this bridge, I want to recognize and honor the experiences that identify me as a Mexican as well as a Mexican-American woman.[1] In some areas of the border, a bridge geographically unites the Mexican and U.S. lands. This bridge helps me to imagine a cultural bridge where I can stand in order to incorporate my experiences in both of these cultures.

However, since I am going to reflect on the use of the Bible in some of my theological articulations and tasks, my identification needs to be more specific. Baptists represent a very diverse group, and through the years I have been related to and influenced by diverse types of Baptists, who differ in some theological positions that lead them, in turn, to different practices, such as baptism and the Lord's Supper, the government of the church, and the role of women in the church. At this time, because of my geographical location, I am immersed in a predominantly conservative to moderate Baptist world. If I want to make an impact in my immediate Baptist world, I have to recognize that theology is not done in a vacuum—not only because it belongs to a particular theologian, but also because it has a target audience.

In my case, my immediate audience is composed of the Latina/o Baptists who are concentrated in South Texas and Mexico. In their summary of beliefs, these Baptists affirm: "The Holy Bible was written by divinely inspired authors, and is the record of God's revelation of himself to humankind."[2] In addition to this formal statement of belief, they also have their own practical concept of the Bible. David Maldonado states that in the lives of *evangélicos/as*, among them Baptists, the Bible has always had a central place.[3] Justo González has described the special way in which Latino/a Protestants carry their Bibles to church with tenderness and affection, and I will add with a certain sense of pride. These Christians who have such a reverence and devotion for the Bible sometimes have been accused of bibliolatry.[4] For most of these Baptists, the whole Bible is the Word of God—sometimes even the covers, the credits, and the footnotes.

Although I have done a significant amount of theological work with this specific group of Baptists (men and women), my primary work is related to the women in this group. These women represent diverse age groups and educational levels. In addition, those in the United States represent diverse nationalities as well as different levels of acculturation, depending on which generation of Hispanics they belong to (first, second, third, etc.).[5]

IS IT TRULY A "GOOD" BOOK?

In many places of the world, the Bible is referred to as the Good News, or, as Justo González has defined it, "the good book."[6] However, for these Baptist women that I have just described, and many other women around the world, the Bible has sometimes been a good book with good news, but, at other times, not so good. I have heard innumerable stories of women, not only in my immediate geographical area but around the world, where the Bible has been used as a tool to attempt to limit and control women. These uses of the Bible have turned it into an oppressive book that, instead of bringing good news for women, seems to be the bearer of bad news for them. Since these women consider the Bible as the word of God, when the Bible is used against them in order to question women's status, call, capability, and competence, it feels as if it is not only the Bible who is against them but also the God of the Bible. This has devastating consequences for women, because through these challenges women are constantly questioning and doubting themselves. The result is a sense of disempowerment that can lead women to be paralyzed: who wants to be against God? I know because I lived with that same sense many years ago.

The real problem here, I believe, lies in issues of authority, interpretation, and theological criteria. While the Bible is received and accepted by this group as a book with divine authority, is it possible for these women to separate the Bible from its many interpretations? If so, how do they do that? Furthermore, what are the theological criteria to dismiss, support, or embrace a particular interpretation?

Since this particular group of women see the complete Bible as the inspired word of God, it will be hard for many among them to follow the strategy of other women theologians, such as Ada María Isasi-Díaz, who proposes a Mujerista hermeneutics that submits the Bible to a Latinas' canon where "we accept as authoritative only biblical texts that are liberative for us."[7] My need for a different strategy may lie in the fact that, according to Isasi-Díaz, this particular group of Latinas to which she refers does not seem to have a close relationship to the Bible. Isasi-Díaz mentions that these Latinas "do not consult the Bible in [their] daily lives. . . . When [they] need help [they] find it not in the Bible but in praying to God and the saints."[8] Her audience or readers allow Isasi-Díaz to articulate a theology where the Hispanic women's experience and their struggle for survival become the starting point and the source of the theological task, and not the Bible.[9]

In contrast to this experience, the relationship between *evangélicas* and the Bible is different. Loida Martell-Otero has expressed it in this way:

> Since mujeres evangélicas stand in the tradition of the Protestant Reformation, the first and most obvious tool we bring to the table is the authority of Scripture. What the Bible says informs and critiques what the larger community may or may not say about a particular subject. The centrality of Scripture is revealed in many ways: in any theological argument put forth in a Hispanic Protestant community, you better have a chapter and verse you can quote to back it up. Our joys, our grief, our suffering, our fiestas, our anger and our triumphs are all expressed at some point with a Bible citation.[10]

Going back to the idea of the "canon within the canon," or what I prefer to call "a canon from the canon," it assumes that the sections of the Bible that a particular group or person find difficult or uncomfortable should be openly dismissed or at a minimum subtly ignored. If I do not like what Paul says about a particular issue, I simply ignore him or I say openly that these sections are not part of the canon.

I believe that many Christians have formed their own "canon from the canon" through their own selective reading of the Bible. In some Protestant circles, the "canon from the canon" may be the lectionary that guides weekly sermons and in a subtle way pushes preachers to preach only from certain sections of the Bible. Some people avoid/ignore the book of Revelation because they do not understand it or are afraid of it. Some people who are against the equality of men and women have their own "canon from the canon," and thus they hardly preach about the powerful women of the Bible. These men, and sometimes women, in a conscious or unconscious way are using their own canon to promote their own theological or ideological agenda about the submission of women. In this agenda, the submission of women, the controversial passages (e.g., 1 Cor. 14:34-35; 1 Tim. 2:9-15) of Paul about women have a predominant place.

Even though most likely all of us have our own "canon from the canon" guided by our own struggles, understandings, and agendas, the issue at a theological table is under which canon are we going to work if we are going to dialogue or reflect together? As a theologian, I need to know and take seriously the canon under which the other person is living his/her Christianity and/or articulating her/his theology. This means that I cannot just dismiss the other person's canon because it does not fit my agenda or because I do not like it.

So, if I am going to take seriously the world of the other person (the reader), as Fernando F. Segovia has strongly suggested, and engage it with the world of the Bible in a responsible and effective way,[11] I need to understand and respect the context of these Baptist Latina women that I work with. This means that, since they see the complete Bible as inspired and authoritative, the passages that have been interpreted as speaking against women in general—such as Genesis 3, I Cor. 14:34-35, and I Tim. 2:9-15—cannot be dismissed or ignored simply as non-authoritative, because for these women and their communities, they are inspired and authoritative. Thus, if I am going to take seriously the world of the Bible as well as the world of these readers of the Bible, I have to deal with these passages and any other passage that seem to have a negative effect on women in general. I need to do it in a way that makes sense to them, according to their realities, with the goal of helping them construct a new meaning where they can find empowerment and liberation.

THE FIELD OF BIBLICAL CRITICISM AND MY THEOLOGICAL TASK

The issues of women are only some of the complicated issues that the person who decides to take the Bible as a whole needs to deal with. Francisco García-Treto offers a good example of another hard issue as he confronts the situation of xenophobia in the Bible. García-Treto, following a similar view of the Bible, highlights that "simply to ignore these passages is not enough."[12] In order to deal with this xenophobia, he analyses the story in Joshua 9 where the Gibeonites faced the possibility of extermination under the hands of the Israelites.

As a starting point, he candidly acknowledges that in these passages the problem lies to a certain extent in interpretations of the Bible, but that "the real problem lies in the undeniable presence of a core of problematic materials in the Bible where the obliteration of 'the other' is put forward as a divine command."[13] How do we deal with these passages about xenophobia? For him, the reader of these passages needs to be an "astute reader [who] can hear not one single and oppressive monologic discourse but a dialogizing voice that subverts and simultaneously opens up the meaning of the text."[14] In this particular passage, García-Treto highlights the alternative voice of the Gibeonites, who with their perspicacity achieved their own survival, and by doing that they encourage oppressed people today to do the same.

In his analysis about the work of García-Treto, Fernando F. Segovia concludes: "In other words, given the nature and usage of the Bible, the question becomes how texts in which oppression of the highest order is presented as a divine imperative can be read as liberative by the children of oppression."[15] Segovia continues: "for García-Treto the aim is . . . the need for the marginalized to become subjects of their own history and the production of a reading on their part that is healing and liberative for all, for dominant and marginalized alike."[16]

Following the suggestions of García-Treto, the woman reader who takes the Bible as a whole, and who is in search of empowerment and liberation, needs to become also an astute reader who, as a subject of her own story, can open up the meaning of the text into a reading that is healing and liberative not only for her but also for all. How does this process happen? And how can I as a theologian help in this task?

It is well-known that the field of biblical hermeneutics has gone through major changes in the last forty years. Fernando F. Segovia, in his essay "And They Began to Speak in Other Tongues," describes these changes as he analyzes four competing contemporary paradigms in the field of biblical criticism.[17]

He starts by analyzing historical criticism, which involves different strategies—such as literary criticism, redaction criticism, and composition criticism—and was the leading paradigm through the mid-1970s. In this paradigm, "the text [is approached] as a means to the author who composed it or the world in which it was composed."[18] In this model, the reader is a universal and objective one.[19] The second paradigm is that of literary criticism, which became a good alternative in the 1980s and 1990s and which involves narrative criticism, structuralism, rhetorical criticism, psychological criticism, reader-response criticism, and deconstructionism. In this paradigm, "the text [is approached] as a message from author to readers,"[20] and the reader continues to be an objective and universal one.[21] Within the same time frame of this second model, a third paradigm of biblical criticism is found: cultural criticism. It includes socioeconomic and ideological analysis, sociological approaches, cognitive dissonance, sociology of knowledge, analysis of social dynamics and roles, anthropological approaches, and comparative societal studies. Here the "text [is approached] as both medium and means . . . to that world in which it was produced,"[22] and the reader continues to be objective, with the difference that in some instances there may be a more contextualized reader.[23]

Finally, Segovia analyses a fourth paradigm called Cultural Studies which is described as "a joint critical study of texts and readers, perspectives and ideologies,"[24] where the text is approached as a construction, with the goal of producing liberation and decolonization. It includes among others, postcolonial studies, border theory, feminist theory, and gender studies. Here the reader is a real flesh-and-blood reader who is ideologically, socially, and historically positioned and engaged and may or may not possess training in criticism and theory. This particular paradigm is diverse, as various readers approach the text from their own respective complex social locations, using different interpretative models and strategies and interacting among themselves in a critical dialogue.[25]

While Segovia manifests his preference for this last paradigm, he is open to a creative use or combination of all the methods for the sake of liberation and decolonization,[26] as long as they take into consideration the contemporary flesh-and-blood reader. In his analysis of Segovia's work, Efrain Agosto observes:

> Segovia suggests that authentic biblical interpretation takes into consideration not just the cultural and historical situation of the original text, but the cultural and historical situation—social location—of the reader. By taking fully into account the context of the modern reader . . . an interpreter thereby allows for the contextualization of culture and experience, both with regard to the ancient text and to the readers of such texts.[27]

To the group of women I work with, all these paradigms and the product of their combination have been key aids in my task of bringing empowerment and liberation to them. At this point, it is important to acknowledge as well the work of women biblical scholars that have also provided an invaluable contribution to this task. These contributions come from different social, geographical, and religious perspectives. They include, among others, the work of Elisabeth Schüssler-Fiorenza,[28] Renita J. Weems,[29] Leticia Guardiola-Sáenz,[30] Gale Yee,[31] and Musa W. Dube.[32] They also include the contributions of organizations such as Christians for Biblical Equality that have sponsored biblical scholarship from an evangelical perspective.[33] Since many of these works are well-known and available to the reader, I will not give a summary of them here. Instead, I would like to proceed by introducing some guidelines that have been useful to both me and the groups of women that I have work with as we relate and deal with the whole Bible in a more positive way.

GUIDELINES TOWARD EMBRACING THE BIBLE AS A GOOD BOOK

As I mentioned previously, as a result of patriarchal and oppressive readings of the Bible, many women around the world see the Bible as a book that sometimes works against them. How is it possible to challenge this perspective?

First, it begins by taking seriously the relationship between the Bible and the particular reader or community of readers. It is important to remember that the reader is a real flesh-and-blood reader who is reading from a particular spiritual, emotional, intellectual, and ideological platform. Also, it is fundamental to detect, acknowledge, and understand under which particular canon this reader or community of readers operates. Having this vital information, I can proceed to see how this reader or community of readers relates to the Bible. A good way to do this is by listening to the readers' stories of pain, struggle, and hope, and how they interact with the text in light of their stories. Do they trust the Bible? Are they angry with the Bible? Do they feel oppressed by the Bible? Do they have the urge to prove that the Bible is right or wrong? Are they open to its message? Why or why not?

Second, after acknowledging this relationship with the Bible, there is a need to explore what is the best way to foster a better relationship with the Bible, meaning one that is open, friendly, peaceful, and productive. If I believe that the Bible is "a good book," how do I help them develop this kind of relationship? I believe it is important to promote the development of the astute reader that García-Treto talks about. An astute woman reader is one who, regardless of her level of education, is able to read/perceive[34] with a good sense of trust or distrust depending on the situation and the biblical interpretation that is articulated.

Being aware that not all women have had the gift of receiving an education, my task as a trained theologian is to make available to them the best resources in the field of biblical scholarship in order to help them find liberation and empowerment. In a sense, my role is one of a hermeneutical translator. As a bicultural person, I understand well the importance of translation. Sometimes translation is done in a literal way, and the real meaning of the word is lost because even though the term may have a similar root or spelling, it does not have the same meaning in the other language. In this case, what is needed is not only a linguistic translator but a cultural translator who can give the real meaning to the words being translated.

Orlando Crespo defines a cultural interpreter or translator as one who has "the ability to interpret these different worlds or cultures to those who cannot fully understand or appreciate them."[35] In light of this, my role as a hermeneutical translator is to translate/interpret/communicate the scholarly resources and developments in the field of biblical hermeneutics in a language and meaning that is understood by these women. In this sense, I, as a theologian engaged with the community, must be multilingual as I speak and articulate different languages: the language of the academy, the language of the religious denomination, and the language of the audience or the people.

As a multilingual hermeneutical translator, I can help these women in their process of empowerment and liberation as I translate valuable concepts that have been produced by the academy into a language that they can understand. As a multilingual translator, I can help also in this process as I translate some of these concepts to denominational leaders in order to increase the awareness about women's struggles and issues.

Third, another important element in the development of this positive relationship with the Bible is establishing some theological criteria that will help these women in setting boundaries to the different interpretations that they may encounter. These theological criteria are related primarily to the person and work of God, and God's revelation in Christ. For instance, if I believe that God is a God of life and peace who wants to complete shalom for me and my community, these concepts will set a boundary to question/reject interpretations that seem to present the opposite for my life. Following this view and strategy, I am not automatically ignoring and dismissing the text or assuming that it is not part of the canon. On the contrary, it means that I need to take the whole text seriously and, guided by my theological criteria about God, recognize that I must do more work with the text. This continuous work will help me to find a way to articulate an interpretation that makes sense to me or to the particular group with whom I am working.

Lastly, I have to recognize my limitations. Since we are limited human beings, we need to recognize that we do not understand everything. Why is this passage there? Is it really the way that God wants us to live or is it warning us about some human weaknesses and vulnerabilities that we have related to issues of power and control? Is this a passage that does not make sense at this point? If so, do we need to recognize that we do not have enough information at this point to deal with it?[36] At the same time, can we give God the benefit of the doubt? Does the fact that the passage seems to be against me necessarily mean that God is against me? Or does it mean that I do not have enough information to deal with it, but I can still believe that God is good and God wants something good for me?

CONCLUDING COMMENTS

In a sense, my task as a theologian in this setting is to help these women to make peace with the Bible. In other words, as my professor of Theological Studies at seminary, Elouise Renich Fraser, would say, I need to help them "To Make Friends with the Bible."[37] As a theologian, I am there to help them understand that God, through the Bible, is their friend and not their enemy. Furthermore, I am there to help them become empowered through the Bible to have better lives that are truly abundant.

I believe that if I engage the readers in their world, and work from their perspectives and issues, then I will help these women in a process of liberation and empowerment that makes sense to them. The results may not necessarily look like or meet my own standards of liberation as an educated, middle class woman, but I need to see them as a step in a process of liberation that is not imposed on them—a process that makes sense to them so that they can embrace it.

From this perspective, my function as a trained theologian is a pastoral one but also a prophetic one. These two functions have to be maintained in a healthy and creative tension. The pastoral function will help me recognize, acknowledge, and respect where in this tension the women are positioned. The prophetic one will help me challenge them to move to the next step in their process of empowerment and liberation. I, as a theologian, need to be sensitive to the group, and be careful not to push them too much; otherwise, they will dismiss me from the group as one who has lost her mind, or as too liberal (whatever this means for them), too academic, or too disengaged from the real views of the community. In light of this, the ideal position of the theologian should be as much as possible as an insider in this particular group but also as an outsider who can bring to the group new concepts from the academy. In this sense, the theologian is one who lives in *"Nepantla"* between communal and academic spaces.[38] I would like to close by sharing two brief stories that illustrate this process of making friends with the Bible.

The setting for the first story is Texas, San Antonio, in particular. In addition to my teaching responsibilities, I direct the Christian Latina Leadership Institute. The institute serves primarily the kind of evangelical woman that I described above. After teaching one seminar that I call "Good News for Women," which deals with the Bible and women, one of the participants told me: "With these concepts you have awakened the giant who was waiting for liberation." The tools and interpretations that she received made sense to her in her own world, and she was able to embrace them in her process of empowerment and liberation.

The setting for the second story is India. After teaching a one-hour Bible study about some guidelines to read the Bible as women, a woman came and with broken English asked me why God did not bless women? This hard question took me by surprise, and to gain some time to think, I asked her what she meant? After listening in detail to the hardships that Indian women go through from the moment of conception until their time of death, I told her that I believe God had blessed women, and I urged her to come to the next Bible studies gathering. For the next four days we dealt with many of the complex passages about women in the Bible. On the last day, she came again and she just told me with a hopeful voice: "God sent me an angel, now I understand," and she left. I never heard again from this woman, or what happened to her, but the work that we did that week made sense to her, and at least in her internal world she started a process of empowerment and liberation by understanding biblical concepts that made sense to her in her reality.

Again, most likely for my standards of liberation, the processes of these two women may be too slow or not very radical, but it is not about me, my concepts, or my sense of timing, but about them, their process, and their world. They started a process of empowerment and liberation where, as Christian women, a vital component is to start "making friends with the Bible," and even more making friends again with the God of the Bible.[39]

NOTES

1. On the concept of bridge, see Leticia Guardiola-Sáenz, "A Mexican-American Politics of Location: Reading from the Bridge," paper presented at the American Academy of Religion Annual Meeting, Philadelphia, PA, November, 1995.

2. See Texas Baptist Convention, https://texasbaptists.org/about/what-we-believe-the-bible, accessed on 6/3/2018.

3. David Maldonado, Jr., "Protestantism," in *Hispanic American Religious Cultures*, Vol. 2, ed. Miguel A. de la Torre (Santa Barbara, CA: ABC-CLIO, 2009), 461–462.

4. Justo L. González, *Santa Biblia: The Bible through Hispanic Eyes* (Nashville: Abingdon, 1996), 118.

5. Orlando Crespo, *Being Latino in Christ: Finding Wholeness in Your Ethnic Identity* (Downers Grove, IL: InterVarsity Press, 2003), 40–53.

6. González, *Santa Biblia*, 115–118.

7. Ada María Isasi-Díaz, *Mujerista Theology* (Maryknoll, NY: Orbis Books, 1996), 150 and 165, n. 7.

8. Isasi-Díaz, *Mujerista Theology*, 148.

9. Isasi-Díaz, *Mujerista Theology*, 148–151.

10. Loida Martell-Otero, "Women Doing Theology: Una Perspectiva Evangélica," *Apuntes* 14,3 (Fall 1994): 76.

11. Fernando F. Segovia, "Towards a Hermeneutics of the Diaspora: A Hermeneutics of Otherness and Engagement," in *Reading from This Place*, vol. 1: *Social Location and Biblical Interpretations in the United States*, ed. Fernando F. Segovia and Mary Ann Tolbert (Minneapolis: Fortress Press, 1995), 70–71.

12. Francisco O. García-Treto, "The Lesson of the Gibeonites: A Proposal for Dialogic Attention as a Strategy for Reading the Bible," in *Hispanic/Latino Theology: Challenge and Promise*, ed. Ada María Isasi-Díaz and Fernando F. Segovia (Minneapolis: Fortress Press, 1996), 74.

13. García-Treto, "The Lesson of the Gibeonites, 74.

14. García-Treto, "The Lesson of the Gibeonites, 74.

15. Fernando F. Segovia, "Toward Intercultural Criticism: A Reading Strategy from the Diaspora," in *Reading from This Place*, vol. II: *Social Location and Biblical*

Interpretations in Global Perspective, ed. Fernando F. Segovia and Mary Ann Tolbert (Minneapolis: Fortress Press, 1995), 317.

16. Segovia, "Toward Intercultural Criticism," 318.

17. Fernando F. Segovia, "And They Began to Speak in Other Tongues: Competing Modes of Discourse in Contemporary Biblical Criticism," in *Reading from This Place*, Vol. 1: *Social Location and Biblical Interpretations in the United States*, ed. Fernando F. Segovia and Mary Ann Tolbert (Minneapolis: Fortress Press, 1995), 1–32.

18. Segovia, "And They Began to Speak," 6.

19. Segovia, "And They Began to Speak," 9–14.

20. Segovia, "And They Began to Speak," 6.

21. Segovia, "And They Began to Speak," 15–20.

22. Segovia, "And They Began to Speak," 6.

23. Segovia, "And They Began to Speak," 20–28.

24. Segovia, "And They Began to Speak," 29.

25. Segovia, "And They Began to Speak," 28–31; Segovia, "Towards a Hermeneutics of the Diaspora," 59.

26. Fernando F. Segovia, "Toward Intercultural Criticism," 329.

27. Efrain Agosto, "Hermeneutics," in *Hispanic American Religious Cultures*, vol. 2, ed. Miguel A. De La Torre (Santa Barbara, CA: ABC-CLIO, LLC, 2009), 653.

28. Elisabeth Schüssler-Fiorenza's most important book is *In Memory of Her: A Feminist Theological Reconstruction of Christian Origins* (New York: The Crossroads Publishing Company, 1983). Other important writings are: *Bread Not Stone: The Challenge of Feminist Biblical Interpretation* (Boston: Beacon Press, 1985); *But She Said: Feminist Practices of Biblical Interpretation* (Boston: Beacon Press, 1992); *Sharing Her Word: Feminist Biblical Interpretation in Context* (Boston: Beacon Press, 1998); and *Wisdom Ways: Introducing Feminist Biblical Interpretation* (Maryknoll, NY: Orbis Books, 2001).

29. Renita J. Weems, *Just a Sister Away: A Womanist Vision of Women's Relationships in the Bible* (Philadelphia: Innisfree, 1988); *Showing Mary: How Women Can Share Prayers, Wisdom, and the Blessings of God* (New York: Warner Books, Inc., 2002).

30. Leticia Guardiola-Sáenz, "Borderless Women and Borderless Texts: A Cultural Reading of Matthew 15:21–28," in *Reading the Bible as Women: Perspectives from Africa, Asia, and Latin America*, ed. Katharine Doob Sakenfield, Sharon Ringe, and Phyllis Bird, *Semeia* 78 (Atlanta: Scholar Press, 1997), 69–81; "Reading From Ourselves: Identity and Hermeneutics Among Mexican-American Feminists," in *A Reader in Latina Feminist Theology: Religion and Justice*, ed. María Pilar Aquino, Daisy L. Machado, and Jeanette Rodríguez (Austin, TX: University of Texas Press, 2002), 80–97; "María Magdalena: Apóstol a los apóstoles," in *Camino a Emaús: Compartiendo el ministerio de Jesús*, ed. Ada María Isai-Díaz, Timoteo Matovina, and Nina M. Torres-Vidal (Minneapolis: Fortress Press, 2002), 15–22.

31. Gale Yee, *Poor Banished Children of Eve: Woman as Evil in the Hebrew Bible* (Minneapolis: Fortress Press, 2003).

32. Musa W. Dube, *Postcolonial Feminist Interpretation of the Bible* (St. Louis: Chalice, 2000).

33. The organization Christians for Biblical Equality publishes the *Priscilla Papers* journal with the goal of disseminating interdisciplinary evangelical scholarship on topics related to the Bible and gender equality. In addition, they publish also the magazine *Mutuality*, which discusses similar perspectives, but with a less academic tone and language, as it is aimed at a more general audience.

34. Here I am including the word "perceive" because many women around the world are not able to read, but they can still wisely perceive and understand when an interpretation or situation is turned against or for them.

35. Orlando Crespo, *Being Latino in Christ*, 116–117.

36. Millard J. Erickson, *Introducing Christian Doctrine* (Grand Rapids, MI: Baker Academic, 2001), 73–74.

37. Elouise Renich Fraser and Louis A. Kilgore, *Making Friends with the Bible* (Scottsdale, PA: Herald, 1994).

38. "*Nepantla*" is a term that means in the middle or the middle space. It is in the Nahuatl language that was spoken by the Nahuas who lived in the central part of Mexico before the conquest. See Lara Medina, "Nepantla" in *Hispanic American Religious Cultures*, vol. 2, ed. Miguel De La Torre (Santa Barbara, California: ABC-CLIO, LLC, 2009), 403–407.

39. Guardiola-Sáenz, "A Mexican-American Politics of Location."

BIBLIOGRAPHY

Agosto, Efrain. "Hermeneutics." In *Hispanic American Religious Cultures*, Vol. 2, edited by Miguel A. De La Torre, 647–656. Santa Barbara, CA: ABC-CLIO, LLC, 2009.

Crespo, Orlando. *Being Latino in Christ: Finding Wholeness in Your Ethnic Identity*. Downers Grove, IL: InterVarsity Press, 2003.

Dube, Musa W. *Postcolonial Feminist Interpretation of the Bible*. St. Louis: Chalice, 2000.

Erickson, Millard J. *Introducing Christian Doctrine*. Grand Rapids, MI: Baker Academic, 2001.

García-Treto, Francisco O. "The Lesson of the Gibeonites: A Proposal for Dialogic Attention as a Strategy for Reading the Bible." In *Hispanic/Latino Theology: Challenge and Promise*, edited by Ada María Isasi-Díaz and Fernando F. Segovia, 73–85. Minneapolis: Fortress Press, 1996.

González, Justo L. *Santa Biblia: The Bible through Hispanic Eyes*. Nashville: Abingdon, 1996.

Guardiola-Sáenz, Leticia. "Borderless Women and Borderless Texts: A Cultural Reading of Matthew 15:21-28." In *Reading the Bible as Women: Perspectives from Africa, Asia, and Latin America*, edited by Katharine Doob Sakenfield, Sharon Ringe, and Phyllis Bird, 69–81. *Semeia* 78. Atlanta: Scholar Press, 1997.

———. "María Magdalena: Apóstol a los apóstoles." In *Camino a Emaús: Compartiendo el ministerio de Jesús*, edited by Ada María Isai-Díaz, Timoteo Matovina, and Nina M. Torres-Vidal, 15–22. Minneapolis: Fortress Press, 2002.

———. "A Mexican-American Politics of Location: Reading from the Bridge." Presentation at American Academy of Religion Annual Meeting. Philadelphia, PA, November, 1995.

———. "Reading From Ourselves: Identity and Hermeneutics Among Mexican-American Feminists." In *A Reader in Latina Feminist Theology: Religion and Justice*, edited by María Pilar Aquino, Daisy L. Machado, and Jeanette Rodríguez, 80–97. Austin, TX: University of Texas Press, 2002.

González, Justo L. *Santa Biblia: The Bible through Hispanic Eyes*. Nashville: Abingdon, 1996.

Isasi-Díaz, Ada María. *Mujerista Theology*. Maryknoll, NY: Orbis Books, 1996.

Maldonado, David Jr. "Protestantism." In *Hispanic American Religious Cultures*, Vol. 2, edited by Miguel A. de la Torre, 461–462. Santa Barbara, CA: ABC-CLIO, 2009.

Martell-Otero, Loida. "Women Doing Theology: Una Perspectiva Evangélica." *Apuntes* 14:3 (Fall 1994): 67–85.

Medina, Lara. "Nepantla." In *Hispanic American Religious Cultures*, Vol. 2, edited by Miguel De La Torre, 403–407. Santa Barbara, California: ABC-CLIO, LLC, 2009.

Renich Fraser, Elouise and Louis A. Kilgore. *Making Friends with the Bible*. Scottsdale, PA: Herald, 1994.

Schüssler Fiorenza, Elisabeth. *Bread Not Stone: The Challenge of Feminist Biblical Interpretation*. Boston: Beacon Press, 1985.

———. *But She Said: Feminist Practices of Biblical Interpretation*. Boston: Beacon Press, 1992.

———. *In Memory of Her: A Feminist Theological Reconstruction of Christian Origins*. New York: The Crossroads Publishing Company, 1983.

———. *Sharing Her Word: Feminist Biblical Interpretation in Context*. Boston: Beacon Press, 1998.

———. *Wisdom Ways: Introducing Feminist Biblical Interpretation*. Maryknoll, NY: Orbis Books, 2001.

Segovia, Fernando F. "And They Began to Speak in Other Tongues: Competing Modes of Discourse in Contemporary Biblical Criticism." In *Reading from This Place*, Vol. 1: *Social Location and Biblical Interpretations in the United States*, edited by Fernando F. Segovia and Mary Ann Tolbert, 1–32. Minneapolis: Fortress Press, 1995.

———. "Towards a Hermeneutics of the Diaspora: A Hermeneutics of Otherness and Engagement." In *Reading from This Place*, Vol. 1: *Social Location and Biblical Interpretations in the United States*, edited by Fernando F. Segovia and Mary Ann Tolbert, 57–73. Minneapolis: Fortress Press, 1995.

———. "Toward Intercultural Criticism: A Reading Strategy from the Diaspora." In *Reading from This Place*, Vol. 2: *Social Location and Biblical Interpretations in Global Perspective*, edited by Fernando F. Segovia and Mary Ann Tolbert, 303–330. Minneapolis: Fortress Press, 1995.

Texas Baptist Convention. "Beliefs: The Bible." At: https://texasbaptists.org/about/what-we-believe-the-bible.

Weems, Renita J. *Just a Sister Away: A Womanist Vision of Women's Relationships in the Bible*. Philadelphia: Innisfree, 1988.

———. *Showing Mary: How Women Can Share Prayers, Wisdom, and the Blessings of God*. New York: Warner Books, Inc., 2002.

Yee, Gale. *Poor Banished Children of Eve: Woman as Evil in the Hebrew Bible*. Minneapolis: Fortress Press, 2003.

Chapter 6

Reading against the Grain

Scripture and Constructive Evangélica Theology

Loida I. Martell

I am a constructive theologian. That is to say, I am intentional about defining my context as I seek to retrieve theological perspectives marginalized by the tradition and critically examine them in light of contemporary issues. I am a bicoastal Puerto Rican evangélica with a background in veterinary medicine who pastors and teaches members of marginalized communities. Being bicoastal means that I reside in "between and betwixt" geographical and cultural spaces. I am a biological and cultural *sata*—the term for "mutt" in Puerto Rico, on which I shall expand below—who does theology through bilingual and multicultural lenses. Ambiguity, a sense of never quite belonging, and a need to continuously define myself because I am always seen as "other" are part of my daily existence.

As a Puerto Rican, I belong to a people who are still colonized—their identities and sovereignty defined and controlled by the sociopolitical, economic, and even religious hegemony of the United States. As such, I lay claim to a historical memory of the rape and plunder of the land and its people with nary a word of protest from any quarter of the world. As recently as the 1970s, the women of the island were used for medical experimentation and young people were assassinated for expressing nationalistic hopes. I am familiar with this silence of collusion by the United States to deceive Puerto Ricans of its past colonial actions. Thus, I come from a despised and humiliated people who live either in a land that no longer belongs to us or in a country that does not want us. I am not so much a diaspora person as I am a *Samaritana*—one who is treated as a stranger in the land of her birth.

I am also an evangélica theologian. The term "evangélica" does not necessarily translate as "evangelical," which in the United States implies a particular theological and at times political position within Protestantism. Rather, "evangélica" in Spanish simply denotes one as a Protestant. In Puerto Rico, few Protestants call themselves "Protestantes," with its implications about protest. Most call themselves "evangélic@s," because they see themselves as a people of "The Book"—*el evangelio* or "good news."[1] Thus, the Bible holds a preeminent place in evangélica theology.

In Latin America and the Caribbean, the various forms of Protestantism introduced through sundry missiological waves were transmuted in their encounter with a popular Catholicism. This particular expression of Catholicism was itself the result of an encounter between Iberian Catholicism—that included Jewish, Moorish, and other cultural-religious roots—and Amerindian and African religious beliefs and practices. These various encounters and their resulting distinctive expressions have been described in various ways, including as a process of *mestizaje*. Mestijaze is a term that gained widespread usage among Latin@ theologians after it was adapted by Virgilio Elizondo. Elizondo defined *mestijaze* as a process in which two or more cultural, religious, and/or biological groups give rise to a new entity but which nevertheless retains fully all the characteristics of the precursors alongside its new expressions.[2] As a result, evangélic@ refers to a popular Protestantism that reflects a worldview arising from the encounter of all these influences.

To speak of missiological Protestant influences means that evangélic@s acknowledge certain religious emphases as part of their tradition, including conversion as a mark of the Spirit's working in their lives; the need to commit publicly and personally to Jesus Christ as Lord and Savior; and the authority of the Bible as "the rule of faith and practice." However, what constitutes "authority" is at times contested and not altogether clear. Recent studies have begun to explore the meaning of authority for various Latin@ religious groups.[3]

I am also a veterinary doctor. My years of training and practice have afforded me with a particular hermeneutical lens for doing theology. For example, during my years in veterinary medical school, I was taught that if I wanted to be a good diagnostician, I should never rely just on my eyes but rather engage all my senses in the examination of my patients. To see only with one's eyes could result in missing critical information. It was driven home to me that we needed to learn to "see" with our hands by palpitating the patient and to run them "against the grain" of a patient's coat. This skill often served me well. It allowed me to "see" diseases and conditions that otherwise my physical eyes would have missed. I translated that skill to my new profession when I became a pastor, and currently as a theologian.

Thus, from my specific social location, I argue that evangélica theology is a constructive effort that approaches Scripture by "reading against the grain." It is a "peripheric reading" that takes seriously the voices of grassroots evangélicas who consider the Bible an authoritative source not because it is "inerrant" or "infallible," but because it is a space in which they encounter the triune God *en lo cotidiano*/in the spaces of everyday life. Reading against the grain honors the communal narratives that arise when evangélicas interweave biblical interpretation with *testimonios* (witness) and *coritos* (short refrains). These communal narratives, in turn, expose and subvert what I call "normatizing myths" leveled against Latinas. Thus, reading against the grain is a salvific process in which evangélicas experience empowerment, healing, and transformation.

READING FROM THIS PLACE: SOCIAL LOCATION

Evangélicas are part of a diverse group of people often erroneously grouped under the broad term "Latin@." In reality, there is no such thing as a Latina or Latino. There are, however, diverse peoples—with diverse histories, cultures, socioeconomic status, religious traditions, and worldviews—who have either primary or secondary ties to Latin America and the Caribbean: Mexicans and Mexican Americans in the North, Central, and South Americans; Cubans, Dominicans, and Puerto Ricans from the Caribbean; and/or, the subsequent generations of such peoples who are born in this country. Regardless of their diverse backgrounds, these peoples experience a dislocation of identity in this country, when they suddenly discover that they are considered "Latina" or "Hispanic" by the demands of the dominant culture. They have reluctantly accepted the designation to represent a shared kinship with those who face myriad challenges of ethnic and linguistic discrimination, poverty, under- and unemployment, poor educational attainment, poor health care, subpar housing, institutional and domestic violence, and marginalization from those things that provide vital connections and quality of life.

By and large, a majority of Latin@s find themselves in this country as a result of a long history of invasion, colonialism, and neocolonialism. This history began with the loss of lands of our indigenous forebears by European military and missiological forces that justified this theft as well as their genocidal impulses with Scriptural and theological warrants. Empire-building did not stop with Spain and Portugal. The United States and other North Atlantic nations have continued such policies under varied names, including Manifest Destiny. Unjust wars deprived Latin@s of our homelands. Treaties have been broken with impunity. Women have been raped and exploited, treated as "things" to be used by whoever has been in power. Our economies are gutted by NAFTA-like policies that exploit the natural and human resources of our native lands in order to enrich the economic elites of empire-building nations. More recently, empire-building is beginning to transcend the traditional nation-state borders and is represented by trans- and multinational corporations. For such corporate entities, we Latin@s are simply "raw material," available for their manipulation.

Regardless of whether the perpetrator has been a sociopolitical or corporate entity, Western Euro-centric Christianity has never been an innocent bystander in this process. Missionaries often entered defeated nations under the protective banner of invading armies. In too many instances, Christianization has been synonymous with "Americanization." The religious traditions of indigenes, and of later Latin@ inhabitants, have been dismissed as demonic or archaic superstitions.[4] The result of this history is that oftentimes Latin@s are considered as people of no value, who contribute nothing to society. We are nothing more than undesirable *sat@s*.

In Puerto Rico, "satos" are mixed-breed dogs; they are mutts. They are kicked to the curb and left without shelter. Periodically, there are campaigns to reduce the population of such "vermin." Latin@s are treated as the sat@s of U.S. society: viewed as impure, vermin, and therefore unwanted. History is dotted with the genocidal impulses of the United States in its attempts to rid itself of its neighbors to the south and its brown inhabitants within. Consider, for example, the so-called "immigration reform" bills and nativistic attacks that seek to dispatch "illegals," the enforced sterilization of Puerto Rican women to control "overpopulation," or U.S. efforts to exploit these peoples for its self-enrichment. Latin@s are considered sat@s, and, as such, are treated as *sobraja* (leftovers) that can be discarded at will.[5]

Yet, while Latin@s proudly lay claim to the mixed inheritance that contributes to a particular worldview—a *cierta manera de ser* (a certain way of being)—we are not sat@s in its pejorative sense. We are a deeply religious people, who believe that God is fully present *en lo cotidiano*, in the space of daily life. It is the space in which the powerless and marginalized seek meaning for, and control of, their lives.[6] Too often male-centric theologies focus on the macro structures of dominance and sin, but lose sight of its impact at the microlevel of everyday living. These are the sites that too often are rendered invisible to the halls of academia and to the theological writings that emanate from the centers of power. Yet, these sites can often be spaces where structural sin and divine grace are most visible. Latin@ theologians, particularly Latinas, have long argued that *lo cotidiano* is the primary space where God is encountered and that, therefore it is the *locus theologicus* for evangélica theology. It is in *lo cotidiano* where they can discern "the grace, justice, presence, and love of God manifested in the everyday occurrences" as they share insights about their experiences of *el Jesús sato* and the power of the Spirit.[7]

Paradoxically, within this "peripheric space," one can gauge the real impact of structural and personal sin in the daily lives of the poor and oppressed. To speak of poverty and give statistics is important as long as one does not forget the real day-to-day stories of loss and survival that statistics translate: as poor women, who often are forced to pay exorbitant fees for substandard food in stores that are never truly accessible to them; as parents, who must send their children to school in the morning never quite sure if they will return alive that evening; as new mothers, afraid to leave their babies in their cribs for fear that rats will chew them alive; and as the myriad ways in which our humanity is diminished and our self-worth erased. Violence is the constant companion of poor Latinas: by a health system that does more to abuse than to heal; by social institutions, including ecclesial bodies that marginalize them; and even within family structures that are supposed to be sanctuaries for them.

Elizabeth Conde-Frazier and others remind us that evangélicas read the Bible from the particularities of their lived realities.[8] It is within the peripheral places of neglect, violence, abuse, poverty, and suffering as well as hope, life, family, and faith that many grassroots evangélicas read Scripture. This is where their stories, in word and song, encounter the stories of the bible. From this place, they articulate their theologies and live out their spiritualities.

READING AGAINST THE GRAIN: POSTCOLONIAL READINGS IN A COLONIZED WORLD

Theology has often been defined as a discourse about God and things pertaining to God. Yet, "discourse" is as much about listening as it is about speaking. I believe that hearing "against the grain" entails listening to the silences, to sense the crevices and liminal spaces that remain hidden in what is espoused, and being attentive to what or who is absent from the conversation. Such skills are particularly important to someone who has pastored among a people who have been silenced by structures of oppression, and whose own cultural and spiritual history has been intentionally rendered invisible by the colonizing powers that have ruled over them, in my case in Puerto Rico.

Theologians have at various times identified Scripture, tradition, experience, and reason among the critical sources and resources for doing theology. While there is no true consensus among theologians about what should be the definitive sources for doing theology, generally the Protestant tradition considers the Bible to be a preeminent authoritative source.[9] Constructive theology, nevertheless, is by its very nature a field that revisits the givens of tradition, particularly the universalized claims made by Euro-centric theologies. It emphasizes contextual and praxeological hermeneutics over universal and abstract claims. As such, constructive theologians have been very much attuned to the recent trends in biblical scholarship that have sought to revisit the veracity and viability of Scripture.

Contemporary constructive biblical hermeneutics have questioned the dependence on historico-critical methodologies, particularly its elevation as *the* method for interpreting texts and its complicity in the oppression of those deemed "other." Subsequently, new paradigms have been proposed. Nevertheless, we Latina evangélica theologians who engage in this constructive work find ourselves in a quandary similar to that of Nyasha Junior's: we too find that there is a dearth of biblical scholarship from an evangélica perspective.[10] Thus, we must creatively engage the Bible, as well as responsibly dialogue with biblical scholars and those from other fields.

Interestingly, the earliest scholars to call for a reading of Scripture from a "Hispanic" perspective were Protestant theologians rather than biblical scholars. Early in the Latin@ theological enterprise, Orlando E. Costas suggested the need for a "Hispanically oriented reading of Scriptures and Christian history"[11] that took seriously the Latin@ realities of conquest, colonialism, migration, and biculturalism. Justo L. González later suggested that the Bible be read "in Spanish" as a "non-innocent" history that deals with issues of power and powerlessness.[12] Subsequently, he published *Santa Biblia*, in which he constructed a paradigm for reading the Bible "through Hispanic eyes." He posited that Latin@s read through the lenses of their identity and commitment to liberative efforts. This identity includes the experience of marginality, poverty, *mestizaje*, and exile—since Latin@s are often considered "aliens" in the context of the United States.[13]

The efforts of these two pioneering scholars to better define what it meant to do theology by reading the Bible "hispanically" resulted in a fruitful and ecumenical conversation among Latin@ biblical scholars and theologians. While those efforts were a critically important step for Latin@ contextual theologies, absent from them were experiences of gender oppression. Furthermore, though these scholars mentioned colonialism as an element to be considered, their "Hispanic readings" were curiously absent of any intentional analysis of colonialism or neocolonialism—either in the history of the Americas or in the present lives of Latin@s.

In light of the geopolitical realities of empire, colonization, and neocolonialism that encompass most of the Two-Thirds world, and the re-inscription of these respective ideologies in the current readings of biblical texts, contemporary Catholic and Protestant biblical scholars and theologians are proposing a move toward a "postcolonial reading" of the Bible, using the tools afforded by postcolonial and cultural studies.[14] "Postcolonial" and postcolonialism are defined in various ways. Fernando F. Segovia defines postcolonial as a field of studies that takes into consideration the reality of empire as an "omnipresent, inescapable, and overwhelming reality in the world." He applies it in biblical studies to see how it affects the production and interpretation of texts, as well as the "real readers" as interpreters.[15] Kwok Pui Lan defines postcolonial studies as a "reading strategy and discursive practice that seeks to unmask colonial epistemological frameworks, unravel Eurocentric logics, and interrogate stereotypical cultural representations."[16] For her, it is a form of criticism that "exposes the relationship between power and knowledge," challenging "imperialist and nationalist claims."[17]

Drawing insights from such varied fields as cultural studies, ideological criticism, and even postmodernism, postcolonial criticism has been incorporated into biblical studies, where it seeks to bring to the fore the voices of those absent from the biblical text, its interpretation, and what Leticia Guardiola-Sáenz calls "flesh-and-blood readers."[18] It evaluates how the Bible often has been used as an instrument for conquest and a tool that has justified the hegemonic move of elite groups to exclude, murder, or otherwise rule over those they consider "other." Thus, Segovia argues that there is a need to "decolonize biblical studies" by addressing the question of "how to read and interpret the Bible in the aftermath of centuries of domination, discrimination, exploitation, and the wholesale displacement and extermination of countless 'others' who stood in the path of Western progress."[19] This approach understands that imperialism, colonialism, and neocolonialism serve as a historical framework for both the production of the text and the context of the reader.

Postcolonial approaches to biblical interpretation offer a promising method for constructive theologians in their use of Scripture. However, I have five concerns with this approach. These are as follows: (1) addressing the dynamics of gender and ethnic oppression; (2) visualizing a postcolonial reading without overcoming colonization; (3) reinscribing colonial academic ties by using the language of the center; (4) addressing the collusion of silence regarding the daily lives of poor women; and (5) analyzing the question of the authority and validity of the Bible.

My first concern is that, in its effort to situate the production and interpretation of the text within the larger geopolitical framework of empire, a postcolonial reading risks rendering invisible the dynamics of gender and ethnic oppression *en lo cotidiano* (in the everyday). In this regard, I believe that Gale A. Yee and Kwok Pui Lan offer insightful approaches.

Yee's use of ideological criticism—defined as a "materialist-feminist reading of the text that understands literature as an ideological production of social praxis which itself is governed by ideology"—underscores that the text is indeed "non-innocent."[20] She argues that in its very production a text is not a simple mirror of the historical world in which it was produced but rather a "construal" of the ideologies of its authors. She defines ideology as "a discourse of meaning, both embedded in social practice and autonomous from it."[21] The text is never passive but rather an interpretation of the inscribed ideological positions that produced it; it is an "ideology of an ideology."[22] Generally speaking, the text represents the ideologies of those in power.

Using various means, these ideologies are promoted as legitimate interpretations of reality and serve hegemonic interests.

Kwok, conscious that a general postcolonial reading may not adequately address the subjugation and gender discrimination experienced by women, particularly women of color, proposes a "postcolonial feminist interpretation of the Bible" that investigates "the deployment of gender in the narration of identity, the negotiation of power differentials between the colonizers and the colonized, and the reinforcement of patriarchal control over spheres where these elites could exercise control."[23] She suggests various ways to achieve this including: (1) a critical awareness of how the Bible has been used as a tool of the imperial interests of the West, in particular its use to "domesticate" women patterned after a white Western ideal of womanhood; (2) an examination of how marginalized women are rendered invisible in the Bible; (3) attention to how political differences create patterns of violence between groups of people; (4) consideration of how difference is used to shape the identity of the "knower" and her/his "situated knowledge"; and (5) the resistance to homogenize "women's interpretive experience" under a false collective "our" that erases the multiplicity of theological voices.[24]

Yee's and Kwok's approaches allow scholars to address the inscribed elements of patriarchy in the text and to remain conscious of how biblical interpretation often reinforces stereotypes about women, particularly women of color. Both approaches are intentional about bringing the issues of gender oppression to the fore as well as seeking viable responses to counteract the injustices against women, particularly poor women of color, that arise from colonizing structures of empire.

The second difficulty I have regarding postcolonial methods of biblical interpretation is whether it is indeed possible to truly visualize a *post*colonial reading if we have not yet overcome colonization. How are we to achieve such a reading in a context of continued colonization? As a Puerto Rican, I can assert that colonialism is alive and well on the island, insidiously undermining our culture and way of life.

On a recent trip to Puerto Rico, I was struck by how our Amerindian and African histories are vanishing from public discourse, privileging Spanish and European history. "Americans" are lauded as the saviors of the Puerto Rican people, and "America" is preached as the promised land in our schools as well as from our pulpits. This reality exists with little or no outrage or protest from the public quarter. I remain struck by the apparent lack of acknowledgment of Puerto Rico's continued colonial status when I read the postcolonial analytical writings of colleagues, though there are allusions to the movements of liberation in Latin America. There is no mention of Puerto Rico's political prisoners, of young people gunned down in cold blood for their political beliefs, of a people cowed by police and military repression, or of other acts of cultural, social, economic, and political genocide systematically carried out against its inhabitants during its tenure of U.S. occupation. For Puerto Rico, there is no "post" colonial reality, only a slow and steady decimation of our cultural heritage and political self-determination.

I am not the only scholar raising concerns about the use of the term "postcolonial." Ella Shohat discusses the roots of the postcolonial studies and the coining of the term of itself, as well as its epistemological relation to the concept of "Third World." In her brief discussion, she posits two strong criticisms in regard to the terminology of "postcolonial."

First, that it is a globalizing term that hides both a spatial difference (Which colonized/colonizer relation are we speaking about—in the so-called First World or the so-called Third World, where such relationships also take place?) and a temporal difference (When did the "post" colonizing event take place, if at all?). This globalizing term tends to "[downplay] multiplicities of location and temporality as well as discursive and political linkages between postcolonial theories and contemporary anticolonial or anti-neocolonial struggles and discourses."[25] Her second criticism is that the term "masks the white settlers' colonialist-racist policies toward indigenous people," policies that carry on against indigenes in the Americas and in other nation-states. Its terminology "leaves no space . . . [for] Fourth World peoples dominated by both First World multinational corporations and by Third World nation-states."[26] These "internal" as well as "external" colonialisms are realities with which one must contend.

What do we mean, then, when we refer to "post" colonialism? If by the term scholars mean to imply "a time after colonialism and temporally" and refer to "a post-independence of the former colonial world," then the terminology poses a problem because for "two-thirds of the world, colonialism is not dead."[27] However, as Shohat points out, if "post" is meant to imply not "after" but "going beyond," then perhaps more precise terminology such as "post-anticolonial critique" is desirable.[28]

A third concern is related to the preceding discussion. Postcolonial theory arises from European theoretical discourse. In this sense, it is not just a critique; it is also a "contested space."[29] To what degree do we re-inscribe our colonial academic ties by inadvertently attempting to use the master's tools to dismantle the master's house?[30] This concern is only underscored when I observe that we, as biblical scholars and theologians of color, state that our concern in postcolonial critique is to seek to be attentive to the voices of the margins. However, what I often find to be the case is that we continue to be in dialogue with, and speak the language of, the center.

For example, consider the consultation between Latin@ biblical scholars and theologians held during a session of the American Academy of Religion—a locus that represents the oft-colonizing world of the academy.

Why not have such conversations in the pews, the ghettos, and the streets of our respective communities? It is not an impossible task, as recent theological consultations of my denomination have proved. Biblical scholars, theologians, and educators, together with pastors and lay people, hold such consultations to great effect and create engaging and energetic conversations. Kwok and others have noted that a truly postcolonial optic must engage grassroots women. Andrea Smith and other Native American scholars have noted that a true liberating hermeneutic must take place not within the academy but rather within the community as a whole.[31] Otherwise, the postcolonial optic simply becomes another means to make invisible and silenced the truly marginalized and colonized.

My fourth concern as I seek liberating methods of biblical interpretation is related to what I consider the "collusion of silence." Here I am using "collusion" in a different manner than Yee does. She uses the word to describe women's internalization and consent in their own subordination and oppression.[32] As a constructive theologian, I am cognizant of the importance of the interpretive history *surrounding* the Bible as a tool of oppression, invasion, and destruction, as well as the ideological history *embedded* in it that marginalizes and excludes some in support of others' hegemonic interests. However, here I want to direct myself to the power of silence to which I have been a witness and its impact upon the fabric of the daily lives of poor women.

This particular collusion of silence is one that allows us to ignore the fact that in our country women and children go hungry, reside in unheated homes, and cannot afford adequate medical care. It is a collusion that permits atrocities to be committed against black, Latina, Amerindian, and Asian women's bodies with little or no public outcry. It permits certain Latinos who are in positions of leadership to sexually harass Latinas, and yet continue to be celebrated as icons of the community. It is this collusion of silence that continues to reign among Latin@ evangélica churches which refuse to acknowledge or speak about the presence of gays and lesbians in our midst in a strange dance of "don't ask, don't tell" deniability. Latina evangélicas know too well about these silences. They are familiar with the efforts to silence them. How do we instead ensure that we listen to the silences, that we become acutely aware of the crevices where the absent are present, and that we acknowledge "the voice of the other... who has long suffered the unjust invasion and oppression" not just in the text but also in the real world that we inhabit?[33]

This brings me to my fifth concern regarding biblical hermeneutics and postcolonial, as well as other liberating, approaches to it: *textual* criticism in its various configurations, which has the potential of questioning the validity and authority of the Bible. Is that criticism representative of the way grassroots evangélicas, women of color, and oppressed people read and interact with the biblical text? In the antebellum South, slaves interpreted the Bible in ways that provided an alternative and liberating message compared to the interpretation proposed by their white slave masters; thus the "authority" of the Bible lay somewhere beyond the text. In sharing with women from my church and communities, it seems to me that the authority and centrality of the Bible are a given, not because of fundamentalist presuppositions or naïve faith, but because in some way, through its narratives, those who give it that authority have heard from it a saving word from God.

Agosto and Conde-Frazier have noted that "authority" is often ascribed to the Bible, or to a particular passage, not because of some *a priori* theoretical assumptions regarding inerrancy or infallibility, but rather because the stories that evangelic@s encounter in some way speak to their realities, subsequently empowering them to transform their lives.[34] The text rings true. Thus, Scripture, which has admittedly been used to justify atrocities, to perpetrate the theft of lands and destroy indigenous people, to enslave and dominate countless others, has also functioned as a source of subversive transformation for the powerless. In many cases, it has been the means by which people have affirmed their humanity in dehumanizing circumstances. The question then arises: how and why is the Bible, which has served as a tool of colonization and marginalization, also a "book of salvation" for evangélicas and other powerless and marginalized people?[35] Why do evangélicas believe that in its pages they encounter the living triune God, that in it *Dios está aquí/* God is present to them?[36]

My response to these questions is to engage not just the text but also the voices of grassroots evangélicas who have been so formative in the theological development of those of us who grew up in the church by "reading against the grain." To read against the grain is to critically evaluate how evangélicas interact with the Bible through prayer, *testimonios*, and *coritos* in their social location in the margins. Theirs is what I have denoted a "peripheric reading." In listening to them, I can perceive how Scripture has become a source of comfort and challenge, inspiration, and prophetic transformation.

This reading against the grain does not intend to preclude a postcolonial or, as I prefer to call it, an anticolonial analysis of a text. I believe it to be an important tool, along with Yee's ideological criticism and Guardiola-Sáenz' astute use of cultural studies to note the importance of border motifs. Yet, as Segovia has noted, each one of these methods should never be considered *the* optic, but *a* method to be used, along with others as we seek to hear the multivocal interpretations of both the text and the readers, each speaking to other. As an evangélica, I would be remiss if I ignored the importance of the discerning presence of the Holy Spirit, whose guidance speaks to us as a community as we seek to understand the text and ourselves in light of the text, our real experiences, and our contexts.

READING AGAINST THE GRAIN: LISTENING THROUGH *TESTIMONIOS* AND *CORITOS*

For evangélicas, the Bible is a foundational and authoritative source of their theological reflection, because it provides a way for them to understand and give voice to their experiences as poor, marginalized, forgotten, invisible, and powerless women. Consequently, reading against the grain in evangélica theology entails listening to how they read and incorporate Scripture. The most explicit way this is done is through *testimonios*.

Testimonios are a form of communal storytelling in which women share their experiences about their encounters with God *en lo cotidiano* (in their daily lives). They are not simply a verbal re-telling of experiences. They are how women live their faith. Testimonios reveal that for them Scripture is not simply a book to be read, but a living testament that is to be interpreted and incorporated into their daily lives. It is an incarnational, pneumatological, and praxis-centered reading. A hermeneutical cycle ensues in light of this encounter. On the one hand, evangélicas interpret their experiences in light of insights from the biblical text. On the other hand, their social location allows them to interpret the texts in light of their experiences.

Coritos are testimonios in song. They are short musical refrains, usually based on Scripture, that can either be lamentations or songs of praise. Often evangélicas turn to song when a spoken *testimonio* can no longer fully express what is in their hearts. This was borne out for me recently when I interviewed grassroots evangélicas. I asked them to share an experience that they could identify as "God *presente* (being with them)" and how they ascertained that experience as being truly the presence of the divine. In each instance, as they shared their stories of financial crisis, illness, death, and abandonment, they would reach a point in which their words failed to express the depth of their experience. It would be at that point that each of them would break into song. This tendency to sing their faith once led the Rev. Rafael Martell, the (now retired) pastor of the Iglesia Bautista Cristiana de Soundview in New York City, to describe Latin@s as "un pedazo de música andante (a portion of walking music)."

Interweaving Scripture, testimonio, coritos, and prayers—which can be concise testimonios—produce a holistic narrative that is communal in nature. While Scripture can be read in the privacy of one's home, its full interpretive value becomes evident in the degree to which evangélicas publically share their *testimonios*, sing their songs, and come to an understanding of what the biblical text and their experiences mean. These narratives underscore the notion that Scripture is polyvalent and that, therefore, a multivocal hermeneutic is required to provide space for enriched and nuanced meanings of the text. When texts are read and interpreted communally through the lens of marginality, these texts shed light on themes not normally highlighted by theologians from the center.

For example, the story of the Samaritan woman, so often interpreted as a woman of "loose morals" chastised by Jesus—though the text itself says nothing to support such conjecture—means something very different to Latinas who rely on men for their well-being, but who are often abused and abandoned by them. Migrant workers who work in stooped positions for eighteen hours a day, or women who work for indecent wages in the "needlework industry" stooped for hours sewing by hand or over machines, interpret the text about the woman "stooped" quite differently.[37] They understand what it means to be ignored until they dare to claim their rights. These women know what it is to reside in a place that does not want them, but is willing to exploit them. From such locations, many experience what it means to trust in the saving hand of Jesus who comes to liberate them and help them live their lives with their backs straightened. So they sing:

Venid a mi todo el que estáis trabajados, todo el que esté cansado /
Os haré descansar /
Toma mi yugo sobre vosotros y aprended de mi que soy manso /
y os haré descansar.[38]

The process of communal narration opens up space for the voices of many, as well as respecting the many voices in the text. This is what I refer to as a "peripheric reading against the grain."

These communal narratives demonstrate that evangélicas consider Scripture as authoritative because it is a saving word *from* God. It is considered a word from God because its stories resonate with the personal experiences of evangélicas. For example, the many stories of healing resonate with evangélicas who often have no access to adequate medical care. Conde-Frazier tells the moving story of a group of women who meet in the bathroom of their church after the regular service and how they interpreted the passage about the hemorrhagic women through the lens of the sexual assault that one of them experienced.[39]

When I read that same passage, I think of my neighbor who had a cyst drained from her breast on numerous occasions but was never given anesthesia; or the young woman who went to her first gynecological examination and was humiliated by the laughter and bawdy comments of the examining doctor and other medical personnel because she was an eighteen-year-old virgin. The description by Mark that the hemorrhagic woman had suffered much at the hands of physicians is a familiar refrain for evangélicas, for they too have been abused by a health system that too often has been racist and culturally insensitive.[40]

Stories about loss of life, dislocation, healing, feeding, overcoming storms, and raising the dead are not metaphors or legends for women whose sons are shot while sitting on their stoops, who have lost their jobs and face eviction, or who have risked their lives crossing the border. Rather, scriptural *testimonios* are about real events that witness to the God who continues to act in their present lives and within their communities through the power of the Holy Spirit. Thus, they sing:

Oye o Dios mi clamor /
A mi oración atiende /
Desde el cabo de la tierra clamaré a ti cuando mi corazón desmaye /
Llévame a la roca que es más alta que yo /
Porque tú has sido mi refugio, Señor/ Porque tú has sido mi refugio.[41]

As they share their communal narratives, the Spirit moves in their midst and beyond. The Spirit brings these Scriptural testimonies to life and gives them wisdom and understanding as they read. It is through the power of the Spirit that they experience liberation and transformation. They also receive *una palabra que redarguye* (a word of conviction that challenges) the sinful structures that not only surround them but also that they have internalized in wounding ways. The Spirit provides insights that allow the women to read the texts in subversive and prophetic ways that counter-hegemonic narratives. Through the Spirit, this convicting word becomes a well of living water.[42]

Thus, these communal narratives open up dialogical spaces where evangélicas, particularly the poor and marginalized, encounter God. On the one hand, God speaks to them through Scripture. On the other hand, they interrogate the text, bringing to it the questions and concerns that arise from their social location. The insights gleaned from this dialogical process— incorporating context and experience, clarifying meanings, and creating new interpretive horizons— are passed on as *testimonio* that teaches to the community of faith, to those outside of the immediate community, and to new generations of believers/ readers. Thus, as the saying puts it, *La palabra confirma lo que el testimonio de la comunidad afirma* (the Word that is vivified through the Spirit confirms that which the community of faith's experience has affirmed). The communal narratives are testimonios that God's promises are true and can be trusted.[43]

I do not believe that it is a coincidence that many of the stories about the poor, marginalized, or oppressed in the Bible are about nameless people. It is easy for those in power to impose their images and values onto the nameless and powerless. These are "stereotypes"—the essentializing of traits to define a group, using value-laden adjectives.[44] Thus, for instance, the Johannine story of the Samaritan woman, rather than being about the exploitation of a nameless woman, often becomes the cautionary tale of a woman who has prostituted herself, as so many contemporary scholars describe her. I coined the phrase "normatizing myths" to refer to these stereotypes and to underscore how those from the centers of power and privilege articulate often-coded public discourses about those conceived as "other."[45] Latinas know these myths well. Latinas are often referred to as "illegals," "wetbacks," "welfare octomoms," who "rob decent deserving folk" of needed resources. Their bodies are eroticized, and their minds infantilized. Their very presence is considered an affront to those at the centers of discourse. These myths are a form of institutionalized violence that dehumanizes and disempowers Latinas.

Their experience is similar to the woman who enters Simon's house and weeps at Jesus' feet (Luke 7:36-50). Most biblical exegetes, including white feminists, assume that the nameless woman is a sinner and a prostitute, although there is nothing in the text to indicate that she is a prostitute. In fact, Judith K. Applegate specifically notes that the text does not mention the word "prostitute." However, she then proceeds to list the reasons why the pericope implies that the woman is one.[46] Reading the text against the grain—from the perspective of the marginalized, the poor, the voiceless; of women treated as *sobrajas*, discounted, and invisible—provides a hermeneutic of suspicion against such an interpretation. Nothing in this "feminist analysis" seems to support Applegate's claims, nor similar pejorative views expounded by other scholars, about the woman in the story.

Further analysis reveals that the Greek syntax of the text simply implies that the woman is *known in the city* as a sinner.[47] Latinas, who have so often been maligned and stereotyped as *satas*, resonate with the story of this woman. We too find ourselves entering places where we are not wanted nor welcomed, weeping bitter tears. We too have been subject to the ridicule of those who thought themselves better than us, those who wondered how God could abide the presence of such *sobrajas*. That Jesus ultimately upholds the dignity of the woman and compares her worth to the unworthy behavior of Simon is a subversive reversal in a story about those who think they know better or think they are better because of their class and gender. That she is lifted up and granted shalom is a transformative word of salvation and hope for the *satas* of the world.

Thus, the communal narratives of Scripture, testimonio, and coritos bring to light the falsehood of normatizing myths and assert the humanity of the dehumanized. When evangélicas sing:

Dios está aquí /
tan cierto como el aire que respiro /
tan cierto como en la mañana se levanta el sol /
tan cierto que cuando le hablo /
Dios me puede oír.[48]

they remember that they are not *sobrajas*, not drains on a system. They affirm that God is present because they are fully human, fully *hijas de Dios* (daughters of the living God), and beloved members of *la familia de Dios* (God's family). Death, violence, hunger, marginalization, and loss do not have the final word in their lives. When they participate in these communal narrations, they remember and affirm that God is the God of life who faced the worst in the human condition and responded with a resounding "No" in the resurrection of Jesus. *Dios está aquí* (God is here), just as God has been with the marginalized, forgotten, and oppressed throughout time. This is the God evangélicas claim, not the God of oppressors, colonizers, conquerors, or patriarchy. They sing to this God of life who is present in the spaces that they inhabit.[49]

CONCLUDING COMMENTS

Douglas John Hall has defined theology as an encounter of stories: ours with God's.[50] If this is so, then I believe that a valid way to engage Scripture as an evangélica constructive theologian is to read it against the grain through communal narratives. If the principle of epistemological priority of the poor espoused by theologians of liberation is correct, then an effective way to "read against the grain" is to listen to the voices of the absent and silenced, the voices of the suffering poor. In the evangélica churches, this means listening to the collective wisdom of women who provide us with a theological foundation through their communal narratives of Scripture, *testimonies*, and *coritos*.

This does not mean that one is to ignore or eschew the critically important work of biblical and theological scholars. Rather, if one is to take seriously an anticolonial reading of Scripture—which biblical scholars of color have, I believe, rightly proposed—then one needs to hear the voices of the colonized and make note of how they have used Scripture to resist the very forces that would colonize them, as well as critically assess how Scripture has been complicit in the colonizing process. Such a reading must widen its scope and listen to voices heretofore not included, voices that come from beyond the circles of the academy, and must be attentive to the polyvalent nuances and multiple colonized realities.

These variations can be lost when grouped in almost homogenous ways under a generalized rubric of "postcolonial." Among other things, such a rubric hides the continuing theft and genocide of native peoples in internal colonizations, the ongoing colonial realities imposed by nations in the East as well as in the West, and the oppression of poor women of color throughout the global two-thirds worlds. Postcolonial analyses that are not careful about these nuanced differences inadvertently can become complicit with hermeneutic readings that legitimize the oppression, marginalization, and genocide of communities, as well as the continued despoliation of our environment.

In proposing a reading against the grain from an evangélica perspective, that is pneumatological and communal, it is not my intention to set aside the wonderful work of my colleagues in biblical studies and theological hermeneutics. Rather, I propose an additional tool, one that ensures at the very least the incorporation of the larger nonacademic community, and in particular, the voices of grassroots evangélicas. Reading against the grain is not a naïve reading, nor a romanticized understanding of grassroots popular faith. It is, rather, a humble listening to the Spirit blow and a seeking to discern even though at present we can only see "through a mirror darkly" (1 Cor. 13:12). It is a reading that is not satisfied simply with being affirmed. It is one that seeks above all to be transformed in holistic ways. It acknowledges that, as much as we seek to do justice, we will always come "short of the glory of God" (Rom 3:23). Therefore, we seek from the Spirit, and from the Spirit's speaking through the tongues of others, new insights and new perspectives that *redarguyen* (challenge) us out of our comfort zones.

I have often heard or read about how certain "texts of terror" or narratives about "anonymous" characters are minority perspectives. It often sounds like such narratives accidentally slipped through the fingers of the dominant gatekeepers. I do not believe this to be the case. To read against the grain is to believe that each and every narrative in the biblical text has a purpose and a message. The "minority voices"—those of women betrayed and of people destroyed—are the constant witnesses to us that the "least of these" must never be overlooked, that the weakest of voices must never be silenced.

Such voices stand as witnesses to human injustice and greed, no matter how much we want to mythologize Scripture into a grand history of faith and generosity of spirit. It is the constant narrative of people surviving, and even overcoming, those who would rob them of lands, life, and hope, and doing so by whatever means possible, including religious ones. Those narratives are the pointers that tell us that we are to look even deeper for the nonstories, the counter-narratives, and the silent and invisible ones. For each tale of injustice and violence, there are hundreds of nameless ones whom we can only perceive "illegibly," if only we run our hands "against the grain" over the text.[51]

If we learn to read Scripture in this way, it becomes a way of life. We learn to hear the non-voices around us—the stories never passed down of slaves, of native peoples destroyed, of comfort women abused and thrown aside as refuse, of slaves trafficked who have become the engine of nations' economic booms, and countless others. We learn to read against the grain and so acknowledge our complicity in the world's injustice. We learn not to take comfort in a false Christianity of unholy sanctity that allows us to pretend to be religious, while we grow deaf to the cries of the suffering and exploited around us. In Spanish we have a saying: *No hay peor ciego que el que no quiera ver* ("None is more blind than the one who refuses to see"). To read against the grain is to see with more than our eyes and to refuse to be blind. It is the willingness to run our hands against the texture of life itself and to hear the blowing of the Spirit with our hearts. It is to confess our complicity and ask the Spirit to transform us, to transform the world around us, and make us agents of change and justice for the Reign of God. It is, I think, to place our hope in a true "post"-coloniality.

NOTES

1. I am using the -@ ending in "evangélic@s" to note gender-inclusive language. Thus, evangélic@ is equivalent to evangélica/o.

2. See Virgilio Elizondo, *Galilean Journey: The Mexican American Promise* (Maryknoll, NY: Orbis Books, 2000), 5–7.

3. On such explorations, see Efraín Agosto, "Reading the Word in America: US Latino/a Religious Communities and Their Scriptures," in *MisReading America: Scriptures and Difference*, ed. Vincent L. Wimbush with the assistance of Lalruatkima and Melissa Renee Reid (Oxford: Oxford University Press, 2013), 117–164. This piece brings together a presentation on "Seeking Guidance from the Word: U.S. Latino/a Religious Communities and Their Scriptures," given by Efraín Agosto, Brian Clark, Elizabeth Conde-Frazier, and Jacqueline Hidalgo, at the Reading Scriptures, Reading America Conference, sponsored by the Institute for Signifying the Scriptures and its Scriptural Ethnologies Project, Claremont Graduate University (October 16, 2009).

4. It should be noted that many dedicated missionaries today, conscious of this tainted history, have attempted to be supportive of the liberation efforts, as well as cultural and national distinctiveness of host countries. Others, however, continue a policy of paternalism, equating the "gospel" with "Americanization."

5. For a fuller discussion on sat@s, see Loida I. Martell-Otero, "Of Satos and Saints: Salvation from the Periphery," *Perspectivas* 4 (Summer 2001): 8–9. For information on the forced sterilization of Puerto Rican women, see Helen Rodríguez Trias' pioneering work, which exposed this practice, *Women and the Health Care System Sterilization Abuse* (New York: Barnard College, 1978) and *Eliminating Health Disparities: Conversations with Latinos* (Santa Cruz, CA: ETR Associates, 2003). See also Annette B. Ramírez de Arrellano and Conrad Seipp, *Colonialism, Catholicism, and Contraception: A History of Birth Control in Puerto Rico* (Chapel Hill: The University of North Carolina Press, 1983).

6. For a fuller discussion of "lo cotidiano," see Daniel H. Levine, *Popular Voices in Latin American Catholicism* (Princeton: Princeton University Press,

1992); Ada María Isasi-Díaz, *Mujerista Theology: A Theology for the Twentieth-Century* (Maryknoll, NY: Orbis Books, 1996); and María Pilar Aquino, "Theological Method in U.S. Latino/a Theology: Toward an Intercultural Theology for the Third Millennium," in *From the Heart of Our People: Latino/a Explorations in Catholic Systematic Theology*, ed. Orlando O. Espín and Miguel H. Díaz (Maryknoll, NY: Orbis Books, 1999), 38.

7. Elizabeth Conde-Frazier, "Latina Women and Immigration," *Journal of Latin American Theology* 3 (2008): 60, 62. See Loida I. Martell-Otero, "Encuentro con el Jesús Sato: An Evangélica Soter-ology," in *Jesus in the Hispanic Community: Images of Christ from Theology to Popular Religion*, ed. Harold J. Recinos and Hugo Magallanes (Louisville, KY: Westminster John Knox, 2009), 77–78.

8. Elizabeth Conde-Frazier, "Evangélicas Reading Scriptures: Readings from Within and Beyond the Tradition," in *Latina Evangélicas: A Theological Survey from the Margins*, ed. Loida I. Martell-Otero, Zaida Maldonado Pérez, and Elizabeth Conde-Frazier (Eugene, OR: Cascade Books, 2013), 71. See also Leticia Guardiola-Sáenz, "Border-crossing and Its Redemptive Power in John 7:53–8:11: A Cultural Reading of Jesus and the Accused," in *Transformative Encounters: Jesus and Women Re-viewed*, ed. Ingrid Rosa Kitzenberger (Leiden: Brill, 2000), 271.

9. See Kwok Pui-Lan, *Postcolonial Imagination and Feminist Theology* (Louisville, KY: Westminster John Knox, 2005), 7; and José David Rodríguez, "Hispanic Theology's Foundational Challenges," in *Hidden Stories: Unveiling the History of the Latino Church*, ed. Daniel R. Rodríguez-Díaz and David Cortés-Fuentes (Decatur, GA: AETH, 1994), 127–128. Cf., Douglas John Hall, *Thinking the Faith: Christian Theology in a North American Context* (Minneapolis: Fortress Press, 1989), 258.

10. Nyasha Junior, "Womanist Biblical Interpretation," in *Engaging the Bible in a Gendered World: An Introduction to Feminist Biblical Interpretation in Honor of Katherine Doob Sakenfeld*, ed. Linda Day and Carolyn Pressler (Louisville, KY: Westminster John Knox, 2006), 40–41. I have tried to honor the scholarship of Latina Protestant biblical scholars in this essay such as Leticia Guardiola-Sáenz and others. While Efraín Agosto is male, I believe he needs to be cited, because he has contributed important insights to Pauline scholarship as well as critical work regarding the use of the Bible in the evangélic@ community.

11. Orlando E. Costas, "Hispanic Theology in North America," in *Struggles for Solidarity: Liberation Theologies in Tension*, ed. Lorine M. Getz and Ruy Costa (Minneapolis: Fortress Press, 1992), 72.

12. Justo L. González, *Mañana: Christian Theology from a Hispanic Perspective* (Nashville: Abingdon, 1990), 75–80, 84–85.

13. Justo L. González, *Santa Biblia: The Bible Through Hispanic Eyes* (Nashville: Abingdon Press, 1996).

14. It would seem that while Orlando Costas anticipated this movement, due to his premature demise in 1987, he never had the opportunity to explore his intriguing comment about reading the Bible "Hispanically."

15. Fernando F. Segovia, *Decolonizing Biblical Studies: A View from the Margins* (Maryknoll, NY: Orbis Books, 2000), 123, 125.

16. Kwok, *Postcolonial Imagination*, 2–3, 64. For a greater discussion on postcolonial studies in general, as well as criticism for the use of its terminology, see Fawzia Afzal-Khan and Kalpasa Seshadri-Crooks, eds., *The Pre-Occupation of Postcolonial Studies* (Durham, NC: Duke University Press, 2000).

17. Kwok, *Postcolonial Imagination*, 2–3, 64.

18. Guardiola-Sáenz, "Border-crossing," 270.

19. Segovia, *Decolonizing*, 125.

20. Gale A. Yee, *Poor Banished Children of Eve: Women as Evil in the Hebrew Bible* (Minneapolis: Fortress Press, 2003), 9.

21. Yee, *Poor Banished Children of Eve*, 27.

22. Yee, *Poor Banished Children of Eve*, 22.

23. Kwok, *Postcolonial Imagination*, 9.

24. Kwok, *Postcolonial Imagination*, *passim*.

25. Ella Shohat, "Notes on the 'Post-Colonial'," in *The Pre-Occupation of Postcolonial Studies* (Durham, NC: Duke University Press, 2000), 131.

26. Shohat, "Notes on the Post-Colonial," 129, 132. For more on this important topic, see Jace Weaver, ed., *Native American Religious Identity: Unforgotten Gods* (Maryknoll, NY: Orbis Books, 1998), particularly the essays by Jace Weaver, "From I-Hermeneutics to We-Hermeneutics: Native Americans and the Post-Colonial," 1–25, and Steven Charleston, "From Medicine Man to Marx," 155–172. See also Robert Warrior, "Canaanites, Cowboys, and Indians," *Union Seminary Quarterly Review* 59, no. 1–2 (2005): 1–8, and Andrea Smith's response, "Decolonizing Theology," *Union Seminary Quarterly Review* 59, no. 1–2 (2005): 63–78.

27. Weaver, "From I-Hermeneutics to We-Hermeneutics," 13. Shohat concurs. See "Notes on the Post-Colonial," 132.

28. Shohat, "Notes on the Post-Colonial," 134.

29. Weaver, "We-Hermeneutics," 14. Shohat, 135.

30. Audre Lorde, "The Master's Tools Will Never Dismantle the Master's House," in *Sister Outsider: Essays and Speeches*, 2nd ed. (Berkeley: Crossing Press, 2007), 112.

31. Kwok, *Postcolonial Imagination*, 84, citing Musa Dube's experience with African women. Andrea Smith, "Walking in Balance," in *Native American Religious Identity: Unforgotten Gods*, ed. Jace Weaver (Maryknoll, NY: Orbis Books, 1998), 179.

32. Yee, *Poor Banished Children*, 16–17.

33. Leticia Guardiola-Sáenz, "Reading from Ourselves: Identity and Hermeneutics among Mexican-American Feminists," in *A Reader in Latina Feminist Theology: Religion and Justice*, ed. María Pilar Aquino, Daisy L. Machado, and Jeanette Rodríguez (Austin: University of Texas Press, 2002), 94.

34. Agosto et al., "Seeking Guidance," 52. Conde-Frazier, "Evangélicas Reading Scriptures," *passim*.

35. Justo L. González, "Historia de la interpretación bíblica," in *Lumbreras a Nuestro Camino*, ed. Pablo Jiménez (Miami, FL: Caribe, 1994), 114.

36. For the importance of the notion of *presencia* in evangélica theology, see Loida I. Martell-Otero, "My GPS Does Not Work in Puerto Rico: An Evangélica

Spirituality," *American Baptist Quarterly* 30, no. 3–4 (Fall-Winter 2011): 4–6. Also, Loida I. Martell-Otero, "From Satas to Santas: Sobrajas No More—Salvation in the Spaces of the Everyday," in *Latina Evangélicas*, 39–40.

37. Félix Muñoz-Mas, "Gender, Work, and Institutional Change in the Early Stage of Industrialization: The Case of Women's Bureau and the Home Needlework Industry in Puerto Rico, 1940–1952," in *Puerto Rican Women's History: New Perspectives*, ed. Félix V. Matos-Rodríguez and Linda C. Delgado (Armonk, NY: M.E. Sharpe, 1998), 181–205. On a personal note, I remember the years my mother worked sewing a completed and stuffed animals for 10 cents in order to help our family make ends meet. Contra Muñoz-Mas' indications, nothing seemed to be regulated in this industry. She worked long hours for a pittance, and often brought in her younger sister to help meet her quota. My father, in the meantime, often held two jobs to support his family during that same period. Women are not the only ones "stooped over."

38. Based on Matthew 11: 28–30 (the Spanish Reina Valera version): "Come to me all of you who are overworked and are weary / I will give you rest / Take my yoke upon you and learn from me; for I am gentle / and I will give you rest."

39. Conde-Frazier, "Latina Women and Immigration," 68–74.

40. See Council of Scientific Affairs, "Hispanic Health in the United States," *Journal of American Medical Association* 265, no. 2 (January 9, 1991): 248–252. See also: Marsha D. Lillie-Blanton and Charisse Lillie, "Re-examining Federal and State Roles in Assuring Equitable Access to Health Care," in *Achieving Equitable Access: Studies of Health Care Issues Affecting Hispanics and African Americans*, ed. Marsha D. Lillie-Blanton, Wilhelmina A. Leigh, and Ana I. Alfaro-Correa (Washington, DC: Joint Center for Political and Economic Studies, 1996), 163–200; José I. Lavastide, *Health Care and the Common Good: A Catholic Theory of Justice* (Lanham: University Press of America, 2000), 58–60, 71–76; Monica E. Peek et al., "Racism in Health Care: Its Relationship to Shared Decision-making and Health Disparities: A Response to Bradby," *Social Science and Medicine* 71, no. 1 (July 2010): 13–17.

41. From Psalm 61:1-3 (VRV): "Hear my cry, O God; listen to my prayer. From the ends of the earth I will call on you, when my heart is faint. Lead me to the rock that is higher than I/ For you are my refuge [O Lord/ for you are my refuge]." (English translation partly based on NRSV).

42. Agosto et al., "Seeking Guidance," 53.

43. Agosto et al., "Seeking Guidance," 54.

44. Yee, *Poor Banished Children*, 16.

45. Daisy L. Machado, "Voices from *Nepantla*: Latinas in U.S. Religious History," in *Feminist Intercultural Theology: Latina Explorations for a Just World*, ed. María Pilar Aquino and María José Rosado-Nunes (Maryknoll, NY: Orbis Books, 2007), 93, calls such myths "historical imagination." They are "how those in the dominant group of a nation who have power to tell its history perceive the other."

46. Judith B. Applegate, "'And She Wet His Feet With His Tears': A Feminist Interpretation of Luke 7:36-50," in *Escaping Eden: New Feminist Perspectives on the Bible*, ed. Susan Lochrie Graham and Pamela Thimmes (Washington Square, NY: New York University Press, 1999), 78.

47. John J. Kilgallen, "Forgiveness of Sins (Luke 7: 36-50)," *Novum Testamentum* 40, no. 2 (April 1998): 106.
48. "God is here, as certain as the air that I breathe, as certain as the sun rises each morning, so certain that when I speak God can hear me." (My translation).
49. Martell-Otero, "My GPS," 4–9.
50. Hall, *Thinking the Faith*, 89.
51. Umberto Eco, *The Name of the Rose*, trans. William Weaver (San Diego: Harcourt, Inc., 1980), 11.

BIBLIOGRAPHY

Afzal-Khan, Fawzia, and Kalpasa Seshadri-Crooks, eds. *The Pre-Occupation of Postcolonial Studies*. Durham: Duke University Press, 2000.

Agosto, Efraín. "Reading the Word in America." In *MisReading America: Scriptures and Difference*, edited by Vincent L. Wimbush, 117–64. Oxford: Oxford University Press, 2013.

Applegate, Judith B. "'And She Wet His Feet with His Tears': A Feminist Interpretation of Luke 7:36-50." In *Escaping Eden: New Feminist Perspectives on the Bible*, edited by Susan Lochrie Graham and Pamela Thimmes, 69–80. New York: New York University Press, 1999.

Aquino, María Pilar. "Theological Method in U.S. Latino/a Theology: Toward an Intercultural Theology for the Third Millennium." In *From the Heart of Our People: Latino/a Explorations in Catholic Systematic Theology*, edited by Orlando O. Espín and Miguel H. Díaz, 6–48. Maryknoll, NY: Orbis Books, 1999.

Charleston, Steven. "From Medicine Man to Marx." In *Native American Religious Identity: Unforgotten Gods*, edited by Jace Weaver, 155–172. Maryknoll, NY: Orbis Books, 1998.

Conde-Frazier, Elizabeth. "Evangélicas Reading Scriptures: Readings from Within and Beyond the Tradition." In *Latina Evangélicas: A Theological Survey from the Margins*, edited by Loida I. Martell-Otero, Zaida Maldonado Pérez, and Elizabeth Conde-Frazier, 73–89. Eugene, OR: Cascade Books, 2013.

———. "Latina Women and Immigration." *Journal of Latin American Theology* 3, no. 2 (2008): 54–75.

Costas, Orlando E. "Hispanic Theology in North America." In *Struggles for Solidarity: Liberation Theologies in Tension*, edited by Lorine M. Getz and Ruy Costa, 63–74. Minneapolis: Fortress Press, 1992.

Council of Scientific Affairs. "Hispanic Health in the United States." *Journal of American Medical Association* 265, no. 2 (January 9, 1991): 248–252.

Eco, Umberto. *The Name of the Rose*. Translated by William Weaver. San Diego: Harcourt, Inc., 1994.

Elizondo, Virgilio. *Galilean Journey: The Mexican American Promise*. Maryknoll, NY: Orbis Books, 2000.

González, Justo. "Historia de la interpretación bíblica." In *Lumbreras a Nuestro Camino*, edited by Pablo Jímenez, 79–118. Miami, FL: Caribe, 1994.

———. *Mañana: Christian Theology from a Hispanic Perspective*. Nashville: Abingdon Press, 1990.

———. *Santa Biblia: The Bible through Hispanic Eyes*. Nashville: Abingdon Press, 1996.

Guardiola-Sáenz, Leticia. "Border-crossing and Its Redemptive Power in John 7: 53–8:11: A Cultural Reading of Jesus and the Accused." In *Transformative Encounters: Jesus and Women Re-viewed*, edited by Ingrid Rosa Kitzenberger, 267–291. Leiden: Brill, 2000.

———. "Minorities in the Midst of Affluence." In *The Many Voices of the Bible*, edited by Sean Freyne and Ellen Van Wolde, 86–92. Concilium 1. London: SCM Press, 2002.

———. "Reading from Ourselves: Identity and Hermeneutics Among Mexican-American Feminists." In *A Reader in Latina Feminist Theology: Religion and Justice*, edited by María Pilar Aquino, Daisy L. Machado, and Jeanette Rodríguez, 80–97. Austin: University of Texas, 2002.

Hall, Douglas John. *Thinking the Faith: Christian Theology in a North American Context*. Minneapolis: Fortress Press, 1989.

Isasi-Díaz, Ada María. *Mujerista Theology: A Theology for the Twentieth-Century*. Maryknoll, NY: Orbis Books, 1996.

Junior, Nyasha. "Womanist Biblical Interpretation." In *Engaging the Bible in a Gendered World: An Introduction to Feminist Biblical Interpretation in Honor of Katherine Doob Sakenfeld*, edited by Linda Day and Carolyn Pressler, 37–46. Louisville: Westminster John Knox Press, 2006.

Kilgallen, John J. "Forgiveness of Sins (Luke 7: 36-50)." *Novum Testamentum* 40, no. 2 (April 1998): 105–116.

Kwok, Pui-Lan. *Postcolonial Imagination and Feminist Theology*. Louisville: Westminster John Knox Press, 2005.

Lavastide, José I. *Health Care and the Common Good: A Catholic Theory of Justice*. Lanham: University Press of America, 2000.

Levine, Daniel H. *Popular Voices in Latin American Catholicism*. Princeton: Princeton University Press, 1992.

Lillie-Blanton, Marsha D., and Charisse Lillie. "Re-examining Federal and State Roles in Assuring Equitable Access to Health Care." In *Achieving Equitable Access: Studies of Health Care Issues Affecting Hispanics and African Americans*, edited by Marsha D. Lillie-Blanton, Wilhelmina A. Leigh, and Ana I. Alfaro-Correa, 163–200. Washington, DC: Joint Center for Political and Economic Studies, 1996.

Lorde, Audre. "The Master's Tools Will Never Dismantle the Master's House." In *Sister Outsider: Essays and Speeches*, 2nd ed. Berkeley: Crossing Press, 2007.

Machado, Daisy L. "Voices from *Nepantla*: Latinas in U.S. Religious History." In *Feminist Intercultural Theology: Latina Explorations for a Just World*, edited by María Pilar Aquino and María José Rosado-Nunes, 89–108. Maryknoll, NY: Orbis Books, 2007.

Martell-Otero, Loida I. "Encuentro con el Jesús Sato: An Evangélica Soter-ology." In *Jesus in the Hispanic Community: Images of Christ from Theology to Popular*

Religion, edited by Harold J. Recinos and Hugo Magallanes, 74–91. Louisville, KY: Westminster John Knox Press, 2009.

———. "From *Satas* to *Santas:Sobrajas* No More—Salvation in the Spaces of the Everyday." In *Latina Evangélicas: A Theological Survey from the Margins*, by Loida I. Martell-Otero, Zaida Maldonado Pérez, and Elizabeth Conde-Frazier, 33–51. Eugene, OR: Cascade Books, 2013.

———. "My GPS Does Not Work in Puerto Rico: An *Evangélica* Spirituality." *American Baptist Quarterly* 30, no. 3–4 (Fall-Winter 2011): 256–275.

———. "Of Satos and Saints: Salvation from the Periphery." *Perspectivas* 4 (Summer 2001): 7–38.

Muñoz-Mas, Félix. "Gender, Work, and Institutional Change in the Early Stage of Industrialization: The Case of Women's Bureau and the Home Needlework Industry in Puerto Rico, 1940–1952." In *Puerto Rican Women's History: New Perspectives*, edited by Félix V. Matos-Rodríguez and Linda C. Delgado, 181–205. Armonk, NY: M.E. Sharpe, 1998.

Peek, Monica E., et al. "Racism in Health Care: Its Relationship to Shared Decision-making and Health Disparities: A Response to Bradby." *Social Science and Medicine* 71, no. 1 (July 2010): 13–17.

Ramírez de Arrellano, Annette B., and Conrad Seipp. *Colonialism, Catholicism, and Contraception: A History of Birth Control in Puerto Rico*. Chapel Hill: The University of North Carolina Press, 1983.

Rodríguez, José David. "Hispanic Theology's Foundational Challenges." In *Hidden Stories: Unveiling the History of the Latino Church*, edited by Daniel R. Rodríguez-Díaz and David Cortés-Fuentes, 125–129. Decatur, GA: AETH, 1994.

Rodríguez Trias, Helen. *Eliminating Health Disparities: Conversations with Latinos*. Santa Cruz, CA: ETR Associates, 2003.

———. *Women and the Health Care System Sterilization Abuse*. NY: Barnard College, 1978.

Segovia, Fernando F. *Decolonizing Biblical Studies: A View from the Margins*. Maryknoll, NY: Orbis Books, 2000.

Shohat, Ella. "Notes on the 'Post-Colonial.'" In *Pre-Occupation of Postcolonial Studies*, edited by Afzal-Khan Fawzia and Kalpasa Seshadri-Crooks, 126–139. Durham: Duke University Press, 2000.

Smith, Andrea. "Decolonizing Theology." *Union Seminary Quarterly Review* 59, no. 1–2 (2005): 63–78.

———. "Walking in Balance." In *Native American Religious Identity: Unforgotten Gods*, edited by Jace Weaver, 178–198. NY: Orbis Books, 1998.

Warrior, Robert. "Canaanites, Cowboys, and Indians." *Union Seminary Quarterly Review* 59, no. 1–2 (2005): 1–8.

Weaver, Jace. "From I-Hermeneutics to We-Hermeneutics: Native Americans and the Post-Colonial." In *Native American Religious Identity: Unforgotten Gods*, edited by Jace Weaver, 1–25. Maryknoll, NY: Orbis Books, 1998.

Yee, Gale A. *Poor Banished Children of Eve: Women as Evil in the Hebrew Bible*. MN: Fortress Press, 2003.

Chapter 7

Darkening the Image
Another *Allegory of the Beauty of the Shulamite*[1]

Elaine Padilla

I am dark and beautiful,
O daughters of Jerusalem,
As the tents of Kedar,
as the curtains of Solomon.

—Song of Songs 1:5, my translation

Darkness, "the other" of light, is often construed as the negation of beauty and good; as such, it is associated with immorality and evil. The "dark side" corrupts social mores and virtues, for darkness is a symbol of sin versus purity. In politics, this antitype translates into the dark-skinned body that can easily become the scapegoat needed for cleansing society from corruption. In the case of a foreigner or stranger of dark skin, her divergence from common constructs of racial and ethnic categories can further impact these misidentifications. To counterargue this ideology on the basis of Christian teaching would be to believe and act in ways that affirm the value of being made in the image of God.

However, this theological statement when thinking of gender, race, and ethnicity can pose some problems. For instance, when having skewed constructions of identities, such as dark skin as inferior to light skin, what God-talk on the doctrine of the *imago Dei* can serve to challenge this Manichean metaphysics of light versus darkness? For this, as Latina theologian Michelle A. González has argued, being according to the divine image can no longer remain monolithic, symbolically equated to the white color and the male gender.[2] Furthermore, since the God of Christianity has been colonized, there is a need for *darkening* the divine image, in order to reconsider thereby the symbolic language on souls and their redemption. Fortunately, one would not need to depart much from the Christian theological tradition in order to rescue the "dark side" of God.

Such darkened radiance of the *imago Dei*, in this essay, shines forth through the depths of an*other's* allegory: that of the Shulamite's imaging of God according to her dark skin. This sensitive task of thinking theologically about the racial process of *darkening* affirms the Shulamite's multiple ethnicities attributed to her. In doing so, the essay challenges the synthetizing and polarizing tendencies of "whitening" processes embedded in Christian aesthetics. The chapter aims at punctuating the dynamic process that stems from multiple origins that pluralize selves with its potential for disrupting the one dominant image. In that vein, the chapter seeks to resist the temptation to favor one ethnic and racial category over others, to construct yet another category, or to affirm a romanticism of racial integration.

The Shulamite and teachings on the *imago Dei* darken via early Christian commentaries based on allegorical interpretations of the Shulamite of the Song of Songs and read with present U.S. *latinidades* in view.[3] Prompting the reader to raise questions with which to discover parallel *othering* circumstances primarily between the Shulamite and Latinas/os, this chapter seeks to unearth artifacts with ethnic undertones buried in Christianity since the patristic era. The aim is to use contextual hermeneutical lenses with which to create a kaleidoscopic reflection on the concept of darkness that can rescue Christian theology from its historical contempt toward women's dark bodies.[4]

DARK S(K)INS

Sin is black as virtue is white. All those white men, fingering their guns can't be wrong. I am guilty. I don't know what of, but I know I'm a wretch.

—Franz Fanon, *Black Skin, White Masks*[5]

Race is fundamental to theology, for, as Michelle González argues, one cannot ignore the role it already plays in our understandings of the self and God.[6] Since social dynamics and tensions occur at the communal level, the many ethnic backgrounds that compose them need to be explored in tandem with what she describes as "a worldview that holds the material and the spiritual worlds as organically interconnected."[7] Racial processes equally impact both dimensions. A narrative that is fruitful for this kind of theological study on ethnicity and gender is the book of *Song of Songs*, and, in particular, the figure of the dark-skinned and anonymous female lover known as *hashulammit* or the Shulamite (Songs 6:13). Especially, since the color of her skin resembles "the curtains of Solomon" and, most poignantly as well, "the tents of Kedar" (Songs 1:5).

She whose name is related to the root of the name Solomon (*slm*) and to the name or epithet of the goddess Ishtar might also be a woman from *Shunem*.[8] Historically, she has held the protagonist role of the female counterpart and beloved of King Solomon, and hence has been given the title of wife, "the Solomoness." Yet, in deriving from the female name of *Shelem*, as in the goddess *Shala* or *Shulmanitu* or *Ishtar*, her provenance and thus her ethnicity become equally significant components of her identity. Admittedly, presuming *Shunem* as an identifier of her ethnic background is no easy task. The evidence of *Shulem* as a possible variant of *Shunem* as well as details on the historical background of this place of origin are scanty. From the point of view of intertextuality, one explanation for this territory can be in terms of the land apportioned to the tribe of Issachar at the time of the Hebrew conquest (Joshua 19:18). This would be the origins also of both Abishag, the beautiful young girl who waited and cared for David in his old age (1 Kings 1:1-4, 15) and the Shunamite woman of means who offered lodging to the prophet Elisha and his servant Gehazi and whose son Elisha brought back from the dead (2 Kings 4:8-37, 8:1-6).

One conclusion can be that the name *hashulammit* symbolizes a type of ethnicity for which her pigmentation becomes polemical. On the one hand, the Shulamite is described as a beautiful black woman in the text. On the other, commentators attenuate the issue of her skin color, which can indicate what Marvin H. Pope considers to be an inherent struggle with her ethnicity.[9] One finds: the Greek adjective employed in the Septuagint is *melaina*, which can be rendered as *nigra* (black) or *fusca* (dark) in the Latin, and the conjunction *kai*, which can mean several things—among them: "and," "even," "also," "namely," "but," and "indeed"—in relationship with *kalei* or the female adjective of beautiful. While the statement could have meant "Black am I and beautiful," many early commentators, as some Bible versions still do, combined the two terms "dark" and "but," which mitigated the meaning and posited an adversative relation between blackness and beauty: "I am dark *but* beautiful."[10]

According to Origen, her skin color, which refers also to her ancestry, is the reason why she pleads before the maidens for her *kalos* to be acknowledged, for her people, the great people of Kedar, to be viewed as beautiful. He describes her as offering an apology, as if saying:

> "I am indeed dark—or black—as far as my complexion goes, O daughters of Jerusalem; but, should a person scrutinize the features of my inward parts, then I am beautiful. For the tents of Cedar, which is a great nation," she says, "also are black, and their very name of Cedar means blackness or darkness. The curtains of Solomon likewise are black; but that blackness of his curtains is not considered unbecoming for so great a king in all his glory. Do not reproach me

for my colour, then, O daughters of Jerusalem, seeing that my body neither lacks natural beauty, nor that which is acquired by practice."[11]

That her kinfolk from the area of *Shunem* were identifiably black, and generally would have earned the reproach of others, cannot be verified from the text itself. Yet, that she seems to be serving as a disruptive trope of the darkening-other can be further deduced from the tension that the text produces when she compares herself simultaneously with "the tents of Kedar" and the "curtains of Solomon."

Upon describing her skin color as black and then comparing her beauty to the "tents of Kedar," she most likely was making an assertion of assumed *otherness*. Furthermore, by pairing her Ishmaelite lineage with that of the favored patriarch Isaac that the curtains of Solomon represented (Gen. 16, 17 and 21), she was possibly making a statement to identify herself with the dominant lineage. This aesthetic expression of ambiguous attitudes and self-identification toward the dark-others can also be evident in early commentaries. Origen almost apologetically argues that Kedar is "a great nation," descendants of Ishmael (Gen. 25:13), which people were also blessed.[12] Gregory the Great, perhaps well familiar with the commentary work of Origen, yet seeking to vindicate her marginal ancestry, corrects his views by saying: "And the tents of Kedar belonged to Essau."[13]

These clues carefully laid out in these texts can provide the developmental background for an aesthetic of darkening that can prove challenging to thinking race theologically. In order to illustrate, in early theological constructs, dark skins represented those who had fallen away from the teachings and standards of orthodoxy. For Gay L. Byron, Blacks alongside the Ethiopians and Egyptians represented the "extremes" and "'most remote' manifestations of Christian identity."[14] The phrase "from the ends of the earth," which Origen employed when comparing the Shulamite with the queen of Sheba, can support this point.[15] While this argument cannot be made in all certainty, it can be underscored that *Shunem* itself, as much of the Northern Kingdom in biblical times, appears to figure the outskirts of the prescribed faith of Israel. Hence, like the once royal Canaanite city perhaps suspected of harboring worshippers of Ishtar, her dark skin takes on allegorical and tropological contours, symbolizing the place of "return" or "repentance" denoted by the term "leap" that can favor processes of lightening ancestries (Songs 6:13).

To fit in the plan of redemption, the black beauty of *Shunem* would have to play the role of the heathen in need of conversion or of the wayward wife expected to return home. For example, Nicholas of Lyra argued that *Shunem* represents periods of time in which the Hebrew people were called to return, starting with the Babylonian captivity until the time of Jesus. More metaphorically still, it signifies the return to "Sulamitis," what he translates as perfection, "original condition of perfection" or the "original wholeness" of their faith.[16] As if referring to stages in the walk of faith, from the old life to the new, would her beauty then compare to the "curtains of Solomon" only by means of assimilating herself to the privileged identity of the one nation or ethnicity that would translate into belief in an orthodox Christian faith? Already in an incipient manner Gregory of Nyssa assumes this position when describing Jerusalem or the City of God as the place where all foreigners are made "fellow tribesmen"—"Babylonians become Jerusalemites, and the harlot [Rahab] a virgin, *and the Ethiopians bright*, and Tyre the city on High."[17] Note the parallels drawn between morality, territories, and ethnicities that can implicitly be indicative of early Christian attitudes toward the dark-skinned.

This turn to salvific history drawn from geopolitics and the redistribution of ancestral backgrounds can be most problematic, especially when gesturing toward ethnic tensions in the text, when strangeness, perhaps of the Canaanite type, is stamped on skin pigmentations in need of "leaping" or evolving. While for some, early theologies such as these may offer a contribution to early positive developments of concepts of the beauty of negritude by the very fact that it is acknowledged (e.g., Ernst Benz), like Pope one might ponder how they also plaster blackness "with a whitewash of highly questionable quality."[18] A false logic ensues: why would not her skin be an external indicator of her internal moral ugliness?

Invariably, with early allegorical biases translating dark skins into sins and vices, demons and evil, heresies, and sexual threats, the color symbolism of darkness was turned into an aesthetic sensibility that rejected her identity at its core—her inherent goodness.

- Origen, as welcoming of her heritage as he was, considers her skin color to be a metaphor for how "darkened with exceeding great and many sins" the Ethiopians were and how what he also calls "the inky dye of wickedness" comes to represent those *"beyond the rivers of Ethiopia."*[19]
- For Gregory of Nyssa, "the evening darkness of the west and the morning darkness of the east" is nothing other than "the place where evil begins and the place where evil ceases" that must meet the *Sun of Justice* by noonday.[20] He had previously allegorized this concept by using the Shulamite as a type to interpret Rom. 5:6-8 and the thoughts of St. Paul.[21] Injustice for him takes on the form of dark skins, and of evil human beings symbolizing unclean spirits, as in the model of Bede the Venerable.[22]
- Similarly, Gregory the Great compares her dark skin with her previous sinful state as a Gentile, "She ponders what she was. She ponders what she has become. And she acknowledges her past faults lest she be proud, acknowledges her present conduct lest she be ungrateful, and says: *I am black but beautiful*. She is 'black' through what she deserves but beautiful

through grace; black through her past conduct but beautiful through her subsequent way of life."[23]
- Origen goes as far as to conclude that the blackness of her skin might not image God. Indeed, in God there is no darkness.[24] Her true beauty lies beyond corporeal and temporal dimensions of reality. While being black, her soul is in the image of eternity, a "rational form and a spiritual likeness."
- As for Gregory of Nyssa, this could mean that the bride must not have been *truly* black, for she was shaped by the radiant hands of God. She rather became black, "stained all over with some dark and gloomy color."[25] When formed, she was "a copy of the true light, far removed from the marks of darkness and resplendent in its likeness to the beauty of its archetype."[26] Hence, in this early commentary work, violence against her ethnic background comes as this moralizing discourse succeeds at turning the Shulamite's darkness into a symbol of shame and guilt.

These narratives when compared to others of similar content can serve as examples of how women of dark skin could readily be objects of contempt. For instance, in a dream described in the apocryphal *Acts of Peter* that Marcellus has of an "Ethiopian woman," she appears as a "most evil-looking" black woman (*nigram*) "dressed in filthy rags" and "dancing with an iron collar about her neck and chains on her hands and feet."[27] Marcellus proceeds to encourage Peter to cut off her head and all her limbs into pieces, an order that a man looking like Peter immediately obeys. Thereupon, with much amazement, Marcellus wakes up from his dream. Byron rightly points to the "ethnic and color-symbolic language" made synonymous with the collar and chains as well as the representation of an enemy worthy of decapitation and dismemberment. Because her dark body—ethnic identity and gender—is specifically depicted as evil or demonic (*daemonis*), early rhetoric such as this can be indicative of prevalent attitudes and textual patterns of exclusion.

Against the Shulamite in particular, textual violence comes also under the guise of *luminosity*, her becoming lovely and beautiful only by means of whitening herself, that is, doing away with her dark alterities. For how else could she *reform* herself if not by becoming more like God, or shall we say the colonizer? Similar to the spiritual process of masculinization of the woman in the Gospel of St. Thomas (v. 114), so it occurs with the whitening of *imago Dei* of the dark-skinned woman in early Christian literature. Blackness became that which those seeking perfection had to overcome. For this dark-skinned beauty to regain her divine image, she must undergo a process of luminosity that leads her away from disobedience and unbelief and into a paradisiacal state of purity (the same as that prior to the fall).

Consequently, when she puts darkness away, then the Shulamite's light and splendor "will be restored" to her and the blackness for which the maidens have reproached her "will be banished" from her completely, so that she "shall be accounted worthy to be called *the light of the world.*"[28] For William of St. Thierry, Solomon's dark-skinned bride would not even receive her kiss, and "until, by riddance of her *Egyptian blackness* and rejection of the *customs of a barbarous nation*, she might become worthy of access to the royal bridechamber."[29] Her "radiant beauty" can be recovered as the light of grace removes all traces of blackness, the night that obscures it, says Gregory of Nyssa.[30] Only in this sense it can be said that her beauty is properly her own.

When considering the implications of these early Christian views on naming the other ethnically in tandem with Byron's insights on how the categories of "insiders" and "outsiders" are being conferred moral qualities of black/evil and light/justice, one would need to recognize how orthodoxy has been colonized. The dominant Christian tradition has aligned itself with power structures of conquest of the Greco-Roman type that set in place aesthetic misrecognitions of being human. With a concept like the *imago Dei* serving alongside these impulses as an equally powerful tool of oppression (if not a *totem*)—a symbol that can be said to have arisen from principles fostered in early Christian thought—the negative implications compound when further promoted in modern concepts such as "racial purification," once employed, for the purposes of this study, during the periods of modern conquests as well as during colonial and neo-colonial times.

COLONIZING PENDULUMS

A brief study on the *latinidades* of the Americas, particularly because of their mixed- and dark-hued ancestries, can serve to show how the above theological underpinnings can pose a challenge to a present-day reading of the Song of Songs. The act of identifying the good in ethnic groups often gets entangled in a complex web of de/gradations of beauty. To be named *kalos* is an effort, if not a plea, that, like that of the Shulamite, is quite characteristic of peoples whose lands have been conquered and colonized yet find themselves residing in the territorial limits of their colonizers.[31]

The work of George R. Andrews on Afro-Caribbean and Latin American identities can serve to illustrate the dangers of deracialization and assimilation, and also the subversions and deviations with which those being named have responded.[32] It explores the pendulum shifts between whitening and darkening processes among populations—with cultural, political, and economic implications—at least since 1880. With a combined challenge in the pursuit of citizenship in the formerly enslaved populations and a boom in export economy, each shift was determined by a struggle between the need to satisfy the demand for labor and international trade and the opposing reactions of native populations. The balance, at least initially, tilted toward the former, once racial identities and distinctions also became tightly knitted to foreign economic interests.

In order to succeed, the educated elites first had to create an aura of prosperity and social advancement attractive to white European immigrants. While Blacks, mestizos, Indians, and mulattos were targeted for Europeanization, reports on local newspapers and magazines also show that for many elites a transfusion of blood was necessary to counteract the "jungle" effect caused by the defects of "our blacks and Indians."[33] Whitening was necessary, as Raimundo Nina Rodrigues reports, since those almost incapable of becoming civilized would have "to constitute themselves as civilized peoples."[34] Furthermore, as Fernando Ortiz puts it, "since the 'black race' has proven itself to be 'more delinquent than the white situated in the identical social position . . . white immigration is what we should favor.'"[35] In the meantime, economically, a great impact was felt by the educated Blacks and mulattos seeking advancement and the same opportunities as the European whites. They often encountered closed doors to symbolic structures of cultural capital: "refusal of admission to restaurants, theatres, barbershops, hotels and other public facilities; private (and occasionally, prestigious public) school's refusal to enroll their children; social clubs' refusal to admit them; and, most damaging of all, open or veiled job discrimination," argues Andrews.[36]

All along a counterfeit process of darkening was taking place at the hands of the rising industrial powers of the United States—an influence primarily seeking to impact the economic level. Offering job opportunities to those willing to bargain for lower wages, U.S. export economy attracted mostly the uneducated mulattos and blacks. A report on the United Fruit Company on the Costa Rican magazine *Reportorio Americano* (1923), says that, "Hondurans will be buried beneath a Haitian republic . . . Instead of 700,000 light-colored Hondurans, we will have 4,000,000 dark Antelleans . . . [,] the Atlantic coast will be transformed into a solid mass of soot, and the Caribbean Sea into a Charcoal Sea."[37] This seemingly anti-Europeanizing agenda equally served to endanger the well-being of these developing territories, since it ultimately intended their impoverishment and the demise of their economic autochthony. It also helped set up the foundation for a system of dependency upon, if not blatant assimilation to an already U.S. racist economy.[38]

In the United States, whitening processes based on gradations of color, employed by some to debase the beauty inherent in Indian and African ancestry (including the myth of full miscegenation or "whole racial integration" into "white/non-white" categories that continue to this day[39]), fuel the embers of racialized aesthetics for the purposes of discrimination according to class.[40] These taxonomies reify feelings of guilt and ambiguity among members of darker skin and of lighter complexion. Whitening processes colloquially known as *mejorar la raza* (to better the race) entice both to engage in behaviors that enable them to *pass* as white. Nevertheless, Jorge argues, this is a mere illusion, since U.S. American society does not acknowledge these distinctions and categorizes all Latina/os, regardless of their phenotype, in the non-white category.[41] Conversely, to assimilate oneself to the Afro-American culture as a gesture of solidarity may prove problematic. Northwestern European standards of biogenetics that conveniently ensued in the perpetual and self-perpetuating "one-drop rule," "one black ancestor rule," or the rule of hypodescent would remain unchallenged, as Carlos A. Fernández argues.[42]

In either case, when loyalties to white or black categories are enforced, misrepresentations of identities are perpetuated and ostracism aimed at those challenging this taboo system is maintained.[43] Taxonomies maintain oppressive means of authentication and internalization and can lead to all sorts of external as well as internal forms of discrimination. When these remain unchallenged, processes of eradication of multiple ancestries continue to abet the colonial hierarchy that ultimately upholds a false image of being American—Anglo purity, superiority, and "natural" rights.[44] In this regard, darkening processes that acknowledge "racially mixed people" can serve to put in question what Teresa K. Williams calls "the one-dimensional racial structure upon which America has founded and built its national identity."[45]

The celebration of the fullness and diversity of Latinao peoples, as one example, can hold its commitment to embracing African ancestry, yet also abstaining from assimilation and integration processes of old and new that reify false moralities.[46] In order to destabilize the replica, the monolithic, and the false homogeneity of European ethnicities, one can highlight intersubjective processes such as *négritude*, creolization, maroonness, *mulataje*, *métissage*. Bearing in mind these transitions, pollutions, deviations, anomalies, and transmutations, combined with biological, social, and co-constructive *naming* processes, intersubjective relationships can be viewed as positively playing a role in what George Kitahara Kich calls the "ongoing adaptation to a changing world."[47]

These terms will always be limited and heavily weighed down by the gruesome history of colonial rape, dislocation, erasure, injury, genocide, discrimination, and much more. None can hold supremacy and exactitude. Each can connote whitening as well as darkening, depending on the vantage point. Each can be equally used for discrimination as well as for commitment to, elaboration of, and paying tribute to the fullness and diversity of Latinao ancestries. However limited, these terms seek to voice the good and beautiful in their various hues of mixture. These include true living relationships between past and present histories of near and far continents; memories of free and enslaved as well as of wandering and nomadic peoples; ancient and modern ways of living; languages, customs, music, and dance; food and tastes—an utter demystification of racial and ethnic purity.

Would an acknowledgment of the beauty expressed in the array of hues serve to debilitate a morality aiming at *being called white as snow*, as with the process of luminosity illustrative of the patristic writings? Embodying ambiguity allows for journeying into spaces of lived experiences, a process of marginalization and victimization overturned by one of "resistance and assertion,"[48] and ultimately overcoming "strict societal rules" and disrupting social and cultural constructions of "racial boundaries."[49] Without a sharp split between dark and light, perhaps there would be no need for blackness to reach out for a false universal erroneously disguised as whiteness. Thus, a way forward into darkening the self, as in reconstructing theological concepts like the *imago Dei*, could be via a process of darkening in the sense of acknowledging mixture, so that the self can reside comfortably, within her multiethnic skin. The self, by being darkened by the admission of all racial mixture, can subversively reassert its impurity to disrupt prescriptive categories of becoming divine.

Dancing into darkness
Leap, leap,
    O Shulamite!
Leap, leap,
    and let us gaze on you.
How will you gaze
    on the Shulamite
In the dance of the two camps?
(Song of Songs 6:13, translation mine)

Theologically, as J. Kameron Carter has shown, modernity inherited the biological racism of the Enlightenment that became the means of unifying people for the purposes of preserving the "sovereign social body."[50] Racism was founded upon what for Immanuel Kant meant the creation of an ethical community that resembled Christ's discontinuity with his humanity (Jewish race). Elevated above from any particularity, this community, which ultimately becomes a cosmopolitan one, would in the end beautify or bring to perfection the human race with its establishment of justice, right, and "perpetual peace."[51] The good character of the European ideal would promote "this good society" by means of the moral progress of each of the human species (based on race),[52] with the Germans being superior. Ultimately, it aimed at the eradication of multiplicity.

Consequently, unless ethnically mixed bodies resist, they can fall into the trap of moralities that draw from, keep intact, and energize racial taxonomies.

As the "good" becomes synonymous with the "white" race (defined by "whiteness"), race serves as a sovereign tool fashioned for redistribution of social value from the least to the most polluted. In the unconscious of the *homo occidentalis*, being black, Franz Fanon argues, "symbolizes evil, sin, wretchedness, death, war, and famine."[53] With Satan being the ugly ruler of the world of shadows, the master of the night, while God, on the other hand, being bright, and represented as a beautiful white dove, would not levels of *naming oneself* likely become contingent upon assimilation? For Fanon, by aligning dark skins with satanic powers, *negritude* causes feelings of guilt and shame. Hence, all attachments to *negritude* need to be rejected, whitened, so that bodies can be acceptable in the eyes of those seeking to colonize consciousness. The image of whiteness disguised as *luminous* turns opaque dark alterities and enforces sharp dualisms refusing to affirm the whole of being beauti*fully* human.

A re-reading of Song of Songs and of the Sulamite thus is also necessary. As in theologies of color, rather than positing darkness at the opposite extreme of the *imago Dei*, its symbolic use in Christian teachings can be reconstructed through an array of tinted lenses in order to loosen definitions of being human from moralizing and assimilating constructs.[54] With new narratives on God, as Charles Long has rightly concluded, theological significations can make room for a *reality of opacity* that indicts the normative rhetoric of transparency that intensifies the gaze upon dark skins (for use) and demystifies the dark other alongside God.[55] In Latinao thinking in particular, to affirm such divinely given opacity can mean to likewise graciously embrace the multiplicity of fleshliness and dynamic character of human existence in relation to the divine mystery.

With this in mind, one can note how Gregory of Nyssa is also inclined to use another metaphor for the divine mystery with which to reflect on multiplicity in his sermon on Songs 3:1-4 and 5:2: *luminous darkness*. As he puts it, "The revelation of God to the great Moses began with light as its medium, but afterwards God spoke through him through the medium of a cloud, and when he had become more lifted up and more perfect, he saw God in darkness."[56] Might the Shulamite's desire to image God also resemble the ascent of Moses to the mountain in the sense of embracing her luminous opacity? In so doing, could she be viewed as leaping deeper and dancing into the darkness, thus as entering into another dimension of the archetype, becoming divine in the likes of the ambiguities that would accompany light mixing with the dark hues of the divine matrix?

For Nyssa, the world of phenomena guides the soul, a personification of the Shulamite, into the world of the *"night,"* "the divine night," "darkness," "the Invisible," or "the *dark cloud.*"[57] Furthermore, as if entering this *dark cloud* that Nyssa calls "the innermost shrine of the knowledge of God," there she can dwell in a state of becoming "entirely seized about by the divine darkness."[58] With regard to his previous interpretations, he adds that, while she was initially "cast into darkness by unenlightened beliefs," she, in her desire to draw close "to the fount of light," is capable of washing away "the darkness of ignorance." By this process she can then be "already surrounded by the divine night, in which the Bridegroom draws near but is not manifest."[59] Might darkening yield a closer embrace within the divine *luminous darkness*, which, while resulting in unknowing,[60] could also serve as a metaphor for the divine mixture (continuous movements from black to white and white to black) that she herself can come to affirm?

Could this ambiguous act of leaping and even dancing into the dark cloud not only symbolize the enactment of the mystery of her flesh but also aid in freeing God from the grips of conquest and colonization? Quite likely, since for Nyssa, when recognizing herself as beautiful (Songs 1:8), the Shulamite, as with the rest of humanity, comes to understand how she has been made "in the likeness of incorruptible Beauty, an impress of the true Deity."[61] Already Carter in conversation with Albert J. Raboteau explores a similar path when using the concept of opacity to describe how the invisibility of the eternal Logos (archetype) becomes visible (a type) in black existence and faith as an icon would. It subverts imposed designations of being morally ugly. Likewise bringing into the conversation Gregory of Nyssa and Bonaventure, Carter argues that opacity signifies a free participation that brings a fleshly expression (active) to what has been divinely impressed (passive) and that discloses "the surface of the Infinite."[62] This iconic existence, for him, is dynamic and opaque, in that there is something that escapes the human gaze, progressively uncapturable, that to me radiates through the flesh shining forth the multiple.

OF TONES AND RHYTHMS OF FLESH

Culipandeando la Reina avanza,
y de su inmensa grupa resbalan
meneos cachondos que el gongo cuaja

—Luis Palés Matos, *Majestad Negra*

However, in order to arrive there, one would need to disrupt the colonization of typologies, for night and day, darkness and light, black and white, *noumena* and *phenomena*, flesh and spirit, or heaven and earth are not sharp opposites. Perhaps through his use of terms such as the luminous darkness Nyssa sought to do away with seeming oppositions such as these. Yet, he falls short even so, since luminosity still finds itself minimizing the beauty of flesh. Thus, an earthen process would still be needed to henceforth challenge a *hyper*metaphysics used to inscribe a "beyondness" that distances God too far from the created order. The trope of dark bodies is needed, especially since dark women are often tropologically labeled as evil and sinful by being deemed closest to the earth.[63] The movement of going deeper into the cloud cannot simply be from the sensual to the spiritual. In reconstructing Nyssa, then imaging God according to a luminous darkness could neither translate into abandoning all creatureliness nor giving up all finitude.[64] One may thus find in Gregory of Nyssa an ally insofar as he can aid us in illustrating the complexity of divine epiphany in the beauty of the created order, perhaps as in the darkening of luminosity via which human bodies with all their array of colors become an icon of God.

In seeking to challenge the split between the *noumena* and *phenomena* figured in the conquered "God," one would need to propose a more generous view toward female bodies: a crossing over and subversion of categories without doing away with each of their distinctiveness.[65] As in the work on the Songs of Richard Kearney, being an icon would not erase distinctions, for the Shulamite (as a type of God) crosses over "without consuming or being consumed by" the other.[66] She is transfigured in relation to the other, while likewise remaining herself. Beyond Kearney, one might speak of the divine imaging also mirroring her beauty. While being an excess of it, might not the divine reflection also be according to the multiplicity of flesh in an incomprehensible way?

Reading early commentators once again from the present to the past with an intent to darken the imaging processes, one can note how "the tents of Kedar" *and* "the curtains of Solomon," as Origen argues, point to the curtains that adorn the tabernacle, which are black and glorious.[67] Like the tabernacle, which resembles *"the Word made flesh,"*[68] these curtains are made according to *"the pattern of the true tabernacle."*[69] Speaking specifically of the Shulamite, he says, "she doubtedless means the glory and beauty of those curtains which cover over that *tabernacle, which God had pitched, and not man."*[70] These curtains are black themselves, "since they were woven of goats' hair,"[71] meaning flesh! That their material is of goats' hair is significant, for it denotes a ruggedness and the frailty of the flesh that equally affirms her divine archetypical composition. Hence, the glory of the icon shines through darkened flesh and iconizes itself also via darkness.

Furthermore, the flesh is plural, for the curtains are likened to the "countless churches scattered all over the world, and huge gatherings and multitudes of peoples,"[72] which can point to a celebration of the multiple ancestries of the Shulamite, thus her dark alterities. Likewise, for Origen, "this black and beautiful one,"[73] the Shulamite, becomes a type of the church, for her ancestral stock is composed of "the races of the whole world."[74] Rather than describing her alterities as oppositional (the tents of Kedar versus the curtains of Solomon, as Gregory the Great and Gregory of Nyssa would[75]), one could point to an element of earthly heterogeneity in the Shulamite as a type of dark luminosity. Such heterogeneity would be characteristic of the many hues of black curtains that beautifully adorn the tabernacle in the tones of goat skins.

This reading of the mystery of multiple flesh shining forth through the icon would implicitly be rejecting, along with Carter, the perfecting capacity of a dominant racial category to exercise a universal rationality that outlives the "excess of bodily particularity" of dark-skinned bodies.[76] It can set in motion a reversal of whitening processes by which, as he also argues, "The reconstituted and enlightened body politic completes the task of the (perfect) 'race-ing' of the body." Beyond Carter, this excess might point to a way out of the "black/white," "human/non-human," "God/creation" sharp binaries. Thus, while the texts are not exempt from readings that remain problematic, these contain sufficient disruptive patterns toward social attitudes with which to transgress constrictive social imaginaries.

Hence, with an impulse to darken the *imago Dei* in the sense of mixing, could human beauty be defined more multi*pliably* in relation to the dust that also shapes it? That is, could the Shulamite be set free to *darken* herself in relation to her natural world orders? Perhaps the Shulamite's dark skin can shine through as an icon of the female persona of the "Majestad Negra" or the black majesty of the *night* and ambiguously locate herself in relation to the "Danza Negra" of Luis Palés Matos. She, as a symbol of the black dance, could liberate the Black dancing Ethiopian woman who appeared in the dream of Marcellus narrated in the apocryphal *Acts of Peter*. She rhythmically vibrates with the impulse of the created order already imbued with the spirit world, as she finds herself in the divine dark chambers of *Night*. Her body is a continuum and instrument of passage, as she enjoins the nocturnal animals, with sounds tu-cu-tú, to-co-tó, pru-pru-prú, cro-cro-cró reminiscent of Africa. The subversive black dance, out of sight of the enslaving masters, also pays homage to this polymorphic heritage flowing through the veins of her darkened existence. In her body, African and Antillian woods, the Calabó y bambú and Bambú y calabó, used for the instrumentation of the dance, come together and change orders—none prior to the other, higher than the other, opposite to the other.

The dancing body becomes the icon of divine mystery, freedom, equality, fullness of humanity. "Culipandeando la Reina avanza," writes Palés Matos. She, the black queen of the Caribbean *Shunem*, would represent rebellion against whitening processes, the imposed dress codes and dances of Louis XV, a reversal to the Victorian ideal, perhaps also a resistance to the orthodox Christian faith?[77] This black beauty—even as a loved bride, sister, daughter, or mother—sensuously swivels her hips and moves forward, at the rhythm of the drums. The sun that has beaten tirelessly upon her curved flesh pulsates through her blood because of her strenuous labor. Her body suffers the ignominy of more than one ancestry, one stereotype, one dominant religious heritage. Yet, her very skin pigmentation in the end becomes the song celebrating her heterogeneity. That which has been the cause of enslavement becomes the very means of symbolic freedom from the colonizing way of being human.

This other allegory of the black beauty of Songs, one celebratory of her diverse earthly hues, array of skin colors and rhythms, can prove to strengthen the discourse. For a Latinao imaginary of multiplicity, alongside other multiethnic self-identifying embodiments, can further enfeeble the impulse toward whitening hermeneutics. Rather than seeking to flee from the moral ugliness imposed upon the Shulamite (via warring between two camps: the tents of Kedar" and "the curtains of Solomon"; luminosity and darkness; the earth below and the dark cloud above), a Latinoa multiplicity can question the polarizing processes in imaging God. This it can do by honoring the vast array of humanities, skin colors, phenotypes, ethnicities, and cultures housed in the bodies of *Latinaos* themselves. Luminosity and darkness indeed dance about in a type of luminous darkness, but as in moving choreographically in defiant resistance without dishonoring or silencing any ancestry.

The aim is a robust argument for having the dancing Shulamite remain center stage in Christian theology, even after suffering the ignominy of colonial dominance, of multiple historical conquests, latent in the Scriptures and in Christian commentaries, and later used as instruments of Enlightenment and still operative to this day. Like la *majestad negra*, the Shulamite could be a figure that darkens these whitening processes in the Scriptures themselves. Why not make use of her possible multiple ethnicities, her dark alterities, to disrupt a theological discourse ridden with oppression reified time and again in its privileging of dominant images seeking to colonize darkness? How else should she enter into the *luminous darkness*, her whiteness mixed with darkness, if not by darkening within luminosity itself?[78]

FINAL MUSINGS...

Recovering the Shulamite as an icon of the luminous darkness dislodges the kind of othering that operates under the principles of a metaphysics of whiteness, the impulse of colonization that not only subdued people groups, racially exterminating them and raping their women but also pillaged their land. By positing the divine mystery of being dark-skinned also in relation to the natural world orders, of an incomprehensible God alongside the beauty of the dark universe in which humans are also made, the *imago Dei* becomes decolonized, that is darkened, by the heterogeneous origins that further disturb settled categories of race, ethnicity, and gender. This *other* allegory is thus needed. The Shulamite in the image of the tents of Kedar and the curtains of Solomon can refer to a mode of being human that correlates with the human mystery of diverse shapes, pigmentations, and forms of existence, dark alterities of being a woman of color, not too distant from the *dark cloud* that houses divinity.

Similarly, self-conscious of their multi*pliable*-belongingness, Latinaos can hold heterogeneity as an antidote to the passé U.S. segregating interpretative lenses, even as they wrestle with its inherent tensions. Being of more than one genus, one history, one religion, one point of reference, they are outsiders—aliens, strangers—as much as insiders. Their bodies celebrate their divinely enfleshed markings of multiple centers and margins, like the Shulamite's flexible inhabiting of ethnic categories of those of being "darkened by the sun" (Songs 1:6) alongside those with shades of "black" and "dark" (Songs 1:5 according to various translations).

Promising in this interplay between darkness and light is the challenge to ethnocentric and racist tendencies within and beyond Latinao communities (with diverse economic, cultural, social, political, and educational impacts) that can likewise serve to construct conscientious aesthetic models of human and divine fleshly becomings. By de-ghettoizing darkness and light (as metaphysical elements), an intersubjective inhabiting of races (and genders) across temporalities and spaces can be affirmed in order to further disturb colonizing taxonomies and systems of controls. The hope is to put forth another imaginary by means of allegorizing the Shulamite, whose beauty reflects a composition of the many origins that her body inhabits, and to call her *black and beautiful* according to an *imago Dei* whose archetype is incomprehensible even as it is beguilingly darkened by a plurality of shapes characteristic of the divine icon.

NOTES

1. I want to thank the Louisville Institute for their support in writing this essay. Here my emphasis is on the Afro-Caribbean heritage and identity. For essays where I integrate indigenous views and religious practices, another component of Caribbean heritage, see: "Expanding Space: A Possibility of a Cavernous Mode of Dwelling," in *Contemporary Issues of Migration and Theology*, Christianities of the World, ed. Elaine Padilla and Peter C. Phan (New York: Palgrave McMillan, 2013), 53–72; "Flower and Song: A Comparative Study on Teotlizing in Aztec Theology and Karl Rahner's View of Divine Self-Disclosure," in *Comparing Faithfully: Insights for Systematic Theological Reflection*, ed. Michelle Voss Roberts (New York: Fordham University Press, 2016), 46–65.

2. Michelle A. González, *Afro-Cuban Theology: Religion, Race, and Identity* (Gainesville/Tallahasee: University Press of Florida, 2006), 121. For a feminist

overview of the doctrine of the *imago Dei*, see also her book, *Created in God's Image: An Introduction to Feminist Anthropology* (Maryknoll, NY: Orbis Books, 2007).

3. See, for example, a definition of *mujerismo* hermeneutics in Ada María Isasi-Díaz, "'By the Rivers of Babylon': Exile as a Way of Life," in *Mujerista Theology* (Maryknoll, NY: Orbis Books, 1996), 35–36, esp. 38.

4. For other feminist views on the Song of Songs, see: Athalya Brenner, *The Song of Songs: A Feminist Companion to the Bible*, First Series (Sheffield: Sheffield Academic Press, 1993, 2001); and Athalya Brenner and Carole R. Fontaine, *The Song of Songs: A Feminist Companion to the Bible*, Second Series (Sheffield: Sheffield Press, 2000). See, in particular, the essay by Carole R. Fontaine: "The Voice of the Turtle: Now It's *MY* Song of Songs," in the second series, and her brief illustrations under the section "*Beautiful and Black as...*" (179–181), where she seeks to provide a brief analysis on class conflicts in light of some urban experiences of African American women comparable to understandings of cults of ancient goddesses.

5. Franz Fanon, *Black Skin, White Masks* (New York: Grove Press, 2008), 118.

6. González, *Afro-Cuban Theology*, 122.

7. González, *Afro-Cuban Theology*, 137.

8. See Marvin H. Pope, *Song of Songs*, The Anchor Yale Bible (New Haven & London: Yale University Press, 1977), 596–600.

9. Pope, *Song of Songs*, 307.

10. See, for example: William of St. Thierry, *Exposition on the Song of Songs*, Cistercian Fathers Series 6, trans. Mother Columba Hart OSB (Kalamazoo: Cistercian Publications, 1968), 38; Gregory the Great, *On the Song of Songs*, Cistercian Studies Series 244, trans. Mark DelCogliano (Collegeville, Minnesota: Liturgical Press, 2012), 133.

11. Origen, *The Song of Songs, Commentary, and Homilies*, Ancient Christian Writers, trans. and ed. R. P. Lawson (Mahwah, NJ: Newman Press, 1956), 91.

12. Origen, *The Song of Songs*, 91–93.

13. Gregory the Great, *On the Song of Songs*, 133.

14. Gay L. Byron, *Symbolic Blackness and Ethnic Difference in Early Christian Literature* (London-New York: Routledge, 2002), 1 and 33. For a Greek understanding of the foreigner that can have implications for theological views on race, see Aristotle's *Politics*, chapter 3, questions on "citizenship," "the state," "the sovereignty of the people," and "the best men."

15. Origen, *The Song of Songs*, 97 (emphasis his).

16. Nicholas of Lyra, in *The Song of Songs: Interpreted by Early Christian and Medieval Commentators*, trans. and ed. Richard A. Norris Jr., The Church's Bible (Grand Rapids, MI: William B. Eerdmans, 2003), 251.

17. Gregory of Nyssa, *Homilies on the Song of Songs*, Writings from the Greco-Roman World, trans. Richard A. Norris (Atlanta: Society of Biblical Literature, 2012), 53–54. Emphasis mine.

18. Pope, *Song of Songs*, 310. In this section on the color black, he makes reference to Rev. Jacob A. Dyer, "The Biblical Attitudes toward Race and Color," unpublished paper (cf. 309).

19. Origen, *The Song of Songs*, 103.
20. Gregory of Nyssa, *Homilies*, 69.
21. Gregory of Nyssa, *Homilies*, 53.
22. See St. Bede the Venerable, in *The Song of Songs: Interpreted*, 43.
23. Gregory the Great, *On the Song of Songs*, 135 (emphasis his).
24. Origen, *The Song of Songs*, 112.
25. Gregory of Nyssa, *Homilies*, 55.
26. Gregory of Nyssa, *Homilies*, 57.
27. *Acts of Peter 22*; in *Acta Apostolorum Apochrypha*, 2 vols., ed. Ricardus A. Lipsius and Maximilus Bonnet (Hildesheim: G. Olms, 1959), 1:69–70; quoted in Byron, *Symbolic Blackness*, 17.
28. Origen, *The Song of Songs*, 109.
29. William of St. Thierry, *Exposition on the Song of Songs*, 10 (emphasis mine).
30. Gregory of Nyssa, *Homilies*, 53.
31. See, for example, Albert Memmi, *The Colonizer and the Colonized* (Boston: Beacon Press, 1965).
32. George Reid Andrews, *Afro-Latin America, 1800–2000* (Oxford: Oxford University Press, 2004), esp. 117–190.
33. Winthrop R. Wright, *Café con Leche* (Austin: University of Texas Press, 1990), 72; quoted in Andrews, *Afro-Latin America*, 119.
34. Celia Maria Marinho de Azevedo, *Onda negra. Medo blanco. O negro no imaginário das elites—século XIX* (São Paolo, 1987), 141–144; Raimundo Nina Rodrigues, *Africanos no Brasil* (São Paolo: Ed. Nacional, 1985), 4; quoted in Andrews, *Afro-Latin America*, 119.
35. See Alejandro de la Fuente, "Negros y electores: Desigualdad y políticas raciales en Cuba, 1900–1930," in *La nación soñada: Cuba, Puerto Rico, Filipinas ante el 98*, ed. Consuelo Naranjo Orovio, et al. (Aranjuez, Spain: Ediciones Doce Calles, 1996), 170; Avi Chomsky, "'Barbados or Canada?' Race, Immigration, and Nation in Early Twentieth-Century Cuba," *Hispanic American Review* 80:3 (2000): 426; quoted in Andrews, *Afro-Latin America*, 119.
36. Andrews, *Afro-Latin America*, 126.
37. Alberto Masferrer, "¿Será ya el principio del fin?" *Reportorio Americano* (San José, 14 May 1923), 50–51; quoted in Andrews, *Afro-Latin America*, 139.
38. See Eduardo H. Galeano, *Las venas abiertas de America Latina* (Mexico City: Siglo XXI, 2009); in English, *Open Veins of Latin America: Five Centuries of the Pillage of a Continent* (New York: Monthly Review Press, 1997).
39. Andrews, *Afro-Latin America*, 173–190.
40. See Sherezada "Chiqui" Vicioso, "Discovering Myself: Un Testimonio," in *The Afro-Latin@ Reader: History and Culture in the United States*, ed. Miriam Jiménez Román and Juan Flores (Durham-London: Duke University Press, 2010), 263; Angela Jorge, "The Black Puerto Rican Woman in Contemporary American Society," in *The Afro-Latin@ Reader*, 270.
41. Jorge, "The Black Puerto Rican Woman," 272.
42. Jim Crow forced people of mixed ancestry to adhere to "the one-drop rule," so the "white/non-white" paradigm has been fueled by a phobia for multiple ancestries.

For was it not until 1967 that the Supreme Court of the United States considered unconstitutional the remnant of the miscegenation laws (Loving vs. Virginia)? See Carlos A. Fernández, "Government Classification of Multiracial/Multiethnic People," in *The Multiracial Experience: Racial Borders as the New Frontier*, ed. Maria P. P. Root (Thousand Oaks, London-New Delhi: Sage Publications, 1996), 15–36.

43. See Bailey, *The New Face of America*, 29–55.

44. Ironically, prior to the U.S. civil war, the prevailing sentiment was anti-British. Now that the tables have turned, the national sentiment rooted in the Mayflower and later the Ellis Island narratives serve as the basis for "whitening processes" based on ancestry.

45. Teresa Kay Williams, "Race as Process: Reassessing the 'What Are You?' Encounters of Biracial Individuals," in *The Multiracial Experience*, 193.

46. See González, *Afro-Cuban Theology*, 36-44.

47. George Kitahara Kich, "In the Margins of Sex and Race: Difference, Marginality, and Flexibility," in *The Multiracial Experience*, 270.

48. Kich, "In the Margins of Sex and Race," 272.

49. Bailey, *The New Face of America*, 10, 99.

50. J. Kameron Carter, *Race: A Theological Account* (Oxford: Oxford University Press, 2008), 67; see also 79–122.

51. Carter, *Race*, 108.

52. Carter, *Race*, 109.

53. Fanon, *Black Skin, White Masks*, 167.

54. For instance, God has already taken on the flesh of African American experiences as a "Black God," of those of the Native American as a "Red God," and even of women of color. See James Cone, *God of the Oppressed* (Maryknoll: Orbis Books, 1997); Vine Deloria Jr., *God Is Red: A Native View of Religion* (Golden, CO: Fulcrum Publishing, 2003); and Delores Williams, *Sisters in the Wilderness: The Challenge of Womanist God-Talk* (Maryknoll: Orbis Books, 1995). See also the challenge that González puts forth regarding "black/white" racial paradigms in her book *Afro-Cuban Theology*, specifically pp. 34–50.

55. Charles H. Long, *Significations: Signs, Symbols, and Images in the Interpretation of Religion* (Minneapolis: Augsburg Fortress Press, 1986), esp. 107, 193–197.

56. Gregory of Nyssa, *Homilies*, 339.

57. Gregory of Nyssa, *Homilies*, 193.

58. Gregory of Nyssa, *Homilies*, 341.

59. Gregory of Nyssa, *Homilies*, 342–343.

60. Gregory of Nyssa, *The Life of Moses*, The Classics of Western Spirituality, trans. Abraham J. Malherbe and Everett Ferguson (New York and Mahwah: Paulist Press, 1978), 94–97.

61. Gregory of Nyssa, *Homilies*, 75.

62. Carter, *Race*, 152–154.

63. See, for example, González' overview of women's critique in *Created in God's Image*, 121–132. For another feminist interpretation of transcendence intricately related to the cosmos, see Mayra Rivera, *The Touch of Transcendence: A*

Postcolonial Theology of God (Louisville-London: Westminster John Knox Press, 2007).

64. Gregory of Nyssa, *Homilies*, 195.

65. An author that can be helpful in understanding the notion of *luminous darkness* is Nicholas of Cusa, who makes use of a coincidence of opposites to describe the effect of uniting opposites through terminology that transcends pure comparison and that exceeds composition and synthesis of the terms by affirming both the negative and affirmative aspects of it. See Nicholas of Cusa, *Nicholas of Cusa: Selected Spiritual Writings*, The Classics of Western Spirituality, ed. Bernard McGinn (Mahwah: Paulist Press, 1997); for an introduction to his thinking, see his argument on maximum and minimum and on plurality and unity, especially pp. 89–90.

66. Richard Kearney, *The God Who May Be: Hermeneutics of Religion* (Bloomington: Indiana University Press, 2001), 54.

67. Origen, *The Song of Songs*, 93.

68. Origen, *The Song of Songs*, 93 (emphasis his).

69. Origen, *The Song of Songs*, 105 (emphasis his).

70. Origen, *The Song of Songs*, 105 (emphasis his).

71. Origen, *The Song of Songs*, 106.

72. Origen, *The Song of Songs*, 106.

73. Origen, *The Song of Songs*, 100.

74. Origen, *The Song of Songs*, 98. Another personification of the Shulamite appears in William of St. Thierry's commentary. For him, the daughter of Pharaoh of Egypt was the wife whom Solomon took. Presumably, like the Shulamite, he argues, she was visibly black. See William of St. Thierry, *Exposition on the Song of Songs*, 10.

75. See Gregory the Great, *On the Song of Songs*, 133; Gregory of Nyssa, *Homilies*, 51–53.

76. Carter, *Race*, 90.

77. Here one cautiously embraces *la poesía negrista* or black poetry of Luis Palés Matos, for, along with Magali Roy-Féquière, one could argue that he highlights the creole identity to the point that "black pleasure" may be celebrated "without an understanding of black pain" (see *Women, Creole Identity, and Intellectual Life in Early Twentieth-Century* [Philadelphia: Temple University Press, 2004], 228). Yet, to fully agree with her view would be to miss the subversive impulse of these verses. Not only are the images of slave labor (and possibly rape) implicitly stated here but missed in her analysis, but also with his poetry Palés Matos situates the Caribbean peoples between whitening and darkening processes, the tug of war between Europeanism and Americanization. Its location points to times when pockets of African resistance remained in urban centers. Viewed as negating control, order, reason, and discipline, these *danza negra* and *majestad negra* would allegedly be the antithesis of "whiteness" and thus representatives of barbarism. As Andrews argues, in exhibiting deep African roots of clothing of slaves and "riotous dancing and drumming contests," as in the carnivals, the lower classes would "turn the tables on their social betters" (Andrews, *Afro-Latin America*, 123–125).

78. For Gregory of Nyssa, the Shulamite's turn into a radiant light points to continence and virginity that refuse all carnal pleasure. The problem is that he views

sexuality with contempt. See Gregory of Nyssa, *Homilies*, 204–205. As Fanon questions, is not the color white the symbol of "justice, truth, and virginity?" and thus the opposite of what dark skins symbolize?

BIBLIOGRAPHY

Andrews, George Reid. *Afro-Latin America, 1800–2000*. Oxford: Oxford University Press, 2004.
Brenner, Athalya. *The Song of Songs: A Feminist Companion to the Bible*. First Series. Sheffield: Sheffield Academic Press, 1993, 2001.
Brenner, Athalya and Carole R. Fontaine, *The Song of Songs: A Feminist Companion to the Bible*. Second Series. Sheffield: Sheffield Academic Press, 2000.
Byron, Gay L. *Symbolic Blackness and Ethnic Difference in Early Christian Literature*. London-New York: Routledge, 2002.
Carter, J. Kameron. *Race: A Theological Account*. Oxford: Oxford University Press, 2008.
Cone, James. *God of the Oppressed*. Maryknoll: Orbis Books, 1997.
Chomsky, Avi. "'Barbados or Canada?' Race, Immigration, and Nation in Early Twentieth-Century Cuba." *Hispanic American Review* 80:3 (2000): 415–462.
de la Fuente, Alejandro. "Negros y electores: Desigualdad y políticas raciales en Cuba, 1900–1930." In *La nación soñada: Cuba, Puerto Rico, Filipinas ante el 98*, edited by Consuelo Naranjo Orovio, et al., 163–178. Aranjuez, Spain: Ediciones Doce Calles, 1996.
Deloria, Vine, Jr. *God Is Red: A Native View of Religion*. Golden, CO: Fulcrum Publishing, 2003.
Dyer, Jacob A. "The Biblical Attitudes toward Race and Color." Unpublished paper.
Fanon, Frantz. *Black Skin, White Masks*. New York: Grove Press, 2008.
Fernández, Carlos A. "Government Classification of Multiracial/Multiethnic People." In *The Multiracial Experience: Racial Borders as the New Frontier*, edited by Maria P. P. Root, 15–36. Thousand Oaks, London-New Delhi: Sage Publications, 1996.
Galeano, Eduardo H. *Las venas abiertas de America Latina* (Mexico City: Siglo XXI, 2009). English trans: *Open Veins of Latin America: Five Centuries of the Pillage of a Continent*. New York: Monthly Review Press, 1997.
González, Michelle A. *Afro-Cuban Theology: Religion, Race, and Identity*. Gainesville/Tallahasee: University Press of Florida, 2006.
———. *Created in God's Image: An Introduction to Feminist Anthropology*. Maryknoll, NY: Orbis Books, 2007.
Gregory of Nyssa. *Homilies on the Song of Songs*. Writings from the Greco-Roman World. Trans. Richard A. Norris. Atlanta: Society of Biblical Literature, 2012.
———. *The Life of Moses*. The Classics of Western Spirituality. Trans. Abraham J. Malherbe and Everett Ferguson. New York and Mahwah: Paulist Press, 1978.
Gregory the Great. *On the Song of Songs*. Cistercian Studies Series 244. Trans. Mark DelCogliano. Collegeville, Minnesota: Liturgical Press, 2012.

Isasi-Díaz, Ada María. "'By the Rivers of Babylon': Exile as a Way of Life." In *Mujerista Theology*, 35–48. Maryknoll, NY: Orbis Books, 1996.
Jorge, Angela. "The Black Puerto Rican Woman in Contemporary American Society." In *The Afro-Latin@ Reader: History and Culture in the United States*, edited by Miriam Jiménez Román and Juan Flores, 269–275. Durham-London: Duke University Press, 2010.
Kearney, Richard. *The God Who May Be: Hermeneutics of Religion*. Bloomington: Indiana University Press, 2001.
Kitahara Kich, George. "In the Margins of Sex and Race: Difference, Marginality, and Flexibility." In *The Multiracial Experience*, edited by Maria P. P. Root, 263–276. Thousand Oaks, London-New Delhi: Sage Publications, 1996.
Lipsius, Ricardus A., and Maximilus Bonnet, eds. *Acta Apostolorum Apocrypha*. 2 vols. Hildesheim: G. Olms, 1959.
Long, Charles H. *Significations: Signs, Symbols, and Images in the Interpretation of Religion*. Minneapolis: Augsburg Fortress Press, 1986.
Marinho de Azevedo, Celia Maria. *Onda negra. Medo blanco. O negro no imaginário das elites—século XIX*. São Paolo: Paz e Terra, 1987.
Masferrer, Alberto. "¿Será ya el principio del fin?" *Reportorio Americano* (San José, 14 May 1923): 50–51.
McGinn, Bernard, ed. *Nicholas of Cusa: Selected Spiritual Writings*. The Classics of Western Spirituality. Mahwah: Paulist Press, 1997.
Memmi, Albert. *The Colonizer and the Colonized*. Boston: Beacon Press, 1965.
Nina Rodrigues, Raimundo. *Africanos no Brasil*. São Paolo: Ed. Nacional, 1985 [1932].
Norris, Richard A., Jr., trans and ed. *The Song of Songs: Interpreted by Early Christian and Medieval Commentators*. The Church's Bible. Grand Rapids, MI: William B. Eerdmans, 2003.
Origen. *The Song of Songs, Commentary, and Homilies*. Ancient Christian Writers. Trans. and ed. R. P. Lawson. Mahwah, NJ: Newman Press, 1956.
Padilla, Elaine. "Expanding Space: A Possibility of a Cavernous Mode of Dwelling" In *Contemporary Issues of Migration and Theology*, Christianities of the World, edited by Elaine Padilla and Peter C. Phan, 53–72. New York: Palgrave McMillan, 2013.
———. "Flower and Song: A Comparative Study on Teotlizing in Aztec Theology and Karl Rahner's View of Divine Self-Disclosure." In *Comparing Faithfully: Insights for Systematic Theological Reflection*, edited by Michelle Voss Roberts, 46-65. New York: Fordham University Press, 2016.
Pope, Marvin H. *Song of Songs*. The Anchor Yale Bible. New Haven & London: Yale University Press, 1977.
Rivera, Mayra. *The Touch of Transcendence: A Postcolonial Theology of God*. Louisville-London: Westminster John Knox Press, 2007.
Roy-Féquière, Magali. *Women, Creole Identity, and Intellectual Life in Early Twentieth-Century*. Philadelphia: Temple University Press, 2004.
Vicioso, Sherezada "Chiqui." "Discovering Myself: Un Testimonio." In *The Afro-Latin@ Reader: History and Culture in the United States*, edited by Miriam

Jiménez Román and Juan Flores, 262–265. Durham-London: Duke University Press, 2010.
William of St. Thierry. *Exposition on the Song of Songs*. Cistercian Fathers Series 6. Trans. Mother Columba Hart OSB. Kalamazoo: Cistercian Publications, 1968.
Williams, Delores. *Sisters in the Wilderness: The Challenge of Womanist God-Talk*. Maryknoll: Orbis Books, 1995.
Williams, Teresa Kay. "Race as Process: Reassessing the 'What Are You?' Encounters of Biracial Individuals." In *The Multiracial Experience*, edited by Maria P. P. Root, 191–210. Thousand Oaks, London-New Delhi: Sage Publications, 1996.
Wright, Winthrop R. *Café con Leche*. Austin: University of Texas Press, 1990.

Chapter 8

La Guadalupe, The Bible, Pentecost

Nancy Pineda-Madrid

The work of a theologian is to interpret religious symbols so as to shed light on God's active presence among us. Symbols, of their very nature, possess an organic character. They can be neither produced nor invented. As Paul Tillich observes:

> [Symbols] grow out of the individual or collective unconscious and cannot function without being accepted by the unconscious dimension of our being .... Like living beings, they grow and they die. They grow when the situation is ripe for them, and they die when the situation changes. ... They die because they can no longer produce a response in the group where they originally found expression.[1]

No doubt, that among U.S. Latina/o Catholics today one of the most undeniable examples of a vital religious symbol is that of Our Lady of Guadalupe. In Latina/o Catholic communities in Mexico, the United States, and beyond, December 12 celebrations that honor her often rival the celebration of Christmas. In the last few decades, a growing number of theologians, myself included, have advanced distinct readings of Guadalupe's theological significance, many of these underscoring connections to biblical texts, metathemes, and metanarratives.[2] In this study, I want to consider the role of the Bible in advancing a theological interpretation of Guadalupe. More specifically, how might the biblical account of Pentecost inform our theological reading of Guadalupe? And, why might developing this connection be important for theological work?[3]

There is a need for theologians to reflect on Guadalupe as a *religious* symbol, by which I mean a symbol that bears the capacity to illuminate our need for salvation as well as "the way of salvation."[4] Accordingly, a theological interpretation of Guadalupe—and for that matter of any religious symbol—needs to resonate with the narratives of the Bible, needs to be situated within the multidimensional context of a particular living community of faith, needs to be rooted in faith in Christ, and, finally, needs to deepen our journey toward eschatological fulfillment by encouraging our embrace of justice and mercy. What kind of theological reading of Guadalupe will encourage a more just and merciful world? And relatedly, how do I as a theologian understand the authority of the Bible in my theological work?[5]

The Bible rightly commands an exceptional place of authority in my theological work. For me, along with other people of faith, the scriptures are not only sacred, but also, in a way that cannot be fully explained, the scriptures hold a transcendent authority. Through biblical texts people of faith hear God speaking, revealing God's self in the narratives and verses of the biblical text. However, the authority of the Bible comes neither from within itself nor from the events of which it bears an account; rather, its authority comes from persons, through the experience of the Holy Spirit, through a relationship with Christ Jesus, and through the believing community of faith inaugurated by Christ, his apostles, and disciples. The biblical text enables believers to develop a more intimate relationship with the triune God and the community of faithful disciples. This point bears particular importance in this chapter as it attempts a connection between Guadalupe and Pentecost.

Even though for believers the scriptures will always remain authoritative, this must not be understood in an absolute way. The Bible is, on the one hand, the inspired word of God, and, on the other hand, the work of human beings. Indeed, the Bible contains many passages that bear the stain of patriarchy and kyriarchy, and these passages have been used to undermine the dignity of human beings (particularly women, people of color, people who are poor, people from the LGBTQ community) as well as the sacredness of all creation. To clarify what I mean by the authority of the Bible is always a complex and demanding endeavor,[6] one implicit in the work of this study.

Building on the work of U.S. Latino/a scripture scholars and theologians, this study argues that the biblical account of Pentecost may serve as an "interpretive key" to the theological meaning of Guadalupe. By "interpretive key" I refer to Pentecost as an extended narrative and theme that recurs in the scriptures, with each recurrence demonstrating particular features.[7] I will make the argument that Pentecost resounds in the "event of Guadalupe," that is, an experience of Guadalupe that captivates not only our minds but also our imagination and affect in such a way that we desire a deeper relationship with God. If Guadalupe is seen as one of the various iterations of Pentecost, then we discover in the event of Guadalupe the movement of the Holy Spirit calling us to greater life. This approach offers an interpretation distinct from those which examine Miguel Sánchez's use of Revelation 12 as a model for Guadalupe. Guadalupe, when viewed through the prism of Pentecost, does reveal a rich array of theological insight.

Before rereading Pentecost in light of Guadalupe, it is imperative to appreciate the threshold contributions that have already been made by two U.S. Latino/a scripture scholars and one theologian. Building on the work of Mexican-born diocesan priest Miguel Sánchez (1596–1674),[8] yet moving in different directions with it, three scholars—Jean-Pierre Ruiz, Timothy Matovina, and David Sánchez—have examined his use of Revelation 12 as an inspiration for Guadalupe. These contributions, which comprise the first section of this study, set the stage, in that they examine the originating biblical connection between Guadalupe and Revelation 12. That said, recall that there are two texts identified as the originating Guadalupe narrative, one written in Spanish by Miguel Sánchez in 1648, titled *Imagen de la Virgen María*, and a second written in Nahuatl most likely by Luis Laso de la Vega in 1649, commonly titled the *Nican Mopohua*.[9] Since Sánchez's version explicitly and transparently employs Revelation 12, it is the focus of the first section.

Two more U.S. Latino/a theologians, Virgilio Elizondo and Orlando Espín, in their reading of the Guadalupe narrative and devotion, develop a pneumatological connection. Examining this pneumatological connection is the focus of the second section of this study. My own contribution stands on the shoulders of these five scholars (Miguel Sánchez, Luis Laso de la Vega, Jean-Pierre Ruiz, Timothy Matovina, and David Sánchez). In the third and final section, I offer a rereading of the Pentecost episodes with the purpose of illustrating how Guadalupe might be understood within the Pentecost trajectory.

GUADALUPE AND REVELATION 12

Over the course of almost two decades, three scholars, Jean-Pierre Ruiz, Timothy Matovina, and David Sánchez, have each examined Miguel Sánchez's published account of the apparition, *Imagen de la Virgen María*, with particular attention to his use of Revelation 12. As all note, this biblical connection has not been widely considered by U.S. Latino/a theologians.

In his study of 1999, "The Bible and U.S. Hispanic American Theological Discourse," biblical scholar Jean-Pierre Ruiz observes that U.S. Latino/a theologians, by and large, have not attended to, much less developed, the hermeneutical implications of reading the Guadalupe narrative as an intentional rereading of Revelation 12.[10] Ruiz makes clear that Miguel Sánchez used Revelation 12 to create a theological grounding and compelling narrative for the Guadalupe story, which previously existed only as an oral tradition.

According to tradition, Guadalupe appeared several times to Juan Diego on a hill named Tepeyac. Ruiz observes that Sánchez's narrative

> ... begins with an introductory exegesis of Revelation 12, followed by an extensive verse-by-verse exposition of correspondences between the biblical text and the Mexican Guadalupe. Next, Sánchez gives an account of the events at Tepeyac, a description of the image, and an elaborately detailed, phrase-by-phrase reading of Revelation 12, which simultaneously renders a "reading" of the hierophany at Tepeyac. . . . Thus, at great length, Sánchez proposes that the woman clothed with the sun of Revelation 12 corresponds to the image of Our Lady of Guadalupe, and that this chapter of the Apocalypse furnishes the key to understanding the apparitions and the image, and their significance for Mexico.[11]

Ruiz offers multiple examples of this Revelation 12-Guadalupe parallel, and then offers a further comparison with a second text, Laso de la Vega's account, the *Nican Mopohua*. This second account of the apparition is the one much more widely cited by U.S. Latino/a theologians today because it foregrounds the perspective of the indigenous. Throughout his chapter, Ruiz asks us to consider, what did each author intend with his version of the Guadalupe story? In terms of Sánchez's account, Ruiz shows how Sánchez wrote it with the purpose of affirming and furthering the goals of the *criollo* class, that is, those born in Mexico who were descendants of the conquistadores and, for the most part, comprised a class with land, money, and power. Thus, Sánchez did not intend for it to support the interests of the Nahuatl-speaking indigenous population in Mexico.[12]

The goal of this chapter (and several of his other publications), as Ruiz makes clear, is to call his readers' critical attention to the sociopolitical contexts in which biblical texts are read, interpreted, and received, especially since these are almost always separated from one another temporally, culturally, politically, etc.[13] Ruiz argues that the interpretation of biblical texts must be done in a manner that: (1) respects the integrity of an other's religious experience and traditions; (2) is open to new experience because it "can speak in ways that shed light on ancient texts, giving birth to fresh meanings";[14] (3) does not attempt to speak for an "other" as this bears the "potential for ideological manipulation";[15] and (4) is open to the possible "value and significance of popular readings of the Bible,"[16] since these too can help us better understand ourselves.

For well over two decades, theologian and historian Timothy Matovina has published books and many articles addressing the apparition of Guadalupe. However, his substantive engagement with Miguel Sánchez's work dates from his article of 2003, "Guadalupe at Calvary: Patristic Theology in Miguel

Sánchez's *Imagen de La Virgen María* (1648)."[17] Matovina observes that Sánchez was a well-educated patristic theologian and pastor, stating that "his primary concern was to examine the Guadalupe narrative and the evangelization of Mexico vis-à-vis the wider Christian tradition, particularly the writings of St. Augustine and other Church Fathers and the image of the 'woman clothed with the sun' in Revelation 12."[18] Throughout his article, Matovina provides a substantial analysis of the ways that Sánchez uses Revelation 12, noting that his central thesis identifies the woman in Revelation 12 as Mary and thus also as Guadalupe. This same woman is identified with the church as well.

From Matovina we learn that Sánchez's theological method imitates that of Augustine, "particularly through engaging biblical typologies and presuming the contemporary Church [certainly the Mexican Church] was the fulfillment of biblical prophecy."[19] Correspondingly, divine providence figures prominently in Sánchez's vision of Guadalupe. In point of fact, Sánchez maintains that Revelation 12 foretold Guadalupe's appearance in the wake of the brutal conquest of Mexico and, further, that this text described in detail the visual image of Guadalupe. As Matovina makes clear, even the conclusion of Sánchez's work draws on the last verses of Revelation 12 and the beginning of chapter 13, to reflect on "the ongoing cosmic battle for the soul of Mexico."[20] Moreover, Sánchez makes ample use of biblical analogies, drawing connections between the Guadalupe story and passages in Genesis related to the Garden of Eden, Noah, and the flood, as well as passages in Exodus related to Moses, particularly Mount Sinai and the Ark of the Covenant. Even though Revelation 12 is the foundational text employed, Matovina shows that Sánchez's use of biblical texts extends beyond this given text.

What Matovina intends is to advance a critical reappraisal of Sánchez's contribution for the purpose of deepening theological studies of Guadalupe. In particular he notes:

> Further study is needed to assess with greater precision Sánchez's knowledge and use of patristic sources, the extent of patristic influences on *Imagen de la Virgen María*, and how subsequent Guadalupe preachers and writers selectively employed, developed, and altered Sánchez's core ideas. . . . Just as the renewed study of the Church Fathers was a key intellectual precursor to the Second Vatican Council, the *ressourcement* of Guadalupan and other Latin American theological works is a crucial step in the project of developing theologies that are rooted both in the life and faith of Latino/Latina communities and in the wider Christian tradition.[21]

He observes that U.S. Latino/a theologians who write on Guadalupe, typically using the *Nican Mopohua* rather than Sánchez's work, nonetheless employ Sánchez's themes, whether they are conscious of doing so or not. From the study of Sánchez, theologians will glean an appreciation of the Guadalupe tradition as a model for adapting not only patristic thought "but also patristic theological methods to meet contemporary ecclesial and societal needs."[22] So, while Matovina's primary focus concerns "the knowledge and use of patristic sources," he likewise sees the study of Sánchez as essential to helping theologians consider more critically how to, and how not to, interpret what is transpiring in the world—past, present, or future—when considered in light of the biblical text and its context.

In 2008, scripture scholar David Sánchez published his book *From Patmos to the Barrio: Subverting Imperial Myths*. In this work, he develops a sustained analysis linking three historical moments that draw out the hermeneutical implications of the relationship between Revelation 12 and different forms of the Guadalupan myth. His thesis is that "people living on the margins of power—specifically in imperial, colonial, and neocolonial contexts—will challenge the centers of power in patterned ways over time and culture."[23] Beginning with the sources informing Revelation 12, David Sánchez shows how myths are developed by dominant power (colonial power) so as to legitimize their dominance and then picked up by the powerless (the colonized) in their resistance movements. The colonized appropriate a myth that seemingly supports the dominant and re-invent it, creating a countermyth for the purpose of subverting dominant power. David Sánchez draws out the ways we see this manifest in the Bible and in biblical interpretation, particularly in Revelation 12.

Using postcolonial theory, he shows how Revelation 12 is a countermyth, "a retelling, reconfiguration, and subversion of the Greco-Roman Dragon Slayer myth" which was central to Roman imperial power in the first century.[24] For example, Sánchez argues that during the colonial period, there was a myth advanced by Mexico's most prominent leaders, the *peninsulares*, namely, those born in Spain but living in Mexico and occupying the positions of highest power. Over time, this myth came to be identified with the Virgin of Remedios, a Spanish Marian devotion that gained prominence toward the end of the sixteenth century among the Spaniards living in Mexico. During the same time period, tensions deepened between the *peninsulares* and the *criollos* (Spaniards born in Mexico), one of whom was the theologian and pastor, Miguel Sánchez. The *criollos*' devotion to Guadalupe during this period grows. It was Miguel Sánchez who "planted that all-powerful ideological seed by subverting the very myth used to de-center him and other [*criollos*] of the Americas."

This, indeed, gives us a clue as to why Miguel Sánchez appropriated the text of Revelation 12 in his work. Revelation 12, like the countermythology of Miguel Sánchez in the *Imagen [de la Virgen María]*, sought to undermine not the structures of oppression but the ideologies that stood behind those structures."²⁵ What David Sánchez claims is that in Miguel Sánchez's *Imagen de la Virgen María* we find not the call to "outright rebellion" but instead "a more subtle and perduring form of resistance—ideological resistance."²⁶ While this is but one of several examples, it offers a clear representation of what David Sánchez is hoping to accomplish.

A fundamental goal for David Sánchez is to heighten our recognition of the ways that power remains deeply entrenched in the social order in the form of myths employed on behalf of power and, relatedly, to heighten our awareness of how readers are as important as texts in the endeavor to interpret. He argues, "The process of relocating our interpretive points of departure from texts to our distinctive social locations is not simply an intellectual enterprise but is the primary impetus for the construction of discourses that initiate the process of liberation and decolonization."²⁷ His aim is to interrogate "interpretations of the center" in a manner that exposes "oppression and misrepresentations,"²⁸ and by so doing to advance a more just world through support for socially situated knowing that makes greater human freedom possible.

In highlighting the work of these three scholars—Ruiz, Matovina, and (David) Sánchez—what becomes evident are some of the more prominent ways in which connections have been made in contemporary scholarship between Guadalupe and Revelation 12. Moreover, while Revelation 12, dating back to the work of Miguel Sánchez (1648), has been the foundational biblical text in the Guadalupe narrative, it is not the only biblical text employed by Miguel Sánchez or by other scholars in the intervening centuries.²⁹

GUADALUPE AND THE HOLY SPIRIT

Over the course of many years, Latino theologians, particularly Virgilio Elizondo and Orlando Espín, have explored the connection between Guadalupe and the Holy Spirit. Arguably, their writings reveal a strong allusion to a Guadalupe–Pentecost connection, even though this is not stated explicitly. Since my aim is to develop an explicit connection between Guadalupe and Pentecost, it is crucial to lay the groundwork for this in the contributions of Elizondo and Espín.

A Guadalupe–Holy Spirit connection is evident from the time of Elizondo's earliest work. In his 1978 dissertation, *Mestizaje*, Elizondo draws parallels between the calvary of the Mexican people at the hands of Cortés's conquest and the calvary of Jesus. He interprets Guadalupe as a resurrection experience, in which the death wish of indigenous Mexico becomes a life wish—that is, a desire not only to survive but to thrive. Guadalupe inaugurates the "glory of the birth of LA RAZA," states Elizondo.³⁰ If we believe that the Holy Spirit is the giver of life, as is professed in the Nicene Creed, then for Elizondo, Guadalupe clearly mediates the presence of the Holy Spirit. Inasmuch as Guadalupe embodies meaning at the level of symbol for both "Iberian Catholics and native Mexicans," she gave and gives life to a new community. Both the image and the narrative of Guadalupe seamlessly incorporate significant elements of Nahua and Catholic religious symbolism.

The "event of Guadalupe" is not only an event in 1531 but an event that continues and thrives in our own time among Mexicanas/os, Latinas/os, and other devotees from around the world. Elizondo contrasts the Spanish missionaries' narrow and dogmatic understanding of religious truth with that exemplified in the "event of Guadalupe." The event of Guadalupe refers to the experience of being moved by the image and/or text in a way that enhances one's faith and draws one into a closer relationship with God (conversion). In theological nomenclature, Elizondo's distinction may be described as the difference between *didache* or teaching (Spanish missionaries' approach) and *kerygma* or proclamation (event of Guadalupe).[31]

Elizondo describes the missionaries' style of evangelization as one of dominating and coercive practices, while the event of Guadalupe appealed to the people through a compelling and radiant beauty. As humans, we naturally desire beauty, "it feeds our hearts and souls," it compels us to it. For Elizondo, the event of Our Lady of Guadalupe offers us an experience of divine beauty, an experience which we joyfully and freely seek. *Flor y canto* (flower and song), an indigenous way of entering into divine truth, represents that which draws us and lifts our hearts. Thus, the event of Our Lady of Guadalupe extends to us "[t]he humanizing and liberating beauty of the divine experience"[32] Guadalupe continues to function as a symbol, says Elizondo, that animates the struggle for liberation and for new life, which is a primary attribute of the Holy Spirit.[33]

In *Guadalupe: Mother of a New Creation* (1997), Elizondo draws out many dimensions of the Guadalupe story that parallel Pentecost episodes in the book of Acts. In this book Elizondo identifies Guadalupe as an American Gospel but does not explicitly identify Guadalupe with Pentecost. Yet, given his reflections on her, there is a strong basis to link Guadalupe to Pentecost in his work. In great detail, he examines the multidimensional conversion and transformation of the church inaugurated by the Guadalupe apparition. Beginning with Juan Diego, it is the poor and rejected who initiate the conversion of the church as a whole, the conversion of the Spanish and the indigenous.[34] He writes:

> At Tepeyac no one is to be rejected. Tepeyac becomes the most sacred space of the Americas precisely because of the unlimited diversity of peoples who experience a common home there. Precisely because everyone is welcomed there

and experiences a sense of belonging, is listened to with compassion and senses the energy of true universal fellowship, the face of God is clearly seen while the heart of God is experienced intimately and tenderly. This is what makes Tepeyac so sacred—it is not a sacredness that scares, separates, and divides but the sacredness of the holiness of God that allures, brings together, and unifies.[35]

The Guadalupe story which takes place at Tepeyac, like the episodes of Pentecost, gives birth to a new way of being church. I hear echoes of Pentecost throughout Elizondo's claims.

While to date he has not developed this idea in a sustained manner, Orlando O. Espín has suggested that Guadalupe does not refer to Mary of Nazareth, the mother of Jesus, but rather to the Holy Spirit. He credits others with sharing this idea with him. In the introduction to one of his books and in a chapter of an anthology he co-edited, he explores what it means to associate Guadalupe with the Holy Spirit.[36] According to Espín:

> ... some of us have argued that it is time to look again at the Guadalupe apparition story and subsequent devotion from the perspective of pneumatology, with a careful analysis of the cultural, historical, and sociopolitical rootings of the symbols involved—including the very appropriation of the otherwise Spanish Marian symbols and categories in early colonial Mexico and thereafter. Perhaps it is time to seriously question if Guadalupe is (or has ever been) really Marian or is in fact pneumatological for the majority of Latinos/as. I am not suggesting that Mary is the Holy Spirit (a theologically impossible affirmation). I am, however, asking whether the Virgen of Guadalupe is Mary of Nazareth at all. Indeed, I am proposing that a pneumatological reading of the Guadalupe story and devotion would enrich a Latino/a theology of grace and sin (besides opening up important new vistas in mainstream Christian theologies of the Holy Spirit).[37]

While he advances a quite provocative insight, he does not sufficiently clarify how he would support his claim. What does it mean theologically to say that Guadalupe is not a Marian apparition? Granted that theologians, myself included, often extend their understanding of Guadalupe well beyond what is strictly Marian. Even so, that is not the same as severing the Guadalupe-Mary identification. According to tradition, devotion to Guadalupe began just after 1531, almost 500 years ago. With the contributions of Miguel Sánchez and Luis Laso de la Vega, we have an unambiguous written identification of Guadalupe with Mary, which was very likely part of an oral tradition that preceded their works.[38] To sever this identification would be a monumental theological and pastoral undertaking. What then is to be made of the long-standing effective history of devotees who understand Guadalupe to be

Marian? Although I would not dismiss Espín's approach, I am skeptical and think there may be other ways of proceeding.

Both Elizondo's and Espín's work highlight a serious challenge: the tension between, on the one hand, the extraordinary devotion of generations of Mexicans and Latinos/as to Guadalupe, a form of devotion that, some have argued, is only rightly directed to God; and, on the other hand, a fervent identification of Guadalupe with Mary all the while recognizing that Guadalupe-Mary is not God. How can this be understood other than as a dissonance between practice and belief? What to make of this theologically? If Guadalupe is pneumatologically significant, might thinking in terms of the "event of Guadalupe" hold promise? Indeed, the event of Guadalupe continues to occur time and again for believers who experience the sacred through Guadalupe. Might Guadalupe best be understood as one more of the many Pentecost episodes (plural) narrated in the book of Acts?

GUADALUPE AND PENTECOST

Pentecost may be reread in the narrative and event of Guadalupe because the book of Acts leaves this as a possibility and because Guadalupe resonates, at a fundamental level, with the biblical account of Pentecost. Clearly, this assertion builds on the work of Latino/a scholars, even though it is a claim that develops in an uncommon direction. This assertion likewise rests on the work of two scripture scholars, Earl Richard and Robert C. Tannehill, and their reading of Pentecost.[39] While I have thus far mentioned two versions of the Guadalupe narrative (Sánchez and Laso de la Vega) that overlap in many respects, here I draw on Laso de la Vega's *Nican Mopohua*, which is much more widely known. Guadalupe resonates with Pentecost on a thematic level and on a paradigmatic level as well.

In the study of Luke-Acts, scripture scholars rarely note that the Pentecost episode of Acts 2 "is not limited to the Jerusalem community;"[40] however, there are multiple manifestations of the Spirit, a pivotal point made by both Tannehill and Richard. In Luke-Acts, the Holy Spirit plays an increasingly significant role following Jesus' departure. In addition to Acts 2, other manifestations of the Holy Spirit take part in Pentecost, each playing a primary role in marking a beginning: among them, "4:31 (community at prayer), 8:14f. (Samaritan mission), 10-11 (Cornelius episode), 19:1f. (John's disciples), and Luke 3:21-22 (Jesus' baptism). Also important are the Spirit's coming upon Mary (Luke 1:35), the prophetic figures and disciples who are 'filled with the Spirit,' and Paul's reception of the Spirit (Acts 9:17)."[41] These manifestations establish a fundamental thematic pattern that is suggestive. As Richard observes: "The Pentecost theme acquires an iterative character and function; that is, the Spirit's manifestations participate, by their repetitive features, in the paradigmatic Pentecost experience and yet, through their unitive character, transcend this episode and represent the outpouring of the Sprit in the ends-days."[42] This pattern bears importance because it signals the possibility, well beyond what is recorded in Acts, for the outpouring of the Spirit in other situations in a manner in continuity with the Pentecost event of Acts 2. If the characteristics that distinguish Pentecost are present in Guadalupe, then might she be one of many manifestations of the Holy Spirit in continuity with Pentecost?

The most compelling argument may be found in the thematic parallels between Pentecost and the Guadalupe narrative as recorded in the *Nican mopohua*. Before Pentecost, the disciples of Jesus were filled with fear. The Romans had brutally crucified Jesus, the one in whom the disciples had placed their hopes and dreams for a better tomorrow. Even though Jesus had arisen from the dead, and even though he had appeared to them many times, still they knew fear. At Pentecost, that fear is transformed into courage and zeal for mission, accompanied by an inexorable awareness of God's abiding grace. The first verses of Acts 2:1-4 (NAB) read:

> When the time for Pentecost was fulfilled, they were all in one place together. And suddenly there came from the sky a noise like a strong driving wind, and it filled the entire house in which they were. Then there appeared to them tongues as of fire, which parted and came to rest on each one of them. And they were all filled with the Holy Spirit and began to speak in different tongues, as the Spirit enabled them to proclaim.

These verses record a radical transformation. Four prominent Pentecost themes, which Tannehill identifies and develops at length, are abundantly evident in Guadalupe: (1) promise and presence; (2) power and zeal for mission; (3) the movement from death to life; and (4) the gift of the Spirit is a progressive reality.

(1) Promise and Presence. Even before Pentecost, we learn from Jesus that the Spirit has been promised by God many times (Acts 1:4-5) and, later, that the Spirit will be poured out "on all flesh" (Acts 2:17). God has promised to send the Spirit; Jesus promises his followers the Spirit; and, even before Jesus, John the Baptist announces the promise of the Spirit. When Jesus shares this promise with his disciples, he tells them that this promised gift of the Spirit is imminent. In the Gospel of Luke and in the Book of Acts we learn that this promise is for the disciples and their children and beyond, meaning the gift of the Spirit will be poured out "on all flesh."[43]

Guadalupe can be identified as an American Pentecost because her image and story reflect the presence of the Spirit. Through her intercession, those devoted to her experience her presence as a consolation. She represents an ongoing gift. According to the *Nican Mopohua*, Guadalupe tells Juan Diego, an indigenous middle-aged man: "Listen and hear well in your heart, my most abandoned son: that which scares you and troubles you is nothing; do not let your countenance and heart be troubled; do not fear . . . sickness or anxiety. Am I not here, your mother? Are you not under my shadow and my protection? Am I not your source of life? Are you not in the hollow of my mantle where I cross my arms? Who else do you need?"[44] To this day, the original *tilma* (apron) that bears her image remains in the Basilica of Our Lady of Guadalupe in Mexico City. Many continue to seek her out and take comfort in her presence. In the Basilica, devotees often leave a memento (e.g., a lock of hair, an *exvoto-milagro* [a small metal medallion representing a healing], a picture, among other mementos) as a way of recognizing her constant presence.

(2) Power for Mission. At Pentecost, the gift of the Spirit is power for mission. The Spirit vigorously initiates and continually renews a zeal for the gospel mission. Indeed, the whole of the book of Acts addresses the overly abundant outpouring of the Spirit. The gift of the Spirit fuels a mission universal in scope, thus crossing racial, class, ethnic, religious, economic, and sexual orientation lines—in other words, all boundaries erected by human beings. It is mission directed at every nation under heaven. The coming of the Spirit effects an immediate result, namely a robust proclamation of God's presence which freely invites conversions in large numbers as well as generously gifts all with the powerful experience of God's grace.[45]

Guadalupe's image and narrative had a most inconspicuous beginning. Yet, over time her image and story gradually spread, exciting those who experienced it, and evoking an ever-increasing devoted following.[46] Why? Through the image, the indigenous, the mestizos, as well as the criollos began to see a future for themselves and their children. As the *Nican mopohua* illustrates, Guadalupe offered an image that all of these groups could identify with religiously, racially, culturally, linguistically, on every level. Even more profoundly, through Juan Diego, the Christian Catholic Church leadership came to know what it means to have a universal mission. Juan Diego helped the bishop to learn the universality of the mission of the Spirit. Guadalupe spoke to Juan Diego in a language and using a symbol system, *flor y canto* (flower and song), that was his own.[47] This generated a zealous power for mission.

(3) From Death to Life. After the Acts 2 account of Pentecost, the rest of the Book of Acts teaches us that the disciples' fear gives way to bold, zealous action. While fear deadens the soul, the gift of the Spirit melts fear and draws out zeal, energy for the future. The Spirit releases power for mission and mission offers a release from sin.[48] In Tannehill's words:

> God's transcendence is displayed in the world when a surprising grace or a surprising justice appears that transcends, and may contradict, human intentions and powers. The Pentecost speech [Peter's interpretation of Pentecost] is primarily the disclosure to its audience of God's surprising reversal of their intentions, for their rejection has ironically resulted in Jesus' exaltation as Messiah, spirit-giver, and source of repentance and forgiveness.[49]

This radical reversal, from death to life, from fear to bold zealous action, marks Pentecost.

How does Guadalupe generate energy and excitement? What does the *Nican Mopohua* suggest to us about how she turns a "death wish" into a "life wish"? Her image and narrative signal a new dawn, and a new awakening. Guadalupe recognized Juan Diego at the most fundamental level, and this recognition enabled belief in God in a way that was credible among the indigenous. This image did not obliterate the indigenous' drive for life but affirmed it. The image and the narrative transformed despair into hope for new life. The indigenous experienced a kind of resurrection. The indigenous and the Spanish came to see new possibilities, in that she spoke and speaks to both. Both see themselves in her image.

Some view her skin color as that of a Spaniard; others, as that of an indigenous person; and still others, as that of a mestiza, a mixture of the two—a reality that was only beginning to emerge in the Americas. She is said to have appeared ten years after the brutal conquest. As a mestiza, she signals the resurrection and birth of a new people and a future life for the indigenous, some of whom believed they would be obliterated. In addition, the Guadalupe image takes in the whole cosmos, that is, the stars of her mantle, the rays of the sun around her image, the moon upon which she stands—all these representing prominent gods of the Nahuas. These gods are not obliterated in her image, they continue in the new age that is dawning. This representation of the Nahuas gods (in the image of Guadalupe) becomes part of a new cycle. An indigenous hieroglyph on her dress above her womb indicates that she is pregnant and carrying the center of the universe within her, an image with arguably Christological significance. This image ushers in a new age, recognized as the Sixth Sun by the indigenous.[50]

(4) The Gift of the Spirit is a Progressive Reality. The divine promise of the Spirit as gift is a progressive reality, one that continues well beyond the biblical period.[51] While Pentecost places the gift of the Spirit under a magnifying glass, the Pentecost episode of Acts 2 is not the final realization of this gift. It is an ever-expanding process. The Gospel of Luke and the Acts of the Apostles teach us that the coming of the Spirit is to be "understood as a divine promise that is realized progressively, but only partially, in Acts as a whole."[52] The Book of Acts offers only a partial account of the gift of the Spirit. As Tannehill rightly argues, "The narrative encourages belief that God's promise to pour out the Spirit 'on all flesh' is meaningful and relevant even though it exceeds present experience, for it can be linked to a series of new breakthroughs that move toward the final goal."[53]

What if Guadalupe is one of these present breakthroughs? Guadalupe may well be an American Pentecost, because many experience her as faithful to her promise of presence, as stirring them to mission beyond their initial conception, and as transforming what is dead within them and bringing forth new life. Guadalupe may be an example of the gift of the Spirit as a progressive reality. In her devotees, she draws forth the will to live and thrive, along with the belief that life is worth living even in the face of evidence to the contrary. Guadalupe encourages Christian believers to hope. She invites us to see, in the human lives that God restores now, evidence that God's reign is at hand and that the power of the Spirit lives. Pentecost resounds in Guadalupe.

NOTES

1. Paul Tillich, *Dynamics of Faith* (New York: Harper Torchbooks, 1957), 42–43.
2. Gerald O'Collins, SJ and Daniel Kendall, SJ, *The Bible for Theology: Ten Principles for the Theological Use of Scripture* (New York: Paulist Press, 1997), 7.
3. I thank Dr. Mary Rose D'Angelo for her insightful reading of this text and for her suggestions. I am likewise grateful to Dr. Christopher Matthews, Dr. Richard Lennan, and Dr. Francine Cardman for their suggestions.
4. Josiah Royce, *The Sources of Religious Insight* (Washington, D.C.: Catholic University of America Press, 2001 [1912]), 17.
5. O'Collins and Kendall, *The Bible for Theology*, 6–39.
6. O'Collins and Kendall, *The Bible for Theology*, 8–11.
7. O'Collins and Kendall, *The Bible for Theology*, 27–28.
8. Timothy Matovina, "Guadalupe at Calvary: Patristic Theology in Miguel Sánchez's Imagen de La Virgen María (1648)," *Theological Studies* 64:4 (December 2003): 796.

9. While tradition dates the apparition of La Virgen de Guadalupe to Juan Diego at Tepeyac in December of 1531, the accounts of this apparition do not appear in print until 1648. See Miguel Sánchez, *Imagen de la Virgen María, Madre de Dios de Guadalupe: Milagrosamente aparecida en la ciudad de México: Celebrada en su historia, con la profecía del capítulo doce del Apocalipsis* (México City: Viuda de Bernardo Calderón, 1648). Reprinted in Ernesto de la Torre Villar and Ramiro Navarro de Anda, eds., *Testimonios históricos Guadalupanos* (México City: Fondo de Cultura Económica, 1982), 152–267. In 1649 Luis Laso de la Vega published another account of the apparition commonly known as the *Nican mopohua*. *Nican mopohua* literally means "Here is recounted" in Nahuatl. Nahuatl is the language of the Nahuas, a tribe of Meso-American indigenous people of sixteenth-century Mexico. They are commonly, but erroneously, identified as the Aztecs. For an English translation of the *Nican mopohua*, see *The Story of Guadalupe: Luis Laso de la Vega's 'Huei Tlamahuiçoltica' of 1649*, ed. and trans. Lisa Sousa, Stafford Poole, and James Lockhart, Nahuatl Studies Series 5 (Stanford: Stanford University Press, 1998). Generally speaking, scholars today recognize Laso de la Vega as the author of the *Nican mopohua*. However, the origins of the narrative account have been and continue to be disputed with at least three versions, each attributed to different authors, namely, Luis Laso de la Vega, Miguel Sánchez, and Antonio Valeriano. For a discussion of the different versions and the political interests that each furthered, see D. A. Brading, *Mexican Phoenix: Our Lady of Guadalupe: Image and Tradition across Five Centuries* (Cambridge, UK: Cambridge University Press, 2001), 58–70, 81–95, 129–32, 273–80, 342–60.

10. Jean-Pierre Ruiz, "The Bible and U.S. Hispanic American Theological Discourse: Lessons from a Non-Innocent History," in *From the Heart of Our People: Latino/a Explorations in Catholic Systematic Theology*, ed. Orlando O. Espín and Miguel H. Díaz (Maryknoll, NY: Orbis Books, 1999), 100–120.

11. Ruiz, "Bible and U.S. Hispanic American Theological Discourse," 106.

12. Ruiz, "Bible and U.S. Hispanic American Theological Discourse," 107.

13. For example, see Jean-Pierre Ruiz, *Readings from the Edges: The Bible & People on the Move* (Maryknoll, NY: Orbis Books, 2011); Jean-Pierre Ruiz, "Reading between the Lines: Toward a Latino/a (Re)configuration of Scripture and Tradition," in *Futuring Our Past: Explorations in the Theology of Tradition*, ed. Orlando O. Espín and Gary Macy (Maryknoll, NY: Orbis Books, 2006), 83–112.

14. Ruiz, "The Bible and U.S. Hispanic American Theological Discourse," 115.

15. Ruiz, "The Bible and U.S. Hispanic American Theological Discourse," 116.

16. Ruiz, "The Bible and U.S. Hispanic American Theological Discourse," 116.

17. Timothy Matovina, "Guadalupe at Calvary," 795–811; "Theologies of Guadalupe: From Spanish Colonial Era to Pope John Paul II," *Theological Studies* 70(1) (March 2009): 61–91; Timothy Matovina, "The Origins of the Guadalupe Tradition in Mexico," *The Catholic Historical Review* 100(2) (Spring 2014): 243–270.

18. Matovina, "Guadalupe at Calvary," 797.

19. Matovina, "Guadalupe at Calvary," 801.

20. Matovina, "Guadalupe at Calvary," 806, 801–805.

21. Matovina, "Guadalupe at Calvary," 809, 810.
22. Matovina, "Guadalupe at Calvary," 811.
23. David A. Sánchez, *Patmos to the Barrio: Subverting Imperial Myths.* (Minneapolis, MN: Fortress Press, 2008): 4.
24. Sánchez, *Patmos to the Barrio*, 5–6.
25. Sánchez, *Patmos to the Barrio*, 74.
26. Sánchez, *Patmos to the Barrio*, 75.
27. Sánchez, *Patmos to the Barrio*, 124–125.
28. Sánchez, *Patmos to the Barrio*, 125.
29. See Matovina, "Theologies of Guadalupe: From Spanish Colonial Era to Pope John Paul II."
30. Virgilio Elizondo, *Mestizaje: The Dialectic of Cultural Birth and the Gospel* (San Antonio, TX: Mexican American Cultural Center, 1978), 422.
31. For a discussion of *kerygma*, see Rudolph Bultmann, *Kerygma and Myth: A Theological Debate*, ed. Hans Werner Bartsch, trans. Reginald Horace Fuller (New York: Harper & Row 1961).
32. Virgilio Elizondo, *Guadalupe: Mother of the New Creation* (Maryknoll, NY: Orbis Books, 1997), 72.
33. Elizondo, *Mestizaje*, 422–24.
34. Elizondo, *Guadalupe: Mother of the New Creation*, 59, 84–97, 102, 109, 114, 120.
35. Ibid., 112–13.
36. Orlando O. Espín, "An Exploration into the Theology of Grace and Sin," in *From the Heart of Our People: Latino/a Explorations In Catholic Systematic Theology*, ed. Orlando O. Espín and Miguel H. Díaz, (Maryknoll, NY: Orbis Books, 1999), 137–40; Orlando O. Espín, "Introduction," in *The Faith of the People: Theological Reflections on Popular Catholicism* (Maryknoll, NY: Orbis Books, 1997), 6–10.
37. Espín, "An Exploration into the Theology of Grace and Sin," 138.
38. For a discussion of the oral tradition, see Matovina, "The Origins of the Guadalupe Tradition in Mexico," 243–270.
39. Earl Richard, "Pentecost as a Recurrent Theme in Luke-Acts," in *New Views on Luke and Acts*, ed. Earl Richard, 133–149 (Collegeville, MN: Liturgical, 1990); Robert C. Tannehill, *The Narrative Unity of Luke-Acts: A Literary Interpretation.* Vol. 2: *The Acts of the Apostles* (Minneapolis: Fortress Press, 1986).
40. Richard, "Pentecost as a Recurrent Theme in Luke-Acts," 133.
41. Richard, "Pentecost as a Recurrent Theme in Luke-Acts," 135.
42. Richard, "Pentecost as a Recurrent Theme in Luke-Acts," 135.
43. Tannehill, *Narrative Unity of Luke-Acts*, 12, 30.
44. Elizondo, *Mother of the New Creation*, 15–16.
45. Tannehill, *Narrative Unity of Luke-Acts*, 12, 26–30, 39.
46. Matovina, "The Origins of the Guadalupe Tradition in Mexico," 243–270.
47. See the following: Elizondo, *Guadalupe: Mother of the New Creation*; Matovina, "Guadalupe at Calvary"; and Matovina, "Theologies of Guadalupe."
48. Tannehill, *Narrative Unity of Luke-Acts*, 29.

49. Tannehill, *Narrative Unity of Luke-Acts*, 37.
50. Elizondo, *Guadalupe: Mother of the New Creation*.
51. Elizondo, *Guadalupe: Mother of the New Creation*, 13, 29–33.
52. Elizondo, *Guadalupe: Mother of the New Creation*, 29–30.
53. Elizondo, *Guadalupe: Mother of the New Creation*, 31.

BIBLIOGRAPHY

Brading, D. A. *Mexican Phoenix: Our Lady of Guadalupe: Image and Tradition across Five Centuries*. Cambridge, UK: Cambridge University Press, 2001.

Bultmann, Rudolph. *Kerygma and Myth: A Theological Debate*. Ed. Hans Werner Bartsch. Trans. Reginald Horace Fuller. New York: Harper & Row 1961.

de la Torre Villar, Ernesto and Ramiro Navarro de Anda, eds. *Testimonios históricos Guadalupanos*. México City: Fondo de Cultura Económica, 1982.

Elizondo, Virgilio. *Guadalupe: Mother of the New Creation*. Maryknoll, NY: Orbis Books, 1997.

———. *Mestizaje: The Dialectic of Cultural Birth and the Gospel*. San Antonio, TX: Mexican American Cultural Center, 1978.

Espín, Orlando O. "An Exploration into the Theology of Grace and Sin." In *From the Heart of Our People: Latino/a Explorations In Catholic Systematic Theology*, edited by Orlando O. Espín and Miguel H. Díaz, 153–171. Maryknoll, NY: Orbis Books, 1999.

———. *The Faith of the People: Theological Reflections on Popular Catholicism*. Maryknoll, NY: Orbis Books, 1997.

Matovina, Timothy. "Guadalupe at Calvary: Patristic Theology in Miguel Sánchez's Imagen de La Virgen María (1648)." *Theological Studies* 64(4) (December 2003): 795–811.

———. "The Origins of the Guadalupe Tradition in Mexico." *The Catholic Historical Review* 100(2) (Spring 2014): 243–270.

———. "Theologies of Guadalupe: From Spanish Colonial Era to Pope John Paul II." *Theological Studies* 70(1) (March 2009): 61–91.

O'Collins, Gerard SJ and Daniel Kendall, SJ. *The Bible for Theology: Ten Principles for the Theological Use of Scripture*. New York: Paulist Press, 1997.

Richard, Earl. "Pentecost as a Recurrent Theme in Luke-Acts." In *New Views on Luke and Acts*, edited by Earl Richard, 133–149. Collegeville, MN: Liturgical, 1990.

Royce, Josiah. *The Sources of Religious Insight*. Washington, D.C.: Catholic University of America Press, 2001 [1912].

Ruiz, Jean-Pierre. "The Bible and U.S. Hispanic American Theological Discourse: Lessons from a Non-Innocent History." In *From the Heart of Our People: Latino/a Explorations in Catholic Systematic Theology*, edited by Orlando O. Espín and Miguel H. Díaz, 100–120. Maryknoll, NY: Orbis Books, 1999.

———. "Reading between the Lines: Toward a Latino/a (Re)configuration of Scripture and Tradition." In *Futuring Our Past: Explorations in the Theology of*

Tradition, edited by Orlando O. Espín and Gary Macy, 83–112. Maryknoll, NY: Orbis Books, 2006.

———. *Readings from the Edges: The Bible & People on the Move*. Maryknoll, NY: Orbis Books, 2011.

Sánchez, David A. *Patmos to the Barrio: Subverting Imperial Myths*. Minneapolis, MN: Fortress Press, 2008.

Sánchez, Miguel. *Imagen de la Virgen María, Madre de Dios de Guadalupe: Milagrosamente aparecida en la ciudad de México: Celebrada en su historia, con la profecía del capítulo doce del Apocalipsis*. México City: Viuda de Bernardo Calderón, 1648.

Sousa, Lisa, Stafford Poole, and James Lockhart, eds. and trans. *The Story of Guadalupe: Luis Laso de la Vega's 'Huei Tlamahuiçoltica' of 1649*. Nahuatl Studies Series 5. Stanford: Stanford University Press, 1998.

Tannehill, Robert C. *The Narrative Unity of Luke-Acts: A Literary Interpretation*. Vol. 2: *The Acts of the Apostles*. Minneapolis: Fortress Press, 1986.

Tillich, Paul. *Dynamics of Faith*. New York: Harper Torchbooks, 1957.

Chapter 9

Liberation Hermeneutics in Jewish, Christian, and Muslim Exegesis

A Latino/a Perspective

Rubén Rosario Rodríguez

Interaction between the world's major religions is an inescapable fact of life in today's globalized societies. Therefore, dogmatic reflection demands clarity on the relationship of Christianity to other faiths. Judaism, Christianity, and Islam share a broad range of cultural and historical influences, but they also share a history of religious exclusivism manifested as political violence. Despite this long and troubled history of conflict, however, the shared historical and cultural ties between Judaism, Christianity, and Islam facilitate comparative theological work.[1]

As a Latino/a theologian employing a liberation hermeneutic, I confront religiously motivated political violence with the claim that the three great monotheistic traditions share an underlying belief that God requires liberation for the oppressed, justice for the victims, and—most demanding of all—love for the political enemy. While attempting a comparative theology in conversation with Judaism and Islam, this chapter is a work of Christian theology and as such seeks neither to convert the other nor to reinterpret the other's religious traditions from a Christian perspective. My more modest goal is to model religious pluralism and cooperation by retrieving distinctly Christian sources that nurture tolerance and facilitate coexistence with other religions. The strategy adopted in this work seeks to recover texts within the Christian biblical tradition that foster dialogue and patience in the midst of religious conflict as a foundation for mutually beneficial discourse with Judaism and Islam.

AN EXERCISE IN COMPARATIVE THEOLOGY

Comparative theology, a growing sub-discipline within Christian theology, is defined in diverse ways, but always distinguished by a methodological commitment to the thoughtful consideration of and engagement with other religious traditions. It is differentiated from the theology of religions, broadly understood as reflection on the reality of other religions in light of the particular claims of a particular faith, because it engages in intellectual reflection on God from an explicitly pluralistic perspective by affirming a range of theological perspectives, even while granting primacy to one particular understanding of God. In other words, the theology of religions approach views the reality of religious pluralism as a challenge to the internal coherence of exclusivist theological claims and attempts to account for pluralism through internal theological rationalization.

A normative assumption of comparative theology is that theology is inherently hermeneutical and that a primary task of theologians is to interpret the truth claims of a religious tradition for a particular time and place. Accordingly, this work embraces a model of comparative theology that presumes we can know God better by studying traditions in their particularity, while asserting that no single theological interpretation of divine revelation can claim absolute authority over another. As such, comparative theology is a constructive enterprise grounded in a particular confessional faith perspective, yet engaged in thorough comparative analysis of two or more religious traditions, moving beyond a simple comparison of doctrines toward a critical reconstruction of a tradition's own doctrines as a direct result of this comparative work.[2]

Without postulating a neutral, confession-less conception of Ultimate Reality that undermines the foundational truth claims of traditional theologies—such as the uniqueness of Christ in the doctrine of the Incarnation or the Qur'an's affirmation that "there is no god except the one God" (5:73)[3]—a comparative theology requires a methodological humility that recognizes in other religions "the truth that is God, insofar as this can be apprehended by a faith that seeks understanding."[4]

A major assumption of this investigation is that underlying all three monotheistic faiths is some form of the doctrine of "revelation," a technical term for the concept that knowledge of God originates in a divine act whereby something previously unknown (or ambiguously apprehended) about God is disclosed, along with the personal assurance of faith that the content of this revelation is reliable. In all three Abrahamic faiths, the transmission of this revealed message occurs via the medium of sacred texts, grounded in the theological claim that these texts are uniquely related to God in both origin and normativity, and thus authoritative for shaping worship, communal life, and moral behavior. Religious traditions preserve collections of "holy scripture," not just as narratives about past events important for the community's identity, nor merely as classic works of human literary creativity, but because they believe that the human authors of these texts convey a divinely generated communication.

The doctrine of revelation implies some form of the doctrine of divine hiddenness (*Deus absconditus*), which states that if God exists, God does not make this existence sufficiently clear and available to all. According to seventeenth-century philosopher and mathematician, Blaise Pascal, God remains hidden in order to nurture the virtue of humility as a necessary first step on the path toward wisdom: "God being thus hidden, any religion that does not say that God is hidden is not true, and any religion that does not explain why does not instruct. Ours does all this. *Verily thou art a God that hidest thyself.*"[5] Pascal says God is hidden not just because God cannot be grasped by our senses but also because God chooses to hide from those who seek power, status, and dominance over others—for knowledge of God can give little satisfaction to those who desire worldly power. This latter judgment even includes those who seek to know God solely through reason and intellect.

Faith is God's chosen medium for knowing and engaging humanity. While reason enables one to know that God exists from the beauty, complexity, and order of creation, knowing God as a rational possibility is not the same as knowing God intimately through faith: "God wishes to move the will rather than the mind. Perfect clarity would help the mind and harm the will. Humble their pride."[6] Therefore, whether in Judaism, Christianity, or Islam, some variance of the doctrine of the hiddenness of God leads to the conclusion that the full mystery of God cannot be contained by human theological formulations.[7]

This investigation presumes that the Abrahamic religions affirm belief in one God and that this God has chosen to reveal God's self in distinct and culturally particular, though not mutually exclusive, ways. Despite tragic histories in which missionary and proselytizing theologies rationalized political violence, all three Abrahamic religions share a more fundamental theological belief—the hiddenness and mystery of the revealed God—that enables genuine peaceful discourse between the religions. If God is ultimately understood as mystery—a mystery whose truth is known only through an act of divine self-revelation (whether mediated through Moses, Jesus, or Muhammad)—then the sacred scriptures of each tradition are most properly understood as a *human* witness to a divine act of revelation. The implications for comparative theology arising from these two doctrines—revelation and the hiddenness of God—coupled with the limits these doctrines place on human knowledge of God and God's will for humankind cannot be overstated.

WHY LIBERATION HERMENEUTICS?

In the North American context, U.S. Latino/a theology stands as a vibrant example of a contextual theology employing liberation hermeneutics in articulating an alternative form of Western Christianity in which the particularities of culture are respected, yet no single cultural manifestation of Christianity becomes normative for all Christians. Here, I introduce critical issues raised by U.S. Latino/a theologians on the subject of biblical hermeneutics, identify some of the chief contributors to this discussion, and synthesize major points of agreement for a distinctively Latino/a theology of liberation as a point of departure for articulating a comparative theology encompassing Jewish, Christian, and Islamic perspectives. By affirming that these particular experiences, cultural contexts, and traditions of interpretation play crucial roles in theological construction,[8] nascent theological movements like U.S. Latino/a theology ably demonstrate how the driving concerns of Europe and North America—atheism and secularization—differ greatly from the issues motivating the majority of Christians in the world.

Based on a 2007 Pew Research Center study, the growth of the U.S. Hispanic population has transformed North American religion, with Latino/as accounting for over 35 percent of the Roman Catholic Church in the United States and two-thirds of Latino/as (68 percent) identifying themselves as Roman Catholics.[9] The second largest Latino/a Christian group is evangelical Protestants who comprise an estimated 15 percent of the U.S. Hispanic population. While the Hispanic presence in North America predates the founding of the United States, Latino/a theological voices within the church and the academy have been marginalized—even silenced—for much of this history. Thus, while properly located within the Western Christian tradition, U.S. Latino/a theology has emerged as a critique from the margins, questioning historically, culturally, and ethnically dominant forms of Christianity.

Liberation theologies set aside all pretense of "impartiality" by arguing that Christians are called to make a preferential option for the poor and marginalized because in the scriptures God acts on behalf of the weak and abused of human history. This reading of scripture leads the church to make political commitments in solidarity with the oppressed, seeking the historical transformation of oppressive situations and social orders. Epistemologically, liberation theology recognizes that all theological reflection is contextual—inevitably intertwined with the interests and desires of a particular culture, ethnic group, or social class—and cautions that theological traditions have often been used to legitimate oppression. Therefore, there exists a methodological commitment to a "hermeneutics of suspicion" as a check upon the tendency of ideology and tradition to distort truth.

In the North American context, the voices of U.S. Latino/a theologians provide an alternative to the dominant perspectives within the academy and the church. The experience of marginalization has led Latino/a theologians to build coalitions and work in solidarity to articulate a collaborative, ecumenical, and multicultural theology. Certain recurring themes within the work of Latino/a theologians locate this movement at the margins—yet still within—the Western Christian tradition.

Latino/a Theology: Recurring Themes

First, U.S. Latino/a theologians identify *revelation* as the primary source of Christian theology. Specifically, the ultimate source of Christian faith and Christian doctrine is the man named Jesus, known through the witness of the New Testament. Implied in this affirmation, however, is the recognition that the scriptures are not the *unmediated* word of God, but a *human* witness to the revelation of God in the man Jesus, called the Christ of God. Thus, while the New Testament is a reliable—even inerrant—witness to God's historical self-revelation, "the same cannot be said for any interpretation of the Bible."[10] Such a liberative reading "takes the Bible into its own hands and away from those in control of the present order, reading it from its own perspective rather than from the perspective of the powerful."[11]

Second, U.S. Latino/a theologies affirm the role of *culture* as an important source for theology. The Christian faith is preserved in the collective memory of the people of God in solidarity with the historical witness of the New Testament, embraced as the foundational, normative narrative about the life, ministry, death, and resurrection of Jesus. However, this witness does not stand outside or above culture but is revealed in the midst of culture. In other words, there is no irreconcilable gap between God's act of self-revelation and humanity's capacity to understand and obey this revelation. For revelation, "in order to be claimed as revelation, must also be a human cultural event."[12]

Not surprisingly, the Incarnation becomes a central locus of Latino/a theological reflection: "God encounters us through humanity, acting in its midst. Hispanics identify deeply with Jesus, not because of his divinity, but because of his humanity. In Jesus, God takes on a face of flesh and bone. Such a God we can understand; and we know that he can understand us, too."[13] The hermeneutics of liberation that inform and guide U.S. Latino/a theology discloses an intimate relationship between the God of the Bible and the people of God such that the people encountered in the Bible are not historically or culturally distant but are received as "fellow sufferers, fellow pilgrims or sojourners, fellow visionaries."[14]

Third, a point of reference for Latino/a theologizing is *popular religion*, defined as the concrete religious practices of the people of God arising independently of church teaching and discipline, often in resistance to the institutional church. Consequently, Latino/a theology not only affirms the scriptures and official tradition as reliable sources of God's self-revelation but also the popular beliefs and practices of the laity as vessels for the Holy Spirit (Joel 2:28; Acts 2:1-13).

Due to its roots in Latin American history and culture, Latino/a Christianity in the United States has been indelibly shaped by the Iberian Catholic conquest of the New World in the fifteenth and sixteenth centuries. Therefore, the syncretistic religious practices of the people of Latin America, which combine the Christian symbols and rituals of the Iberian Catholic conquerors with indigenous forms of spirituality as well as the religions of African slaves, are an important resource for understanding Latino/a Christianity.

Ultimately, despite tensions between popular religion and official tradition, a dialogical relationship exists between church hierarchy and the people, through which Latino/as have "managed to preserve and re-interpret significant elements of their shared worldview" while also disseminating "many of the doctrinal contents of popular Catholicism, though sufficiently adapted (*and* concealed) in forms acceptable to the modern ecclesiastical realities."[15]

Fourth, while U.S. Latino/a theology has consistently critiqued culturally dominant Christian traditions, Latino/a theologians also affirm the normative role of *tradition* in Christian theology. As demonstrated by its emphasis on popular religion, U.S. Latino/a theology occupies the "borderlands" between official church structures and popular practices, yet Latino/a theologians struggle to affirm both their inherited confessional commitments and their distinctly Latino/a forms of piety.

Again, a hermeneutics of liberation informs Latino/a theological reflection on tradition reception, with the understanding that what is transmitted as tradition "is," in the words of Orlando Espín, "what one Christian community, though not necessarily another, decided was more important or indispensable. All Christian communities, aware of it or not, choose what they think is most necessary from a wider pool of contents witnessed and traditioned to them by others."[16] Latino/a theology concedes the interested perspective of every theological tradition and encourages intersubjective conversation as a corrective against the tendency to universalize particular points of view, thus viewing theology as an inherently communal and discursive practice.

Fifth, and finally, a concern uniting Latino/a theologies is a commitment to *liberative social praxis*. Christian ethics from a Latino/a perspective begins with the preferential option for the poor: an intentional act of solidarity with, by, and for the poor, marginalized, and disenfranchised in society. It should be noted that the term "preference" in the phrase "preferential option for the poor" as used by liberation theologians is not the primary dictionary definition of "preference" as "favor shown to one person or thing over another or others." Rather, the language of the Latin American Bishops' statement, at the Second Episcopal Conference in 1968, Medellín employs the legal definition of the term, meaning "a prior right or claim to something" (*Oxford English Dictionary*). In other words, the use of the word preferential is not intended to mean that God loves the poor more; rather, because of their immediate and undeniable suffering, the church must give *priority* to the needs of the poor.

Not only does this faith commitment entail a critique of the dominant political and economic structures, it also questions the dominant European and North American paradigms governing the academic and public conversation on pressing social issues. The problem with this dominant discourse is that it perpetuates the metanarrative of a supposedly color-blind, universal, and objective ethical norm. Such hermeneutical naïveté fails to account for the dominant culture's own biases and prejudices or its role in marginalizing—even repressing—minority views. However, as De La Torre argues, "marginalized communities of color have long recognized that no ethical perspective is value free. The subjectivity of Eurocentric ethical thought can be lifted by the academy to universal objectivity because the academy retains the power to define a reality that secures and protects their scholastic privilege."[17] Striving for concrete and attainable social justice, Latino/a theological reflection begins within the social, historical, and cultural context of Latino/a Christianity grounded in the day-to-day life experience of Latino/as attempting to live the Christian Gospel in a society that to this day is still defined in terms of racial, gender, economic, and ethnic inequalities.

Latino/a Theology: Transformative Social Praxis and the Biblical Tradition

Justo L. González, an ordained Methodist minister, historian, and theologian, stands as one of the chief progenitors of Latino/a theology in the United States. In González's analysis, two major themes unite the Latino/a theology movement in the United States: (1) the socio-historical context of Latino/as in the United States, described as a community "in exile," as a point of origin for theological reflection and (2) a commitment to resist European and North American cultural hegemony by articulating contextualized theologies committed to liberative social transformation.[18]

As the theology of an exiled people, Latino/a theology is grounded in hope—not an eschatological, future-directed panacea—but hope as a motivating, God-given promise to work with humanity for a more just tomorrow. Consequently, as the theology of an alien and exploited people trapped in a daily struggle for survival, Latino/a theology defines liberation in concrete historical terms with tangible social change as its goal. However, this commitment to transformative social praxis does not merely arise from within the Latino/a experience of marginalization and exploitation but is interwoven into the Latino/a reception of the Christian biblical tradition.

This methodological commitment leads to the realization that the social context of many biblical narratives mirrors contemporary Latino/a experiences of dislocation and exile (along with the social injustices that accompany such conditions). In other words, Latino/a readings of the Bible resonate with God's preferential option for the poor and marginalized as illustrated in the Exodus narrative, the prophetic literature, and the preaching of Jesus, mainly because the liberative dimension is *already* present within the biblical canon as a core component of God's self-revelation. Thus, when the church embraces a reading of the Bible from the perspective of an exiled community, it can overcome the temptation to manipulate the reading of sacred texts in implicit support of an unjust status quo and enact the biblical imperative for justice and peace in all human affairs. Such a liberative reading also resists the dominant academic and ecclesial narratives that claim objective detachment and universality of truth claims by emphasizing the perspectival nature of all biblical interpretations.

THE PROPHET JONAH: A CASE STUDY IN COMPARATIVE LIBERATIVE HERMENUTICS[19]

One avenue for furthering religious pluralism and tolerance is to utilize justice as a religious norm that transcends confessional particularity, thereby providing some standard the various religions can employ in evaluating their own truth claims as well as those of others.[20] This approach recognizes that genuine pluralism depends on free and mutually beneficial dialogue between participants and argues that so long as certain political and economic inequalities persist, pluralism remains a chimera.[21] As Mark Heim observed, however, employing justice as a transcultural norm raises its own set of problems: "What constitutes injustice, what counts as removing it, and what will actually affect the removal are all matters over which we know there are the most vehement disagreements."[22]

Rather than positing a universal standard of justice for evaluating all religious claims, my goals are more humble and limited in scope. On the assumption that it is more productive to engage in comparative theological discourse where multiple shared norms already exist, I limit my comparative study to the three Abrahamic religions. Without dismissing the possibility of a comparative theology between theistic and nontheistic religions, this investigation simply proposes a case study between the three Abrahamic religions—given that they share so much scripturally, culturally, and even doctrinally—as a means of testing the value of utilizing justice as a norm for comparative theology.

Liberation theology emphasizes orthopraxis (correct action) over orthodoxy (correct belief), thereby judging a religious tradition's core teachings by how well that tradition embodies the moral demands of its theological doctrines. This stands in contrast with more spiritualized readings of the Christian tradition that focus on a person's individual relationship to God in isolation from the communal context in which human life is lived and faith experienced. This balancing of belief with praxis is grounded in the religion of the Hebrew Bible, especially the admonition of the prophets, who equated genuine worship of YHWH with maintaining just social relations: "What does the Lord require of you but to do justice, and to love kindness, and to walk humbly with your God?" (Mic 6:8, NRSV).

Theologically, liberationists define injustice and oppression as a breach of communion with God and with one another; this presumes that humanity is created for communion. Whatever fractures the fundamental community of humanity in and with God is sin. Conversely, restoration of community brought about by divine forgiveness cannot exist without justice. In other words, faith communities cannot enact forgiveness by ignoring sin, since genuine repentance and transformation are demanded by and result from divine forgiveness. While the gospel cannot be reduced to justice, there is no understanding of the gospel that does not include justice.

The same can be said, *mutatis mutandis*, about Judaism and Islam. In other words, a liberationist emphasis on orthopraxis—specifically praxis that liberates the oppressed and establishes social justice—does not reject traditional spiritualities, or the more contemplative, even mystical, dimensions of faith. Rather, liberation spirituality understands that proper accounting of justice is grounded in the gift of divine forgiveness, and therefore refuses to sever love of God from love of neighbor.

This investigation interprets the book of the prophet Jonah as a paradigmatic narrative for addressing religious pluralism and political violence. Jonah, a canonical text for both Judaism and Christianity, is also important in Islam: it is the only one of the twelve Minor Prophets of the Hebrew Scriptures/Old Testament to be named in the Qur'an. This brief but revered narrative is a prophetic text whose central protagonist is a Jewish nationalist who reluctantly delivers a warning from YHWH to the imperial occupiers of Israel, the Assyrians, then becomes angry with God for showing mercy toward them. The presence of this surprisingly subversive text within the canon destabilizes the pervasive nationalism of the Hebrew Scriptures and provides a paradigm for resisting the violence that often typifies interactions between competing religious traditions.

Jonah as Unique among the Prophetic Writings

The book of Jonah is unique within the prophetic writings of the Hebrew Bible.[23] First, unlike the other books of the prophets, this book is not a collection of the prophet's sayings but a collection of narrative vignettes about Jonah. Though he is never called a prophet in the story, tradition has linked the character of "Jonah" in this narrative to the historical prophet "Jonah," who lived during the time of King Jeroboam II (Jon 1:1; 2 Kings 14:23-27). Consequently, Jonah's place in the canon of the Hebrew Scriptures, as one of the Twelve (Minor) Prophets, warrants comment. Tradition has located Jonah among the Twelve Prophets on the assumption that Jonah is the son of Amittai mentioned in the book of Kings and therefore a contemporary of Jeroboam II (c. 786–746 BCE), accounting for its place in the canon alongside the prophets Hosea and Amos and serving as confirmation that, "despite its narrative nature, it was not regarded as part of the biblical historiography, but rather of the prophetic literature."[24] However, as a prophetic text, Jonah is unlike any other in the Hebrew canon.

Prophetic books typically consist of the word of God to the people of Israel as mediated by the preaching of the prophet (marked off by the phrases "Thus says the Lord" and "the Word of the Lord"), the prophet's response—often a word of protest in the form of a prayer or lamentation—to God, as well as a brief biographical or autobiographical segment locating the prophet at a specific moment in Israel's history.[25] The book of the prophet Jonah includes only one biographical tidbit (Jon 1:1), contains a lengthy prayer tenuously connected to the rest of the narrative (2:2-9), and presents only the briefest message from God, a message not directed to the people of Israel: "Now the word of the Lord came to Jonah son of Amittai, saying, 'Go at once to Nineveh, that great city, and cry out against it; for their wickedness has come up before me'" (1:1-2).

Instead, the prophet Jonah is commissioned to speak the word of God to Gentiles, and not just any Gentile nation but the people of Nineveh, the capital of the Assyrian Empire, responsible for the conquest and exile of the northern kingdom of Israel in 721 BCE. Not surprisingly, Jonah is reluctant to travel to the land of his political enemies to deliver a prophetic warning from God and flees to the West by boarding a boat to Tarshish "away from the presence of the Lord" (1:3). Eventually, Jonah accepts God's call and delivers YHWH's prophetic warning. Jonah's sermon is similar in form to other prophetic preaching in the Hebrew Bible, communicating YHWH's judgment against the people of Nineveh, but it is distinguished by its brevity (five words in Hebrew, eight in English): "Forty days more, and Nineveh shall be overthrown!" (3:4).

Though ultimately obedient, Jonah's terse and brief word from God suggests continued reluctance on the part of Jonah. The fact that all the citizens of Nineveh, even the animals, repent and are forgiven by YHWH, does not reflect Jonah's great oratorical skill, nor stems from his virtue as one of God's chosen prophets. Rather, Jonah's all-too-brief sermon succeeds despite Jonah's wishes, since it is clear from the narrative that Jonah—contrary to God's express intention—wants and expects the destruction of Nineveh and all its inhabitants. Yet, by sparing the city of Nineveh, the author of the book of Jonah emphasizes a theme present in other prophetic texts: YHWH's sovereignty over Israel and all the nations.

Jonah: Story and Message

The story begins with God commanding Jonah to travel to the city of Nineveh in order to preach against their evil ways (1:1-2). Yet, unlike the archetypal Hebrew prophet who is a paragon of faithful obedience (even in the face of persecution), Jonah directly disobeys God by boarding a ship headed to Spain, traveling west instead of east (1:3). God, who is sovereign over all of nature and all of humanity, sees Jonah's disobedience and immediately raises a storm against the ship. The Gentile sailors were frightened and each prayed to his god; then, they threw cargo overboard in an effort to save the ship, and all the while Jonah slept in the hold. The captain wakes Jonah, orders him to pray to his god, that perhaps they might all be spared (1:4-6).

On the assumption that the storm is divine punishment for the sins of someone aboard the ship, the sailors cast lots to determine who is responsible and when the lots reveal Jonah is to blame, the sailors confront Jonah: "Tell us why this calamity has come upon us. What is your occupation? Where do you come from? What is your country? And of what people are you?" (1:8). To this Jonah replied: "I am a Hebrew. I worship the Lord, the God of heaven, who made the sea and the dry land" (1:9). However, instead of immediately throwing Jonah overboard, the Gentile seamen are presented as men of good conscience and piety, so that, when Jonah tells them the storm will abate when they throw him into the sea, they hesitate and pray to Jonah's God, YHWH: "Please, O Lord, we pray, do not let us perish on account of this man's life. Do not make us guilty of innocent blood; for you, O Lord, have done as it pleased you" (1:14). Once Jonah is cast overboard, the storm immediately ceases and the ship's crew is moved to worship YHWH by making vows and offering sacrifices (1:16). The prophet of God is disobedient, while the Gentile sailors come to genuine faith.

What is the didactic purpose of having one of God's prophets painted in such a negative light while the non-Israelites demonstrate admirable piety? Like Jesus' parable of the Good Samaritan, in which the priest and the Levite walk past the injured man on the side of the road while the Samaritan lends assistance (Luke 10:25-37), the one expected to obey God's word (Jonah) acts contrary to God's will while the Gentile sailors respond to YHWH with obedient gratitude. The author of the book of Jonah, writing to an Israelite audience, clearly has words of criticism for the people of Israel—embodied in Jonah and his exclusivist attitude—and confronts them with YHWH's love for all peoples and all nations.

Yet, despite Jonah's disobedience, YHWH does not abandon Jonah, instead commanding a great fish to swallow him, "and Jonah was in the belly of the fish for three days and three nights" (Jon 1:17). Jonah, whether motivated by fear for his life, or in thanksgiving for being rescued from the sea, turns to God in prayer. Traditionally identified as a prayer of thanksgiving, Jonah's prayer drives home the message that "Deliverance belongs to the Lord" (2:9), emphasizing themes central to Israel's core testimony concerning YHWH's sovereignty, justice, and compassion. Whether meant sincerely or not, Jonah's prayer is answered when God speaks to the fish and has it spew Jonah onto dry land (2:10).

What follows is a moment of recapitulation, where contrary to most prophetic texts, YHWH speaks the *same* word to one of the prophets. In scripture, a disobedient prophet is likely to meet with immediate punishment, like the prophet killed by a lion (1 Kings 13:20-32). Yet Jonah's entire narrative is an exercise in divine patience and forbearance. Instead of being punished, Jonah is saved from calamity then offered a second chance. This time Jonah obeys and starts walking east toward Nineveh, as expected from one of the Hebrew prophets, and signaled by the phrase "according to the word of the Lord" (Jon 3:3). So, for the one and only time in the Hebrew Bible, a prophet of Israel is sent by YHWH to preach the word of God to Gentiles. Without chastising Jonah for his disobedience, YHWH simply repeats his commandment to Jonah to preach repentance to the people of Nineveh, underscoring YHWH's concern for non-Israelite peoples.

Israel's biblical testimony contains other passages in which YHWH's concern for other nations is communicated (Amos 9:7; Isa 19:23-24), but nowhere else is one of God's prophets commissioned to minister the non-Israelite world. Clearly, this mission was so important to YHWH that he overlooked Jonah's disobedience in order to bring about Nineveh's conversion: "When God saw what they did, how they turned from their evil ways, God changed his mind about the calamity that he had said he would bring upon them; and he did not do it" (Jon 3:10). Furthermore, since it is God's will that Nineveh repent of its evil ways, no amount of disobedience—or half-hearted obedience (as in the brevity of Jonah's sermon noted above)—can undermine God's will. Once again reinforcing the core testimony of Israel concerning YHWH's sovereignty over all nations and compassion toward all people, the story of Jonah bears witness to the power of the word of God as the entire populace of Nineveh, from the king to the animals, responds with the same sincere piety as the Gentile sailors (1:16).

The story concludes with the inevitable confrontation between YHWH and the disgruntled prophet, as Jonah turns to God in defiant prayer: "O Lord! Is not this what I said while I was still in my own country? That is why I fled to Tarshish at the beginning; for I knew that you are a gracious God and merciful, slow to anger, and abounding in steadfast love, and ready to relent from punishing. And now, O Lord, please take my life from me, for it is better for me to die than to live" (4:2-3). Finally, the source of Jonah's anger and disobedience is laid bare for all to see: Jonah, as a Torah-believing prophet of Israel, knew that YHWH is a God of mercy and compassion (Exod 34:6-7; Ps 106:40-45), but as an Israelite, Jonah did not want forgiveness and compassion toward his enemies, the Assyrians.

Like a petulant child, Jonah followed this temper tantrum by walking to the edge of the city to wait for forty days to "see what would become of the city" (Jon 4:5). Then YHWH had a bit of fun with Jonah. God made a plant grow quickly to shade Jonah from the hot desert sun, which pleased Jonah. The very next day, God destroyed the plant, greatly angering Jonah and driving him to repeat his pathetic, childish plea: "It is better for me to die than to live" (4:8). When God asked Jonah what right he had to be angry about the bush, Jonah replied he was "angry enough to die" (4:9), to which YHWH replies: "And should I not be concerned about Nineveh, that great city, in which there are more than a hundred and twenty thousand persons who do not know their right hand from their left, and also many animals?" (4:11). The story ends abruptly, and like one of Jesus's parables, leaves the reader pondering layers of meaning and multiple interpretations.

CONCLUDING COMMENTS

A consistent theme of inclusion and compassion in Jonah's tale transcends confessional particularity, not just as it is preserved in the Hebrew canon, but as part of the liturgy of rabbinic Judaism, in the Christian Bible and in the Muslim Qur'an.

In contemporary Judaism, the book is read every year in its entirety on Yom Kippur, the Day of Atonement. In this liturgical context, the text affirms that God's forgiveness extends to all nations and peoples. Thus, in spite of the postexilic book of the prophet Nahum that celebrates the fall and destruction of Nineveh and the Assyrian Empire, Jonah's narrative has been used to develop the theological theme of *teshuva*, the ability to repent and be forgiven by God.

In the same way, Jonah's Qur'anic narrative is very similar to the Hebrew Bible story: the Qur'an describes Jonah as a righteous preacher of the message of God who fled from his mission because of its overwhelming difficulty, but who repents and carries out his mission to preach God's word to the people of Nineveh.

In Christianity, as previously mentioned, the sign of Jonah (Matt 12:38-42; 16:1-12; Luke 11:29-32) has been interpreted as prophetic prefiguring of Jesus's death and resurrection, and, until the liturgical reforms of the Second Vatican Council (1962–65), sections of Jonah were read as part of the Holy Saturday liturgy. Today, these are incorporated into the readings for the season of Lent. In Greek Orthodoxy, the entire book continues to be read as part of the Holy Saturday liturgy, and in the mainline Protestant denominations, Jonah remains part of the three-year lectionary cycle during Epiphany and Easter. However, despite this prevailing interpretation linking Jonah's three-day travail inside the fish to Jesus's three days in the tomb, it is significant that, like Jesus's parable of the Good Samaritan, the Lukan account of the sign of Jonah is linked to the righteousness and obedience of Gentiles ("the queen of the South" in verse 31 and "the people of Nineveh" in verse 32), lifting up a Gentile nation as an example of how one ought to respond to the word of God with repentance and sincere piety.

Finally, Jonah's place in Islam also emphasizes the theme of divine compassion, as evident from this Qur'anic summary of the book of Jonah:

And Jonas was one of the messengers.
When he fled towards the laden Ark.
He cast lots, but was one of the losers.
Then the whale swallowed him, and he was to blame.
Had he not been one of those who glorified [Allah];
He would have stayed in its belly until the day they will be resuscitated.
Then We cast him out in the wilderness while he was sick.
And made to grow over him a gourd tree.
And We sent him forth to a hundred thousand or more.
They believed, and so We accorded them enjoyment
   for a while. (Sura 37:139-148)[26]

Not only is Allah's compassion directed at the disobedient prophet (who is to blame), Allah also extends compassion to the unbelievers to whom Jonas was sent to deliver God's message, and just as in the canonical text of the Hebrew Bible, God spares the "hundred thousand or more."[27] In Sura 10, named after Jonah (Yunus), the people of Nineveh are lifted up as exemplars of faith: "How is it, then, that no town believed so that its belief would profit it, except the people of Jonah? When they believed, We removed from them the punishment of disgrace in the present life and allowed them to enjoy life for a while" (Sura 10:98).

While representing a literary tradition distinct from the Hebrew Bible, there is a thematic consistency to the Qur'anic Jonah that allows A. H. Johns to conclude: "The people of Jonah, although at first they disbelieved, were given time to repent. Accordingly, the message to Muhammad is that if his people are not yet punished, there is a reason for it: there is still time for them to believe and their faith to avail them. Muhammad is not to give in to frustration as did Jonah"; thus, the Qur'an "presents symbols, imagery and a prophetic message that is a [thematic] counterpart to that of the biblical Book of Jonah."[28]

Each of the three Abrahamic religions affirms there is only one God and that on the basis of our shared humanity—as creatures in the image and likeness of God—we are intended to live in fellowship with God and with one another. The God that spoke to Jonah is a God that placed life—human and animal life—above politics and religion, and challenged the nation of Israel to reconsider its role in the covenant with God. As Naim Ateek states, it is to "the credit of the Hebrew religion [that] the book was retained and included in the canon."[29] God's justice cannot be reduced to a human conception of justice, whether an Israelite or Assyrian justice, but transcends the limits of human perspectival thinking in the name of a common humanity created by the one true God. The biblical witness, originating with the Hebrew Bible, but broadened to include the Christian New Testament and the Muslim Qur'an, understands creation as an act of divine grace, and values humanity by virtue of the fact that humans are created to live in covenant with God. Theologically speaking, the value and dignity given is a gift originating in the act of creation that can never be lost nor taken away.

While most liberation theologies have emphasized God's work of historical liberation, as in the Exodus narrative, or the divine imperative for justice, as in the prophetic and Deuteronomic traditions, another consistent theme found in the biblical testimony about the one true God is God's abounding compassion.

Consistently, this compassion manifests itself in love toward the enemy: whether in YHWH's rebuke of the prophet Jonah for desiring the death of all Nineveh's inhabitants (Jon 4:11) despite knowing that God is "a gracious God and merciful, slow to anger, and abounding in steadfast love, and ready to relent from punishing" (4:2); in Christ's commands to love the enemy and turn the other cheek (Matt 5:39, 5:44); or in Allah's (who is called "the Gracious, the Merciful") instruction to treat others as you would your closest kin: "O believers, be dutiful to Allah and bearers of witness with justice; and do not let the hatred of a certain group drive you to be unequitable. Be equitable; that is nearer to piety, and fear Allah. Allah is fully aware of what you do!" (Sura 5:8), for "Allah enjoins justice, charity and the giving to kindred; He forbids indecency, evil and aggression. He admonishes you that you may take heed" (Sura 16:90).

It is God's desire that humanity live in peace with one another and that God's justice as revealed in the sacred scriptures—be it the Tanakh, the New Testament, or the Qur'an—guide and instruct all human relations. These sustained biblical themes of liberation, justice, and compassion are sufficient to put into practice an ethical norm for negotiating religious differences that engenders respect and tolerance without resorting to violence. Despite differences of interpretation as to how God's justice is defined and applied in all circumstances, even within the same confessional tradition, the sacred texts are abundantly clear that God prefers life over death, justice over injustice, peace over strife, nonviolence over violence.

NOTES

1. See María Rosa Menocal, *The Ornament of the World: How Muslims, Jews, and Christians Created a Culture of Tolerance in Medieval Spain* (New York: Back Bay Books, 2002), for a history of the cultural dialogue that took place in Medieval Spain between Muslims, Christians, and Jews that created a culture of tolerance and peaceful coexistence.

2. See: David Tracy, "Comparative Theology," in *The Encyclopedia of Religion*, Vol. 14, ed. Mircea Eliade (New York: MacMillan Publishing Co., 1987), 446–55; Francis X. Clooney, S.J., *Comparative Theology: Deep Learning Across Religious Borders* (Malden, MA: Wiley-Blackwell, 2010); David B. Burrell, *Towards a Jewish-Christian-Muslim Theology* (Malden, MA: Wiley-Blackwell, 2011).

3. *The Qur'an: A Modern English Version*, trans. Majid Fakhry (Reading, UK: Garnet Publishing, 1997). Unless otherwise noted all citations from the Qur'an are from this translation.

4. Clooney, *Comparative Theology*, 111–112.

5. Blaise Pascal, *Pensées*, trans. A. J. Krailsheimer (New York: Penguin Books, revised edition 1995), F 584. All citations from the *Pensées* use the Fragment numbers from this translation. Pascal here alludes to Isaiah 45:15, "Truly, you are a God who hides himself, O God of Israel, the Savior" (NRSV).

6. Pascal, *Pensées*, F 234.

7. For a discussion of the hiddenness of God in the three Abrahamic religions, see Walter Brueggemann, *Theology of the Old Testament: Testimony, Dispute, Advocacy* (Minneapolis: Fortress Press, 1997), 333–357; David B. Burrell, *Knowing the Unknowable God: Ibn-Sina, Maimonides, Aquinas* (Notre Dame, IN: University of Notre Dame Press, 1986); John Dillenberger, *God Hidden and Revealed: The Interpretation of Luther's Deus Absconditus and Its Significance for Religious Thought* (Philadelphia: Muhlenberg, 1953); Martin Buber, *Eclipse of God: Studies in the Relation Between Religion and Philosophy* (London: Victor Gollancz, 1953); and Ebrahim Azadegan, "Ibn 'Arabi on the Problem of Divine Hiddenness," *Journal of the Muhyiddin Ibn 'Arabi Society* 53 (2013): 49–67.

8. For an introduction to the issues regarding the contextual character of theology see Stephen B. Bevans, *Models of Contextual Theology* (Maryknoll, NY: Orbis Books, 1992), 11–22; Stephen B. Bevans and Roger P. Schroeder, *Constants in Context: A Theology of Mission for Today* (Maryknoll, NY: Orbis Books, 2004), 10–72; and Robert J. Schreiter, *Constructing Local Theologies* (Maryknoll, NY: Orbis Books, 1985), 1–21, 75–94.

9. The Pew Forum on Religion and Public Life and the Pew Hispanic Center, *Changing Faiths: Latinos and the Transformation of American Religion* (Washington, DC: Pew Research Center, 2007); see: http://www.pewhispanic.org/files/reports/75.pdf.

10. Justo L. González, *Santa Biblia: The Bible through Hispanic Eyes* (Nashville: Abingdon Press, 1996), 12.

11. Fernando F. Segovia, "Hispanic American Theology and the Bible: Effective Weapon and Faithful Ally," in *We Are A People! Initiatives in Hispanic American Theology*, ed. Roberto S. Goizueta (Minneapolis: Fortress Press, 1992), 43.

12. Orlando O. Espín, *Idol and Grace: On Traditioning and Subversive Hope* (Maryknoll, NY: Orbis Books, 2014), 19.

13. Luis G. Pedraja, *Jesus is my Uncle: Christology from a Hispanic Perspective* (Nashville: Abingdon, 1999), 62.

14. Segovia, "Hispanic American Theology and the Bible," 49.

15. Orlando O. Espín, *The Faith of the People: Theological Reflections on Popular Catholicism* (Maryknoll, NY: Orbis Books, 1997), 141. Emphasis in the original.

16. Espín, *Idol and Grace*, 9.

17. Miguel De La Torre, *Latina/o Social Ethics: Moving beyond Eurocentric Moral Thinking* (Waco, TX: Baylor University Press, 2010), xi.

18. See my analysis of Justo L. González's use of the Bible in "Sources and En Conjunto Methodologies of Latino/a Theologizing," in *The Wiley Blackwell Companion to Latino/a Theology*, ed. Orlando O. Espín (Malden, MA: Wiley-Blackwell, 2015), 58.

19. I first suggested utilizing the book of the prophet Jonah as a model for tolerance and nonviolence between competing religions in "*De orilla a orilla*: The Ecumenical Theology of Luis Rivera Pagán," *Journal of Hispanic/Latino Theology* 18 (2012): 26–34. A note of thanks to Dr. Rivera Pagán who, in responding to my paper, introduced me to the work of Naim Stifan Ateek. Ateek describes Jonah as the first Palestinian liberation theologian in *A Palestinian Cry for Reconciliation* (Maryknoll, NY: Orbis Books, 2008), 67–77. Though differing from Ateek on several key points, this work benefits greatly from his analysis of Jonah as a canonical witness that "condemns all narrow, restrictive, or exclusive theologies" (77).

20. See Paul F. Knitter, "Toward a Liberation Theology of Religions," in *The Myth of Christian Uniqueness: Toward a Pluralistic Theology of Religions*, ed. John Hick and Paul F. Knitter (Maryknoll, NY: Orbis Books, 1987), 178–200.

21. See Rubén Rosario Rodríguez, "Liberating Epistemology: Wikipedia and the Social Construction of Knowledge," *Journal of Religion and Theology* 26 (2007): 173–201.

22. S. Mark Heim, *Salvations: Truth and Difference in Religions*, Theology in Global Perspective (Maryknoll, NY: Orbis Books, 1995), 76.

23. For an introduction to the issues surrounding Jonah's placement in the Hebrew canon, its categorization as a prophetic book over against other genres, and related issues of authorship, dating, and canonical status, see: James Limburg, *Jonah: A Commentary* (Louisville, KY: Westminster/John Knox, 1993), 19–36; Jack M. Sasson, *Jonah*, Anchor Bible, 24B (New York: Doubleday, 1990), 9–29; and Uriel Simon, *Jonah*, The JPS Bible Commentary (Philadelphia: The Jewish Publication Society, 1999), vii-xliii.

24. Simon, *Jonah*, xiv.

25. For an introduction to Hebrew prophetic literature, see James M. Ward, *Thus Says the Lord: The Message of the Prophets*. (Nashville: Abingdon, 1991), 13–33; see also: Abraham Joshua Heschel, *The Prophets* (New York: Harper Perennial Classics, 2001), 3–31; and Walter Brueggemann, *The Prophetic Imagination* (Minneapolis: Fortress Press, 1978), 44–61.

26. See Brannon M. Wheeler, *Prophets in the Quran: An Introduction to the Quran and Muslim Exegesis* (London: Continuum, 2002), 168–72.

27. For a detailed analysis of Jonah in the Qur'an, see A. H. Johns, "Jonah in the Qur'an: An Essay on Thematic Counterpoint," *Journal of Qur'anic Studies* 5 (2003): 48–71.

28. Johns, "Jonah in the Qu'ran," 68.

29. Ateek, *A Palestinian Christian Cry for Reconciliation*, 72.

BIBLIOGRAPHY

Ateek, Naim Stifan. *A Palestinian Cry for Reconciliation*. Maryknoll, NY: Orbis Books, 2008.

Azadegan, Ebrahim. "Ibn 'Arabi on the Problem of Divine Hiddenness." *Journal of the Muhyiddin Ibn 'Arabi Society* 53 (2013): 49–67.

Bevans, Stephen B. *Models of Contextual Theology*. Maryknoll, NY: Orbis Books, 1992.

Bevans. Stephen B., and Roger P. Schroeder. *Constants in Context: A Theology of Mission for Today*. Maryknoll, NY: Orbis Books, 2004.

Brueggemann, Walter. *The Prophetic Imagination*. Minneapolis: Fortress Press, 1978.

———. *Theology of the Old Testament: Testimony, Dispute, Advocacy*. Minneapolis: Fortress Press, 1997.

Buber, Martin. *Eclipse of God: Studies in the Relation between Religion and Philosophy*. London: Victor Gollancz, 1953.

Burrell, David B. *Knowing the Unknowable God: Ibn-Sina, Maimonides, Aquinas*. Notre Dame, IN: University of Notre Dame Press, 1986.

———. *Towards a Jewish-Christian-Muslim Theology*. Malden, MA: Wiley-Blackwell, 2011.

Clooney, S.J., Francis X. *Comparative Theology: Deep Learning across Religious Borders.* Malden, MA: Wiley-Blackwell, 2010.
De La Torre, Miguel. *Latina/o Social Ethics: Moving beyond Eurocentric Moral Thinking.* Waco, TX: Baylor University Press, 2010.
Dillenberger, John. *God Hidden and Revealed: The Interpretation of Luther's Deus Absconditus and Its Significance for Religious Thought.* Philadelphia: Muhlenberg, 1953.
Espín, Orlando O. *The Faith of the People: Theological Reflections on Popular Catholicism.* Maryknoll, NY: Orbis Books, 1997.
———. *Idol and Grace: On Traditioning and Subversive Hope.* Maryknoll, NY: Orbis Books, 2014.
Fakhry, Majid, trans. *The Qur'an: A Modern English Version.* Reading, UK: Garnet Publishing, 1997.
González, Justo L. *Santa Biblia: The Bible through Hispanic Eyes.* Nashville: Abingdon Press, 1996.
Heim, S. Mark. *Salvations: Truth and Difference in Religions,* Theology in Global Perspective. Maryknoll, NY: Orbis Books, 1995.
Heschel, Abraham Joshua. *The Prophets.* New York: Harper Perennial Classics, 2001.
Johns, A. H. "Jonah in the Qur'an: An Essay on Thematic Counterpoint." *Journal of Qur'anic Studies* 5 (2003): 48–71.
Knitter, Paul F. "Toward a Liberation Theology of Religions." In *The Myth of Christian Uniqueness: Toward a Pluralistic Theology of Religions*, edited by John Hick and Paul F. Knitter, 178–200. Maryknoll, NY: Orbis Books, 1987.
Limburg, James. *Jonah: A Commentary.* Louisville, KY: Westminster/John Knox, 1993.
Menocal, María Rosa. *The Ornament of the World: How Muslims, Jews, and Christians Created a Culture of Tolerance in Medieval Spain.* New York: Back Bay Books, 2002.
Pascal, Blaise. *Pensées.* Translated by A. J. Krailsheimer. New York: Penguin Books, revised edition 1995.
Pedraja, Luis G. *Jesus is my Uncle: Christology from a Hispanic Perspective.* Nashville: Abingdon, 1999.
The Pew Forum on Religion and Public Life and the Pew Hispanic Center. *Changing Faiths: Latinos and the Transformation of American Religion.* Washington, DC: Pew Research Center, 2007. See: http://www.pewhispanic.org/files/reports/75.pdf.
Rosario Rodríguez, Rubén. "*De orilla a orilla*: The Ecumenical Theology of Luis Rivera Pagán." *Journal of Hispanic/Latino Theology* 18 (2012): 26–34.
———. "Liberating Epistemology: Wikipedia and the Social Construction of Knowledge," *Journal of Religion and Theology* 26 (2007): 173–201.
———. "Sources and *En Conjunto* Methodologies of Latino/a Theologizing." In *The Wiley Blackwell Companion to Latino/a Theology*, edited by Orlando O. Espín, 53–70. Malden, MA: Wiley Blackwell, 2015.
Sasson, Jack M. *Jonah,* Anchor Bible 24B. New York: Doubleday, 1990.
Schreiter, Robert J. *Constructing Local Theologies.* Maryknoll, NY: Orbis Books, 1985.

Segovia, Fernando F. "Hispanic American Theology and the Bible: Effective Weapon and Faithful Ally." In *We Are A People! Initiatives in Hispanic American Theology*, edited by Roberto S. Goizueta, 21–50. Minneapolis: Fortress Press, 1992.

Simon, Uriel. *Jonah*, The JPS Bible Commentary. Philadelphia: The Jewish Publication Society, 1999.

Tracy, David. "Comparative Theology." In *The Encyclopedia of Religion*, edited by Mircea Eliade, 446–455. Vol. 14. New York: MacMillan Publishing Co., 1987.

Ward, James M. *Thus Says the Lord: The Message of the Prophets*. Nashville: Abingdon, 1991.

Wheeler, Brannon M. *Prophets in the Quran: An Introduction to the Quran and Muslim Exegesis*. London: Continuum, 2002.

Chapter 10

Popular Ritual as Liberating Pedagogy

Christopher D. Tirres

One of the defining features of U.S. Latino/a theology has been its focus on faith as it is lived at the everyday level. In a variety of ways, Latino/a theologians have given pride of place to categories like popular religion, popular ritual, and *lo cotidiano*, and this focus has yielded important new methodological insights. Among other things, it has helped to expand our understanding of the biblical "text." As many scholars of Latino/a religion recognize, the Bible is not simply a written document to be read and studied by individual adherents. Rather, it is a living narrative that communities re-imagine, re-construct, and re-enact in light of their own concrete and lived experience. As the late Alejandro García-Rivera suggests, our object of study must be a "living theology." Unlike "textbook theology," a living theology demands that we engage the quotidian and aesthetic dimensions of faith, such as found in the symbols, imagery, and music of the Latino/a faith community.[1]

Latino/a theologians have helped to expand the meaning of the biblical text in large part because they understand the theological endeavor as a consummately contextual affair. Latino/a theologians recognize, in other words, that there is no such thing as an "objective theology," divorced from the particularities of time, place, and interests of power. Instead, they recognize the need to be honest about the historical and social particularities that shape their work. This is, I believe, one of the greatest contributions that a contextual theology such as this can make to a wider theological landscape.

This being said, however, a number of questions are often left unanswered when we speak of Latino/a theology as a contextual theology. Some of these questions include: To what extent is Latino/a theology also a *liberation* theology? What emancipatory aims, if any, inform its contextualist focus? In light of these questions, I would like to revisit one prevalent object of study within U.S. Latino/a theology—popular ritual—in order to rethink the ways in which we understand it as liberating. How, for example, do *posadas, pastorelas,* and *via cruces* represent and reconfigure biblical narratives in such a way that lead to new forms of individual and social growth? How do they embody practices of freedom?

As I will suggest, one important step in answering these questions is to see popular ritual not in terms of what popular ritual "itself" does but rather how ritual organizers and ritual participants engage one another, through the language of ritual, to create ongoing experiences of liberation. This focus on the dialogical and discursive dimensions of popular ritual redirects us back to questions of pedagogy, which have been so central to liberationist thought for several decades now, beginning with the groundbreaking work of Paulo Freire.[2] However, whereas Freire's work is premised largely on the model of linguistic exchange and encounter, my own modest intervention here is to underscore the importance of a pedagogical approach for the more gestural, symbolic, and embodied medium of ritual.

This chapter is divided into four sections. In the first section, I examine some of the challenges that contextual theologies presently face in connecting their contextualist focus with liberationist aims. In the second section, I look specifically at the ways in which some prominent U.S. Latino/a theologians have broached popular ritual as an embodied and enculturated site of liberation. A pressing question has been: In what ways is Latino/a popular ritual liberating? The third section then considers how a pedagogical approach to popular ritual helps us better answer this question. I argue that a renewed focus on pedagogy underscores a pivotal insight that is often lost when interpreting popular ritual: like all integral and authentic forms of liberation, popular ritual is a *process* that grows over time through continued cultivation and engagement. In the final section, I consider some implications that a pedagogical approach to popular ritual has for constructive theology and biblical criticism alike.

CONTEXTUAL THEOLOGIES: CONTRIBUTIONS AND CHALLENGES

In his classic study, *Constructing Local Theologies,* Robert Schreiter describes two types of contextual theologies: those that follow an "ethnographic" approach, which are particularly concerned with identity and social location, and those that follow a liberationist approach, which emphasize the need for social change. As Schreiter makes clear, these two types of contextual theology provide important alternatives to older "translation" and "adaptation" models of theology, which either see culture as static or as a mere reflection of dominant worldviews.[3] I would agree with Schreiter that it is appropriate to place ethnographic and liberationist approaches under a common umbrella of contextual theology. One ongoing challenge, however, is how best to integrate "ethnographic" and "liberationist" approaches. As I see it, within the discourse of U.S. Latino/a theology, there are generally three responses to this challenge.

The first response tends to be suspicious of any kind of ethnographic focus. Critics like Manuel Mejido and Ivan Petrella, for example, have taken issue with U.S. Latino/a theology's turn to aesthetics and culture, both of which would fall under the "ethnographic" category. They hold that U.S. Latino/a theology is not, or has failed to be, a liberation theology in the fullest sense of the term. For Mejido, a turn to ethnographic categories like culture and aesthetics runs counter to the formation of a "critically oriented science"; for Petrella, it detracts from the practical task of creating concrete "historical projects."[4] While I agree with parts of their critique, I think that both authors prematurely foreclose a discussion of the ways in which cultural and aesthetic categories—when approached carefully and critically—can actually shed significant light on the scope and meaning of "integral" liberation.

A second response to this challenge takes a position that is almost the inverse of the first. Whereas critics like Mejido and Petrella fault U.S. Latino/a theology's ethnographic turn as a betrayal of its liberationist aims, some U.S. Latino/a theologians have heartily embraced the ethnographic character of U.S. Latino/a theology, leaving liberationist concerns largely aside. The work of Alejandro García-Rivera moves in this direction, but there are others who share this general sentiment. I have heard other U.S. Latino/a theologians claim, for example, that whereas Latin American liberation theology deals with an "option for the poor," U.S. Latino/a theology reflects more an "option for culture." It seems to me that a distinction as sharp as this—which pits economic concerns against cultural ones—does more harm than good.

What is needed, rather, is a third approach, one that integrates different, yet interrelated, facets of reality, including culture, politics, economics, class, and gender. Fortunately, the majority of U.S. Latino/a theologians today seem to subscribe to such a position. Most would claim that U.S. Latino/a theology is a contextual theology with *both* an ethnographic focus *and* a liberationist focus. As we will see in the next section, the attention that U.S. Latino/a theologians have given to popular religion and popular ritual represents an important first step in integrating both of these aspects. An ongoing challenge, however, is how one justifies this connection and makes it explicit.[5]

POPULAR RELIGION AND POPULAR RITUAL IN U.S. LATINO/A THEOLOGY

Without a doubt, one of the most important contributions that U.S. Latino/a theology has made in forging a more integral approach to liberation has been its focus on popular religion, which may be broadly defined as the "set of experience, beliefs, and rituals which ecclesiastically and socially peripheral groups create and develop in the search for an access to God and salvation."[6] Ethicist Ada María Isasi-Díaz underscores the subversive nature of Latino/a popular religion, noting that: (1) it honors ritual practices and symbols that are often considered marginal to more mainstream expressions of faith; (2) it is syncretic, in that it incorporates meaning from other religious traditions; and (3) it re-interprets "official" religious practices so as to imbue them with new meaning.[7] In this light, Latino/a popular religion may be seen as a complex, transcultural practice that affirms the agency of people who have undergone some form of conquest and who continue to live on the margins of society. Through Latino/a popular religion, adherents are able to draw upon mainstream expressions of faith without having to assimilate to them fully or reject them outright. Latino/a popular religion may be read, then, both as a response to the ravages of conquest as well as a creative act of world-building in its own right.

U.S. Latino/a theologians have given much time and attention to a study of popular religion, and Orlando Espín's large body of work on popular religion is especially exemplary in this regard. In a number of books and articles, Espín notes that three historical strains have contributed to what we now call Latino popular Catholicism: Western Christianity in its Iberian form, native religions of the Americas, and native religions of Africa. Perhaps most original and significant is Espín's analysis on the Iberian roots of popular Catholicism. As Espín shows, the version of Catholicism that came to the Americas in the sixteenth century, especially in Mexico, was not yet *Roman* Catholicism, with all of its anti-Protestant doctrinal polemics but rather a pre-Tridentine and medieval form of *Iberian* Catholicism that was highly ritualistic and symbolic in form.

Iberian Catholicism traded on the patristic understanding of *traditio*, which encompasses much more than our modern notion of "tradition." Whereas a religious "tradition" today is often defined primarily in terms of one's adherence to doctrines and creeds, or "orthodoxy" (Gr. *orthos*, "right" + *doxos*, "opinion"), the medieval understanding of *traditio* also encompassed and foregrounded the importance of "right action," or "orthopraxy." Thus, one's involvement in the liturgical and sacramental practices of one's community, and, indeed, in one's daily life, was just as important as one's adherence to the ancient creedal definitions of the church. *Traditio*, then, was coextensive not only "with what Christians believed" but also with "how they worshipped, and how they lived."[8] At its best, *traditio* represented a total way of life.

Significantly, this Iberian form of Catholicism was the primary expression of Christianity in the New World well up until a century *after* the Council of Trent (1545–63). What is more, even after the doctrinal debates of Trent began to take root in the Americas, such debates took place primarily only at the level of the Spanish and *criollo* elites. At the popular level, Iberian Christianity continued to perdure. As Espín puts it, "the vast majority of people did not participate in [the] official, doctrinal world" of the universities and Episcopal synods. Rather, "[f]or common folk (and for much of the clergy), essential doctrine was embedded in the ordinary."[9]

This insight—that "essential doctrine was embedded in the ordinary"—has been a key point of departure for many Latino/a theologians, especially those who are Catholic. Espín, for one, has gone on to explore the doctrinal implications of this idea, arguing that Latino popular Catholicism, like the pre-Tridentine Iberian Catholicism before it, may organically embody the *sensus fidelium*, or the collective "sense of the faithful."[10] As he argues, the *sensus fidelium* should be understood as an integral source of the Christian tradition, right alongside scripture and conciliar documents.[11]

While the expressions and meanings of popular religion have, no doubt, varied from place to place over the centuries since the conquest of the Americas, the link between lived faith and theology has continued to be foundational for Latino/a Catholics. Other Catholic theologians, such as Roberto Goizueta, Virgilio Elizondo, and Ada María Isasi-Díaz, have offered variations on this theme, showing how a careful study of "ordinary" faith practices may contribute to a deeper understanding of human *praxis* (Goizueta), *mestizaje* (Elizondo), and ethical struggle (Isasi-Díaz).

Methodological Implications

For the purposes of this chapter, I would like to turn to the methodological implications of making popular religion—and, by extension, popular ritual—a central point of departure. In her excellent survey on U.S. Latino/a theology, María Pilar Aquino comments on the overall significance of Latino/a popular Catholicism for theological method. "Latino/a popular Catholicism," she states, "embraces the faith of the people and thus constitutes the locus and central code for interpreting the tensions inherent in human life." Underscoring this point, Aquino adds: "The whole structure of the faith finds rationality, order, and coherence in popular Catholicism's contents, symbols, rituals, and languages."[12]

This focus on popular religion has led to new ways of thinking about liberation. As Latin American and U.S. Latina feminists have pointed out, early

Latin American liberation theology tended to give "priority only to global social phenomena." The idea of liberation was often tied, for example, to the success (or failures) of left-wing political parties. As a result, as Aquino argues, "daily life and the relationship between men and women were regarded as of secondary importance."[13] Latin American and U.S. Latina feminists have addressed this deficiency, pointing out that liberation has as much to do with the public sphere as is does with the private sphere. They have also underscored the importance of *lo cotidiano*, or daily life, as a constitutive moment for any liberating praxis.

Systematic theologian Roberto Goizueta recognizes the significant contributions of U.S. Latina feminists, and he shares their critique of the public-private split. Significantly, however, he has gone one step further to argue against what he sees as reductive interpretations of liberation that "instrumentalize" liberation to political ends. Goizueta argues that Latino popular religion points to a noninstrumental liberating praxis—one that is communal, relational, and highly aesthetic. As such, it resists being reduced to a discreet goal or product. The following passage, which emerges, in part, out of Goizueta's first-hand experience of the Good Friday rituals at the San Fernando Cathedral in San Antonio, Texas, is indicative of his basic starting point. In "[m]y own experience of Latino communities," he writes,

> I have witnessed a type of empowerment and liberation taking place which, at least initially and explicitly, seems to have relatively little connection to any social or political struggles. Indeed, in many cases, empowerment and liberation are not explicit goals at all. Seemingly, the only explicit goals are day-to-day survival and, especially, the affirmation of relationships as essential to that survival.[14]

Goizueta suggests that the operative human praxis here is not a (Marxian) "revolutionary praxis" that was indicative of early Latin American liberation theology. Rather, according to Goizueta, what we witness here is a more symbolic praxis of resistance, which Goizueta refers to as an "aesthetic praxis" of accompaniment (*acompañamiento*). In the context of popular ritual, "empowerment and liberation are not explicit goals at all." Instead, liberation surfaces in the ritual act itself. In the ritual experience of Good Friday, for example, the Latino/a faithful—who daily face their own forms of suffering—undergo liberation when they share in the embodied, symbolic, and enculturated experience of "walking with" the suffering Jesus. In such a case, liberation does not have an explicit *telos*, but it is implicitly and communally embodied in ritual acts of solidarity, accompaniment, and cultural presence.[15]

This idea, that the symbols and rituals of Latino popular religion prove liberative insofar that they help to "resist" cultural assimilation, is often echoed by other Latino/a theologians. Pastoral theologian Virgilio Elizondo, for example, comments on the cultural damage that was done to the Mexican-American people through their "double-conquest"—first, the conquest of ancient Mexico by Spain in 1521, and, second, the conquest of northern Mexico by the United States in the 1840s. These events "forced the native population and their succeeding generations into a split and meaningless existence," marking a "mortal collective catastrophe of gigantic death-bearing consequences." "Yet," Elizondo adds:

> the people have *religious symbols* and the reinterpretation of old ones which have connected the past with the present and projected into the future. The core religious expressions as celebrated and transmitted by the people are the unifying symbols in which the opposing forces of life are brought together into a harmonious tension so as to give the people who participate in them the experience of wholeness.... Where formerly there was opposition, now there is reconciliation and even great yet, synthesis. This is precisely what gives joy and meaning to life, indeed makes life possible in any meaningful sense regardless of the situation. It is in the celebration of these festivals of being and memory that the people live on as a people.[16]

As Elizondo suggests here, Latino/a popular religious symbols and rituals have served as "unifying" forces that sublate internal tensions, thus offering an "experience of wholeness" and "synthesis." This Hegelian-sounding formula points in the direction of liberation without directly mentioning it. For Elizondo, popular religion proves liberative insofar that it resists the dominant culture, through an affirmation of a people's agency, identity, and dignity.

What we see in both of these cases is an emphasis on Latino/a popular religion and popular ritual as forms of cultural resistance. This interpretation no doubt holds much merit, especially in light of the fact that Latino/a popular rituals are often intentionally performed in public spaces. They are infused with elements that reflect Latino/a culture, be it traditional songs, the use of the Spanish language, or common ritualized practices, such as touching or kissing a statue. It is difficult to imagine, for example, a *posada* without the back-and-forth melodies of "Pidiendo Posada," a *Jueves Santo* without the call-and-response refrains of "Caminemos con Jesús," a *via crucis* without soldiers yelling "¡Muévete!" and "¡Camina!," or a *Pésame* without a moment in which congregants touch or kiss a cross or statue of the fallen Christ. Such cultural elements affirm and lift up a people often looked down upon by a wider—and whiter—public. In this light, popular ritual may be seen as liberative, insofar as it stands as a counterhegemonic discourse to the dominant culture.

Risks

As important as this insight is, however, it runs into some possible risks, two of which I will mention here. First, there is oftentimes so much stress placed on the cultural dimensions of popular religion that little is said about the ways in which it may creatively transgress other important aspects of reality. How, for example, might the embodied actions of popular ritual also break down barriers of class, race, and sexuality? And how can we connect these creative transgressions back to the question of cultural resistance? Stated another way, through the experience of popular ritual, one may undergo multiple types of transformations, including affective, cultural, intellectual, moral, or spiritual conversions.[17] The point here is that a cultural resistance, which manifests itself in a new form of cultural awareness, is but one possible form of liberation, among many, that popular ritual may engender.

A second risk has to do with the ways in which Latino/a theologians sometimes portray Latino/a popular religion as being liberative "in itself." At times, the prevailing assumption is that because Latino/a popular religion perdures in a world in which it is often shunned, it is liberative by its very presence. One may be left with the impression, then, that popular religion is, by its own devices, doing the hard work of liberation or that it is intrinsically liberating.

Latina feminist and *mujerista* theologians, however, have cautioned against such an interpretation. They have helped to show that, while popular religion is indeed a central part of the lived experience of the people, it may, at times, contribute to various forms of oppression. While not wanting to minimize or dismiss popular religion altogether, *mujerista* theologian Ada María Isasi-Díaz points out that "popular religiosity has elements that legitimize the oppression of Latinas."[18] Similarly, María Pilar Aquino has argued that "[a]lthough devotions express liberating impulses that have helped the poor masses in their struggle to survive . . . , it is also true that this same popular religiosity contains elements that legitimate submission to the oppressor. Because this environment has been basically patriarchal and *machista*, it is not surprising that women's religious expression also contains these elements."[19]

I second these concerns and would like to add a further word of caution: when saying that popular religion is itself liberating, one may lose sight of the ways in which popular religion functions as an ongoing, dialogical, and pedagogical *process*. This becomes especially relevant, I believe, when considering perhaps the most significant form of popular religion: popular ritual.[20] If we approach popular ritual as liberating in itself, we may overlook not only all the planning, oversight, and intentions brought forth by pastoral leaders, but also, the active, dialogical, and dynamic process of imaginative engagement and encounter on the part of participants. Both of these aspects, I would argue, point to a central feature of popular ritual—its function as pedagogy.

A PEDAGOGICAL APPROACH TO POPULAR RITUAL

In the context of popular ritual, what do I mean here by pedagogy? In the first place, it should not be too hard to recognize that popular rituals like *posadas*, *pastorelas*, and *via cruces* serve a very basic pedagogical function: they tell Bible-related stories. In so doing, they serve as a kind of teaching or catechetical aid, especially for children. These narratives socialize participants into a larger group ethos. At this basic level of education, the pedagogical function of popular ritual serves a formal and somewhat didactic function: information is transferred from one group to the next, namely, from ritual teachers to ritual learners.

However, the pedagogical dimension of popular ritual may also be understood in a more critical and dialogical way. A critical pedagogy foregrounds the way in which popular ritual makes biblical narratives relevant to everyday life. In recent years, social scientists such as Alyshia Gálvez, Karen Mary Davalos, and Wayne Ashley have offered some compelling ethnographies that examine how popular rituals, like the *via crucis*, often reconstruct biblical narratives in a way that brings adherents to a new level of understanding about their own relationship to the biblical narrative.[21] Ritual participants often experience the *via crucis* as an overlay between their cultural heritage, on the one hand, and Jesus's life that is made tangible in the present, on the other. Pedagogically speaking, one could say that popular rituals like the *via crucis* may serve as forms of *concientización* that open participants up to a new understanding of themselves and their connection to a larger narrative of suffering and salvation.

What I would like to add to this insight is that *the manner in which* this reinterpretation and reconstruction is carried out is crucial. In other words, we should always ask: What is the quality of reinterpretation and reconstruction in any given ritual context? In what particular ways are participants invited into a new understanding of their own connection to the biblical narrative? How is this process set up, and to what end? It is here that the role of the pastoral educator becomes especially important, and it is here that we can begin to see more clearly the importance of pedagogy to the liberation process.

On the one hand, we know that there is no guarantee that a community's engagement with popular ritual will automatically yield moments of *concientización*, transformation, or healing. Even among the most socially minded and theologically astute pastoral agents, popular ritual may fall flat. In order to see this, one need not look further than Wayne Ashley's study of the Stations of the Cross at St. Brigid's Church on the Lower East Side of New York City.[22] As Ashley explains in his study, even though the priests at St. Brigid's were highly educated and theologically progressive, a series of missteps actually led to a number of rifts within the community. Much of this had to do with the fact that pastoral leaders sometimes lacked sensitivity to the cultural sensibilities of the Puerto Rican community they served.

For instance, somewhat frustrated with the older and more conservative members of the church, pastoral leaders divided St. Brigid's *via crucis* into two parts, one led by the older members of the congregation and the other by younger members. The idea was that this would help give voice to the younger, more progressive, generation. The result, however, was increased tension between the two generational groups. On another occasion during the Christmas season, church leaders wanted to make the point that the true meaning of Christmas was being killed by consumerism, so they symbolically placed Santa Claus in a coffin. While the idea behind their actions may have been prophetic, the manner in which it was presented led to confusion and fear, especially among children. At other points in the life of the church, pastoral leaders sometimes failed to remain sensitive to various cultural elements that were so dear to St. Brigid's Puerto Rican community: saints were removed from the front of the church, and the use of maracas, guitars, and güiro were replaced by a more traditional Catholic sister who played the organ.

On the other hand, one sees a very different kind of pastoral approach at a number of other churches throughout the United States, such the San Fernando Cathedral in San Antonio, Texas; St. Pius V Parish in the Pilsen area of Chicago, Illinois; or St. Pius X Church in El Paso, Texas. Much has been written about each of these places, and, if one digs deep enough, one can certainly find tensions within these congregations as well. On the whole, though, the pastoral leaders in these faith communities have treated planners and participants as equals and have embraced popular expressions of faith in quite exemplary ways.

Past and present pastoral leaders—like the late Virgilio Elizondo, James Empereur, S.J., and Sallie Gomez-Kelly (at San Fernando in San Antonio); Charles Dahm (at St. Pius V Parish in Chicago); and Arturo Bañuelas (at St. Pius X Church in El Paso [now at St. Mark Catholic Church in El Paso])—all exemplify what Thomas Groome calls a "shared praxis" approach.[23] Whether the context is church governance or liturgy, these pastoral agents advocate nonhierarchical, dialogical, and democratic forms of exchange. These pastoral leaders are some of the most radical educators on the scene today—"radical" in the sense that their modus operandi is, *at root*, an embodiment of a liberative praxis.

Furthermore, while pastoral leaders such as these recognize the importance of immediate and concrete social commitments, they also intuitively understand faith formation as a long-term process. Charles Dahm, for instance, underscores the fact that faith formation, at its best, "works more slowly and is less univocal in its definition" than other community organizing methods, such as the one proposed by Saul Alinsky, because it is "more respectful of people at different stages of personal development and social commitment." To be sure, Dahm is not suggesting here that Alinsky-type community activism does not have its place. On the contrary, he makes clear that church-based community organizing, in the tradition of Alinsky and the Industrial Areas Foundation, has led to several positive changes within his own Pilsen neighborhood. What Dahm does seem to be suggesting here, however, is that an integral liberation process must be approached *as* a process, however partial, incomplete, and continuing this process may seem to be. As Dahm puts it, a "creative balance must be struck between organizing around self-interests and organizing to create a vibrant community that will last beyond the mobilization of the moment."[24]

In offering these examples, my point here is not so much to compare and contrast particular churches or church leaders. Instead, it is to underscore the central role that pedagogy plays in contributing to popular ritual that is liberative in the deepest. What is often missing, I would suggest, is more careful attention to the specific ways in which adherents actively engage a cultural product like popular ritual. The question of *how* they do so—whether before the ritual (through inherited stories and practices), during the ritual (as an embodied praxis), or even after the ritual (through reflection upon the ritual)—is, at root, a question of ritual pedagogy. A renewed focus on the question of ritual pedagogy helps to underscore the liberation process *as* a dialogical process that grows over time.

IMPLICATIONS FOR CONSTRUCTIVE
THEOLOGY AND BIBLICAL CRITICISM

I have pointed out two fundamental challenges that U.S. Latino/a theologians often face when theorizing the liberative dimensions of popular religion and popular ritual. The first has to do with the emphasis that is given to the cultural dimensions of popular religion and popular ritual. While such an emphasis may be seen, in one light, as a helpful corrective to the more explicitly political orientation of early Latin American liberation theology, one must, at the same time, be attentive to the ways in which U.S. Latino/a theology may inadvertently *de*-politicize itself. One of the tasks for the next generation of U.S. Latino/a theologians, I believe, is to offer more subtle and nuanced analyses of the ways in which cultural products and practices intersect with questions of politics, as well as with questions of gender, class, and sexuality.

Another significant challenge is rethinking liberation not only as a product but also as a process. While U.S. Hispanic theology may have shifted the focus from politics to culture, it often remains inscribed within a general framework of approaching liberation as a "product"—a *cultural* product, to be sure, but a product nonetheless. As I have suggested, multilayered ethnographies of particular faith communities can shed invaluable light on the concrete, yet often paradoxical, dynamics of popular ritual. Such studies help constructive theologians to move from a general discussion of popular ritual as liberating "in itself" to a more qualified and empirical look at popular ritual as a complex and ongoing process.[25]

While this discussion may appear especially relevant for those U.S. Latino/a theologians who do constructive theology, the basic concerns discussed here may have important implications for those who do biblical criticism as well. Just as U.S. Latino/a constructive theologians have helped to expand our understanding of "liberation" by staying true to the particularities of culture and context, so, too, have U.S. Latino/a biblical critics offered liberative re-readings of the Bible by foregrounding the importance of the hermeneutical context of both the text and the interpreter.

Various projects of reading the Bible "from the margins" have helped to advance what Fernando F. Segovia calls a program of "continued decolonization and liberation, of resistance and struggle" within the discipline of biblical criticism, a discipline that has been "from beginning to end and top to bottom, thoroughly Eurocentric despite its assumed scientific persona of neutrality and universality."[26] In order to confront this, liberationist biblical criticism has put a high premium on a new hermeneutics, a new way of seeing and interpreting the biblical text, as informed especially by contextual readings of the Bible. In this regard, deconstructionist, postcolonial, and intercultural approaches have been important resources in advancing this work.

As important as these developments have been, one could still ask: Aside from the epistemic value of such interpretations, how are these new interpretations deployed within actual communities of faith? How do they take root and grow through an ongoing dialogue between pastoral agents and parishioners? In short, how is the new hermeneutics utilized as a liberative form of pedagogy? These questions, I would argue, have both practical and theoretical implications.

The practical implications are clear: How, if at all, are theologians and biblical critics alike engaging actual communities of faith? Over the years, I have seen this practical concern resurface in myriad ways within the Academy of Catholic Hispanic Theologians of the United States (ACHTUS). Members of ACHTUS continue to wrestle with the question of how best to stay grounded in, and accountable to, their communities of faith. But these questions have theoretical significance as well: How are we envisioning the very task of liberation? Are we conceiving it mostly in terms of a finished "product"—whether cultural (as manifested in particular symbols and rites) or hermeneutical (as manifested in particular liberationist readings of the text)? Or are we also taking into account the manner in which these things are being put to use in concrete and particular cases? Are we being sufficiently attentive to the pedagogical dynamics of liberation as an ongoing encounter between the interpreter and the wider community of faith? Are we looking closely, in other words, at the liberation process *as* a process of continuing personal and communal growth?

While U.S. Latino/a theology has no doubt significantly advanced liberationist discourse in the Americas, it seems to me that more thought needs to be given to liberation as a dynamical, ongoing, and dialogical process. As I have argued, a return to the foundational liberationist theme of pedagogy—this time, critically re-interpreted in light of the gestural, symbolic, and embodied "language" of ritual—may be a step in the right direction.

NOTES

1. Alejandro R. García-Rivera, *A Wounded Innocence: Sketches for a Theology of Art* (Collegeville, MN: Liturgical Press, 2003), viii.

2. Paolo Freire, *Pedagogy of the Oppressed*, trans. M. Ramos (New York: Continuum, 1970).

3. Robert Schreiter, *Constructing Local Theologies* (Maryknoll: Orbis, 1997), 1–16.

4. Manuel J. Mejido, "Beyond the Postmodern Condition, or the Turn toward Psychoanalysis," in *Latin American Liberation Theology: The Next Generation*, ed. Ivan Petrella (Maryknoll, NY: Orbis Books, 2005), 119–146; Ivan Petrella, "Liberation Theology-A Programmatic Statement," in *Latin American Liberation Theology: The Next Generation*, ed. Ivan Petrella (Maryknoll, NY: Orbis Books, 2005), 147–172. For their more pointed critiques of U.S. Latino/a theology and other contextual theologies, see Mejido's "A Critique of the 'Aesthetic Turn' in U.S. Hispanic Theology: A Dialogue with Roberto Goizueta and the Positing of a New Paradigm," *Journal of Hispanic/Latino Theology* 8, no. 3 (February 2001): 18–48 and Petrella's *The Future of Liberation Theology: An Argument and Manifesto* (Surrey, UK: Ashgate, 2004).

5. I take up this question in *The Aesthetics and Ethics of Faith: A Dialogue between Liberationist and Pragmatic Thought* (Oxford, UK: Oxford University Press, 2014).

6. Orlando Espín and Sixto Garcia, "'Lilies in the Field:' A Hispanic Theology of Providence and Human Responsibility," *Proceedings of the Catholic Theological Society of America* 44 (1989): 73.

7. Ada María Isasi-Díaz, *En La Lucha/In the Struggle: A Hispanic Woman's Liberation Theology* (Minneapolis: Fortress Press, 1993), 47–48.

8. Orlando O. Espín, *The Faith of the People: Theological Reflections on Popular Catholicism* (Maryknoll, NY: Orbis Books, 1997), 119.

9. Espín, *Faith of the* People, 120.

10. Espín, *Faith of the* People, 66.

11. One should note that Espín rightly acknowledges several difficulties in attempting to assess the *sensus fidelium* as a collective "intuition." He states:

> The *sensus fidelium* is *always* expressed through the symbols, language, and culture of the faithful, and, therefore, is in need of intense, constant interpretive processes and methods similar to those called for by the written texts of Tradition and scripture. Without this careful examination and interpretation of its means of expression, the true "faith-full" intuition of the Christian people could be inadequately understood or even falsified. (*Faith of the People*, 67).

12. María Pilar Aquino, "Theological Method in U.S. Latino/a Theology: Toward an Intercultural Theology for the Third Millennium," in *From the Heart of Our People: Latino/a Explorations in Catholic Systematic Theology*, ed. Orlando O. Espín and Miguel H. Díaz (Maryknoll, NY: Orbis Books, 1999), 35.

13. María Pilar Aquino, *Our Cry for Life: Feminist Theology from Latin America* (Maryknoll, NY: Orbis Books, 1993), 13.

14. Roberto S. Goizueta, *Caminemos con Jesús: Toward a Hispanic Latino Theology of Accompaniment* (Maryknoll, NY: Orbis Books, 1995), 88.

15. Much could be said about Goizueta's argument, and I have commented on various aspects of it elsewhere. See, for example, Christopher D. Tirres, "'Liberation' in the Latino Context: Retrospect and Prospect" in *New Horizons in Hispanic/Latino(a) Theology*, ed. Benjamin Valentín (Cleveland: Pilgrim Press, 2003), and *The Aesthetics and Ethics of Faith*, especially pp. 58–75.

16. Virgilio P. Elizondo, "Popular Religion as Support of Identity," in *Mestizo Worship: A Pastoral Approach to Liturgical Ministry* by Virgilio P. Elizondo and Timothy M. Matovina (Collegeville, MN: Liturgical Press, 1998), 30–31. Italics are in the original.

17. On this point, I am indebted to the work of Don Gelpi and Daniel Groody. See Gelpi, *The Conversion Experience* (New York/Mahwah, NJ: Paulist, 1998) and Groody, *Border of Death, Valley of Life: An Immigrant Journey of Heart and Spirit* (Lanham: Rowman & Littlefield, 2002), 79–113.

18. Ada María Isasi-Díaz, *En La Lucha/In the Struggle: A Hispanic Women's Liberation Theology* (Minneapolis: Fortress Press, 1993), 48–49.

19. Aquino, *Our Cry for Life*, 179. See also Michelle A. González, *Afro-Cuban Theology: Religion, Race, Culture, and Identity* (Gainesville, FL: University Press of Florida, 2006), especially 102–120.

20. Catherine Bell, *Ritual Theory, Ritual Practice* (Oxford, UK: Oxford University Press, 1992), 20; Goizueta, *Caminemos con Jesús*, 27–28 n. 26.

21. Alyshia Gálvez, *Guadalupe in New York: Devotion and the Struggle for Citizenship Rights among Mexican Immigrants* (New York: New York University Press, 2010), 107–139; Karen Mary Davalos, "'The Real Way of Praying': The Via

Crucis, *Mexicano*, and the Architecture of Domination," in *Horizons of the Sacred: Mexican Traditions in U.S. Catholicism*, ed. Timothy Matovina and Gary Riebe-Estrella (Ithaca, NY: Cornell University Press, 2002), 41–68. This last book, *Horizons of the Sacred*, also contains other compelling ethnographies on Curanderismo (by Luis D. Leon) and Días de los Muertos (by Lara Medina and Gilbert R. Cadena). See also Timothy Matovina, *Latino Catholicism: Transformation in America's Largest Church* (Princeton: Princeton University Press, 2012), 62–72.

22. Wayne Ashley, "The Stations of the Cross: Christ, Politics, and Processions on New York City's Lower East Side" in *Gods of the City*, ed. Robert A. Orsi (Bloomington, IN: Indiana University Press, 1999), 341–366.

23. For the most developed explanation of this concept, see Thomas H. Groome, *Will There Be Faith? A New Vision for Education and Growing Disciples* (New York: HarperOne, 2011), 261–297.

24. Charles Dahm, *Parish Ministry in a Hispanic Community* (New York: Paulist Press, 2004), 262.

25. In making this point, I do not mean to suggest that popular religion and popular ritual cannot be both a product and a process. After all, there is convenient shorthand in saying, for example, that "Latino/a popular ritual liberates." What I am suggesting, however, is that we should never lose sight of the fact that this *is* a shorthand for complex processes of ritualization. See, for example, Bell, *Ritual Theory, Ritual Practice*, esp. 67–93.

26. Fernando F. Segovia, "Toward a Hermeneutics of the Diaspora: A Hermeneutics of Otherness and Engagement" in *Hispanic Christian Thought at the Dawn of the 21st Century: Apuntes in Honor of Justo L. González*, ed. Alvin Padilla, Roberto Goizueta, and Eldin Villafañe (Nashville, TN: Abingdon, 2005), 55.

BIBLIOGRAPHY

Aquino, María Pilar. *Our Cry for Life: Feminist Theology from Latin America*. Maryknoll, NY: Orbis Books, 1993.

———. "Theological Method in U.S. Latino/a Theology: Toward an Intercultural Theology for the Third Millennium." In *From the Heart of Our People: Latino/a Explorations in Catholic Systematic Theology*, edited by Orlando O. Espín and Miguel H. Díaz, 6–48. Maryknoll, NY: Orbis Books, 1999.

Ashley, Wayne. "The Stations of the Cross: Christ, Politics, and Processions on New York City's Lower East Side." In *Gods of the City: Religion and the American Urban Landscape*, edited by Robert A. Orsi, 341–366. Bloomington, IN: Indiana University Press, 1999.

Bell, Catherine. *Ritual Theory, Ritual Practice*. Oxford, UK: Oxford University Press, 1992.

Dahm, Charles. *Parish Ministry in a Hispanic Community*. New York: Paulist Press, 2004.

Davalos, Karen Mary. "'The Real Way of Praying': The Via Crucis, *Mexicano,* and the Architecture of Domination." In *Horizons of the Sacred: Mexican Traditions* in *U.S. Catholicism*, edited by Timothy Matovina and Gary Riebe-Estrella, 41–68. Ithaca, NY: Cornell University Press, 2002.

Elizondo, Virgilio P. "Popular Religion as Support of Identity." In *Mestizo Worship: A Pastoral Approach to Liturgical Ministry*, edited by Virgilio P. Elizondo and Timothy M. Matovina, 23–33. Collegeville, MN: Liturgical Press, 1998.

Espín, Orlando O. *The Faith of the People: Theological Reflections on Popular Catholicism*. Maryknoll, NY: Orbis Books, 1997.

Espín, Orlando O., and Sixto J. Garcia. "'Lilies in the Field': A Hispanic Theology of Providence and Human Responsibility." *Proceedings of the Catholic Theological Society of America* 44 (1989): 70–90.

Freire, Paolo. *Pedagogy of the Oppressed*. Trans. M. Ramos. New York: Continuum, 1970.

Gálvez, Alyshia. *Guadalupe in New York: Devotion and the Struggle for Citizenship Rights among Mexican Immigrants*. New York: New York University Press, 2010.

García-Rivera, Alejandro R. *A Wounded Innocence: Sketches for a Theology of Art*. Collegeville, MN: Liturgical Press, 2003.

Goizueta, Roberto S. *Caminemos con Jesús: Toward a Hispanic Latino Theology of Accompaniment*. Maryknoll, NY: Orbis Books, 1995.

González, Michelle A. *Afro-Cuban Theology: Religion, Race, Culture, and Identity*. Gainesville, FL: University Press of Florida, 2006.

Groody, Dan G. *Border of Death, Valley of Life: An Immigrant Journey of Heart and Spirit*. Lanham: Rowman & Littlefield, 2002.

Groome, Thomas H. *Will There Be Faith? A New Vision for Education and Growing Disciples*. New York: HarperOne, 2011.

Isasi-Díaz, Ada María. *En La Lucha/In the Struggle: A Hispanic Women's Liberation Theology*. Minneapolis: Fortress Press, 1993.

Leon, Luis D. "'Soy una Curandera y Soy una Católica': The Poetics of Mexican Healing Tradition." In *Horizons of the Sacred: Mexican Traditions in U.S. Catholicism*, edited by Timothy Matovina and Gary Riebe-Estrella, 95–118. Ithaca, NY: Cornell University Press, 2002.

Matovina, Timothy. *Latino Catholicism: Transformation in America's Largest Church*. Princeton, NJ: Princeton University Press, 2012.

Medina, Lara, and Gilbert R. Cadena. "Días de los Muertos: Public Ritual, Community Renewal, and Popular Religion in Los Angeles." In *Horizons of the Sacred: Mexican Traditions in U.S. Catholicism*, edited by Timothy Matovina and Gary Riebe-Estrella, 69–94. Ithaca, NY: Cornell University Press, 2002.

Mejido, Manuel J. "Beyond the Postmodern Condition, or the Turn toward Psychoanalysis." In *Latin American Liberation Theology: The Next Generation*, edited by Ivan Petrella, 119–146. Maryknoll, NY: Orbis Books, 2005.

———. "A Critique of the 'Aesthetic Turn' in U.S. Hispanic Theology: A Dialogue with Roberto Goizueta and the Positing of a New Paradigm." *Journal of Hispanic/Latino Theology* 8:3 (February 2001): 18–48.

Petrella, Ivan. *The Future of Liberation Theology: An Argument and Manifest*. Surrey, UK: Ashgate, 2004.

———. "Liberation Theology-A Programmatic Statement." In *Latin American Liberation Theology: The Next Generation,* edited by Ivan Petrella, 147–172. Maryknoll, NY: Orbis Books, 2005.

Schreiter, Robert. *Constructing Local Theologies.* Maryknoll, NY: Orbis Books, 1997.

Segovia, Fernando F. "Toward a Hermeneutics of the Diaspora: A Hermeneutics of Otherness and Engagement." In *Hispanic Christian Thought at the Dawn of the 21st Century: Apuntes in Honor of Justo L. González,* edited by Alvin Padilla, Roberto Goizueta, and Eldin Villafañe, 55–68. Nashville, TN: Abingdon, 2005.

Tirres, Christopher D. *The Aesthetics and Ethics of Faith: A Dialogue between Liberationist and Pragmatic Thought.* Oxford, UK: Oxford University Press, 2014.

———. "'Liberation' in the Latino Context: Retrospect and Prospect." In *New Horizons in Hispanic/Latino(a) Theology,* edited by Benjamin Valentín, 138–162. Cleveland: Pilgrim Press, 2003.

Part III
CONCLUSIONS

Chapter 11

How Do Latino/a Theologians Employ Scripture?

Francisco Lozada, Jr.

How Latino/a theologians employ Scripture[1] in doing theology (or theologizing) is the focus of this chapter. The question is a hermeneutical question, in that it explores how and why Latino/a theologians go about using Scripture in their constructive theological projects.[2] The chapter gets its start with a broad question posed to the contributors: How do you employ Scripture? Toward this end, three major lines of inquiry were advanced as guidelines: (1) a historical approach—how the Bible has been activated and put into effect (or not) in Latino/a Theology; (2) a theological approach—how the Bible has been employed in their own theological constructions; and (3) a comparative approach—how the use of the Bible in Latino/a theology resembles or differs from its use in Latino/a, racial-ethnic, or geopolitical approaches. All essays incorporate one or more of these approaches in their task of theological hermeneutics.

In what follows, a summary will be provided not only to delineate the main ideas of each essay but also to prepare the reader for a brief analysis of how Latino/a theologians employ Scripture within their respective theologizing endeavors. To that end, the summary will integrate two questions that will allow for a better understanding of how the contributors use Scripture. These questions, which will be put to each essay as a way to summarize how and why they employ Scripture in the fashion they chose, are as follows: (1) How does Scripture bear on their theologizing? and (2) What sort of authoritative force is ascribed to Scripture when an appeal is made?

With regard to the first question, two further questions prove helpful: (1) Does Scripture bear on theologizing *directly*, in that Scripture is employed so as to function as a verification to support a conclusion or main point?; or (2) Does Scripture bear on theologizing *indirectly*, employing Scripture through what others say about or how they use Scripture? These two positions are at opposite ends of a continuum, with theologians vacillating between these ends, depending on the theologizing project at hand. With respect to the second question, two further questions are, again, helpful: (1) Does authority suggest that Scripture contains some sort of intrinsic property, such as inspiration or revelation?; or (2) Does authority suggest how Scripture functions in the life and thinking of the Latino/a community, as in the question of whether Scripture is liberative in the life of the community?[3] These two positions are also at opposite ends of a continuum, with theologians vacillating between the ends, depending on the theologizing project at hand.

Both central questions are related, for how one employs Scripture, directly or indirectly, will influence how authority is construed in theologizing and vice versa. Consequently, how theologians engage both these questions will sway their historical, theological, or comparative use of Scripture.[4] Two further comments regarding the analysis that follows are in order. First, I aim to show how each contributor, each Latino/a theologian, employs Scripture in different ways. That is to say, they do not hold to one standard approach or one understanding of authority as normative; rather, what is standard is how the Latino/a community (broadly understood) is brought to bear on the use of Scripture, thus construing Scripture in a plurality of ways that reflect the lived experience of Latinos/as. Second, for organizational purposes, I shall develop the proposed analysis along the major lines of approach noted earlier: first, the historical; then, the theological; finally, the comparative—knowing full well that many of the essays blend different approaches. At the same time, within these major configurations—aside from the first, the historical approach, in which only one study can be situated—I move from those essays that lean toward a direct use of Scripture toward those that lean toward an indirect use.

CRITICAL ANALYSIS: SCRIPTURE IN THEOLOGY—ROLE AND FORCE

A. The Historical Approach

Edgardo Colón-Emeric—"She orders all things suavemente': A Lascasian Interpretation"

This is a critical reflection on the scriptural hermeneutics of Bartolomé de las Casas—the noteworthy sixteenth-century Spanish theologian and defender of the indigenous of the Americas. Hence, Colón-Emeric's essay takes a historical approach—how the Bible has been activated in a particular period of history, which sheds light on the Latino/a theological-hermeneutical question. The question at hand in Colón-Emeric's eyes addresses the dual responsibility of theological hermeneutics: the "church" and the academy. Colón-Emeric asks how to connect reading Scripture from two particular social locations: reading from East Durham, where he conducts Bible study, vis-à-vis reading from Duke University, where he is a professor/scholar. For Colón-Emeric, the answer is found with Las Casas—a *ressourcement latinamente* (a Latino/a ressourcement), a return to "authoritative" sources of Christianity.

For Colón-Emeric, Las Casas is a viable source for U.S. Latino/a theology, given his Iberian roots. It is also viable, moreover, because Las Casas' theological approach is similar to Latino/a theology's orientation: first, toward interculturalism, in dialoguing with other peoples and religions, and second, toward incarnationality, in believing that all humans can express divine will. Thus, Las Casas, for Colón-Emeric, is the embodiment of a *ressourcement latinamente*. Las Casas serves as an authentic source to guide Colón-Emeric in his question of bridging reading Scripture alongside the marginalized and with reading Scripture alongside the privileged. It follows, then, that Colón-Emeric approaches Scripture indirectly, by way of Las Casas' use of Scripture.

Colón-Emeric's first and main procedural move is to provide a reading of Las Casas as a scriptural interpreter. After a brief review of why Las Casas commits himself to the ill-treated Amerindians—namely, to provide a defense of the indigenous of the Americas against such violent evangelism—Colón-Emeric sets out to review two interpretative readings of Scripture by Las Casas. The first centers on Wisdom 8:1—the key text for Las Casas' defense of the indigenous, found in the treatise entitled *The Only Way to Call* (*De unico vocationis modo*). The second deals with Luke 14:15-24, popularly known as the parable of "The Wedding Banquet"—a text also used by Las Casas in the defense against a violent evangelism against the Amerindians.

With regard to Wisdom 8:1, Las Casas, strongly informed by Thomas Aquinas' *Summa Theologiae* and other texts out of the Latin Vulgate, makes a rational argument by appealing to this text ("All natural things want to be directed to their end gently" [*suavemente*]). Focusing on the last word, "gently," Las Casas deduces (rationally) that Wisdom 8:1 calls for a non-violent evangelism regarding the inhabitants of Tuzutlán, Guatemala—an evangelism not by force but by gentleness. Las Casas even draws on the story of Jesus' sending out the twelve (Matt. 10:9-10) as a way to show how Wisdom/God, taking on flesh in Jesus, evangelizes non-violently, as reflected in Matthew. For sure, Las Casas construes Scripture (i.e., Wisd 8:1) in an authoritative way, since the text functions to present a non-violent evangelism toward the indigenous, consonant with God's manner on how to evangelize. Therefore, Colón-Emeric, by sympathetically (a "reading with" strategy)[5] committing himself to Las Casas's reading of Scripture, also construes Scripture in an "authoritative" fashion.

With regard to Luke 14:15-24, Las Casas comes to this text because his adversary, Ginés de Sepúlveda, appropriates it in order to advocate for physical violence toward the indigenous—a step before evangelism is presented to them. For Las Casas, Luke 14:15-24 has been misinterpreted. The phrase that is being misinterpreted for Las Casas is "to compel them to come in" (14:23, NRSV). Sepúlveda reads this text as suggesting violence, while Las Casas reads it as suggesting persuasion. In other words, the text does not mean that physical violence should be used against the indigenous before converting them; rather, it means that a persuasive argument, guided by God's providence, should be obligatory before converting them. Such an argument, based on scriptural authority, is a non-violent reading of how to evangelize. Colón-Emeric calls Las Casas' interpretative reading strategy a hermeneutics of humanity, for it keeps to the tradition that all humans are instruments of the divine will.

Colón-Emeric's reading of Las Casas' use and interpretation of Scripture is one that appeals to Scripture indirectly, thus placing him toward the indirect end of the continuum. In other words, Colón-Emeric's connection to Scripture is by means of what Las Casas has to say and do with Scripture. Such an adoption of Las Casas helps Colón-Emeric bridge his bifurcated reading location—a world with the marginalized and a world with the privileged. His rereading of Las Casas provides him with the principles and concepts that guide him in proposing a hermeneutics of humanity. It indirectly draws out Las Casas' interpretations of certain texts of Scripture in order to apply them to his overall question: how to bridge his two bifurcated reading communities. In so doing, Scripture is authoritative by way of how it functions, principally because Las Casas (*ressourcement latinamente*) establishes an interpretative history that continues to empower the voice of the Latino/a community as it does in the academy. Thus, for Colón-Emeric, Scripture is employed through a rereading of Las Casas' scriptural defense of the indigenous. Thereby Las Casas' approach is a guide for Latino/a biblical hermeneutics. For Las Casas illustrates how one serves as a bridge to two communities.

B. The Theological Approach

Sammy Alfaro – "Reading and Hearing Scripture in the Latina/o Pentecostal Community"

Alfaro looks at the role and employment of Scripture within the Latina/o Pentecostal community. Attention is given to the theological question of how the Latina/o Pentecostal community reads and hears Scripture. This position is anchored in the belief that it is the Spirit who activates reading and hearing for the purpose of informing, guiding, and directing their (Latinos/

as Pentecostals) lives. To accomplish this, Alfaro explores a primary component of Pentecostal theological hermeneutics: the worship service, which provides a window on the use of Scripture. He will support this with a theological reading of Acts 6:1-7 as an illustration of Latino/a Pentecostal biblical interpretation. To be sure, Alfaro sees Scripture as playing a close direct role in theologizing: a sacred, inspired text informing the lives of Latina/o Pentecostals.

To begin with, Alfaro delineates Pentecostal theological hermeneutics, providing an interpretative account of an historic event in the life of the Pentecostal movement in the early 1900s, where the beginnings of such hermeneutics gets its guiding principles. One such principle is that the reader/hearer is informed by the Spirit. That is, the Spirit inspires their understanding of Scripture. The reader/hearer does not come to Scripture objectively but rather subjectively—moved by the Spirit. A second principle is that Scripture is a living text. Scripture is a holy object that functions to instruct, guide, and transform the believer. It is a text that is inspired by God, making it authoritative. The human component in the development of Scripture is not a concern; rather, Scripture, through the Spirit of God, links God's words with the Spirit's manifestation in the community. For instance, Scripture possesses inherent properties, like the doctrine of baptism, and is authorized through a particular reading of Acts, a foundational text for Pentecostal hermeneutics. That is, God, through the Spirit, confers the doctrine of baptism in Acts. It is through a "spiritual reading" or "fuller meaning" of Scripture, inspired and authoritative by the Spirit, that one is allowed to attain a meaning of Scripture.

Second, Alfaro turns his attention to the use of Scripture in a Latina/o Pentecostal *culto* (service) to demonstrate both principles. He does so first with a look at three characteristics of the *culto*: belief in the priesthood of believers; belief in a noncreedal service; and an "open" or "free" liturgy. These characteristics are reflected in the dynamics of the *culto* itself. For instance, Alfaro, drawing from personal experience, highlights how Scripture functions in the Pentecostal service. The inspired Spirit-living text plays a role in each step of the worship service: (1) first, Scripture is read and interpreted by the leader; (2) then, Scripture is heard through the selection of music; (3) next, congregants employ Scripture through special prayer requests; (4) after that, Scripture is correlated with a testimonial thanksgiving; and (5) finally, a reading of Scripture and its preaching take place. The Spirit, with the purpose of transforming the communal life of the community, inspires all of this.

Third, Alfaro interprets Acts 6:1-6 as a way to demonstrate engagement with Scripture. Beginning with an issue at hand—for example, a lack of leadership roles in the Latina/o Pentecostal community due to the cultural and language generational changes facing the Latina/o church—Alfaro draws on similar cultural and language issues facing the early Christian community in Acts 6:1-6. Guided by the Spirit, Alfaro produces a reading of Acts 6:1-6 that provides a possible solution: the Spirit instructs his community—as the Spirit did for the early Christian community—to be open to all sorts of leadership roles, no matter whether it is preaching or setting up chairs, for all are roles "full of the Spirit." If this openness to the Spirit is welcomed, a solution to the cultural and language divide that is occurring in the Latina/o Pentecostal between generations can be solved. Alfaro concludes his essay with a brief word on the importance of the Spirit working not just through the leadership but also throughout the community privately as well as publicly, as in the *culto*.

Alfaro appears to employ Scripture directly in theologizing the Latino/a Pentecostal approach to Scripture. His appeal to it is due to his faith experience as a Pentecostal and his belief in the transforming power of God through the Spirit. The Spirit is the overarching theological principle that guides his hermeneutics as well as the hermeneutics of his community. The essay demonstrates that he construes Scripture as containing inherent properties and that these properties, such as the doctrine of baptism, can be identified in reading Acts through the power of the Spirit. The power of the Spirit is what gives Scripture authority; in fact, the Scripture appears subordinate to the Spirit. In this sense, Alfaro appears to lean a bit toward an indirect appeal to Scripture—authority comes from the Spirit, given how it functions to activate revelation.

At the same time, in employing Scripture in doing theology, Alfaro takes current issues or problems in his community and moves to Scripture to infer the same issues or problems and solutions, as reflected in his reading of Acts 6:1-6. In other words, Scripture is used as a source of data from which central ideas or doctrines are inferred through the power of the Spirit. The interpreter then takes these ideas or doctrines as his or her own and reinterprets them through *testimonios* (testimony/witnessing) and *coritos* (songs with a particular Pentecostal style). This way of employing the text is not exactly a reflection of a fundamentalist way of reading—at least in how it has been traditionally conceived and practiced.

Hermeneutically, Alfaro's reading strategy appears to be one in which the Bible serves as a source for a communitarian understanding of the Christian faith. To be sure, the experience of the Spirit as part of God's people in and out of the Bible discloses anew God's Spirit. Alfaro thus approaches Scripture principally in a direct way, drawing out the Spirit from Scripture, but also in an indirect way (but surely leaning toward the direct end of the continuum), in that the Spirit controls how to use Scripture in the life of the community—privately and publicly. Consequently, Alfaro engages Scripture as authoritative, containing inherent theological properties (e.g., inspiration) informing theological positions.

Nora O. Lozano – "Is It Truly a 'Good' Book? The Bible, Empowerment, and Liberation"

Lozano examines the role of the Bible in her theological-academic context. She does so by employing the metaphor of a bridge. Given that Lozano navigates between two worlds, as a Mexican and a Mexican American, the bridge allows her a place to speak about her social locations both culturally as well as professionally. Lozano's social location begins with an identification of the Baptist tradition. Recognizing the diversity that exists among Baptists, she locates her Baptist institutional affiliation along the lines of a conservative to moderate school. She recognizes that all views and constructions of theology are done from a social location, but she also acknowledges that one's view of the Bible is influenced by one's target audience. In her case, it is Baptist students, women in particular, who believe in the Bible as a holy and inspired book that is essential to their lives and thus authoritative, based on the position that it is God's word in all its properties, including the cover, credits, and footnotes. Her students also are unapologetic of this belief. It is out of this social location that Lozano questions whether the Bible is truly a "good" book.

Lozano begins to address this question with the acknowledgment that the Bible has not always been a "good" book for women. The Bible has been used as a tool of oppression against women in controlling their minds and behavior. When abused women hold on to the theological view that the Bible *is* God, they tend to correlate the view that God is doing the abusing, as Lozano once believed herself. She posits how it might be possible for these women to separate this correlation. To address this issue, Lozano explores the work of other Latina theologians. For instance, one possible solution emerges from the work of Ada María Isasi-Díaz, who argues that the starting point for any theological interpretation of the Bible is experience and struggle. Thus, focusing on women's experience and struggle read against the Bible is a possibility to challenge the idea that the Bible *is* God. Another possible solution, drawing from Loida Martell-Otero, suggests sifting out those texts that are not liberative from those that are to provide a "canon from the canon," as Lozano suggests. Lozano understands that all interpreters work with a "canon from the canon" approach, and she is aware that her "canon from the canon" might be different from others. Both positions are not without limitations, but Lozano argues that one cannot just use one "canon from the canon" to evaluate another's "canon from the canon."

Instead, one has to take seriously the role of the other person (the reader) and their canon—even if their "canon from the canon" is not liberative. In fact, one must take on at times a resistant reading approach to the whole Bible to tease out the liberative and empowerment elements of revelation for all readers. In this sense, Lozano appeals to Scripture directly, in that Scripture is engaged as a whole, examining groups of writings (canon from the canon) and then combining them to be employed in evaluating ethical and theological decisions. On the whole, Scripture is for sure authoritative. It is biblical authority, which believers should use to guide their lives.

After establishing some theological principles for engaging the Bible, particularly among her community, Lozano turns to the critical field of biblical criticism and her respective theological approach to address the question of how to take the whole Bible, not just a "canon from the canon" or selected texts, to draw from for inspiration and liberation. Lozano draws on how Latino biblical scholars (Francisco García-Treto, Fernando Segovia) engage the Bible: how readers need to become more astute with oppressive texts and search for those alternative voices in a story that can provide encouragement to the marginalized today. It is difficult to work with texts, she realizes, when texts function to provide agency to an oppressive community using oppressive subjects in a story. Lozano's position, therefore, is to engage the Bible in such a way that the reader (women readers in particular) becomes the subject rather than the object of their own story. As a theologian, Lozano sees her role as twofold: making women astute readers of the Bible, and making them aware of the various academic approaches to biblical studies, that take seriously the role of the reader in interpretation (historical, literary, and cultural criticisms as well as cultural studies).

Informed by these principles and approaches, Lozano concludes by providing various guidelines to engage the Bible as a whole, especially when certain texts are oppressive to women. First, Lozano recommends taking seriously the Bible and the community of readers. Both components of interpretation should be critically respected and studied in order to understand their various historical and textual worlds. Second she proposes approaching the Bible in an open and friendly posture. In other words, Lozano sees her theological task as a hermeneutical and cultural translator. She is a theological-multilingual translator—translating the revelation of God to her community for liberation and empowerment. Third, Lozano suggests establishing theological criteria—related to the person of Christ, the work of God, and the revelation of God—to set against the interpretation of the Bible. In this way, one can sift what is liberative and what is not. Finally, Lozano argues that it is important to realize the limitations of interpretations; it cannot resolve all questions. At the end, Lozano sees these four guidelines as her strategy to do theology—a theology that is pastoral, providing a way for her community of women to make the Bible their friend, but also prophetic, moving her community toward liberation and empowerment. She concludes with two short personal stories confirming her approach of making friends with the Bible. Lozano's target audience certainly informs her theological approach within the theological context where she is engaging the Bible.

The Bible is evidently employed in her theological construction of her community. For Lozano, her work is strongly targeted toward bringing liberation and empowerment from the Bible to Baptist women. She appeals to the Bible because it is a sacred, inspired, and authoritative text. The Bible is God's revelation, and for some of the women, the Bible is God. The authority does not rest on how the Bible functions per se; its authority comes because it is the Bible. She is not interested—even though many employ a "canon from the canon" principle—just in those texts that are liberative, she also believes in engaging those texts that are oppressive, particularly to the marginalized and to women. She is interested in engaging the whole Bible.

Lozano, using Scripture in reflecting on the task of theologian, sees the role of the Bible from two perspectives. Living between cultures, or living on a bridge between cultures, allows her the vantage point to see the employment of the Bible not only among her academic community but also among academic Latino/a theologians and biblical scholars. From this vantage point, she recognizes and affirms that there are various hermeneutical stances taken by readers. These include resistance and friendliness. Her task as a theologian is to respect both stances and communities of readers (ecclesial and academic) in order to serve as a guide toward liberation and empowerment to all readers. In this sense, Lozano takes a direct approach to the Bible in her theological work and teaching. This approach does not begin with the authoritative Bible, as with her students; rather, it begins with the experiences of the community.

Loida I. Martell-Otero – "Reading Against the Grain: Scripture and Constructive Evangélica Theology"

Martell-Otero employs a theological approach to Scripture. In so doing, she uses a reading strategy of the Bible that she calls "reading against the grain," which she describes in threefold fashion. First, the strategy begins with a delineation of the theologian's social location. This, when applied to her, is presented as follows: a constructive theologian, who thus adheres to the role of subjectivity in the process of doing theology; an evangélica (Protestant), who thus takes seriously the nature and role of Scripture as a self-interpreting text; and a Latina (Puerto Rican), who sees herself as a *Samaritana* (Samaritan) or stranger in the United States. Second, to "read against the grain" suggests an anti-colonial understanding, informed by the daily experience (*lo cotidiano*) of the marginalized. It is not exactly a postcolonial reading for her. A postcolonial reading overlooks many identity factors, such as gender *en lo cotidiano* (in everyday life), nor does it capture a true sense of a "post" coloniality, such as in the case of Puerto Rico. Postcolonialism, for

Martell-Otero, emanates from a European discourse and fails to listen to the voices of the Other, such as how grassroots evangélicas read the Bible. She prefers to see her anti-colonial orientation as one that reads against oppressive or marginalized readings of the text in order to listen to the voices from her community that have been absent in the constructive theology process. Third, the strategy is applied to two theological sources, *testimonios* (communal storytelling) and *coritos* (songs), as a way to bring forth those voices absent in the process of doing Latino/a constructive theology.

Martell-Otero approaches Scripture both as an authoritative source and resource for her community in a spiritual, ecclesial, and scholarly fashion. She does so vacillating between a direct and an indirect engagement with Scripture. On the one hand, Scripture is the sacred, authoritative source and resource that demonstrates the Spirit's working or breathing of God's revelation in one's reading experience with her community. In this sense, Scripture is not so much doing something but rather contains certain properties (i.e., revelation) that need to be activated through the reading experience with her Latina community. On the other hand, she employs Scripture indirectly, given that her Latina experience functions to inform her reading of Scripture or her approach to Scripture.

For Martell-Otero, the appeal to Scripture is part of her theological identity. She describes part of her social location as an evangélica, meaning that a public and personal commitment to Jesus Christ as Lord and Savior explains partially why she attends to Scripture to construct theology. It is within this evangélica community where the lived realities of suffering come together with the Scripture to make sense of life—living in a world where her community is invisible or, as she says, living in the "peripheral places." Scripture is the place where her community encounters God so as to help them continue living—despite the employment of Scripture as a tool of colonization and marginalization—via seeking comfort, inspiration, and transformation. Reading Scripture is based on a trust with Scripture that the saving hand of Jesus will be there to liberate her community as Jesus has liberated those in the text.

Even though Martell-Otero does not construe Scripture as containing some conceptual system for creating doctrine or serving as a lexicon for proposing concepts, as do more traditional evangelical-conservative positions that hold Scripture's content and concepts as a record of revelation, she leans toward a direct employment of Scripture in the sense that it occasions an experience with the divine/God. Her community is "redeemed" by being placed within those narratives in the biblical text that contain the presence of the redeeming agent. Scripture is authoritative because it provides a normative link with the triune God's self-disclosure. It is the rule of faith and practice for her community, and it is authoritative because it is the saving word of God—not because revelation exists in the words or in the intention of the authors but because Scripture speaks to the realities of the community's lives and helps to transform them. Scripture is construed as giving voice to them. This is reflected in their *testimonios* and *coritos* in the context of worship and prayer.

Martell-Otero, therefore, employs Scripture theologically, in the sense that she is constructing a Latino/a theological approach, informed by her cultural (Latina), religious (evangélica), and professional (theologian) identities, from which she engages the Scriptures indirectly. Thus, she constructs a theology of Scripture from her own particular social location. This theological-hermeneutical approach is one cast as "reading against the grain." This approach aims to capture those voices in the biblical narrative and in the lives of evangélicas that have either been silenced or not yet been revealed through a rereading of Scriptures "against the grain." Central to this approach is a global turn. In other words, Martell-Otero takes stock that she, along with her Puerto Rican community, are members of a racialized colonized nation perceived as the Other ("satos" suggesting mutts). This strategic move is part of her delineation of social location, part of her being critically honest on why and how she reads Scripture. At the same time, her community is a religious people, for in the daily life (*lo cotidiano*) of Latinos/as God is present where the Other is located. This dimension of *lo cotidiano* will thus serve as the *locus theologicus* for evangélica theology.

"Reading against the grain" is a theological approach that takes seriously Scripture as sacred and authoritative. It goes beyond being informed by postcolonial criticism but remains very interested in reading the text framed around a center/peripheral binary, with a particular projection of recovering the voice of Latinas through the reading process itself, through *testimonios* and *coritos*. Scripture is thus employed theologically, directly and indirectly, perhaps leaning more toward direct usage, in the sense that it opens up dialogue, with the help of the Spirit, between the world in the narrative and the world of Latinas.

Nancy Pineda-Madrid—"La Guadalupe, The Bible, Pentecost"

Pineda-Madrid's theological proposal focuses on the religious symbol of Our Lady of Guadalupe. She aims to explore this symbol in relation to biblical texts, metathemes, and metanarratives. For Pineda-Madrid, such theological symbolic reconstruction of Guadalupe is necessary for theologians as a way to disclose the power of justice revealed in the Bible—a source in the sense that it links original scriptural revelation with the triune God and the community of faithful disciples. In this sense, Scripture is authoritative and reading Scripture brings readers to link their religious experience with the triune God. Hence, her claim is that the biblical account of Pentecost (Acts

2:1-12) serves as a way to understand the theological meaning of Guadalupe. She begins to support this claim by establishing a conversation with other scholars who have made a connection with Guadalupe, the Holy Spirit, and the biblical text.

Pineda-Madrid's first significant move is a rereading of the analysis of Guadalupe and Revelation 12 by three scholars (Jean-Paul Ruiz; Timothy Matovina; David Sánchez). All are informed by Miguel Sánchez's 1648 account of Guadalupe, called *Imagen de la Virgen Maria*. In so doing, Pineda-Madrid draws on their contributions: the importance of the hermeneutical implications when correlating Guadalupe with Revelation 12; how the relationship between Guadalupe and Revelation 12 serves to transform the world; and the recognition of power and ideology between Guadalupe and Revelation 12. Consequently, the rereading of these scholars by Pineda-Madrid confirms a connection between Guadalupe and the biblical text.

Her second significant move is to examine the connection between Guadalupe and the Holy Spirit. She does this by examining, to begin with, the work of Virgilio Elizondo, who makes a connection between Guadalupe and the Holy Spirit. Guadalupe, like the Holy Spirit, serves as a religious symbol that conceptualizes the struggle for liberation and new life, which is a trait of the Holy Spirit, and that gives life to a new church as the Holy Spirit did at Pentecost (Acts 2). Then, she draws on the work of Orlando Espín, who connects Guadalupe with the Holy Spirit, thus leading her to explore further the pneumatic relationship expressed through the religious symbol of Guadalupe.

Pineda-Madrid's third significant move explores the relationship of Guadalupe and Pentecost—Acts 2. Informed by scholars of Luke-Acts (Earl Richard and Robert Tannehill), she establishes that Guadalupe "resonates" with Pentecost by way of the Lukan thematic characteristics of Pentecost/Holy Spirit reflected in the work of Guadalupe. These are identified as follows: (1) promise and presence—the Spirit, promised by Jesus and present in the devotion to Guadalupe; (2) power for mission—Spirit/Guadalupe as a commitment to transform the world; (3) from death to life—Spirit/Guadalupe inaugurates a new age for its believers; and (4) the gift of the Spirit as a progressive reality—Spirit/Guadalupe points to hope. At the end, for Pineda-Madrid, the biblical account of Pentecost resonates with Guadalupe, as evidenced through these parallel thematic characteristics.

Pineda-Madrid appeals to the Bible because the task of theology, especially for an analysis of religious symbols such as Guadalupe, needs to bring the Bible to bear upon it. In this sense, her appeal vacillates between indirect and direct in constructing theology. She supposes that the religious symbol of Guadalupe resonates with the Bible (Revelation 12 and especially Acts 2). In so doing, the religious symbol is not only grounded in the Christian-biblical tradition but also established among the people, that is, Latinos/as who believe in the symbol of Guadalupe and who continue to experience the power of God as it speaks to them behind the symbol. In this sense, her appeal to Scripture is more direct. At the same time, she draws on how others read Scripture (e.g., Revelation 12 and Acts 2) and their identification of biblical themes reflected in the symbol of Guadalupe. For Pineda-Madrid, these readings draw out the hidden realities of the symbol of Guadalupe and thus address the existential questions Latinos/as are asking today, such as questions of suffering and liberation.

Pineda-Madrid sees the Bible as authoritative in the sense of how it functions. She employs the Bible within an academic/scholarly context, but this does not exclude the spiritual or ecclesial context. As such, the Bible is not a container that holds every word to be the literal word of God, thus making it authoritative. Rather, the authority of the Bible is construed as the means by which readers are connected (e.g., symbols) to the manifestations of God. Pineda-Madrid understands the Bible as authoritative, in that it expresses an occasion of a saving and revelatory event (Pentecost) for an earlier community of believers, just as it continues to do with communities through the religious symbol of Guadalupe, transforming the lives of Latinos/as and other believers.

There is no doubt that Pineda-Madrid employs Scripture directly and indirectly in the theological construction of Guadalupe in relationship to the Bible. In applying it directly, she views Scripture as proposing a transformative event such as Acts 2. When applying it indirectly, she draws on the interpretative tradition of scholars who have engaged these and other texts to establish a connection between the event of Guadalupe with the event of an earlier (ancient) community for believers today. These scholars' works open up these texts for Pineda-Madrid to draw on those themes that resonate with the religious symbol of Guadalupe. Pineda-Madrid authorizes her claim by appeal to these texts, but also by appeal to her community's experience with Guadalupe. These texts show that the Spirit mediates the power of God, who liberates (redeems) believers through Guadalupe. Thus, in delineating her claim that Guadalupe resonates with Pentecost, Pineda-Madrid acknowledges that the Bible is part of doing theology; she is also saying that the Bible is a descriptive source for Christian constructive theology.

Chris Tirres – "Popular Ritual as Liberating Pedagogy"

Chris Tirres turns to a study of popular ritual as an indirect way to rethink the Bible as a living narrative. Like the popular rituals of *posadas*, *pastorelas*, and *via cruces*,[6] the Bible is also re-imagined, reconstructed, and re-enacted by communities. His focus is not on the Bible's direct link to popular rituals; rather, it is on understanding popular ritual's relationship to pedagogy—a pedagogy that aims to serve in a liberating fashion for both Latino/a theologians and biblical scholars. In a way, his theologizing of popular rituals is a proposal suggesting that popular rituals, grounded in the biblical story, are liberative. To illustrate this claim, Tirres takes four steps to show how popular ritual is liberating: its connection to liberation theology; its employment by U.S. Latino/a theologians as liberating rituals; its relationship to a liberative pedagogy; and its possible implications for constructive theologians and biblical critics.

First, Tirres moves to counter the argument that U.S. Latino/a theology fails to take seriously liberation theology's project toward the liberation of the poor as a result of its ethnographic focus on Latino/a culture and aesthetics. Tirres takes the position that U.S. Latino/a theology entails both an ethnographic and liberation focus. It is ethnographic when it focuses on the culture and aesthetics of popular ritual, and it is liberationist when it provides a sense of agency to those who believe in popular ritual. Tirres sees U.S. Latino/a theology as incorporating both foci.

Second, this integrated focus is reflected in the work of U.S. Latino/a theologians (A. M. Isasi-Díaz, S. Garcia, O. Espín, M. Aquino, R. Goizueta, V. Elizondo, T. Matovina, D. Gelpi, D. Groody, M. González). Tirres, informed by their work, understands popular ritual and religion as providing agency for those who have endured conquest and marginality. Popular ritual emerges out of a historical context (pre-Tridentine Iberian Catholicism) embodied by the *sensus fidelium* ("sense of faithful") of the people (in Latin America), uninhibited by the doctrines of orthodoxy by Roman Catholicism in Europe. Popular religion—and by extension popular ritual—thus serves as a locus for U.S. Latino/a theology and serves to liberate. Liberation does not only concern the public sphere of life (economics, politics) with an explicit *telos*—liberation of the poor. Liberation also concerns the private life of people, as through their experiences with public ritual and its resultant effects of solidarity with others, agency, and a sense of identity—all of which Tirres sees as liberative in the tradition of liberation theology. Tirres is aware of reading popular ritual romantically, without taking seriously its implications and risks, such as its role in challenging class, race, and sexuality, its role in seeing itself liberative by its very presence, and its patriarchal elements. For these reasons, Tirres understands popular ritual as liberating but is fully aware that it can function in a problematic way.

Third, after establishing popular ritual as liberating, Tirres makes the claim that popular ritual is connected to pedagogy because it teaches the Bible through the stories in the *posadas, pastorelas,* and *via cruces.* Thus, popular ritual, through pastoral leaders, rhetorically functions in a didactic way, conveying information to ritual learners, as well as in a critical way, raising consciousness of these learners about their identity and about the narrative of suffering represented in the biblical story.

Fourth, Tirres closes with a brief examination of the possible implications of studying public rituals from a cultural perspective for theologians and biblical critics: its oversight in questions of identity factors such as gender, class, and sexuality; and its failure to see liberation as a process rather than an end product. Both of these challenges, as Tirres calls them, extend to biblical criticism as well. He challenges biblical interpreters not to see biblical studies (just like the study of public ritual) as a practice just for the sake of what the text meant. Rather, biblical studies ought to be practiced as a process toward liberation. In other words, the results of biblical studies ought to provide agency through its own particular way of reading the Bible and ought to be taught in such a way as to aim toward the liberation of its community.

Tirres attends to Scripture in an indirect fashion. There is an appeal, but it is not a strong one. The appeal is indirect, in that, like public rituals (*posadas, pastorelas, via cruces*), the Bible serves as a source in order to experience the divine. For this reason, the appeal is that the Bible is giving foundation to the popular ritual. The Bible is authoritative, in that it functions, like the public rituals, to provide liberation to the Latino/a and other marginalized communities. It is a source that leads to liberation as a product (economic liberation) but that also provides agency to the voiceless. Thus, for Tirres, Scripture is construed as an expression of an occasion or an event (e.g., popular rituals) for not only an earlier community but also for a community in the present, as in *posadas, pastorelas*, and *via cruces*. This is not an understanding of Scripture in terms of biblical principles or concepts, but rather in terms of pointing to acts of God in history (e.g., via public rituals), rendering an understanding of Jesus or God as liberator with the hope of transformation of the followers, either privately or publicly. Thus, the Scripture is understood, like popular rituals, as the re-enactment of the stories in the community's own living experience.

As mentioned above, Scripture is employed indirectly. Its minimal employment is not seen as a negative element in his theological proposal; it just does not figure as prominently as it may in other theological proposals that he has constructed or offered by fellow constructive theologians. When it is employed, Scripture is seen more as an illustration regarding how it might aid to better understand popular ritual as a liberating pedagogy. Constructive theology has the task of translating the manifestation of God through popular ritual as well as its expression in the Bible. In other words, Scripture, like popular ritual, mediates the divine into modern understandings. Tirres thus appears to employ Scripture not in a privileged sense over popular ritual but also not quite on a par with it; rather, it appears that Scripture—and only a part of it—plays a slightly subordinate role to other sources like popular ritual, but, for sure, is still important for shaping the identity of its believers.

Michelle A. González – "Biblical Silence: Where Is the Bible in Latino/a Theology?"

González turns her attention to the role of the Bible in Latino/a Theology, particularly among Roman Catholic theologians. The question at hand is why the Bible does not play much of a role among systematic and constructive Roman Catholic Latino/a theologians. She admits that the Bible does not play a primary source in her own theologizing; rather, it is the faith experience of the Latino/a community and the work of critical theology that play such a role. Thus, her engagement with the Bible is very much toward the indirect end of the continuum, particularly when engaged in theologizing. In addressing this issue, she provides a critical evaluation of Latino/a popular religion/theology, critical biblical hermeneutics, biblical scholarship and popular religion, and the role of the Bible in Latino/a theology.

With regard to Latino/a popular theology, González highlights several academic discussions present within Latino/a theology in its search for identity as an academic discipline: Is it (or not) a form of liberation theology or does it just contain elements of liberation theology? Is it simply systematic or constructive theology with a splash of *latinamente*? What brings Latino/a theology together? For her, and for Roman Catholic Latino/a theology as well, popular religion is a unifying factor in doing Latino/a theology. Popular religion provides social and cultural identity to the Latino/a faith communities, thus distinguishing it from liberation theology but also giving Latino theology identity. At the same time, she cautions against a non-critical analysis of Latino/a popular religion, including overlooking those biblical narratives that give popular religion and practices life.

Second, González explores Latino/a biblical hermeneutics to remind Latino/a theologians of issues to consider in their theological projects. Among these are the following: particularizing one's theological project and theology itself; appropriating the biblical texts without a critical evaluation of their reading strategies; reinscribing the marginality of the Latino/a community in constructing theology; and avoiding a critique of the Bible as a whole while employing biblical texts in liberating projects.

Third, González offers a rereading of the popular ritual of San Lázaro (Lazarus) in relationship to Luke's parable of Lazarus and the rich man (16:14-31). San Lázaro is not an "official" saint of the Roman Catholic Church, yet he represents a significant devotion in Cuban/Cuban American religiosity. After a brief history of San Lázaro and its African and Santería influence, she points out how the institutionalized Catholic Church has tried to rewrite this popular ritual history and devotion, thus overlooking how such devotion to "San" Lázaro, who is poor and marginalized in the Lucan story, appeals particularly to Afro-Cubans who relate to that human condition.

Finally, González concludes with a critical reflection on the absence of the Bible in the work of Roman Catholic Latino/a theologians, positing that the Bible is not central or normative.

González is clearly toward that end of the spectrum where Scripture does not play a central role in theologizing. This is true not only of her own theological project overall—indeed, she intentionally uses the lowercase "s" for Scripture—but also, she argues, of the work of Roman Catholic Latino/a theologians in general. Thus, there is no real strong appeal to Scripture for her. It does not represent that "holy" or "sacred" text as it does for other theologians. For this reason, it is not authoritative in the traditional sense of containing a source of "data" to construe doctrines or to support theological concepts, but it does hold on to some authority if it functions in the life of the community toward liberation. The Bible or Scripture gets its authority through interpretation.

Thus, for instance, in her rereading of the popular devotion to San Lázaro, González provides a reading of Luke 16:14-31 that highlights the event not as a condemnation of wealth but rather as a condemnation of those with resources who do nothing to help the poor. She then expresses this interpretation as the reason, perhaps, why so many Cubans/Cuban Americans, and particularly Afro-Cubans, appeal to San Lázaro today, because San Lázaro reminds them of and affirms their own marginality among the wealthy. In this way, González employs the Bible theologically by aiming to explain how and why there is an appeal to San Lázaro. The Bible—that is, Luke 16:14-31 to be specific—functions indirectly yet authoritatively through the faith of the people. It functions to render an explanation why a faithful community seeks a popular religious practice in honoring San Lázaro—namely, for personal and public life transformation.

C. The Comparative Approach

Elaine Padilla – "Darkening the Image: Another Allegory of the Beauty of the Shulamite"

Padilla takes up the theme of darkness and how the history of Christianity has played a role in the darkening of the Shulamite—the female protagonist in the Song of Songs (6:13). The question at hand for Padilla is why the Shulamite goes through a process of "whitening" in Christian aesthetics. Theologically, she argues that such "whitening" also leads to a "whitening" of the image of God. Padilla is interested in rescuing the Shulamite from such a process by affirming her darkness. Thus, the end goal is not to promote a theology that is founded on essentialism in ethnic/racial identity for beings and God, but one that is constructionist and leading to multiple identities of beings and God. The image of God is not that of one color/ethnicity/race but rather that of multiple colors/ethnicities/races. Such a theological position engages Scripture directly, but in a way that sees Scripture (i.e., Song of Songs) as an ideological product that participates in the construction of identity/race/ethnicity. In this latter sense, a comparative approach is adopted in exploring how the Bible in Latino/a theology differs from other racial/ethnic interpretations of the Shulamite.

She begins with an examination of the word "Shulamite," suggesting that the name is related to her representation as "black" based on the phrase, "I am black and beautiful" (1:5, NRSV). Her color becomes polemical among early commentators, who see this "blackness" in a negative light, particularly when they translate 1:5 as "I am black, but I am beautiful," suggesting a negative connotation with the conjunction "but." Early biblical commentators, through their patristic exegesis, reify a negative interpretation of her darkness, linking it to a contrastive syntactical construction and connecting it with immorality and vices. Padilla provides further support by examining how the Shulamite's darkness has been excluded in understanding the image of God, how it has been associated with evil, and how early commentators aimed to whiten her through the ploy of *luminosity*, that is, the process of whitening or doing away with darkness. Such early history of negative representation of "darkness" and gender (she adds) associated with the Shulamite influences a concept of an image of God that promotes whiteness over darkness, as displayed in the colonizing project of the Americas, to which she turns next.

Padilla aims to show how this negative representation of darkness is carried over in the construction of a variety of ethnic/racial identities (*latinidades*) during the colonial period in the Americas. What she demonstrates is that a process of whitening began with the arrival of Europeans. Along with their presence came an ideology of whitening that infiltrated all areas of culture, economics, and politics. What Europeans brought was a heightening of whiteness and a devaluing of darkness. This is also reflected in the United States where a white/nonwhite binary system was established and where, if you fell in between or toward the end of the non-white, you would experience the effects of racialization. Such a process of whitening led to certain policies such as the "one drop rule": if you had "one drop of black blood," you signified Blackness. What Padilla calls for is a move away from such binary racial categories with a move to celebrate *négritude*, creolization, or *mulataje*. Such acknowledgment of the ethnic/racial diversity of one's past and religious history allows for different ways to see concepts such as the *imago Dei* not along one color line but multiple colors lines.

Padilla's main section focuses on a rereading of the Shulamite in the Song of Songs. In this rereading, she challenges modernity's understanding of racism, which is translated into Christian theology and morality: white is good and Black/darkness is evil. For this reason, she argues that looking at the Shulamite and the theme of darkness from the perspective of Latinoa thinking (her nomenclature) can present darkness positively and thus understand God as not having one representation of color (race/ethnicity) but multiple representations of color/ethnicity/race. To support this argument, Padilla first draws on Gregory of Nyssa, who provides an interpretation (Song of Songs 3:1-4; 5:2) of the Shulamite as embracing her "luminous opacity." This interpretation provides a challenge to any ethical binary system that casts darkness as evil and whiteness as good. Padilla then turns to Origen and his interpretation of 1:5, particularly the phrases "the tents of Kedar" and "the curtains of Solomon," suggesting that these phrases refer to the curtains that adorn the tabernacle. The curtains are black and glorious, thus signifying a positive representation of darkness. The images/icons (i.e., tents, curtains) also point to the Shulamite's flesh, based on their material (i.e., goat's hair), and thus signify the plurality of humanity. Both strategic moves by Padilla are meant to reverse any whitening interpretation of the Shulamite. She suggests a possible interpretation of the Shulamite's darkness that is not binary but rather multiple and colorful.

Padilla does not want to fall into the trap of liberating "blackness" by casting it against "whiteness." Rather she, like Gregory of Nyssa and Origen, wants to explore ways the Shulamite's dark beauty opens possibilities to understand *imago Dei* in a multiplicity of hues—to serve as a symbol of freedom for those colonized for their humanness due to their ethnic/racial identity. It is out of Padilla's context of *latinidad*, which celebrates a multiplicity of self-identifying, that emerges a disruptive examination of any ethical binary based on color. The Shulamite, for Padilla, challenges any attempt to see darkness in the negative or to cast it against whiteness. She concludes with a summary of her theological analysis. At the end, she is recovering the Shulamite from her othering by tradition but also using tradition to recover her sense of identity. As Latinos/as celebrate their various "colors" as well as wrestle with those inherent tensions in ethnicity/race, Padilla's rereading of the Shulamite aims to provide a positive representation of her identity.

For Padilla, Scripture is employed in two ways: historically, by examining the history of the Shulamite's reception in patristic exegesis; and theologically, by examining how "darkness" has been constructed in the history of interpretation and how it can be reconstructed in relationship to the *imago Dei*. She leans toward a direct use of Scripture to support her theological claim or project, namely, that darkness is beauty unto itself, as the character of the Shulamite has represented and has been confirmed by early church leaders (e.g., Nyssa, Origen). It is the unearthing of this tradition that she aims to do methodologically. Scripture, or the text of Song of Songs, is seen as a resource. Thus, as a resource, the text has some revelatory impact, opened up by interpreters, like herself, problematizing those interpretations that cast darkness in a negative light. It is the activation by the interpreter that provides the Song of Songs with authority. For this reason, authority is bestowed upon this text not because it contains static inherent properties but because it functions to provide liberative readings, despite its covering up by oppressive, colonizing readings. Her appeal to Scripture (Song of Songs) contributes to an understanding of ethnicity/race as a construction as well as a celebration of diversity and leads her to the story of the Shulamite. For Padilla, the Shulamite represents darkness in the positive. The character herself possesses inherent beauty.

Rubén Rosario Rodríguez – "Liberation Hermeneutics in Jewish, Christian, and Muslim Exegesis: A Latino Perspective"

Rosario Rodríguez takes a comparative look at the shared relationship between Judaism, Christianity, and Islam. For Rodríguez, all three religions have experienced political violence and all three have a quest for liberation. To embark on this comparative analysis, Rodríguez acknowledges that such comparative work is done from a Christian perspective, with no aim to denigrate the other two religions. Thus, Rodríguez wishes to draw on his biblical tradition to seek those texts that foster dialogue among the three religions.

Rodríguez begins this quest by first delimiting his methodological orientation. He makes quite clear that his analysis is not a "theology of religions," which aims to provide a critical reading of two or more religions from a particular theological perspective with a sense of primacy over the other religions. Rather, Rodríguez's approach is a comparative theological approach that studies each religion in their particularity, while at the same time holding to the claim that no tradition has authority over the other. Second, Rodríguez works with the theological assumption that all three religions have sacred and authoritative texts, from which revelation manifests itself through various sacred events such as worship. He recognizes that the task of theology, with its aim to translate this revelation, is always limited. Third, related to the above, is the theological assumption that Judaism, Christianity, and Islam share in common a belief in the hiddenness and mystery of the revealed God. Thus, Rodríguez's claim here is that the sacred Scripture is a *human* witness to revelation, where God is hidden and remains a mystery. In this sense, Rodríguez's comparative approach to the question of employing Scripture is direct and authoritative, in the sense that it contains an inherent property, revelation, with the aim to promote liberation.

With these reading suppositions established, Rodríguez turns to his reading strategy for comparative analysis. Rodríguez espouses a U.S. Latino/a theological position, influenced by a liberation hermeneutics with an emphasis on the importance of cultural particularity and contextuality. In other words, Rodríguez sees Latino/a theology as a representative of recognizing difference and respecting an ecumenical and multicultural approach. First, Latino/a theologians' liberation hermeneutical approach to the Bible allows for a recovering of revelation that challenges oppressive interpretations. Second, Latino/a theologians' emphasis on culture opens a path between the people of the Bible and the marginalized. Third, Latino/a theologians' emphasis on popular religion stresses the importance of the community in the construction of theology. Fourth, Latino/a theologians' focus on tradition allows for the transmission of tradition from all perspectives (i.e., ecclesial and faith of the people). Finally, Latino/a theologians' commitment to liberative social praxis shows that God is liberative for all God's people. At the end, Rodríguez sees these five characteristics reflected in the work of Latino/a theologians as a possible path to do comparative theological work. He sees the Bible, with the many stories that resonate with the experience of Latinos/as, as a source for theologians to translate God's self-revelation not in an objectivist or universalizing fashion but in a particular and liberative one. In this way, Latino/a theologians characteristically mimic what it means to do comparative theology.

To demonstrate this point, Rodríguez provides a case study of the Book of Jonah—a text that appears in the Jewish, Christian, and Islamic Scriptures. In so doing, Rodríguez brings to bear a liberationist perspective, focusing on action and forgiveness as grounds for divine justice with attention to particularity and difference. For Rodríguez, the Book of Jonah is a paradigmatic narrative for engaging religious pluralism and avoiding political violence. His reading highlights a God who, at the end of the story, shows inclusion and compassion—two theological themes that are reflected in all three religions (Judaism, Christianity, and Islam)—not only toward Jonah but also to Gentiles (the inhabitants of Nineveh). These themes are also found in the Qur'anic Scriptures as well as in the Hebrew Bible. Rodríguez's point is that God's revelation will emerge to bring God's compassion to all. The themes of liberation, justice, and compassion can guide all to respect and tolerate difference—not to place one theology above another, but to place all three religions side by side on equal footing. Latino/a theology points to this comparative theology strategy of reading for him.

Rodríguez sees Scripture as a source to promote interreligious dialogue with the goal of avoiding political violence due to religious exclusivism. His rereading of the Book of Jonah from a Christian perspective—but not one that aims to supplant his reading over the other religious interpretative traditions on Jonah—is to highlight those themes of liberation, justice, and compassion that the story calls attention to in his interpretative experience. In this way, the Bible for Rodríguez is a resource to provide a comparative theological construction that leads to liberation. His focus on Latino/a theology, particularly in its methodological influences and distinctiveness, draws on the engagement of liberation hermeneutics with the Bible, particularly its emphasis on particularity and contextuality as factors brought to bear on the Bible. Such principles have allowed Latino/a theologians to explore their respective theological projects with a sense of ecumenism.

Thus, Rodríguez engages the Bible, at least in this essay, directly, leaning toward indirectly. In other words, it is not the only means—I suspect—that can be used as a source for comparative theology, but in this essay, it is employed to show how such a story as Jonah in all three religious traditions draws on the same themes of liberation, justice, and compassion. By drawing on the function of Scripture within various religious contexts, Rodríguez places authority at this end, namely, human interaction with Scripture (as a human witness of God's revelation) identifies revelation. In this sense, Scripture is bestowed with authority because of how it functions.

CONCLUSION

The preceding critical summary of the various studies in this collection points to several distinctive ways in which Scripture is employed by Latino/a theologians: (1) All engage Scripture in one way or another, directly or indirectly, with no correlation between the usage in question and the particular approach employed. (2) All see Scripture as received tradition. (3) All draw their themes from their particular historical context.

Engagement and Approaches

All of the authors engage Scripture directly or indirectly (or somewhere in between) in their theological constructions. When engaged directly, at one end of the continuum, Scripture is construed as containing inherent theological properties, such as inspiration and revelation, which render it authoritative. Scripture functions thereby as a numinous object that theologians (or ecclesial communities) unquestioningly receive as revelatory statements. On the other end of the continuum, when appealed to Scripture indirectly, Scripture is construed not as a sacred object in and of itself (e.g., the Word of God) but rather as a sacred object that discloses a God that liberates or transforms the Latino/a community. Scripture functions thereby as a source of authority that theologians evoke in seeking to interpret toward transformation or liberation of the community. Thus, in direct engagement, authority is not evoked from Scripture; Scripture is authority.

At the same time, theologians who appeal to a direct use may also lean toward the use of revelatory statements in the text (e.g., Alfaro; Martell-Otero; Lozano) as means to transform their community in a liberative way, such as providing the community with agency in their identity. Furthermore, theologians who appeal to Scripture indirectly may also construe Scripture in less authoritative fashion, as providing a counter-narrative to the normative narrative (e.g., González; Tirres; Padilla). It follows, then, that Latino/a theologians appeal to Scripture directly or indirectly and thus construe Scripture in various ways: either as a theological document of and for believing communities or as an ideological document that may or may not serve to provide agency for a community. These two understandings are at different ends of a spectrum, and most theologians—as reflected in this collection—move between these two ends.

Regardless of how theologians employ the Bible, directly or indirectly, such use does not necessarily correlate with a particular approach (theological, historical, comparative). As delineated above, the majority do so from a theological perspective, as part of their work of theologizing (Alfaro, Lozano, Martell-Otero, Pineda-Madrid, Tirres, González). One approaches the Bible from a historical point of view, as part of a historical reconstruction (Colón-Emeric), while the remaining two do so in comparative fashion (Padilla, Rodríguez). Thus, it appears, the way in which a theologian appeals to Scripture depends on the role that Scripture plays in the project in question.

Is Scripture viewed as an unfiltered repository for early Israelite or early Christian history, or (if at all) as a constructed narrative of the ancient world as it stands with a particular point of view or as somewhere in between? The particular approach that is adopted is related to how the theologians see Scripture function (if at all) in the life of the Latino/a community and/or the Latino/a ecclesial community. In other words, does the Bible constitute the central text for theologizing, or not? It also relates to how the theologians see meaning as located in their respective essays, and not necessarily over their theologizing as a whole. Does the meaning of the scriptural text reside within the world behind, in, and/or in front of the text? These latter questions perhaps have more to do with how they employ the Bible, directly or indirectly, over whether their use correlates with their particular approach.

Received Tradition

The essays also show a preference for engaging Scripture as received tradition. In other words, those essays that engage the text as a whole or in part (e.g., a theme thereof) come to Scripture not as a problematic text but rather as a settled text. In other words, the biblical text is employed as it stands. The goal is not to discover the historical, literary, or social worlds out of which the text came. The goal, rather, is to study how Scripture has been used in certain normative oppressive or liberative ways, whether in the Latino/a ecclesial community as way of helping its self-identity as Christians or in the Latino/a community in general as a way of helping its sense of agency and belonging.

What is problematic is the history of interpretation of certain texts/themes. This is not the case for all the essays, but in some Scripture is understood through the studies of other scholars, other Latino/a biblical scholars or theologians, or sources from tradition—from the patristic period to the present. The results of such "exegetical" or interpretive studies are taken to support or hinder their theological proposals, and thus must be challenged. What is more, a few essays draw not from the interpretative tradition of others per se, but from the reading strategies that other Latino/a biblical scholars have employed in their own work, such as the role of social location. Overall, what is employed—the Bible as a whole or a particular text/theme—depends on a prior decision by another about how to construe and use Scripture or a particular text. Such a decision is grounded in a theologian's critical creative decision and rooted in the particularity of the theologian's identity in relation to an ecclesial or academic common life (or both). Thus, Scripture, if employed, is recognized as a text to be trusted as witnesses to the early tradition, with suspicion placed on the text itself and/or its reception history.

Thematization and Context

The essays further reveal thematization from historical circumstances. Such circumstances, however, are not those that underlie the text but rather those that underlie the theologian or the community situation of the theologian, namely, the Latino/a academic, ecclesial, and social contexts. All theologians, in their engagement with Scripture, read for transformation or liberation regarding some aspect within their respective communities. This ranges from a liberation focused on social, economic, gender and sexuality, or ethnic/racial factors to a liberation centered on oppressive texts or readings from the texts or Scripture.

This reading for liberation (more or less) also follows a "reading with" or sympathetic relationship to Scripture. In other words, in the quest for liberation, many of the theologians opted not to problematize the Bible or a particular text. Scripture was seen as a friend or as simply not relevant to the theological project. Scripture was employed as a tool: on the one hand, with little examination regarding whether the tool was the appropriate one or not; or, on the other hand, with some examination analyzing the proper use of the tool. However, whether employing Scripture as a tool for a historical, theological, or comparative approach, the aim is to bring forth a reading that leads to liberation (broadly understood). Some problematized the claim of cultural liberation, where certain factors such as gender or race/ethnicity are not analyzed for their limitations; others employed it in uncontested fashion. However, their theological projects highlight that liberation is an important component in theologizing, and, in this modern and globalized world, in challenging academia, churches, and communities to re-examine their theological priorities.

A CLOSING COMMENT

In closing, these essays expand the vision of how Latino/a theologians employ Scripture. They open up possibilities of how to put Scripture into effect. What they show is that the construct "Scripture" for Latino/a theologians varies from a sacred object to a cultural object with religious/theological views. Scripture may be employed directly or indirectly, authoritative unto itself or through how it functions. What is a constant, at least in these essays, is an aim for liberation. This liberation may involve giving communities agency to liberation concerning changing oppressive structures. The future of Latino/a theological hermeneutics, I believe, will be significant as long there is a desire to seek to comprehend Scripture in relationship to understanding ourselves and the world. Inquiring how Scripture is employed within theological proposals is very important, especially in light of the constant changing culture, for it provides a significant antidote to the need to build "walls" between communities and instead create dialogue among those of different identities/cultures, faiths, and hermeneutics. Modestly being aware of our own interpretive-theological frameworks, we can benefit from understanding another's framework, thus fostering the next step in Latino/a theological hermeneutics.

NOTES

1. A word about nomenclature in this essay: the term "Scripture" is used interchangeably with the terms "Bible" and "text/texts." Scripture is taken to refer to Christian Scripture (Hebrew Bible and New Testament). Each essay uses one or the other term in their own particular way; my aim throughout is to follow the preferred usage and mechanics when speaking of each essay. In addition, I shall keep to the traditional usage of capitalizing "Scripture" and "Bible" for purposes of consistency; this, however, does not necessarily convey any meaning on my part other than the standard convention as a proper noun.

2. This group of Latino/a theologians is a selective group and in no way presented as standing for the totality of Latino/a theologians. The discussion is simply a sample illustration of various ways in which Scripture can be employed by Latino/a theologians. Thus, the range of possibilities employed by Latino/a theologians in this volume is by no means exhaustive.

3. In helping to understand how Latino/a theologians employ Scripture, I found David H. Kelsey's *The Uses of Scripture in Recent Theology* (Philadelphia: Fortress Press, 1975) quite helpful in formulating these two guiding questions.

4. It is important to note here that the essays in this volume are single cases of theologizing. In no way is the analysis below necessarily representative of each theologians' overall use of Scripture in other projects.

5. A "reading-with" approach here suggests that Las Casas's use of Scripture is a guide along the path toward a hermeneutics of humanity for Colón-Emeric. In other words, Colón-Emeric is not resisting Las Casas's use, nor is he engaging Las Casas' use in the sense of critically naming those aspects of Las Casas' hermeneutics that stand between himself (Colón-Emeric) and Las Casas. For a nuanced understanding of the poetics of contextual hermeneutics, see Fernando F. Segovia, "Reading-Across: Intercultural Criticism and Textual Posture," *Interpreting Beyond Borders*, The Bible and Postcolonialism 3, ed. Fernando F. Segovia (Sheffield, UK: Sheffield Academic Press, 2000), 59–83; see also Adele Reinhartz, *Befriending the Beloved Disciple: A Jewish Reading of the Gospel of John* (New York: Continuum, 2001).

6. Generally speaking, *posadas* represent a reenactment of the search for lodging by Mary and Joseph in Bethlehem; *pastorelas*, a reenactment of the shepherds following the star of David to Bethlehem; and *via cruces*, a reenactment of the way of the cross by Jesus.

BIBLIOGRAPHY

Kelsey, David H. *The Uses of Scripture in Recent Theology*. Philadelphia: Fortress Press, 1975.

Reinhartz, Adele. *Befriending the Beloved Disciple: A Jewish Reading of the Gospel of John*. New York: Continuum, 2001.

Segovia, Fernando F. "Reading-Across: Intercultural Criticism and Textual Posture." In *Interpreting Beyond Borders*, The Bible and Postcolonialism 3, edited by Fernando F. Segovia, 59-83. Sheffield, UK: Sheffield Academic Press, 2000.

Chapter 12

Approaching Latino/a Theology and the Bible

Doing Cultural Analysis on an Ethnic-Racial Key

Fernando F. Segovia

Any analysis of the views and uses of the Bible—or the relationship between biblical texts and theological visions—operative in the field of Theological Studies, I have argued, represents an exercise in interpretation. The present project on the conjunction between Latino/a Theology and the Bible constitutes, therefore, a variation on such an exercise. Its particular hue as a variation lies, I have pointed out, in its foregrounding of the ethnic-racial dimension in interpretation. This is evident given its focus on the movement and discourse of Latino/a Theology within Theological Studies and the ways in which this area of studies invokes and deploys the biblical texts in theological reflection. The present project is thus activated, molded, and informed by the problematic of identity in interpretation.

Any such exercise in interpretation, I have further argued, involves a variety of angles of vision: the trajectory of biblical criticism; the tradition of theological construction; and the realm of cultural analysis. As a variation on such an exercise, I have pointed out, the present project on the conjunction of the Bible and Latino/a Theology Bible highlights the racial-ethnic dimension at all three levels of inquiry. This I have set out to show by tracing the path of the academic-scholarly discussion in each case and situating the project within it. This task I have divided into two parts, for material reasons of length as well as discursive reasons of affinity. Having already drawn such a critical mapping with respect to the first two angles of vision, biblical criticism and theological construction (in chapter 1), I now proceed to do so with regard to the third, cultural analysis. I begin, as I have done with the other critical frameworks, with a preliminary word on this line of inquiry.

In effect, the project represents an exercise in the field of cultural studies, in general, and the field of Latino/a studies, in particular. The realm of cultural analysis may be configured in various ways, depending on the perspective from which such analysis is conceptualized and formulated. One such model is to approach it as comprising the entire range of social-cultural formations in any political unit. Such a range of population groups would include the set of dominant ethnic-racial formations as well as the set of minoritized ethnic-racial groups. In the context of the United States, the former segment would be widely perceived, and would perceive itself, as revolving around the concept of "White," while the latter segment would be broadly regarded, and regard itself, in terms of the notion of "minorities." Among the latter groups in the United States, there lies the Latino/a American community—alongside such others as the African American, the Asian American, and the Native American communities.

Within this model, cultural analysis would involve the critical study of social-cultural production in all formations—across the multiple dimensions and components of any such production. This panoply of studies would include the set of studies having to do with the social-cultural production of minoritized ethnic-racial populations. Among such studies, consequently, stands the field of Latino/a American studies in the United States—alongside African American, Asian American, and Native American studies. Within this model, furthermore, cultural analysis would involve the critical study of religious-theological expression as a dimension of social-cultural production in any formation—across the multiple components of any such dimension. This spectrum of studies would include the set of studies dealing with the religious-theological expression of minoritized ethnic-racial groupings. Among such studies, therefore, lies the field of Latino/a Theology as movement and discourse—alongside African American, Asian American, and Native American Theology.

Given this mapping of cultural studies, the present project on interpretation may be viewed as an exercise in Latino/a American religious-theological studies within the field of Latino/a studies. As such, it is an exercise that is marked distinctly by the inflection of ethnic-racial identity at the core of any minoritized formation. This is so, first of all, in light of its focus on the realities and experiences of the Latino/a community in the United States—by way of Latino/a theologians as representatives of this population. It is so, moreover, given the focus on critical study of the social-cultural production emerging from Latino/a realities and experiences—by way of Latino/a theologians as intellectuals in the Latino/a academic-scholarly community. It is so, lastly, given its focus on critical study of religious-theological expression arising from Latino/a realities and experiences—by way of Latino/a theologians as theologians in the Latino/a religious-theological community.

In effect, all participants bear this threefold affiliation. First, they do so as members of the Latino/a population—individuals who are products of the realities and experiences underlying this formation. Second, they do so as members of the Latino/a academic-scholarly guild—scholars who analyze the realities and experiences behind this formation across the gamut of its social-cultural production. Third, they do so as members of the Latino/a religious-theological guild—theologians who focus on the religious-theological dimension of this formation across the range of its components. It was with such background and such concerns in mind that the participants were invited to reflect on a specific, and key, question: the relevance and impact of the biblical texts on their theological visions.

In the course of such reflections, all participants allude to, engage with, and shed light on—in one way or another, to one extent or another—various aspects and features of their material and discursive context. In so doing, all bring out and sift through the social-cultural conditions of Latino/a religious life, in particular, and Latino/a life, in general. Such reflections serve, therefore, as windows onto the realities and experiences of Latinos/as in the United States and Latin Americans in the diaspora. As such, they serve as important contributions to the work of Latino/a studies. With this in mind, I turn to Latino/a studies.

LATINO/A STUDIES: INTRODUCTION

A critical mapping of Latino/a cultural analysis, or Latino/a studies, is imperative. Only then can the path of Latino/a theology as movement and discourse be properly set against the broader canvas of Latino/a studies. Only then can this project in interpretation within Latino/a theology be properly situated within such a comparative framework of Latino/a studies and Latino/a theology. The proposed undertaking, however, is by no means an easy one; quite to the contrary. For one thing, Latino/a studies is a field that has been expanding for decades, ever since its origins toward the beginning of the second half of the twentieth century. Its body of work is forbidding—not only substantial but also complex and conflicted. For another, in the course of such expansion, the field has shown what can only be described as minimal interest in the religious-theological dimension of Latino/a life and social-cultural production. For yet another, since its own inception two decades afterward, the field of Latino/a theology has shown, to the best of my knowledge, what can justifiably be characterized as sporadic and unsystematic interest in Latino/a studies.

In sum, the gap between the two fields of study is considerable. It is also, in my opinion, very much worth addressing. This I should like to begin to do by taking advantage of the present project as a point of entry in this regard. I should thus like to consider the expansion of Latino/a studies. It is a path that I would describe as having developed in swift fashion, along multiple lines, and with keen sophistication. A number of interrelated developments have contributed directly to such growth, among which three in particular should be noted.

The first involves a sharply intensifying process of self-consciousness and self-projection on the part of the Latino/a population in the country. This rise in conscientization and mobilization has yielded an ever more prominent voice as well as an ever more active role in society and culture at large. The second development has to do with the remarkable surge in migration from Latin America to the United States from the decade of the 1970s onward. This phenomenon has led not only to an enormous rise in overall numbers for the Latino/a population but also to a broad diffusion of such numbers throughout the country, from south to north and from west to east. The third development involves a radical transformation of the Latino/a population in the country, beyond numbers, as a result of such migration. This phenomenon has brought about a thorough diversification and intermixing of the Latino/a population throughout the country, insofar as this pattern of displacement and resettlement has gradually come to reflect the whole of the hispanophone Americas—all nations and regions of South America and Central America; all islands of the Caribbean; and all areas as well as states of Mexico in North America.

The social scenario underlying the expansion of Latino/a studies is thus evident: the incipient emergence of conscientization and mobilization has been directly advanced by the ever more numerous and diffuse presence of the Latino/a formation in the United States as well as by the ever more diverse and intermingled composition of such a presence throughout the country. For Latino/a studies the result has been a long and steady, complex and conflicted, academic-scholarly trajectory, leading to its present state of affairs—multidimensional and multidirectional, yet strategically focalized and canalized. Such a path has been traced and analyzed often over the years since its inception. For my purposes in this study, an overall sense of this trajectory suffices, and toward this end, I draw on various critical reflections of it, four in all, taken from different moments of the project.

Three of these reflections represent articles providing a critical review of the scholarly literature or introductions to readers in the field. Following the nature of the genre, they are brief on the whole, but quite informative. All three come from the pen of top scholars in the field, critics with a wide-ranging and long-standing command of the process, all keen observers of Latino/a reality and experience. Furthermore, insofar as they are situated about a decade apart from one another, they cover the entire development of the field, while in process, from its origins to the present. The fourth reflection is conveyed by way of a scholarly monograph designed as a general introduction to the field of studies. As such, it is more extensive and substantial. It is authored by a scholar of the next generation, a critic in full command of the Latino/a presence and trajectory in the country. Following as it does upon the third brief reflection, it provides, with the benefit of hindsight, an up-to-date account of the field.

The first reflection, dating from the year 1997, was written by the late Juan Flores (1943–2014), who served for many years Professor of Social and Cultural Analysis as well as Director of Latino Studies at New York University. This piece, "Latino Studies: New Contexts, New Concepts," captures the development of the field during the first three decades of its existence.[1] The second piece, which hails from the year 2007, functions as the Foreword to the reader *A Companion to Latino/a Studies*, coauthored by the coeditors of the volume, Juan Flores and Renato Rosaldo, the latter of whom was at the time Lucy Stern Professor Emeritus at Stanford University as well as Professor and founder of the Latino Studies Program at New York University.[2] This reflection, while covering some of the same ground as the former piece, does address, a full decade later, what has transpired since and what is envisioned ahead.

The third piece, appearing in the year 2016, serves as the introduction to another reader, *The New Latino Studies Reader: A Twenty-First-Century Perspective*, coauthored by coeditors Ramón A. Gutiérrez, Preston & Sterling Morton Distinguished Service Professor in United States History and the College at the University of Chicago, and Tomás Almaguer, Professor of Ethnic Studies and former Dean of the College of Ethnic Studies at San Francisco State University.[3] This reflection, coming a decade later, brings the field up into the second decade of the twenty-first-century, while casting an eye on the future as well. The final reflection, published in 2019, is provided via the volume *Latino Studies*, written by Ronald L. Mize, Associate Professor of Language, Culture, and Society in the School of Language, Culture, and Society at Oregon State University.[4] While amplifying throughout on major developments and struggles recorded in the previous reflections, I find its preface and conclusion as most relevant for my purposes in this study.[5]

On the basis of these reflections, I would propose a process of academic-scholarly development involving three major phases over the course of six decades. The first phase, encompassing the decades of the 1960s and 1970s, may be described as a period of formation and definition. The second, which would embrace the decades of the 1980s and 1990s, may be characterized as a period of consolidation and maturation. The third phase, accounting for the first two decades of the twenty-first century, the 2000s and 2010s, may be described as a period of transformation and empowerment. As in the case of any mapping of a field of studies, the different phases in question should be seen not as objective divisions but as analytical aids. They are by no means conceived, therefore, as independent and self-contained, set apart by hard-and-fast boundaries; they are, rather, advanced as imbricated and interrelated, marked by boundaries that are porous and flowing.

In tracing these three phases, I follow a threefold sequence of presentation: first, a setting of the scene by providing a sense of historical context, in the country as well as in the world; then, a summary view of the state of the Latino/a population during the period in question; lastly, an examination of the path of Latino/a studies over the course of these years. A word about the first step is in order. In setting the stage behind the trajectory of the Latino/a presence and Latino/a studies, I shall draw on a variety of approaches and models.

With respect to the national scene, I look first at the political realm and then at the public realm. For the political realm, I have recourse to the succession of presidential elections and terms of office. These I view as keen signifiers for the state of affairs in the country during each phase. For the public realm, I turn to the phenomenon of social movements. These I also take as telling indicators regarding the national state of affairs. With regard to the international scene, I examine first the geopolitical framework and then the geopolitical theater of operations. For the geopolitical framework, I set forth various dominant scenarios in place. These I regard as the key components for the fundamental structure underlying the global state of affairs. For the theater of operations, I draw again on the phenomenon of global movements generated by such a structure. These I view as key pointers for the various lines of tension and modes of conflict marking the global state of affairs. Taking both dimensions into account, I shall argue for a historical backdrop comprising a threefold sequence: a period of convulsion in the first phase; in the second phase, a period of stability; a period of convulsion in the third phase.

FIRST PHASE: FORMATION AND DEFINITION

Setting the Historical Context

The first stage of the trajectory would take up the 1960s and 1970s—the second and third decades within the second half of the twentieth century (1950–2000). With regard to the scene at home, these decades comprehend the following four-year periods: (1) 1960–1964, the cut-short administration of John F. Kennedy (1960–1963) followed by the succession of Lyndon B. Johnson (1963–1964); (2) 1964–1968, the presidency of Lyndon B. Johnson; (3) 1968–1972, the presidency of Richard M. Nixon; (4) 1972–1976, the short-ended administration of Richard M. Nixon (1972–1974) followed by the short-lived succession of Gerald T. Ford (1974–1976); and (5) 1976–1980, the administration of Jimmy E. Carter. With respect to the scene abroad, these decades encompass two geopolitical scenarios of high import: the diffusion of the Cold War and the decolonization of the Global South, both of which affect and engage all presidential administrations. The period as a whole may be characterized as one of convulsion, at both levels and by no means unrelated.

At home, there was certainly upheaval. As the uneven path of presidential succession readily reflects, this was a period of traumatic events in the political sphere: early in the 1960s, the assassination of President Kennedy in 1963, at a most delicate time in global affairs; early in the 1970s, the resignation of President Nixon in 1974, in the face of impending articles of impeachment arising from a highly charged congressional investigation. Momentous developments were taking place in the public sphere as well. This was also a time in which a broad spectrum of social movements arose, all engaged in struggles of political activism, protesting against injustice and oppression as well as pressuring for justice and freedom.

There was upheaval abroad as well. First, the world finds itself under the shadow of the Cold War, which had begun at the end of the 1940s and had raged through the 1950s. This was the confrontation between the world of the West, spearheaded by the United States, and the world of the East, led by the Union of Soviet Socialist Republics (U.S.S.R.). This binomial was signified as follows: on the one hand, multiparty liberal democracy, market capitalism, individual rights; on the other hand, one-party socialist republic, central planning (state capitalism), and social rights. Second, the world further finds itself at the climax of the process of decolonization in the Global South, which had begun in the late 1940s and had raged through the 1950s, as the former colonies of the Western imperial powers struggled for liberation and independence. Given the backdrop of the Cold War, this process was inevitably cast in terms of the confrontation between the West and the East, which was thereby extended and waged throughout the globe—from Africa and the Middle East, to Asia and the Pacific, to Latin America and the Caribbean.

Indeed, the United States became involved in two key components of this process, with the express intention of halting the advance of communism. One of these was in Asia and the Pacific. This took place by way of a steady and massive escalation of the Vietnam War, which affected—in various ways— a number of other countries not only in Southeast Asia but also throughout the region. This conflict yielded much destruction, much carnage, and much displacement. The other had to do with Latin America and the Caribbean. This took the shape of an active crusade against the Cuban Revolution and its gospel of revolution, which affected—in various ways—all other countries of the region. This cause led to the spread of guerrilla movements and the proliferation of authoritarian and repressive states under military regimes.

The decolonization process as a whole, and these scenarios in which the United States found itself implicated in particular, generated a wide variety of social movements worldwide, all engaged in geopolitical activism, expressing opposition to and resistance against any continuation or imposition of imperial-colonial domination or power anywhere in the globe. Such movements outside the country had an impact on the social movements within, and vice versa.

Assessing the State of the Latino/a Population

Such convulsions had a substantial impact on the life and fate of the Latino/a presence in the country. On the one hand, out of the Latino/a population arose one of the many social movements of political activism that came together in the country, rallying for justice and freedom in the midst of injustice and oppression. On the other hand, the emerging Latino/a movement was directly influenced by the various social movements of geopolitical activism that had proliferated around the world, taking up the banner of opposition to and resistance against imperialism of any sort. Above all, and quite understandably so, the movement was most affected by such movements in Latin America and the Caribbean, given the long trajectory of relations between the United States and the region.

The Latino/a formation at this point, it should be noted, constituted a fairly small segment of the population. The 1970 Census, which was the first to address the size of this group, reported a total count of 9.1 million, constituting 4.7 percent of the nation. Its methodology, however, was subsequently found to be quite defective. The 1980 Census, which did formulate the question clearly ("Is this person of Spanish/Hispanic origin or descent?"), showed a total of 14.6 million, amounting to 6.5 percent of the population. Later on, its findings were found to be defective as well, though not to the same extent as in the earlier count.[6] In both cases, despite the methodological shortcomings, such figures were allowed to stand, and still do. While small, therefore, the group was clearly growing in size.

Tracing the Path of Latino/a Studies

Out of these struggles of political and geopolitical activism, a panoply of new knowledges and discourses would take shape as well, as activists in the academic-intellectual world began to clamor for research and study, for space and voice, for programs and projects, in fields of studies and institutions of higher learning. Studies involving the Latino/a experience in the country was one of these new epistemic and cultural formations, doing so discursively as well as institutionally through the decade of the 1970s. On this initial stage, Juan Flores sheds much insight. This he does in the first reflection of 1996; subsequently, in the second reflection of 2006, Flores and Rosaldo come back to it. In this later depiction of the first phase, however, one finds, by and large, a restatement of the earlier portrayal, with some expansion here and there. In what follows, I concentrate on the first reflection, while having recourse to the later piece when appropriate.

The initial critical analysis was written in the wake of the times in question and thus enjoys the privileged benefit of hindsight. It was also written at a time of radical transformation in the Latino/a experience in the country and profound transition in the analysis of such experience in Latino/a studies. It was the aim of Flores in this piece, coming as it does after twenty-five years of development, to establish a sense of historical trajectory and social-cultural memory for a new generation of critics. This task of recollection was viewed as imperative, since this new generation was perceived as no longer possessing a living memory of the times and events, as hailing from a very different historical juncture altogether and as facing a very different set of social and cultural shifts and challenges. This analysis Flores develops, I would argue, by identifying—implicitly rather than structurally—key material as well as discursive features of the new field of studies.

Material Characteristics

With regard to material features, two can be directly identified. The first has to do with the question of nomenclature: the name bestowed upon such endeavors at first. On this matter, he points out that the term "Latino" is absent from any description of such studies. The second involves the question of institutionalization: the academic-intellectual venues in which such endeavors were initially based and pursued. On this point, he notes that such studies found a home in university campuses close to the communities in question.

Nomenclature

To begin with, Flores points out, the Latino/a social movement actually involved two variations, which were respectively grounded in, shaped by, and directed by the struggles against racism and discrimination on the part of the communities then established in the country. These were to be found in different parts of the country: Mexican-Americans throughout the Southwest, extending from Texas to California; and Puerto Ricans across the Northeast, with a presence in major cities of the Midwest as well. Consequently, the knowledge and discourse that would emerge out of such movements, as activists pressed for inclusion in the academy, were twofold as well: what would later come to be known as Latino Studies had its origins as Chicano Studies and Puerto Rican Studies.

Institutionalization

In addition, Flores continues, the institutionalization of such knowledges and discourses in the academic-intellectual realm would take place in the context of public urban universities, located in the respective areas of the country and thus close to the communities themselves. Two iconic examples come to mind right away: in 1969, the Mexican-American Cultural Center—renamed in 1971 as the Chicano Studies Center [1971–1980])—was created at UCLA, while in 1973 the Center for Puerto Rican Studies was founded at Hunter College, the City University of New York.

Discursive Characteristics

With respect to discursive features, four can be readily culled, all present in both variations of the movement. First, such studies were closely tied to the idea and ideal of a nation and driven by cultural nationalism as foundational narrative and ideological agenda. Second, their construction subscribed to a view of the world-system with conflict at the core: a global scenario of domination and oppression anchored by a hierarchical order of nations and crisscrossed by an unequal web of power relations among them. Third, their pursuit generated and followed a set of guiding directives, which called for interdisciplinarity in research, collectivity in execution, and grounding in community. Lastly, such studies demanded much original work, along all lines of research, on the part of critics and scholars, given the paucity of material and data, analysis and discussion, on the social conditions and cultural products of the Latino/a experience.

Cultural Project

With regard to the first trait, Flores explains, the adoption of the nation as the driving concept of analysis in these studies carried a twofold reference: it applied not only to the "historical home countries" but also to "the newly formed internal colonies in U.S. barrios."[7] Thus, the concept encompassed, on the one hand, the national entities of Mexico and Puerto Rico, independent state and U.S. territory, respectively, and, on the other hand, the diasporic populations of Mexicans and Puerto Ricans in the United States. As such, essentialism and homogenization prevailed with respect to the "communities" in the formulation of the project. Consequently, little, if any, attention was paid to the complexity of these communities: the different formations of identity to be found within them or the differential relations of power operative among such formations. It was the community as a whole, as a distinct and coherent entity along "national" lines, that mattered.

Global Context

In terms of the second trait, Flores views the elaboration of such studies as very much indebted to the forces and currents of the time: the process of decolonization working its way through the Global South since the end of the 1940s and the intellectual frameworks of anti-colonialism engendered by it. Thus, he argues, "Militant opposition to the Vietnam War, support for the Cuban Revolution, and the Black and Brown Power movements informed the rhetoric and strategic vision of Chicano and Puerto Rican Studies at their inception."[8] Given the driving notion of the "community" along national lines, the Latino/a experience was approached from the perspective of a world-system in conflict, marked by hierarchical order and unequal interactions among nations. As a result, the Latino communities were set against the backdrop of the United States as a national entity and an imperial power. They emerged thereby as internal colonies within the imperial state, made up of migrants from their home countries, which were in turn regarded as under the imperial-colonial framework of the United States. For such communities, a strategy of liberation was in order.

Research Agenda

In terms of the third trait, Flores presents such a strategy of liberation as an exercise in cultural nationalism—a project duly considered and crafted, by no means monolithic but rather multidirectional in mode and scope. "To extrapolate from the many goals and methods proclaimed," he states, "these founding plans called for knowledge production which was to be interdisciplinary in its methodological range, collective in its practice, and tied to the community."[9] First and foremost, such work demanded that critics and scholars remain throughout in close touch with and responsible to the communities. Not only was cultural production to be undertaken for the sake of the community, with liberation in mind, it was also to be carried out from within, as members of the community. In addition, such work had to involve the whole range of the academic spectrum, bringing together the human sciences and the social sciences in the analysis of the communities. Toward this end, any number of fields would be activated; say, for example: the literary and the historical, the psychological and the political, alongside the anthropological and the economic, the legal and the socioeconomic. Finally, such work called upon this varied field of critics and scholars to work together toward the common goal. This was to be achieved by such means as authorial collaboration and focused study groups.

Research Procedure

With respect to the last trait, Flores and Rosaldo note, the project of cultural nationalism envisioned faced a rather significant obstacle in execution: the absence of material sources as well as critical trajectories. The reason was evident: the lack of attention devoted by traditional scholarship, across all fields of study, to the cultural production and the social situation of the Latino/a experience. Such work had to be undertaken virtually from scratch. For the human sciences, on the one hand, this required the creation of an archive. "Thus, Latino/a scholars," the authors state, "were compelled to be both archivist and critic, uncovering the text and offering an interpretation."[10] Excavative work was of the essence. For the social sciences, on the other hand, this entailed the gathering of basic data in such areas as education and healthcare, housing, and labor. "Applied research," the authors add, "was also critical."[11] Fact-finding work proved imperative as well.

A Concluding Evaluation

The upshot of all such efforts was unquestionable growth, material as well as discursive. Looking back years later, Flores describes this period as follows, "By our time there are already ethnic and minority studies programs long in place on many campuses.... There are professional associations, academic research centers and networks, policy institutes, journals scholarly and otherwise, and a proliferation of Websites all devoted to ethnic and minority studies" (1996: 215). The first phase had thus proved enormously creative and productive.

SECOND PHASE: CONSOLIDATION AND MATURATION

Setting the Historical Context

The second stage of the trajectory would cover the 1980s and 1990s—the third middle decade and the final decade of the second half of the twentieth century. In terms of the national scene, these years include the following presidential terms of office: (1) 1980–1984 and 1984–1988, the presidency of Ronald L. Reagan; (2) 1988–1992, the administration of George H. W. Bush; and (3) 1992–1996 and 1996–2000, the presidency of William Jefferson Clinton. In terms of the international scene, a fundamental transition awaited the world as the dominant geopolitical scenarios of the previous phase give way: the Cold War comes to an end and decolonization runs its course. Another scenario, however, rises to the surface: the emergence of neoliberal economics. In contradistinction to the sense of convulsion that had marked the previous two decades, this phase may be described as one of stability, both at home and abroad.

In the country, tranquility now prevailed. In the political realm, the smooth path of presidential succession conveys a far more settled period of time than that of the 1960s and their aftermath. There is nothing akin to the traumatic circumstances surrounding the assassination of President Kennedy, at the height of the Cold War, or the resignation of President Nixon, during a period of profound constitutional crisis. To be sure, momentous events involving the office were not lacking: the assassination attempt on President Reagan and the impeachment trial of President Clinton. By no means, however, do such events—quite aside from the fact that neither was successful—rise to the level of the dangers posed and the disruptions occasioned by the earlier developments. Such was the case in the public realm as well. The social movements of earlier years did continue their struggles and did make gains in so doing. What now prevailed was not so much an ambience of social rupture, the sense of a world coming apart, but rather an aura of social rebuilding, the sense of a world in restoration. As a result, the critical edge of the social movements of activism, while significantly sharpened, was not as strident or as visible as before.

Tranquility prevailed throughout the globe as well. With regard to the Cold War, what began in the early 1980s as a period of heightened confrontation between East and West, with a massive military buildup undertaken by President Reagan, ultimately turned, during the tenure of President Bush, into a surprisingly swift breakup of the Eastern block of nations in 1989 and the formal dissolution of the U.S.S.R. itself in 1991. With respect to decolonization and the Global South, by this time the process had, for the most part, subsided in intensity, as the former colonies of the West attained independence in rapid succession. Such was the case for the United States as well: the two scenarios of this process in which the country had become deeply implicated had also considerably receded from view. At the same time, a new scenario came to be, actually striding both the international and the national realms, that advanced the promise of a better world for all; it would prove enormously consequential in both the short run and the long run.

What ensued upon the end of the Cold War was a sense of euphoria, brought about by the prospect of a world at peace, after almost fifty years of a war that had followed fast upon the end of World War II and that had always bordered on the precipice of nuclear disaster. To be sure, such jubilation and expectation were jolted, almost immediately, by the outbreak of the First Gulf War of 1990–1991, in which an international coalition led by the United States was brought together to invade Iraq after its invasion of Kuwait over a dispute concerning oil. Nonetheless, this military venture, short-lived and broadly backed as it was, did not detract unduly from the general sentiment of a global respite from war. In retrospect, it was an ominous sign of things to come not only in the Middle East but also in the world at large.

What accompanied the winding down of decolonization was a similar sense of jubilation not only throughout the Global South but also across the world, given the respite from confrontation and war across the world. This proved true for the United States, in particular. In Asia and the Pacific, the Vietnam War had come to a formal end in 1975, bringing about the withdrawal of U.S. troops and the possibility of a different state of affairs for the region. In Latin America and the Caribbean, on the other hand, the crusade against Cuba had diminished in fervor, allowing for a return to democratic governments throughout the region in the 1980s. Here too there was a more somber side. Tragically, these decades also register the failure of various such triumphs of liberation, as a number of new countries and governments enter into a spiral of authoritarianism, corruption, and violence, yielding social and cultural breakdown.

With the crisis of capitalism in the mid-1970s, a new economic vision emerged, the project of neoliberalism. The model advanced the ideal of a free market, anchored, inter alia, in a pursuit of global trade, a reduction in government regulation, and a cutback in public spending. The project was first taken up by the United Kingdom and the United States and subsequently imposed on the rest of the world as the panacea for the resolution of all economic evils and the attainment of universal progress for all in its wake. Such a messianic vision did have its travails, rattled as it was by a series of recurrent regional economic crises, chief among them the Asian Financial Crisis or Contagion of 1997. Nonetheless, the vision marched on, in undeterred and resolute fashion, into the new century.

The sense of a world in restoration, a world undergoing social renovation, thus prevailed globally as well. The signs were many and manifest: the turn toward a traditionalist social agenda in the country, the irruption of a geopolitical shift in world affairs marked by relative peace, and the adoption of promising economic restructuring in both spheres. As in the national scene, therefore, the radical edge of the geopolitical movements of activism subsided considerably as well. Such movements certainly continued and intensified, but with neither the same prominence nor the same appeal as before.

Assessing the State of the Latino/a Population

These developments played a significant role in the life and fate of the Latino/a presence in the country. On the one hand, the group would endure directly the untoward consequences of economic transformation at home—the promise of universal progress and welfare did have a downsize. On the other hand, the group would experience directly the effects of economic restructuration throughout Latin America and the Caribbean—dislocation, migration, relocation. This latter development would lead to a fundamental change in terms of composition, distribution, and direction for the Latino/a community.

Indeed, in the course of this second phase, the growth of the community intensified. The 1990 Census, which basically reproduced the question of the 1980 Census, yielded a total of 22 million, or 8.8 percent of the nation. In turn, the 2000 Census, which modified the question to include, for the first time, the term "Latino" (Is this person Spanish/Hispanic/Latino?), accounted for 35 million, or 12.5 percent.[12] In both decades, therefore, the population grew by more than 50 percent, reaching a remarkable 58 percent in the 1990s.[13] By the end of the century, therefore, the growth of the group had become quite pronounced, gaining an ever-larger percentage of the national population. This was but a sign of things to come in the new century.

Tracing the Path of Latino/a Studies

Latino/a studies would inevitably register such developments in the community and the movement as well. For this second stage of the project, both the analysis offered by Juan Flores in the first reflection piece, produced toward the end of this period (1996), and that advanced by Flores and Rosaldo in the second piece, at the beginning of the third stage (2006), are to the point. To set the scene for these reflections, the evaluation of the project advanced by Flores at the end of its initial phase of formation and definition is worth recalling: undeniable growth at all levels of research and inquiry. What these analyses now offer, toward the end of the second phase, is a different assessment altogether: profound transition in the field of studies, generated by a radical transformation in the Latino/a experience. "Despite the deep continuities between the early years and more recent scholarly concerns," argue Flores and Rosaldo, "there have been significant shifts over the decades, which have brought new issues and challenges to the Latina/o Studies agenda."[14]

This shift in development can be captured by tracing the path of the material and discursive characteristics identified in the period of formation and definition. On the material side, both the character and the venue of the field undergo fundamental changes. On the discursive side, similar changes affect the set of four cultural characteristics. For Flores, the reason for such changes is evident: "The main shift marking off the present context of Latino Studies from its previous manifestation twenty-five years ago is perhaps best summed up in the words *global* and *globalization*."[15]

Such globalization is further said to bear a twofold dimension: one involves economics, the result of a restructuring in the system of world capitalism; the other has to do with communications, the result of a revolution in technology. The two dimensions do have a bearing on one another: economic globalization brings about mass migrations; digital globalization allows for sustained interchange in migration, thus keeping the home and diaspora populations in circular and transnational contact. Such is precisely what happens to the Latino/a experience in the United States.

Material Characteristics

Nomenclature

On the first material question of nomenclature, the issue of character, what one now encounters is a project undergoing demographic expansion. Previously, the field had been birthed and informed by the two groups with long historical presence in the country, Mexican-Americans and mainland Puerto Ricans. By the mid-1990s, Flores points to a field moving in two directions at once, one along the lines of multiple perspectives and the other toward a common perspective. The waves of migration unleashed by the forces of globalization bring diversification, given the arrival of "sizable immigrant communities in the United States from most Latin American countries," and dispersal, since, "many of these diasporas, notably the Mexican and the Puerto Rican, have fanned across the country."[16]

As students from all such groups find themselves in campuses throughout the country, the academic focus moves to incorporate such a variety of trajectories and perspectives in different ways: by themselves, relatively independent of one another, through the addition of new concentrations, as in the case of Cuban Studies or Dominican Studies or as layers of the same phenomenon, giving rise thereby to the idea of Latino Studies. This concept, Flores observes, would prove most useful: "It builds on and complements the perspectives, curricular orientations, and programmatic structures of established Chicano and Puerto Rican programs," while it also "allows for some space to mediate issues of inclusion and solidarity sometimes strained in nationality-specific situations."[17]

Institutionalization

On the second material question of institutionalization, the matter of venue, what one finds at this point is a project caught in a crossfire. At first, the field had found a home in urban public universities in the general area, and thus close to the Latino/a communities in question. Toward the end of the second stage, Flores foregrounds a demand for curtailment alongside a demand for representation. Thus, in the traditional academic contexts, there is a struggle for survival, not only for Latino Studies but also for all other variations of Ethnic-Racial Studies as well. Such venues now faced "the iron hand of fiscal constraints and shifting ideological priorities," yielding a policy of "slashing, reducing, and consolidating those very programs and services" (Flores 1996: 205). Downsizing and merging was the message.

At the same time, in the elite universities of the country, remote from the communities, students mounted a struggle for presence, for "new programs, faculty, courses, and resources in these neglected areas of social knowledge" (Flores 1996: 205). Both types of institutions found themselves at the same conjuncture, a highly conflicted cultural climate: "the expressed educational needs of an increasingly non-white student population" versus "the conservative inclinations of many social and educational power brokers" (Flores 1996: 206).

Discursive Characteristics

Cultural Project

In terms of the first discursive trait, the appropriation of a project of cultural nationalism, the impact of such developments was far-reaching. With the emergence of Latino Studies as a working concept bringing together the various dimensions of the Latino/a experience in the United States, the analytical principles of essentialism and homogenization begin to undergo deconstruction. The complexity of the communities starts to manifest itself in manifold ways. Instead of a distinct and coherent entity captured by the term "nation," it was now the concept of transnationalism that rose to the surface. This it did on account of three globalizing factors.

First, the globalization of the Latino/a population, at large as well as in the academy, brought about by the new patterns of migration from Latin America and the Caribbean. Second, the globalization in communications, whereby the new diasporas were able not only to keep in regular touch with relatives at home but also to keep abreast of and influence social and cultural realities in their countries of origin. Third, the globalization of economic restructuration and displacement that lay behind the new state of affairs in Latin America and the Caribbean and the new migrations that emerged as a result. This moment Flores captures well, "Pan-Latino necessarily implies 'trans-Latino,' a more rigorously transnational unit of Latino Studies analysis than even the staunch 'Third World' and anti-imperialist perspective of Latino Studies in its foundation."[18]

Global Context

Regarding the second trait, the conception of a world-system structured around the hierarchical and differential relations of imperial-colonial frameworks, the effects on the pursuit of Latino Studies prove just as profound. A radical change in context and approach, Flores argues, has taken place: the generation that was forged within the broad-based struggle for liberation from imperial-colonial oppression, a lens that was readily applied to the United

States, has been replaced by a generation that is no longer shaped by such a "charged revolutionary aura."[19] In fact, while the new generation does have a sense of continuity with the foundational generation, the passing of time has blurred the connections and disjunctures in question.

What marks the new generation, Flores submits, is its awareness of the process and effects of globalization: how such economic restructuring "willfully moves people to and from determined places" by "adjusting and altering the historical relations among societies and their fragments relocated by impelled migratory movement."[20] As a result, the new generation sees itself as "more intricately tied to economic and political realities in their countries and regions of origin than ever before."[21] Such a novel sense of interconnection yields epistemic clarity: on the one hand, regarding how family, kinship, and household constitute "sets of relations in the home country and in the United States"; on the other hand, regarding the "deep consequences" of "political and economic changes in one country . . . for people in the other country."[22]

Research Agenda

Regarding the third trait, the adoption of guiding directives for the project of cultural nationalism, the effects for the pursuit of Latino Studies are no less profound. Such was the case with the call for interdisciplinary knowledge production. Most significant in this respect was the change wrought by the movements of postmodernism and poststructuralism throughout the entire spectrum of the academy. What had been up to this point relatively bounded and unified disciplines were rendered, through the linguistic and ideological turns in question, into highly interrelated and diverse fields of studies, with a focus on rhetoric and representation as well as on context and agenda. Such diversity of critical approaches and theoretical frameworks made their way into the emerging pursuit of Latino Studies as well.

Thereby, as questions of identity took over, the problematics of gender and sexuality, economics and race, nationality and postcoloniality, complicated enormously the working concept of nation and project of nationalism. Flores is quite to the point here, "The presumed seamlessness and discreteness of group identities characteristic of earlier Latino perspectives have given way to more complex, interactive, and transgressive notions of hybrid and multiple social points of view."[23] The other guiding directives, the call for collective research and community and community ties, were similarly affected. Given such discursive turns, the very notion of a common goal became problematic; similarly, given the ongoing diversification and expansion of the Latino/a community, the new generation was not as closely tied to the communities as before.

Research Procedure

In terms of the final discursive trait, the creation of a cultural archive and a social database, the impact of the material developments, is quite far-reaching as well. The obstacle previously faced by the project of cultural nationalism, the absence of pertinent sources and scholarly traditions, was now compounded by the new developments in method and theory at work in Latino Studies. The new questions of identity immediately amplified the envisioned parameters of any retrieval of an archive or compilation of a database. In effect, the total absence of Latino faces and voices from times past, faced by the earlier generation, could not be replaced now by the absence of any particular segment or dimension of the community. "Whatever we may think of the vocabulary," Flores declares, "reflections on questions of 'hybridity,' 'liminality,' 'transgressivity,' and the like, and the new intellectual horizons they signal, are clearly germane to any contemporary work in Latino Studies."[24] Excavative as well as fact-finding work in Latino Studies had to be reconceived and pursued accordingly.

A Concluding Evaluation

The outcome of all such developments was radical recasting, material as well as discursive. The unquestionable growth advanced by Flores as key signifier for the first phase did not abate; to the contrary, it intensified with the new waves of migration. Such growth, however, now faced a different set of social and cultural forces, which, in turn, presented a different set of challenges for and called for a different set of directions in Latino Studies. Surveying this second phase a few years later, Flores offers a twofold reflection on such recasting.

On the one hand, given the complexity introduced by the new discursive currents, the mode of Latino Studies has to be carefully weighed. Toward this end, Flores ventures a solution: approaching the analysis of the Latino/a formation through the notion of nations as "imagined communities"—a concept advanced by Benedict Anderson, Aaron L. Binenkorb Professor of International Studies, Government and Asian Studies at Cornell University, in his study of 1983 on nationalism, a piece that appeared early on in this second phase of Latino Studies. Such usage entails a sense of the nation as "a malleable, fluid, permeable construct, a group given form by shared imaginaries," thus capturing "the 'national' experience of Latino diaspora in all its ambiguity."[25] On the other hand, given the ideological and financial difficulties faced in the academy alongside the proliferation of possible moorings available throughout the academy, the place for Latino Studies has to be carefully pondered.[26] In this regard, Flores names the quandary: "What the best 'fit' for Latino Studies may be in the present and shifting structure of the U.S. academy is clearly an enigma, especially as none of these umbrellas or potential federations is guaranteed to feel like home in a suspicious, reluctant, and sometimes dog-eat-dog institutional environment."[27]

THIRD PHASE: TRANSFORMATION AND EMPOWERMENT

The third stage of the trajectory would encompass the 2000s and 2010s—the first two decades of the twenty-first century. With respect to the scene at home, these years comprehend the following terms of office: (1) 2000–2004 and 2004–2008, the presidency of George W. Bush; (2) 2008–2012 and 2012–2016, the administration of Barack Obama; and (3) 2016–2020, the presidency of Donald Trump. With regard to the scene abroad, another fundamental transition lay in store for the world by way of a twofold return: the sense of a world at war and the sense of a Global South in turmoil. After the period of stability represented by the second phase of expansion and consolidation, these years may be viewed as a throwback to the atmosphere of convulsion that had characterized the first phase. To be sure, no reprise is ever the same. The sense of convulsion in question is altogether different. Nevertheless, as in the case of the 1960s and 1970s, the new convulsion would also shake the fabric of both the country and the world, indeed to their very core.

Upheaval certainly marked the scene at home. To be sure, on the surface, the smooth path of presidential succession does reflect a sense of enduring stability in the political sphere: no traumatic events surround the office of the presidency. A look at the public sphere, however, reveals a different story. Certain forces afoot in the country would prove disruptive and dangerous, indeed extremely so. One of these did find resonance in the presidency itself; behind the surface, therefore, a momentous, if not traumatic, development was engulfing the office and radiating outward. What were these sources? First, toward the end of the 2000s, the country experienced its greatest economic crisis since the Great Depression of 1929–1941, as its financial system stood on the edge of meltdown, surfacing the fundamental fragility of the economic model in place. Then, toward the end of the 2010s, the country faced its crudest outbreak of white nationalism since the days of the Civil Rights struggles, as its demographic makeup stood on the verge of transformation, revealing a fundamental shift away from its traditional Euro-white composition. Both developments would have weighty consequences.

On the one hand, the Great Recession shakedown of 2008 and beyond, as the economic crisis would come to be known, had severe repercussions for the country for years afterward—housing meltdown, market plunge, high unemployment, rising inequality, among others. On the other hand, the White Supremacy upsurge of 2016 and beyond, as the nationalist resurgence would come to be characterized, had severe repercussions as well, no doubt for years to come—ethnicism and racism, nativism and xenophobia, anti-Islamism and anti-Semitism, among others. The choice of the year 2016 as marker is a reference to the election of Donald Trump, for the rhetorics and politics of Trumpism play a major role in furthering this movement, thereby implicating the presidency directly in its dynamics and mechanics.

In this period of renewed turbulence, social movements of activism have staged a prominent return to the public sphere, though with crucial variations: the traditional movements undergo change and new movements come to the fore. With respect to the historical movements, a twofold stage can be identified. Early on, deeply affected by the economic crisis, they trod on, continuing to pursue their struggles and making gains in the process; subsequently, directly impacted by the nationalist crisis, they begin to regain the sharp edge of earlier times. With regard to the rising movements, a distinction is in order. At first, a variety of groups on the left target the economic elite as responsible for the damage wrought by the dominant economic model; this was the case of Occupy! (2011–2012). Later on, a number of groups on the right, long simmering, target the demographic "other"—ethnic-racial, immigrant, and religious "others"—as responsible for the decline brought upon the country by immigration and diversity; such was the case of the Unite the Right rally in Charlottesville, Virginia (2017). In effect, the aura of social rebuilding underlying the second phase, with its vision of a world in restoration, had now given way to one of social upheaval, with its vision of a world coming apart.

Upheaval also marked the scene abroad. The revived sense of a world at war took shape by way of the outbreak of Islamic radicalism in the Middle East and beyond, while the renewed sense of a Global South in turmoil developed as a result of the detritus of neocolonial domination. Regarding the impact of radical Islam, the jolt delivered by the First Gulf War of 1990–1991, at the commencement of a world at peace, now resurfaced on a massive scale. The period opened with the attack of al-Qaeda, a militant organization, in September of 2001 on various targets in the United States, including the twin towers of the World Trade Center in New York City and the Pentagon in Washington, D.C. What ensued was a series of military interventions in the Middle East on the part of the United States and a shifting set of allies. Regarding the impact of dominant neocolonialism, the travails signified by the recurrent regional crises of the 1980s and 1990s, during the implementation of the utopian vision, were now felt again but on a grand scale. The period started with the neoliberal project very much in force until the explosion of the model in 2008. What followed was a series of shock waves moving from the Global North outward and affecting the economies of the Global South.

The series of military interventions undertaken by the United States and its allies were expansive and consequential. First, there was the Afghanistan War, launched in 2001 and still ongoing, against the Taliban or Islamic Emirate of Afghanistan, for having provided shelter to al-Qaeda. Then, there followed the Second Gulf War, from 2003 through 2011, against Saddam Hussein in Iraq, under accusations of collaboration with al-Qaeda and possession of weapons of mass destruction. Lastly, there came large-scale military action, beginning in 2014 and still continuing, against the Islamic Caliphate proclaimed by ISIS (the Islamic State of Iraq and Syria) or Daesh over large parts of Iraq and Syria, for embarking on a global campaign of social-cultural cleansing. The end result of such interventions was utter chaos throughout the Middle East—widespread material destruction; untold number of fatalities; and massive population displacement. This created a huge flow of migration seeking shelter in Europe and elsewhere. Meanwhile, the threat of radical terrorism on its own soil pervaded the Global North.

The series of economic shock waves proved just as expansive and consequential. The downside of the utopian vision of the free market, bringing the world together as the way to universal human welfare, had already been in evidence for some time: the displacement and migration of large numbers of have-nots as a result of international trade treaties and the loss of traditional sources of agriculture and labor. In the aftermath of the Great Recession of 2008, such displacement multiplied, leading to a marked increase in the flow of migrants to the Global North in search of survival. The flow of migrants from the Middle East was thus joined by similar flows from Africa and Latin America, trying to cross the Mediterranean into Europe or the Mexican border into the United States, respectively. Such an escalation, in turn, brought forth ever greater nativism and xenophobia in the Global North.

All such developments could not but reinforce the perception of a world coming apart, as the specter of social upheaval dislodged the dream of social tranquility. As one would expect, such developments would lead to a reinvigoration of geopolitical movements of activism, spurred on by the multiplication of terrorist organizations and military involvements, as well as migratory tidal waves and ultranationalist agendas. Indeed, as in the 1960s and 1970s, the social movements at home and the social movements abroad would parallel, influence, and reinforce one another—most markedly perhaps in the dialectical exaltation of the Self and the rejection of the Other. All this, one should keep in mind, was taking place in the light of a world approaching the end of modernity, its dynamics and mechanics, in the face of ever-increasing climate change.

Assessing the State of the Latino/a Population

Such convulsions had a profound effect on the life and fate of the Latino/a community. The group would bear directly, and intensely, the consequences of the economic meltdown after 2008 and the nationalist resurgence of 2016—a decline in well-being followed by the onslaught of ethnicism and xenophobia. The group would further witness directly the ramifications of the economic devastation wrought throughout Latin America and the Caribbean—dislocation, migration, and relocation to the North on an even grander scale, followed by ever-sharper rejection, branding, and exclusion. The result would again be fundamental changes within it, most significantly in terms of numbers.

In the third phase, the Latino/a presence has continued to grow vigorously. The 2010 Census, which introduced changes in the formulation of the question (Is this person of Hispanic, Latino, or Spanish origins?), registered a population of almost 51 million, or 16.4 percent of the national count.[28] Mize brings the data up to 2015 and offers a glimpse into the future. By 2015, he points out that the group had reached a total of 54 million and now constituted 17.6 percent of the total population.[29] Looking ahead, he cites the projections of the U.S. Census for the year 2060: the group will come to represent around 30 percent of the country's population. The growth of the community is still remarkable: 43 percent through the 2000s, with close to one-third of the country in four decades. The magnitude of things to come becomes thereby ever more evident. Thus, Mize affirms, such numbers "will rewrite who we think about when we ask the question: who's an American?"[30]

Tracing the Path of Latino/a Studies

All these convulsions would inevitably have a considerable effect on the path of Latino/a studies as well. For this third phase of the project, the accounts provided by Ramón A. Gutiérrez and Tomás Almaguer in 2016 and by Ronald L. Mize in 2019 prove to the point, especially since they appear toward the end of the period. To set the scene for these reflections, the assessment of the project offered by Flores at the end of the middle phase of consolidation and maturation should be recalled: radical recasting of the field, due to a host of new challenges and new issues. This state of affairs both reflections capture. Mize takes it for granted a decade later: "The plurality of Latino/a experiences and the sheer complexity of varied Latino/a lives require polyvocality as the *modus operandi* of Latino/a Studies."[31] It is similarly presupposed by Gutiérrez and Almaguer in their description of the Reader as an "act of alchemy": "a political project that cultivates a broad cultural sense of belonging to a grander community that is created through ancestral links to Latin America."[32] Both reflections also register, and embody, a move beyond deconstruction and diffusion: what I have characterized as transformation and empowerment.

These reflections follow, as one would expect, other patterns of presentation than that of Flores. Nonetheless, the range of material and discursive characteristics distilled from Flores' analysis of the first phase, subsequently applied to the second phase, can be appropriately and gainfully applied to the progression of Latino/a studies in this third phase. The overall result may be summarized as follows. With regard to the material characteristics of character and venue, the question of nomenclature is more amply pursued than that of institutionalization. With respect to the set of discursive characteristics, a range of emphasis is decidedly present.

Material Characteristics

In the case of the material features, the emphasis on naming over placing is evident. On the title for the field of studies, Flores had recorded a move beyond Chicano Studies and Puerto Rican Studies through the adoption of the more inclusive Latino Studies. These reflections note and advance other designations: a nuanced use of "Latino Studies" in Gutiérrez and Almaguer and the use of "Latina/o Studies" in Mize. Both reflect the diversity of the second phase. On the location for the field of studies, Flores had laid out any number of directions in which the field could be integrated, in light of the academic-scholarly retrenchment, economic as well as ideological, at work. These reflections do not take up the fate of such struggles and discussions, but they do cite various developments in this regard.

Nomenclature

On the naming of the field, both proposals follow a process of theorization, albeit limited. Gutiérrez and Almaguer opt for the continued use of "Latino," not as a gendered masculine term, beyond which the discussion had moved, but as an abstract signifier of a collectivity. They refer to their political project by the term *Latinidad*, a designation that is meant to be multinational and multidimensional, encompassing all the national origins of the group as well as all other dimensions of their identity "without erasing racial, class, gender, and sexual differences," often obscured by the "all-inclusive word 'Latina' or 'Latino.'" These terms are deployed, therefore, as reflecting this sense of grand affiliation to the collectivity of *Latinidad*. In the end, it is "Latino" that is activated, as the title of both the volume and the Introduction show.

Mize, in turn, adopts the gendered binomial in inverted fashion, "Latina/o Studies."[33] This he does after tracing the shifts in self-identification over time by the group: following the initial use of "Latino," there followed Latina, Latino/a, Latina/o, Latin@, and Latinx. All of these, he argues, "have sought to challenge the masculinist aspects of the Spanish language."[34] All of these, he adds, are problematic and subject to inevitable revision in the future, in order "to better align experiences with language and identities with names."[35] Mize, it should be noted, is cognizant of the rise of *Latinidad* to signify the collectivity beyond national and social differences—the approach taken by Gutiérrez and Almaguer, among others; this he views as most promising. In the end, he opts for "Latina/o" despite his awareness of what the later Latin@ and Latinx set out to correct—an emphasis on either gender through the use of the slash and the erection of a gender binary, respectively.

In the end, neither choice is, to my mind, properly articulated: Gutiérrez and Almaguer do not explain why "Latino" is preferred over "Latina" as the abstract signifier, and Mize does not account for a return to "Latina/o" with its foregrounding of women. By way of contrast, I would note in this regard the appearance, also at the end of this third phase, of a reference volume devoted to the field as part of the series "Routledge Key Guides" (2019). Its genre was that of the critical dictionary, which seeks to lay out basic concepts and issues in the field, with accompanying bibliography. As title, its co-authors, Frederick Luis Aldama and Christopher González, opted for the use of the most recent appellation, "Latinx": *Latinx Studies: The Key Concepts*.[36] This choice received pointed grounding, as set forth in the Introduction.[37] Two reasons are adduced: comprehensive representation of diversity, "to be inclusive of all genders and sexual orientation," and up-to-date scholarly usage, "to embrace a term generated and deployed by new generation of Latinxs in the US."[38] Behind the move, there also lies the project of *Latinidad*, given their conception of the field as a way to capture "the different threads that make up a resplendent latinidad."[39]

Institutionalization

On the channeling of the field, both proposals are general in scope, with no reference to the administrative and student pressures highlighted by Flores at the end of the second phase. Gutiérrez and Almaguer presuppose a field transformed by the political project of *Latinidad*—conceptualized as "an interdisciplinary field of research" and involving "larger units of Latino studies" rather than group-specific "departments, centers, and programs."[40] They single out two strategic means of institutionalization along these lines. One is the launching of a Latino/a Studies Association in 2014 devoted precisely to such comprehensive and interdisciplinary undertaking.[41] The other is a presentation of the reader as a "teaching tool" designed to introduce "students, teachers, and interested readers" to the field as conceived.

Mize also takes for granted a transformed field, now bringing the project of *Latinidad* fully to the fore. For him, the analysis of *Latinidad* brings the gradual incorporation of national group research to a climax: a vision of "Latina/o Studies as a full-fledged field."[42] This he defines as an "experiment" that brings together "national-origin specialists" and yields "a variegated picture of who Latinos are, including their transnational, mixed race, and comparative contexts"—in effect, a field that is, as Gutiérrez and Almaguer also argue, multinational and multidimensional.[43] Mize also points to a number of strategic means for the institutionalization of this vision, beyond that of the recently formed association: encyclopedia projects; introductions to the field; ethnographic studies involving the coexistence of national-group populations—in effect, a field that is, as described by Gutiérrez and Almaguer, an "interdisciplinary site of academic inquiry."[44] In their respective elaborations of the field at the end of the third phase, both proposals are close, with neither depicting such institutionalization as a site of struggle.[45]

Discursive Characteristics

In the case of the discursive features, a distinctive shift in emphasis is evident. While Flores had devoted more or less equal attention to all four traits in question, these reflections vary significantly in the degree of attention bestowed on the various traits, although both follow, more or less, the same pattern in so doing. For Gutiérrez and Almaguer, it is the first trait, the conception of a cultural project, that becomes the main focus of attention. They do comment as well on the third and fourth traits, the agenda and procedure of research. However, the issue of global context, the terrain of the second trait, is entirely bypassed. For Mize, too, it is the first trait that emerges as primary. The third and fourth also elicit comment, and indeed at greater length. Again, however, the second recedes entirely from view.

Cultural Project

In terms of the question of identity, a further shift can be detected in this phase. The turn of the second phase toward acknowledgment of complexity and conflictedness, away from the essentialism and homogenization of the initial phase, now yields to a focus on the population on the whole. This return to the collectivity is by no means designed as a resumption, innocent or reactionary, of the initial project of cultural nationalism. It is meant, rather, as an attempt to think beyond the project of cultural transnationalism by turning to the Latino/a population, multidimensionally globalized as it is, as a self-conscious and self-interested collectivity. This is what both reflections associate with the project of *Latinidad*. For both, therefore, the project in question is political to the core—a move toward empowerment within the United States.

For Gutiérrez and Almaguer, such is clearly the case: *Latinidad* is explicitly described, as cited earlier, as a "political project." Without a sense of collectivity, they argue, the "cleavages" that mark the community—"social and national differences, levels of assimilation and adaptation to life in the United States, political beliefs, and a sense of belonging to other groups that may be just as important, say to one's religion, to one's town of birth, or to one's gender as an ardent feminist"—would render any possibility of "group cohesion" or "coalition-building" impossible.[46] This, in turn, would work against the goal of empowerment for the community. The emphasis on collectivity thus has a decidedly strategic political objective.

For Mize, the same is true: *Latinidad* is explicitly characterized as "Most often a political project."[47] Its aim, he states, is "to align power through coalition building and shared interests"[48]—in other words, to work toward group empowerment within the national context. At the same time, as the qualifier "most often" indicates, for Mize the project bears a further dimension, no less political to my mind. A further aim is to counter definitions of the group from above, whether imposed by government directives or linguistic usage, by turning to the grassroots instead. It looks at the ways in which *Latinidad* is embodied in the community by way of multiple *latinidades*—that is, it seeks group empowerment from below. The project thus brings to the fore, with national empowerment in mind, the varying senses of identity taking place among the daily lived experiences of the community, "the shared social locations that Latina/os inhabit, regardless of their unique national origins."[49] As such, the sense of collectivity has an additional self-naming or self-defining objective.

Global Context

Regarding the question of global context, silence prevails. The relation of the political project of *Latinidad* to the geopolitical framework of a world-system is not pursued nor is the sense of globalization that followed upon the drive for liberation developed. The focus remains on the national context. In both reflections, this is a context that revolves around power and such power is hierarchical and unequal, as the call for empowerment makes clear. In Gutiérrez and Almaguer, such conflict remains in the background: it is active and pressing, but not named. In Mize, the conflict is brought to the fore: it is named and unpacked. Like all "social locations" of identity, he states, which are the result of unequal social relations, the *latinidades* forged in everyday life take place "within larger systems of oppression and privilege."[50] Such focus on the national context, I would argue, need not prevent the question of the global context from consideration. To the contrary, it can serve as a strategic point of departure for such linkage.

In Gutiérrez and Almaguer, as already set forth, the project of *Latinidad* is put forward as a way to establish and promote the potential political power inherent in such a collectivity. Only by way of unity can the group hope to have an impact on the society and culture of the United States and bring their "collective aspirations of group empowerment" to fruition.[51] This unity is to be forged not by flattening differences but rather by mobilizing them toward a common goal. In Mize, a similar vision for the project of *Latinidad* is at work, but the unity in question is to be wrought from and through the grassroots. It is a unity that is as varied, as contextual, as the grassroots. To my mind, there is no reason why this drive for political power could not be expanded toward the acquisition and exercise of geopolitical power as well, that is, toward the wielding of influence and direction, in the country and for the country, not only with regard to Latin America and the Caribbean but also with respect to the world-system in place. National empowerment would serve thereby as a platform for international empowerment, for a steering of the country at both a hemispheric and global level.

A concrete channel for such exercise of power is suggested by Mize when addressing the phenomenon of transnationalism in the community from the standpoint of a pan-ethnic perspective, such as *Latinidad*. This would entail a different approach to the transnational: not as a connection between a subgroup within the community and its country of origin—a way of living in two countries at once; rather, as a crucible of relations between the United States and the countries of origin as a set—a way of living brought upon the group by historical-global as well as social-cultural forces.

Four strategies for so doing, for grasping such systemic forces and resultant relations, are delineated.[52] Two of these focus on the United States as agent in the process: on the one hand, analyzing the country as a project of expansion that has brought about, through a history of sustained interventions, multiple waves of Latino/a immigration; on the other hand, viewing the country as dependent on markets, resources, and labor in Latin America and the Caribbean, with such labor as racially marked and subject to additional exploitation. The other two strategies look to the migrants as products in the process: on the one hand, examining Latino/a subjectivity as a product of two racial legacies, the Spanish and the Anglo-American; on the other hand, analyzing Latino/a resistance to this trajectory of imposed and racialized migration, whether by way of identity formation or cultural production.

From this perspective of pan-ethnic transnationalism, national empowerment would be used as a platform for international empowerment in two ways. First, the approach would serve to unmask and critique the scenario, hemispheric as well as geopolitical, that has led to the presence and situation of the community in the United States. Second, the approach would offer other points of reference for the community in the United States in the light of a globalized world: cosmopolitanism, rather than nationalism; polyvocality, instead of univocality; and economic, political, and social forms, beyond identity.

Research Agenda

Regarding the question of guiding directives for research, the state of affairs brought about by the impact of the ideological and linguistic turns is taken for granted and incorporated into the vision of *Latinidad*, of the group as a whole. On the one hand, both the differences of identity that mark the group and the diversity of critical approaches used to analyze such differences are acknowledged. On the other hand, both are also redirected toward a common goal through the lens of the collectivity. In the process, the various directives are affected. First, the call for multidisciplinary knowledge production is sustained—it remains no less diffuse in principle, but it is brought closer together in practice under the aegis of an encompassing political project. Second, the call for collective research regains importance—it is now driven by the overriding sense of a common goal provided by the political project. Lastly, the call for close ties between scholars and the community recovers a sense of vibrancy and urgency—it is made imperative by a conception of the political project as forged in the grassroots. This last point I shall develop in the context of research procedure.

Thus, Gutiérrez and Almaguer envision "an interdisciplinary field of research, with all of its complex themes, preoccupations, and intellectual challenges."[53] Throughout, group belonging, consciousness as well as mobilization, would be emphasized, bringing together individuals from throughout the whole of Latin America and the Caribbean, without erasing differences of any sort, through the concept of *Latinidad*, thus "naming this sentiment of affiliation as 'Latina' or 'Latino.'"[54] Such terms, as stated earlier, would not serve to obscure differences, as they have often done in the past but rather to embrace and marshal them. Similarly, Mize affirms the need for the presence of all disciplines within Latino/a Studies in order to "account for Latinas/os' relevance to US society."[55] No field of studies can be spared in examining and assessing the reality and experience of the group in and for the United States. All fields of studies are needed for the empowerment of the collectivity. In neither case, interestingly enough, does one find mention of religious-theological studies, even when, as Mize does, a long list of such fields is provided.

Research Procedure

In terms of the question of fashioning a cultural archive and compiling a social database, in the light of the marginalization of the community on the part of the dominant academic-scholarly guild, the goals of the second phase—the amplification of the envisioned parameters—are, as in the case of the agenda for research, taken for granted and assimilated into the project of *Latinidad*. In assembling both archive and database, no segment or analysis of the population can be left aside. Comprehensivess is of the essence. Such inclusiveness the reflections develop along different, but not dissimilar, lines. While Gutiérrez and Almaguer focus on the broad scope of the field, Mize highlights the wide object of the field. At the same time, Mize concurs with the need for breadth in scope, while Gutiérrez and Almaguer agree with the point of expansiveness in object.

Gutiérrez and Almaguer present comprehensiveness as the driving principle behind the project of *Latinidad* as signified by their *Reader*. They regard the volume along the lines of a course syllabus, "systematically introducing themes with progressive levels of complexity."[56] Inclusiveness is evident in the objectives identified as central to the volume: providing an up-to-date account of the literature, both theoretical and empirical; incorporating the range of differences in the population; and using the research of both Latinas and Latinos. It is evident in terms of content as well. On the one hand, they point to and apologize for gaps in this panoramic vision. Thus, centered on social production, the *Reader* does not address cultural production. Similarly, centered on the use of English, it does not deal with language differences in the population either, many of whom speak in other languages as well, including a number of indigenous languages. On the other hand, they set out to cover a wide spectrum of social production, attending to seven major themes in all.[57] All essays, throughout all sections, it should be noted, are said to stress the goal of cohesion and coalition behind the volume.

Mize sets comprehensiveness at the core of the project of *Latinidad* as signified by his turn to the grassroots. Such inclusiveness is developed in detailed, threefold fashion. I begin with the final step, the expansion of the object of research. He calls for a return to "community-based research and advocacy scholarship."[58] This means, first, attending to the lived everyday experience of the community, "listening to life stories, documenting *testimonios*, and activating narratives."[59] It also means, second, using such research as a tool for resistance, so as to "counter the negative stereotypes, criminalizations, and demonizations" of the group.[60] This is what a *Latinidad* project must undertake, as comprehensively and as inclusively as possible.

Such research and scholarship are placed within the larger critical framework of the political project. As a first step, he argues for moving beyond the language of race in resisting "Anglo racism," given its grounding in a "system of institutions and privileges," a system that "furthers the enjoyment of privilege by a few," even though not all "who can claim Whiteness" share equally in it.[61] The project should turn instead to the language of "new ethnicities" as contextual constructions of identity.[62] This is what *Latinidad* begins to do. As a second step, he argues for appealing to ancestry in such constructions, for "History matters." The project should approach the notion of ancestry not as "an antique to be preserved intact" but as a path of social relations that "connect past and present, while bounding the trajectories of future possibilities."[63] As such, they must be conceptualized "at different levels of lived relations."[64] This is what grassroots *Latinidad* seeks to do, working from below and emphasizing *latinidades*. It is from these two steps that the third follows: a project that is community-based and advocacy-driven.

From this perspective of ethnicity as contextual construction, Mize argues, various consequences follow for analysis. To begin with, one can understand how the system of racial oppression and the process of racialization work: the role of race in everyday practices; the role of discrimination in interpersonal relations; and the role of institutionalized racialized thoughts and actions in the structures of everyday lives. Second, one can also understand how race functions as a "comparative and meaningful signifier" in such a system, both for each community and in relation to other communities. Third, one can further understand how identities "are informed by multipositionalities, an acknowledgment of the plurality of subject positions that inform social identities in terms of race, class, gender, sexuality, coloniality, nation, and citizenship."[65]

A Concluding Evaluation

The result of all these developments, following upon the unquestionable growth constitutive of the first phase and the radical recasting representative of the second phase, has been strategic consolidation. To be sure, growth has continued apace in the community and in the field alike. Likewise, recasting has continued vigorously along multiple dimensions and directions. What one now observes is an attempt to place the field, in all of its expansiveness and diversity, at the service of what I earlier characterized as a strategy of focalization and canalization—a political project with transformation and empowerment of the community in mind within the context of the United States. In the light of this project, a look ahead proves insightful. Here the year 2016 marks a watershed moment.

Appearing in 2016 and thus prior to the advent of Trumpism, Gutiérrez and Almaguer approach this political project with what strikes me as an altogether uplifting sense of enthusiasm. Thus, they harp on the "excitement that surrounds the political and cultural possibilities of *Latinidad*, the demographic expansion of Hispanics and Latinos as an ethnic group, and the emergence of the field of Latino studies as an interdisciplinary and transnational field of study."[66] The future for the field, and the community, shines brightly. The political project is viewed as promising, as a way to make an impact in the country.

Published in 2019 and thus well into the age of Trumpism, Mize comes to the project with what comes across to me as a decidedly foreboding sense of urgency. He writes, "The political language of 'putting America first' is precisely the language designed to exclude Latina/os from their rightful place," and indeed "Latina/os find themselves increasingly unwelcome in Trump's America."[67] The future for the field, and the community, has turned threatening. The political project is regarded as indispensable, as a way to stem the tide in the country. On this, Mize is to the point: "It is these forms of resistance and resiliency in political coalitions of Latinidad that can fuel voter drives, social movements, alternative economies, mutual assistance, and progressive social change."[68]

LATINX STUDIES AND LATINO/A THEOLOGY: CONJUNCTION

Having outlined the various phases that mark the path of Latino/a studies, I should like to trace, phase by phase, the concomitant paths of biblical studies and theological studies, in general, as well as the development of Latino/a biblical criticism and theological construction, in particular. Such tracing will yield a critical mapping of the relationship between Latino/a studies and Latino/a theology. Such mapping, in turn, will lead to a pointed situating of the project within this comparative framework and thus within the realm of cultural analysis. Indeed, the project may be said to come at an important moment and to enjoy a significant position in such a mapping. In terms of timing, it appears at the start of the 2020s. It has thus been in the making over the last years of the third phase and confronts a period of time yet to unfold and yet to be captured. In terms of function, it can serve as a window onto both the past and the future. It may be approached as a reflection of the élan of the third phase and as a venture into a world defined by the specter of Trumpism.

I should like to begin this critical mapping by summarizing the academic-scholarly flows of the three fields in question over the course of the three phases of Latino/a studies. The first two, I take from my overviews of biblical studies and theological studies in my introduction to this volume. The third is drawn from my overview of Latino/a theology to follow.

The first flow involves the trajectory of biblical criticism in general. I have argued for a process of change in this field of studies in terms of major shifts in method and theory. Grafted onto the three-phase model of Latino/a studies, this flow would proceed as follows: (1) from breaking away from established traditions of the discipline; (2) through expanding in multiple directions, by way of a transition from discipline to field; (3) to becoming a thoroughly diversified field of study, with calls to address the major crises of the day. The second flow has to do with the path of theological construction in general. I have argued for a process of change in this field in terms of key shifts in turns and formations. Following the three-phase model of Latino/a studies, this flow would run as follows: (1) from a turn to political consciousness and the rise of a series of formations attending to the political realm both inside and outside Europe, with the latter yielding variations of Liberation Theology; (2) through a turn to the church as global reality and the emergence of two formations dealing, respectively, with the church as non-confessional, Ecumenical Theology, and the church as inter-religious, Planetary Theology—alongside, to be sure, the development of early and new variations of Liberation Theology; (3) to, as I shall suggest below, the rise of a variety of new theologies of a political bent.

The third flow concerns Latino/a theology. I will argue below that this movement also witnesses, in criticism and construction alike, a process of change in terms of presence and production. Adapted to the three-phase model of Latino/a studies, this flow would proceed as follows: (1) from a state of non-existence in the academic-scholarly world; (2) through a solid beginning along liberationist lines in theology and interdisciplinary lines in criticism; (3) to a veritable explosion of work in both respects along multiple directions. The present project in interpretation, therefore, takes shape well into this third stage of explosion and diversification. In what follows, I proceed to unpack these various flows in greater detail.

First Phase of Latino/a Studies—1960s and 1970s

At the end of the 1970s, the shape of both biblical studies and theological studies had begun to move in significant new directions. On the one hand, biblical criticism was beginning to move away from the contours of traditional historical criticism through early ventures into literary criticism and sociocultural criticism. Such ventures remained, by and large, formalist and objectivist in nature. At the same time, the first steps in ideological criticism were being taken as well through developments in feminist criticism as well as materialist criticism. These developments took on a perspectival turn, yet, within such a turn, remained largely objectivist in scope. On the other hand, theological construction shows the movement of political theology outside the European scenario in full swing, as Liberation Theology in Latin America and the Caribbean moves in all sorts of directions, including biblical interpretation.

During this first phase of Latino/a studies, a period of formation and definition marked by vigorous growth against a historical context of convulsion, nothing comparable can be found in Latino/a theology, whether by way of biblical criticism or theological construction. Both areas of studies still lay in the future. At the same time, I would note, the realm of religion and theology does not figure at all within the parameters of interest and research in Latino/a studies. In the envisioned project of cultural nationalism, no room is made and no need is expressed for such studies, despite the call for a broad-based interdisciplinary research agenda and a similarly broad-based research procedure by way of cultural archive and social database.

Second Phase of Latino/a Studies—1980s and 1990s

At the conclusion of the 1990s, the configuration of both theological studies and biblical studies had changed considerably. With regard to the biblical arena, the field had undergone major transformations. Three observations are in order. To begin with, the early turns to literary criticism and sociocultural criticism had grown in vigorous fashion and developed along multiple lines. While literary criticism was deeply influenced by the linguistic turn, expanding beyond formalism and objectivism, sociocultural criticism continued under the spell of scientific objectivism. In addition, the impact of the ideological turn had proved far-reaching: ethnic-racial criticism and queer criticism emerged in the 1980s and empire-postcolonial criticism followed in the 1990s. Lastly, all variants of ideological criticism, early and new alike, had become increasingly complex and sophisticated as well as multivocal and interactive. They had also left behind the objectivism of earlier days and turned to constructivism.

With respect to the theological scene, the field had witnessed a decided shift as well. Four observations are in order. First, the path of Liberation Theology in Latin America had witnessed first a period of expansion in the 1980s and then one of crisis in the 1990s.[69] Second, this path had also taken a decidedly global turn, taking root throughout the rest of the Global South as well as among minoritized groups in the Global North. Third, the élan of liberation had also come to the fore, in ever more vibrant and pointed fashion, in Feminist Theology, in both the Global North and the Global South. Lastly, the global configuration of Christianity had led to the rise of an ecclesial vision beyond denominational boundaries, Ecumenical Theology, and alongside multireligious traditions, Planetary Theology.

Latino/a Theological Construction

As point of origins for the rise of theological movements among minoritized groups in the Global North, the work of James Cone and the tradition of Black Theology take pride of place. Such efforts, taking place as they do in the transition from the 1960s to the 1970s, parallel the foundational septennium for Liberation Theology (1967–1973) advanced in the introductory piece: *Black Theology and Black Power* and *A Black Theology of Liberation* came back to back, in 1969 and 1972, respectively.[70] Latino/a theology came to be a decade later, more directly influenced by Liberation Theology, as it spread beyond the borders of Latin America.

Elizondo's *The Galilean Journey* in 1983 serves as point of origins, and thus as point of departure for the set of foundational works that followed in rapid succession through 1990 and the publication of González's *Mañana*. This group of authors included: Andrés Guerrero,[71] Ada María Isasi-Díaz and Yolanda Tarango,[72] Allan Figueroa Deck,[73] and Herold J. Recinos.[74] The movement would gather strength through the 1990s, as the number of faces and voices, publications and projects, steadily multiplied. Such growth is pointedly signified by the appearance of various edited collections: in 1992, *We Are A People! Initiatives in Hispanic American Theology*, edited by Roberto Goizueta; in 1996, *Hispanic/Latino Theology: Challenge and Promise*, edited by Ada María Isasi-Díaz and Fernando F. Segovia; in 1997, *Teología en Conjunto: A Collaborative Hispanic Theology*, edited by José David Rodríguez and Loida Martell-Otero.[75]

Many in this movement had recourse to the Bible in their work, certainly so in its early stages; some profusely so. Almost all subscribed to a religious-theological optic, in which the Bible was assigned an exalted status as holy scripture and approached as the inspired, revelatory, and authoritative Word of God. Consequently, the Bible was treated as the measure for critique of the social-cultural realm, but in no way as a measure subject to critique in and of itself from the social-cultural side. A salient exception in this regard was Isasi-Díaz, who, as a follower of Feminist Theology, viewed the voice of women as constituting a higher authority than that of the Bible in their struggle for liberation.[76] Little contact, if any, was established with the academic-intellectual tradition of criticism.

Latino/a Biblical Criticism

As point of origins for the emergence of racial-ethnic criticism among minoritized groups, pride of place belongs to the work of Cain Hope Felder and the tradition of African American hermeneutics. Such ventures take place in the transition from the 1980s to the 1990s: the monograph *Troubling Biblical Waters: Race, Class, and Family* and the edited collection of essays titled *Stony the Road We Trod* appeared back to back, in 1989 and 1992, respectively.[77] Latino/a American criticism quickly followed suit.

The first attempts came in the 1990s, as a number of critics began to reflect on various dimensions of such an approach. This group included early on, Gilbert Romero (1991);[78] later on, Jean-Pierre Ruiz (1995)[79] and Francisco García-Treto (1996).[80] My own early work along these lines would use these reflections as a mapping toward the articulation of a Hispanic American hermeneutics.[81] All such work appealed directly to contemporary developments in method and theory in the field, above all in literary criticism. In so doing, Latino/a criticism largely kept its distance from any type of religious-theological reading, opening the way thereby to a more constructive view of the Bible and a critique of the texts themselves.

Concluding Comment

During the second phase of Latino/a studies, a period of development and maturation signified by diversification of foci and approaches within a historical backdrop of restoration, the formative phase of Latino/a theological construction and biblical criticism takes place, the former in the 1980s and the latter in the 1990s. Latino/a theological visions followed by and large the foundational "national" model of Latino/a studies. This it did in two ways: focusing on the historical formations of the community, Mexican-Americans (Elizondo; Guerrero) and Puerto Rican Americans (Recinos) or addressing the community as undifferentiated, whether as a whole (Figueroa Deck; González) or as a part (Isasi-Díaz). The impact of the linguistic and ideological turns would come later.

Latino/a critical approaches already reflected the impact of both turns on the field. While speaking of the community as a whole, early critics drew on strands within literary criticism—such as structuralism (Romero), reader response (Ruiz), and poststructuralism (García-Treto), as well as within ideological criticism—such as ethnic-racial criticism (Segovia). Such engagement would deepen with the passing of time. As was the case at the end of the first phase, here too, I would note, the dearth of attention to the realm of religion and theology in Latino/a studies persisted. The deconstruction and diffusion of the initial project of cultural nationalism by way of multiple problematics of identity resulted in calls for corresponding amplification of the research agenda and the research procedures, the cultural archive as well as the social database. At no time, however, was there a need mentioned or space cleared for religious-theological studies.

Third Phase of Latino/a Studies: 2000s–2010s

At the end of the 2010s, the shape of theological studies and biblical studies had undergone further key developments. In terms of biblical criticism, the expansion of ideological criticism continued apace. While earlier approaches had gained in complexity and sophistication, new variations appeared on the scene, focusing on other unequal relations of power in society and culture, such as disability criticism and ecological criticism. Throughout, multivocality and interactivity were the norm. To this one should add two other approaches. One is political criticism, which seeks to bring texts and interpretations to bear, across the spectrum of critical approaches, on key issues and discussions involving national or international affairs. The other is global criticism, which brings together, with varying aims, critics from across the globe to work together on the biblical texts and contexts. Here I would place my own call for a global-systemic approach, whose focus would encompass: the world-system in place; the fundamental crisis posited at the core of this system; and the set of crises accounting for such a fundamental rupture. To those originally mentioned (inequality, climate, migration), I would now add any number of others, such as nationalism, surveillance, and health.

In terms of theological construction, an overview of these two decades along the lines of Rosino Gibellini is sorely missed. I will venture a number of suggestions. First, neither of the movements mentioned within the formation of Ecumenical Theology could be said to have panned out as such. Second, Liberation Theology in Latin America had not regained its vibrancy after the crisis at the end of the century. To be sure, its name was still invoked, given the sharp rise in economic inequality worldwide,[82] while new voices called for a refoundational moment, a radical reconceptualization and reformulation of its critical vision and mission in light of changed conditions at both the social-cultural and the academic-scholarly level.[83] Third, the spread of global theology in the wake of a globalized Liberation continued undiminished, as did that of Feminist Theology.[84] Lastly, new variations on political theology had emerged, addressing issues and discussions of the times in conversation with other fields of study: empire and postcoloniality,[85] economics,[86] ecology.[87]

Latino/a Biblical Criticism

Racial-ethnic biblical criticism experienced much growth during these years, not only in terms of individual traditions but now also in terms of efforts to bring such traditions together in critical dialogue and projects. One such venture took place within the context of the Society of Biblical Literature, through the formation of a program unit on "Minoritized Biblical Interpretation" within the structure of its Annual Meetings. This professional space made it possible for critics from the various traditions to address issues of importance in the field, in the communities, and in the country. Another venture took place through the publication of a first volume along these lines, *They Were All Together in One Place? Toward Minority Biblical Criticism.*[88] This work, edited by Randall Bailey, Benny Tat-siong Liew, and myself as senior representatives of the various racial-ethnic traditions, raised the problematic of working together by way of the concept of minoritization and the field of Minority Studies. It drew an initial mapping of the contours and objectives of this approach, provided examples of such work, and analyzed the visions and strategies at work in such studies.

Within this context, the tradition of Latino/a American criticism underwent swift development. It did so both by doing interpretation from a Latino/a perspective, howsoever defined, and by reflecting on the character of such interpretation. Both of these critical currents were picked up in a volume that sought to capture the state of affairs of this tradition, *Latino/a Biblical Hermeneutics: Problematics, Objectives, Strategies*, edited by Francisco Lozada and myself.[89] This work brought together sixteen scholars to address the question, "What Does It Mean to Be a Latino/a Critic?"—a number that in itself reflected the shift underway. This set of responses the volume set against the trajectory of Latino/a criticism as portrayed by a variety of reflections upon the movement produced since the turn of the century.[90]

These studies revealed a broad spectrum of visions and missions in the present and the future. Three comments are in order. As had been the case from the beginning, these studies kept their distance—not altogether but overwhelmingly so—from a religious-theological reading: most bypassed, problematized, or questioned any such reading. As from the beginning, moreover, the vast majority joined forces with ongoing developments in method and theory in the field as a whole: calling for closer interaction with racial-ethnic, materialist, and global south approaches; foregrounding the need for the integration of feminist perspectives at the core of the undertaking; and following postmodernist approaches to identity in any definition of the term "latino/a" itself. Lastly, as had been the case from the beginning as well, all studies, in varying degrees, insisted on a view of criticism as grounded in and pursued for the community. Toward the end of this third phase, a monograph by Francisco Lozada, *Toward a Latino/a Biblical Interpretation*, offered an overview of this critical endeavor and a charter for its future direction as well, emphasizing diversity in both approaches and identities.[91]

Latino/a Theological Construction

Racial-ethnic theological studies also witnessed extensive growth during this phase. This it did certainly in terms of the individual traditions in question. At the same time, collaborative efforts took place as well, especially toward the beginning of this period. Thus, the year 2001 saw the publication of two such endeavors. The first was *A Dream Unfinished: Theological Reflections on America from the Margins*, edited by Eleazar Fernandez and Fernando F. Segovia, which brought together theologians from the various traditions to reflect on their locus within and toward the social-cultural context of the United States.[92] The second was *Ties that Bind: African American and Hispanic American/Latino/a Theologies in Dialogue*, edited by Anthony Pinn and Benjamín Valentín, which addressed a broad set of concerns and issues affecting both traditions. Later on, in 2009, another collection from Pinn and Valentín followed, *Creating Ourselves: African Americans and Hispanic Americans on Popular Culture and Religion*.[93]

Latino/a theological studies moved away from its initial appeal to and use of the Bible. As a result, it did not proceed to engage in ideological critique of the Bible or to establish links with their biblical counterparts. As the question of the status and role of the Bible was relegated to the background, the possibility of interaction with critical approaches to the Bible receded as well. Theological thinking moved in any number of other directions. Certainly, theologizing in a feminist vein developed exponentially as well, as signaled early on by *A Reader in Latina Feminist Theology: Religion and Justice*, edited by María Pilar Aquino, Daisy L. Machado, and Jeannette Rodríguez.[94] Other currents included political theology,[95] postcolonial theology,[96] and aesthetic theology.[97] To be sure, the tradition of Liberation had by no means abandoned, but this banner was now pursued largely without reference to its traditional second mediation—the turn to the biblical texts and the ecclesial traditions for insight and direction.

Toward the end of the period, two publications both signify and register the growth of the tradition. The first of these, from 2015 and edited by Orlando O. Espín, is a compilation of the state of affairs of the field by way of the handbook genre, *The Wiley Blackwell Companion to Latino/a Theology*.[98] As such, it deals with twenty-six topics encompassing the contexts, traditions, and realities of the Latino/a community. The second, published in 2020, is an overview, along the lines of Francisco Lozada's survey of criticism, of the path of Latino/a theology from inception, *Introducing Latinx Theologies*, coauthored by Miguel De La Torre and Edwin David Aponte.[99]

Concluding Comment

During the third phase of Latino/a studies, a period of transformation and empowerment marked by a political strategy of centering and channeling toward national advancement and influence within a historical scenario of convulsion, Latino/a theological construction and biblical criticism undergo an expansionist stage. Latino/a theological visions moved beyond their initial nationalist and homogenizing tendencies to embrace any number of directions, paralleling the second stage of Latino/a studies with its move toward deconstruction and diffusion of identity. In the process, the foundational links to Liberation Theology were revised and recast along other lines of political and geopolitical reflection and involvement. In so doing, the formative focus on the biblical texts and biblical interpretation were increasingly sidestepped.

Latino/a critical approaches deepened its formative tradition of engagement with ongoing currents in method and theory in biblical studies by turning to new ideological models of inquiry, also paralleling thereby the deconstruction and diffusion of identity at work during the second stage of Latino/a studies. In the process, the established pattern of abstaining from explicit religious-theological reading prevailed, with scant attention paid to the question of Scripture as Word of God. In so doing, the question of critical identity, of the status and role of Latino/a criticism, was embraced and problematized. Yet again, I would note, the realm of religion and theology hardly figures within the parameters of interest and research in Latino/a studies. The political strategy of a *Latinidad* called upon all variations of the field, all studies of *latinidades*, to advance the standing of the group as a whole in the national sphere. Yet, in such an agenda of and for *Latinidad* no room was opened and no need was declared for the inclusion of religious-theological studies.

A salient exception is very much worth mentioning, given its assessment of the field. This was a piece written toward the beginning of this third phase by Davíd Carrasco,[100] Neil L. Rudenstine Professor for the Study of Latin America at Harvard University, in the *Reader* edited by Flores and Rosaldo. It came in response to a formal invitation to write on the topic of Latinas/os and Religion. The introductory paragraphs capture the problem of representation.[101] On the one hand, Carrasco registers a critique of the field regarding its stance on religion, "How could a field of study which worked to illuminate the 'historical continuum' of various Latino cultural projects, that prided itself on being of the people, for the people and by the Latino peoples, so successfully ignore the religious dimensions of Latino life?" On the other hand, he accepts the assignment "with gratitude and hope" as a way of breaking through what he characterized as this "nonsense of Latina/o Studies."

LATINO/A THEOLOGY AND THE BIBLE: SITUATING THE PROJECT WITHIN LATINO/A STUDIES

The charting of cultural analysis by way of Latino/a studies over the six decades of its existence as a field of studies—from its inception in the 1960s through its configuration in the 2010s—has yielded a critical trajectory of three phases of development, each encompassing a duration of two decades. This mapping has further shown how, over the entire course of this trajectory, Latino/a studies has bypassed, in systematic and sustained fashion, the realm of religious-theological studies and thus, ultimately, the dimension of religion and theology as well. Such a stance, whether adopted intentionally or not, does have implications.

It signals that the critical study of religious practices and theological beliefs among the Latino/a population was regarded as tangential, inconsequential, to the field of studies. It signals further that such practices and beliefs were viewed as peripheral, distractive, in the social and cultural life of the Latino/a group itself. Thus, all fields of study were called to action in furthering the shifting goals behind the project of Latino/a studies, but this one. Such omission is nonsense indeed, as Carrasco put it. I would go further. It represents a critical faux pas of the highest order. Even if this were a case of casual oversight rather than deliberate choice, it constitutes, to my mind, a reflection of the traditional attitude of dismissal regarding matters of religion and theology in the world of the academy and scholarship. Such omission, consequently, would have to be approached and evaluated in ideological terms.

Set against this background, the comparative charting of Latino/a theology has revealed a similar trajectory, but with a distinct lag in development. This I would put as follows. In the first, formative and defining, phase of Latino/a studies, the 1960s and 1970s, the movement and discourse of Latino/a theology had not yet come into being. Then, during the second, consolidating and maturing, phase of Latino/a studies, the 1980s and 1990s, Latino/a theology experienced its foundational period—along the nationalistic and homogeneous lines marking the first phase of Latino/a studies. Lastly, in the third, transformative and empowering, phase of Latino/a studies, the 2000s and 2010s, Latino/a theology underwent an expansionist phase—following the deconstructive and diffuse lines that characterized the second phase of Latino/a studies. In effect, Latino/a theology has stood throughout a full phase behind Latino/a studies. This mapping has also shown how Latino/a theology has, in fairly sustained and systematic fashion as well, refrained from critical interaction with the field of Latino/a studies. Such a position, whether adopted self-consciously or not, does have implications as well.

It indicates that the critical study of religious practices and theological beliefs within the Latino/a population was conducted as independent, self-contained, within the field of studies. It signals, further, that such practices and beliefs were treated as unrelated, unconnected, to the broader social and cultural life of the Latino/a group. Such a modus operandi also amounts to nonsense and does constitute a critical faux pas of the highest order. Even if this were the result of an instinctive rather than considered decision, it amounts, in my opinion, to a conception of its own discourse and import as out of place in the academic-scholarly world at large, and hence an appropriation of its perception of and attitude toward attitude toward religion and theology. Such distantiation would, again, have to be subjected to ideological critique.

In the light of both trajectories, the locus of this project in Latino/a theology can be better pinpointed and explained. The project is crafted during the third phase of Latino/a studies and thus belongs to the expansionist stage of Latino/a theology. As such, it clearly exhibits the deconstructive and diffuse character of this expansion. It calls upon a variety of theological scholars, from a variety of ecclesial and constructive traditions, to address the question of the Bible in the process of theologizing. A key objective, therefore, is to highlight diversity. The project seeks to capture a sense of the spectrum of opinion regarding the Bible, its status and role, in the field of theological construction, beyond the traditional confines of biblical criticism.

From the standpoint of cultural analysis, such a diversity of positions would represent reflections of the social-cultural context of construction in Latino/a theology as well as the social-cultural context of the Latino/a group itself, insofar as the community stands behind the formulation of such visions and the theologians themselves form part of this community. In effect, their approaches to and deployments of the Bible would be viewed as expressions of the social and cultural life of this minoritized ethnic-racial group—not only in terms of the scholars who advance them but also in terms of the communities within which they dwell and work. Such expressions would thus be treated like all other expressions of Latino/a studies and Latino/a life. They would stand alongside all other modes of social-cultural analysis and all other modes of social-cultural production. They would be treated no differently from critical studies of the human sciences or the social sciences in Latino/a studies. Such expressions would thus be duly integrated, rather than bypassed, into the ongoing project of Latino/a studies. This inclusion would, in turn, serve to break through the critical faux pas, the nonsense, that has prevailed regarding the realm of religion and theology in both critical studies and theological studies.

CONCLUDING WORD: A LOOK FORWARD

I have in this study set forth the backdrop for and place of this project on the views and uses of the Bible in Latino/a theology from the perspective of a third field of study, besides those of biblical criticism and theological construction, that I see as framing this movement and discourse, cultural analysis. I have in so doing foregrounded the ethnic-racial dimension that stands at the center of this exercise, as the product of a minoritized ethnic-racial group in the United States, by turning to Latino/a studies, a variation of cultural studies in the United States, as the critical framework for such analysis. In effect, I have argued that Latino/a theology should be seen and should see itself as a constitutive dimension of Latino/a studies. I have shown in this regard how the path of Latino/a theology correlates with that of Latino/a studies. I have further shown how this project in Latino/a theological construction reflects the latter's second phase of diversification regarding critical problematics and approaches. What I should like to do at this point, by way of conclusion, is to offer suggestions for the future in light of the path signaled by this project.

A first line of direction would involve adopting the impetus behind the third phase of Latino/a studies. This move would require shifting—not abandoning, but integrating—from a mode of deconstruction and diffusion to a mode of focusing and mobilization, with the aim in mind of enhancing the political presence and power of the community in the national scene. Generally, the question to ponder would be how to orient the religious-theological production in all areas of study comprised by Latino/a theology, including theological construction and biblical criticism, toward the advancement of the group, its welfare and influence, within the culture and society of the United States. Specifically, the question would focus on how to marshal biblical interpretation to serve such ends or, to put it otherwise, how to give such interpretive undertaking a political turn, so that it can address key issues and discussions in the national scene in such a way as to profit and forward the Latino/a community.

A second line of direction would include developing close critical acquaintance of and dialogue with the field of Latino/a studies and its broad spectrum of concerns and pursuits. Such an undertaking, one would hope, would be accompanied by a similar disposition from this field in turn. Generally, the question to consider is how the realm of religion and theology, and its critical analysis, relates to and interacts with the broader social and cultural parameters of the Latino/a community, and their critical analyses. Specifically, the question would attend to the activity of biblical interpretation, whether in the field of Latino/a theology, in particular, or in the Latino/a community, as a whole. With regard to the former, for example, how does such an exercise in interpretation relate to the field of literary criticism in Latino/a studies? With respect to the latter, what do attitudes toward the Bible, its status and role, in the community tell us about its social and cultural situation?

A third line of direction would involve extending the call for close critical acquaintance and dialogue beyond the field of Latino/a studies to include further fields of study: other variations of minoritized ethnic-racial studies, such as African American, Native American, and Asian American Studies; the joint study of such groups in Minority Studies, and the long-standing field of ethnic-racial studies as such. Generally, the question to address would be how the realm of religion and theology has been pursued in critical studies dealing with other minoritized groups in the United States and how to bring together all such investigations with the aim of joint advancement vis-à-vis the dominant society and culture of the United States. Specifically, the question would weigh how any such comparative or joint study of biblical interpretation would be of assistance toward this end. A factor to keep in mind here is the history and presence of biblical overtones in the rhetorical and mythological arsenal of the nation.

A final line of direction would entail facing the future, not only alongside Latino/a studies but also alongside minority studies, for the next phase of development. This is a most pressing undertaking. Generally, the question to weigh is how to deploy the realm of religion and theology and its critical study to deal with the explosion of nationalism throughout the world, with its accompanying symptoms of "othering": ethnicism and racism as well as nativism and xenophobia. Specifically, the question would foreground the role of biblical interpretation in so doing. With regard to the national context, this entails dealing not only with the phenomenon of Trumpism, its ideology and rhetoric, but also with its inevitable repercussions for years to come, since the long-repressed and now-surfaced disdain for the "Other" will not retreat easily. Such a task would form part of the drive for greater political empowerment inside the country. With regard to the global scene, this implies dealing with such forces throughout, especially in terms of minoritization. Such a task would form part of the effort toward greater political empowerment outside the country.

In sum, this is a tall order for the future; it is also an indispensable and ineluctable one. The present project represents, I would again submit, but a modest endeavor in this regard. It is only through the accumulation of such modest endeavors, however, that the larger vision of centering and mobilizing, nationally and internationally, can begin to make a dent. If there is a specter of othering in the air, there is, and there must be, a specter of liberation as well. In this task, religion and theology should have a major role to play, as should biblical texts and biblical interpretations, and here I see a call to action for the movement and discourse of Latino/a theology in the interest of Latinidad at home and abroad.

NOTES

1. Juan Flores, "Latino Studies: New Contexts, New Concepts," *Harvard Educational Review* 67 (1997): 208–222. It was reprinted in Juan Flores, ed., *From Bomba to Hip-Hop: Puerto Rican Culture and Latino Identity*, Popular Cultures, Everyday Lives (New York-Chichester: Columbia University Press, 2000): 205–218.

2. Juan Flores and Renato Rosaldo, "Foreword," in Juan Flores and Renato Rosaldo, eds., *A Companion to Latino/a Studies*, Blackwell Companions to Cultural Studies (Malden, MA: Blackwell Publishing, 2011 [2007]): xxi–xxvi.

3. Ramón A. Gutiérrez and Tomás Almaguer, "Introduction," in *The New Latino Studies Reader: A Twenty-First Century Perspective*, ed. Ramón A. Gutiérrez and Tomás Almaguer (Berkeley: University of California Press, 2016).

4. Ronald L. Mize, *Latina/o Studies*, Short Introductions Series (Cambridge, UK-Medford, MA: Polity Press, 2019). This volume reflects, as the first paragraph of its Preface (viii–xi) makes clear, the new era inaugurated by the election of Donald J. Trump in 2016.

"The election of Donald J. Trump in 2016 did not bode well for those under consideration in this short introduction. Latinos in the United States number 54,232,205 according to the 2015 US Census Estimate. They constitute the third-largest Latin American 'nation' (behind Brazil and Mexico). Yet Trump secured his election by imploring White voters to expel, in his words, 'the bad *hombres*,' and more specifically 'Mexican rapists and criminals'" (Mize 2019: viii).

5. Mize, "Preface" and "Conclusion: The Future of the Latina/o Studies Field," *Latina/o Studies*, viii-xi and 123–136, respectively.

6. For information on the Censuses of 1970 and 1980, see D'Vera Cohn, "Census History: Counting Hispanics," Pew Research Center. Social & Demographic Trends, 3 March 2010. In: www.pewsocialtrends.org/2010/03/03/census-history-counting-hispanics-2/. On percentage of the population, see Antonio Flores, "Facts on US Latinos, 2015. Statistical Portrait of Hispanics in the United States," *Pew Research Center. Hispanic Trends*, 18 September 2017. In: https://www.pewresearch.org/hispanic/2017/09/18/facts-on-u-s-latinos/#hispanic-rising-share.

7. Flores, "Latino Studies," 212.

8. Flores, "Latino Studies," 207. More specifically, he states, "The guiding theoretical premises," he states, "were adopted directly from thinkers like Frantz Fanon, Amilcar Cabral, and of course Lenin, with Black nationalism, Pedro Albizu Campos, and even José Vasconcelos and Octavio Paz being more immediate intellectual sources" (212).

9. Flores, "Latino Studies," 216–217.

10. Flores and Rosaldo, "Foreword," xxii.

11. Flores and Rosaldo, "Foreword," xxii.

12. For information on the Censuses of 1990 and 2000, see D'Vera Cohn, "Census History: Counting Hispanics."

13. On the rate of growth in the nineties, Mize (*Latino/a Studies,* 126) cites the following reference: Luis R. Fraga, et al., *Latinos in the New Millennium: An Almanac of Opinion, Behavior, and Policy Preferences* (New York, NY: Cambridge University Press, 2012).

14. Flores and Rosaldo, "Foreword," xxiii.

15. Flores, "Latino Studies," 208.

16. Flores, "Latino Studies," 208.

17. Flores, "Latino Studies," 209.

18. Flores, "Latino Studies," 209.

19. Flores, "Latino Studies," 207. Yet, Flores adds, "further ebbs and flows may eventually reconnect the university-based struggle to such systemic types of social confrontation."

20. Flores, "Latino Studies," 209.

21. Flores, "Latino Studies," 209.

22. Flores and Rosaldo, "Foreword," xxiii.

23. Flores, "Latino Studies," 210.

24. Flores, "Latino Studies," 212.

25. Flores, "Latino Studies," 213. See Benedict Anderson, *Imagined Communities. Reflections on the Origin and Spread of Nationalism* (London: Verso Books, 1983).

26. Five such developments, and hence five possibilities for situating Latino Studies, are mentioned: (a) the variety of long-existing programs in ethnic and minority studies—such as Chicano or Puerto Rican Studies; (b) the availability of professional venues and outlets geared toward ethnic and minority studies—from associations to centers to publications; (c) third, the rise of new disciplines and areas of study with similar concerns—like cultural studies or multicultural studies; (d) the movements for change exerting pressure in established area studies or interdisciplinary programs—such as American Studies, Latin American Studies, and Caribbean Studies; and (e) the spaces carved by forces for change in traditional disciplines, now in crisis. See Flores, "Latino Studies," 215.

27. Flores, "Latino Studies," 215.

28. On percentage of the population in 2010, see Antonio Flores, "Facts on US Latinos, 2015."

29. On the rate of growth in the 2000s, Mize (*Latino/a Studies*, 126) cites again the work of Fraga, *Latinos in the New Millennium*. On the population and percentage of Latinos/as in the country by 2015, see Mize, *Latino/a Studies*, 126.

30. Mize, *Latina/o Studies*, 126. He adds, "The reality is that many in the United States are unwilling to face a demographic inevitability that will make the White majority the minority as early as 2037 or, more conservatively estimated, by 2042.

31. Mize, "Conclusion," 123. He goes on to add: "Multiple voices, multiple experiences, none reducible to the other is simply the way forward if Latina/o Studies is to remain responsive to the diverse communities it serves."

32. Gutiérrez and Almaguer, "Introduction," 1.

33. The problematic of naming is taken up in the first chapter of the volume; see Mize, "What's in a Name? Hispanic, Latino: Labels, Identities," *Latina/o Studies*, 1–13.

34. Mize, "What's in a Name," 6. He explains further in this regard, "Latina/os in the United States, recognizing the problematic gendered nature of Spanish-language rules and practices, have sought since 1977 to shed both the U.S.-government-imposed definition of "Hispanic" and the flawed assumption that masculine forms of names are stand-ins or universal designators."

35. Mize, "What's in a Name?," 7.

36. Frederick Luis Aldama and Christopher González, *Latinx Studies: The Key Concepts*, Routledge Key Guides (New York and London: Routledge, 2019). Aldama is Arts and Humanities Distinguished Professor of English at the Ohio State University; González is associate professor of English and director of the Latinx Cultural Center at the Utah State University.

37. Frederick Luis Aldama and Christopher González, "Introduction," in *Latinx Studies: The Key Concepts*, Routledge Key Guides (New York and London: Routledge, 2019) viii–xii.

38. Aldama and González, "Introduction," viii. The authors go on to describe the decision further as a way of siding with scholars who see such a choice as "a powerful bottom-up claiming of language in ways that demonstrate inclusivity."

39. Aldama and González, "Introduction," ix.

40. Gutiérrez and Almaguer, "Introduction," 1.

41. For the Mission Statement of the Association, see: https://latinxstudiesasso ciation.org/home/mission-statement/.

The Statement outlines a threefold objective: (a) promoting the research and teaching of Latino/a studies; (b) advocating on behalf of Latinas/os; (c) encouraging positive policy change related to Latinas/os. In so doing, it adopts an expansive definition of Latinas/os: long-established communities as well as more recent arrivals. Lastly, it further adopts an expansive focus of analysis: examining the connections between the U.S. Latinas/os and transnational and/or diasporic Latin American and Hispanic Caribbean communities. https://latinxstudiesassociation.org/home/mission-statement/.

42. Mize pursues the question of channeling in a separate chapter: "The Arrival of Latina/o Studies: Bringing in Central American, Cuban, and Dominican Studies," 46–60 (Chapter 4). On this description, see p. 46.

43. Mize, "Arrival of Latina/o Studies," 59.

44. Mize, "Arrival of Latina/o Studies," 60.

45. That institutionalization remains a site of struggle is clear from a recent student protest at Harvard University; see Kate Taylor, "Denying a Professor Tenure, Harvard Sparks a Debate over Ethnic Studies," *The New York Times* 2 January 2020:A12. In effect, the denial of tenure to Professor Lorgia García Peña, described as one of the few professors in Latino and Caribbean Studies, brought charges by minority students of neglect in terms of academic-scholarly programs as well as tokenism in terms of institutional commitment to diversity. The story goes on to mention the presence of similar complaints in a number of other universities.

46. Gutiérrez and Almaguer, "Introduction," 2.

47. Mize, "What's in A Name," 138 n. 5.

48. Mize, "What's in A Name," 138 n. 5.

49. Mize, "What's in A Name," 7.

50. Mize, "What's in A Name," 7.

51. Gutiérrez and Almaguer, "Introduction," 2.

52. Here Mize ("What's in A Name," 8) draws on the work of María Josefina Saldaña-Portillo ("From the Borderlands to the Transnational? Critiquing Empire in the Twenty-first Century," in Juan Flores and Renato Rosaldo, eds., *A Companion to Latino/a Studies* [Malden: Blackwell, 2007], 502–512).

53. Gutiérrez and Almaguer, "Introduction," 1.

54. Gutiérrez and Almaguer, "Introduction," 1.

55. Mize, "Conclusion," 124.

56. Gutiérrez and Almaguer, "Introduction," 1.

57. The major themes of the *Reader* are worth mentioning: (1) What Do Names Mean?; (2) The Origins of Latinos in the United States; (3) The Conundrums of Race; (4) Work and Life Chances; (5) Class, Generation, and Assimilation; (6) Gender and Sexualities; (7) Gender and Sexualities; (8) Latino Politics.

58. Mize, "Conclusion: The Future of the Latina/o Studies Field," 125.

59. Mize, "Conclusion: The Future of the Latina/o Studies Field," 125.

60. Mize, "Conclusion: The Future of the Latina/o Studies Field," 125

61. Mize, "Conclusion: The Future of the Latina/o Studies Field," 123–124.

62. Here Mize explicitly invokes the work of Stuart Hall ("New Ethnicities," in David Morley and Kuan-Csing Chen, eds., *Stuart Hall: Critical Dialogues in Cultural Studies* [New York: Routledge, 1996], 441–449).

63. Mize, "Conclusion: The Future of the Latina/o Studies Field," 124.

64. Mize, "Conclusion: The Future of the Latina/o Studies Field," 124.

65. Mize, "Conclusion: The Future of the Latina/o Studies Field," 125.

66. Gutiérrez and Almaguer, "Introduction," 10.

67. Mize, "Conclusion: The Future of the Latina/o Studies Field," 125.

68. Mize, "Conclusion: The Future of the Latina/o Studies Field," 136.

69. Tombs (*Latin American Liberation Theology*, v–vi, 203–205, 273–274) characterizes its irruption in the 1970s as "The Preferential Option for the Poor: 1970–1979," its expansion in the 1980s as "The God of Life: 1980–1989," and its uncertainty in the 1990s as "Crisis of Hope: 1991–1999." In the 1980s Liberation, he argues, amplified its scope and softened its tone, addressing new areas of concern and taking on a more pastoral hue (203–205). In the 1990s, he adds, Liberation experienced, despite much productivity and initial systematization, declining attraction and questions about its future (273–274). The following statement is to the point: "The 1990s marked the end of Liberation Theology as a vibrant and organised theological movement" (274).

70. James H. Cone, *Black Theology and Black Power* (Maryknoll: Orbis Books, 1969) and *A Black Theology of Liberation* (Maryknoll: Orbis Books, 1972).

71. Andrés Guerrero, *A Chicano Theology* (Maryknoll: Orbis Books, 1987).

72. Ada María Isasi-Díaz and Yolanda Tarango, *Hispanic Women, Prophetic Voice in the Church: Toward a Hispanic Women's Liberation Theology* (San Francisco: Harper & Row, 1988.

73. Allan Figueroa Deck, *The Second Wave: Hispanic Ministry and the Evangelization of Culture* (New York: Paulist Press, 1989).

74. Harold J. Recinos, *Hear the Cry! A Latino Pastor Challenges the Church* (Louisville: Westminster/John Knox, 1989.

75. Roberto Goizueta, ed., *We Are A People! Initiatives in Hispanic American Theology* (Minneapolis: Fortress Press, 1992); Ada María Isasi-Díaz and Fernando F. Segovia, eds., *Hispanic Latino Theology: Challenge and Promise* (Maryknoll: Orbis Books, 1996); José David Rodríguez and Loida Martell-Otero, *Teología en Conjunto: A Collaborative Hispanic Theology* (Louisville: Westminster John Knox, 1997).

76. For a critical analysis of biblical hermeneutics in her work, see Fernando F. Segovia, "Mujerista Theology: Biblical Interpretation and Political Theology," *Feminist Theology* 20 (2011): 1–7.

77. Cain Hope Felder, Troubling Biblical Waters: Race, Class, and Family (Maryknoll: Orbis Books, 1989); and Cain Hope Felder, ed., Stony the Road We Trod: Essays in African American Hermeneutics (Maryknoll: Orbis Books, 1992).

78. C. Gilbert Romero, *Hispanic Devotional Piety: Tracing the Biblical Roots*, Faith and Culture Series (Maryknoll: Orbis Books, 1991).

79. Jean-Pierre Ruiz, "Beginning to Read the Bible in Spanish: An Initial Assessment," *Journal of Latino/Hispanic Theology* 1 (1994): 28–50.

80. Francisco García-Treto, "The Lesson of the Gibeonites: A Proposal for Dialogic Attention as a Strategy for Reading the Bible," in *Hispanic/Latino Theology: Challenge and Promise*, ed. Ada María Isasi-Díaz and Fernando F. Segovia (Minneapolis: Fortress Press, 1996), 73–85.

81. For a delineation of such a hermeneutics, see: Fernando F. Segovia, "Toward a Hermeneutics of the Diaspora: A Hermeneutics of Otherness and Engagement," in *Reading from this Place. Volume 1: Social Location and Biblical Interpretation in the United States*, ed. Fernando F. Segovia and Mary Ann Tolbert (Minneapolis: Fortress Press, 1995): 57–74. For a cartography of Latino/a contributions, see Fernando F. Segovia, "Toward Intercultural Criticism: A Reading Strategy from the Diaspora," in *Reading from This Place: The Global Scene*, ed. Fernando F. Segovia and Mary Ann Tolbert, *Reading* (Minneapolis: Fortress Press, 1995), 303–330.

82. See, for example, Gustavo Gutiérrez and Cardinal Gerhard Ludwig Müller, *On the Side of the Poor: Liberation Theology* (Maryknoll, NY: Orbis Books, 2015). The German original appeared the year before: *An der Seite der Armen: Theologie der Befreiung* (Ausburg: Sankt Ulrich Verlag GmbH, 2015).

83. Here the work of Ivan Petrella is essential: *Beyond Liberation Theology: A Polemic* (London: SCM Press, 2018); *The Future of Liberation Theology: An Argument and Manifesto* (London: Ashgate Publishing, 2014).

84. See, for example: William A. Dryness and Oscar García-Johnson, eds., *Theology without Borders: An Introduction to Global Conversations* (Grand Rapids: Baker Academic, 2015) and John Parratt, ed., *An Introduction to Third World Theologies* (Cambridge: Cambridge University Press, 2004).

85. See, for example, Catherine Keller, Michael Nausner, and Mayra Rivera, eds., *Postcolonial Theologies: Divinity and Empire* (St. Louis: Chalice Press, 2004).

86. Here the work of Joerg Rieger is to the point; see, e.g., *No Rising Tide: Theology, Economics and the Future* (Minneapolis: Fortress Press, 2009).

87. Among such works, see: Krista E. Hughes, Dhawn B. Martin, and Elaine Padilla, eds., *Ecological Solidarities: Mobilizing Faith and Justice for an Entangled World* (University Park: Penn State University Press, 2019).

88. Randall C. Bailey, Benny Tat-siong Liew, and Fernando F. Segovia, eds., *They Were All Together in One Place? Toward Minority Biblical Criticism* (Atlanta: SBL Press, 2009).

89. Francisco Lozada and Fernando F. Segovia, eds., *Latino/a Biblical Hermeneutics: Problematics, Objectives, Strategies*, Semeia Studies (Atlanta: SBL, 2014).

90. For a reading of this trajectory, see the Introduction: Fernando F. Segovia, "Approaching Latino/a Biblical Criticism: A Trajectory of Visions and Missions," in *Latino/a Biblical Hermeneutics: Problematics, Objectives, Strategies*, Semeia Studies, ed. Francisco Lozada and Fernando F. Segovia (Atlanta: SBL, 2014), 1–44.

91. Francisco Lozada, *Toward a Latino/a Biblical Interpretation*, Resources for Biblical Studies 91 (Atlanta: SBL Press, 2017).

92. Eleazar Fernandez and Fernando F. Segovia, eds., *A Dream Unfinished: Theological Reflections on America from the Margins* (Minneapolis: Fortress Press, 2001).

93. Anthony Pinn and Benjamín Valentín, *Creating Ourselves: African Americans and Hispanic Americans on Popular Culture and Religion*, Post-Contemporary Interventions (Durham: Duke University Press, 2009).

94. María Pilar Aquino, Daisy L. Machado, and Jeannette Rodríguez, eds., *A Reader in Latina Feminist Theology: Religion and Justice* (Austin: University of Texas Press, 2002).

95. See, for example, Benjamín Valentín, *Mapping Public Theology: Beyond Culture, Identity, and Difference* (London: Bloomsbury T&T Clark, 2002).

96. See, for example, Mayra Rivera, *The Touch of Transcendence: A Postcolonial Theology of God* (Louisville: Westminster John Knox Press, 2007).

97. See, for example, Roberto Goizueta, Christ Our Companion: Toward a Theological Aesthetics of Liberation (Maryknoll: Orbis Books, 2009).

98. Orlando O. Espín, ed., *The Wiley Blackwell Companion to Latino/a Theology*, Wiley Blackwell Companions (Malden, MA and Oxford: John Wiley & Sons, 2015).

99. Miguel De La Torre and Edwin David Aponte, *Introducing Latinx Theologies* (Maryknoll: Orbis Books, 2020). This is a revised edition of an earlier volume: *Introducing Latino/a Theologies* (Maryknoll: Orbis Books, 2001).

100. Davíd Carrasco, "Cuando Dios y Usted Quiere: Latina/o Studies between Religious Powers and Social Thought," in *A Companion to Latino/a Studies*, ed. Juan Flores and Renato Rosaldo, Blackwell Companions to Cultural Studies (Blackwell Publishing: 2011 [2007]), 60–76.

101. Carrasco, "Cuando Dios y Usted Quiere," 60–61.

BIBLIOGRAPHY

Aldama, Frederick Luis and Christopher González. *Latinx Studies: The Key Concepts*. Routledge Key Guides. New York and London: Routledge, 2019.

Anderson, Benedict. *Imagined Communities. Reflections on the Origin and Spread of Nationalism*. London: Verso Books, 1983.

Aquino, María Pilar, Daisy L. Machado, and Jeannette Rodríguez, eds. *A Reader in Latina Feminist Theology: Religion and Justice*. Austin: University of Texas Press, 2002.

Bailey, Randall C., Benny Tat-siong Liew, and Fernando F. Segovia, eds. *They Were All Together in One Place? Toward Minority Biblical Criticism*. Atlanta: SBL Press, 2009.

Carrasco, Davíd. "Cuando Dios y Usted Quiere: Latina/o Studies between Religious Powers and Social Thought." In *A Companion to Latino/a Studies*, edited by Juan Flores and Renato Rosaldo, 60–76. Blackwell Companions to Cultural Studies. Blackwell Publishing: 2011 [2007].

Cohn, D'Vera. "Census History: Counting Hispanics." *Pew Research Center. Social & Demographic Trends*, 3 March 2010. In: www.pewsocialtrends.org/2010/03/03/census-history-counting-hispanics-2/.

Cone, James H. *Black Theology and Black Power*. Maryknoll: Orbis Books, 1969.
———. *A Black Theology of Liberation*. Maryknoll: Orbis Books, 1972.
De La Torre, Miguel, and Edwin David Aponte. *Introducing Latino/a Theologies*. Maryknoll: Orbis Books, 2001.
———. *Introducing Latinx Theologies*. Maryknoll: Orbis Books, 2020.
Dryness, William A. and Oscar García-Johnson, eds. *Theology without Borders: An Introduction to Global Conversations*. Grand Rapids: Baker Academic, 2015.
Espín, Orlando O., ed. *The Wiley Blackwell Companion to Latino/a Theology*. Wiley Blackwell Companions. Malden, MA and Oxford: John Wiley & Sons, 2015.
Felder, Cain Hope. *Troubling Biblical Waters: Race, Class, and Family*. Maryknoll: Orbis Books, 1989.
———, ed. *Stony the Road We Trod: Essays in African American Hermeneutics*. Maryknoll: Orbis Books, 1992.
Fernandez, Eleazar and Fernando F. Segovia, eds. *A Dream Unfinished: Theological Reflections on America from the Margins*. Minneapolis: Fortress Press, 2001.
Figueroa Deck, Allan. *The Second Wave: Hispanic Ministry and the Evangelization of Culture*. New York: Paulist Press, 1989.
Flores, Antonio. "Facts on US Latinos, 2015. Statistical Portrait of Hispanics in the United States." *Pew Research Center. Hispanic Trends*, 18 September 2017. In: https://www.pewresearch.org/hispanic/2017/09/18/facts-on-u-s-latinos/#hispanic-rising-share.
Flores, Juan. "Latino Studies: New Contexts, New Concepts." *Harvard Educational Review* 67 (1997): 208–222. Reprinted in *From Bomba to Hip-Hop: Puerto Rican Culture and Latino Identity*, edited by Juan Flores, 205-218. Popular Cultures, Everyday Lives. New York-Chichester: Columbia University Press, 2000.
Flores, Juan and Renato Rosaldo. "Foreword." In *A Companion to Latino/a Studies*, edited by Juan Flores and Renato Rosaldo, xxi–xxvi. Blackwell Companions to Cultural Studies Malden, MA: Blackwell Publishing, 2011 [2007].
Fraga, Luis R., et al. *Latinos in the New Millennium: An Almanac of Opinion, Behavior, and Policy Preferences*. New York, NY: Cambridge University Press, 2012.
García-Treto, Francisco. "The Lesson of the Gibeonites: A Proposal for Dialogic Attention as a Strategy for Reading the Bible." In *Hispanic/Latino Theology: Challenge and Promise*, edited by Ada María Isasi-Díaz and Fernando F. Segovia, 73–85. Minneapolis: Fortress Press, 1996.
Goizueta, Roberto. *Christ Our Companion: Toward a Theological Aesthetics of Liberation*. Maryknoll: Orbis Books, 2009.
Goizueta, Roberto, ed. *We Are A People! Initiatives in Hispanic American Theology*. Minneapolis: Fortress Press, 1992.
Guerrero, Andrés. *A Chicano Theology*. Maryknoll: Orbis Books, 1987.
Gutiérrez, Gustavo and Cardinal Gerhard Ludwig Müller. *An der Seite der Armen: Theologie der Befreiung*. Ausburg: Sankt Ulrich Verlag GmbH, 2015.
———. *On the Side of the Poor: Liberation Theology*. Translated by Robert A. Krieg and James B. Nickoloff. Maryknoll, NY: Orbis Books, 2015.

Gutiérrez, Ramón A. and Tomás Almaguer. "Introduction." In *The New Latino Studies Reader: A Twenty-First Century Perspective*, edited by Ramón A. Gutiérrez and Tomás Almaguer, 1-18. Berkeley: University of California Press, 2016.

Hall, Stuart. "New Ethnicities." In *Stuart Hall: Critical Dialogues in Cultural Studies*, edited by David Morley and Kuan-Csing Chen, 441–449. New York: Routledge, 1996.

Hughes, Krista E., Dhawn B. Martin, and Elaine Padilla, eds. *Ecological Solidarities: Mobilizing Faith and Justice for an Entangled World*. University Park: Penn State University Press, 2019.

Isasi-Díaz, Ada María and Yolanda Tarango. *Hispanic Women, Prophetic Voice in the Church: Toward a Hispanic Women's Liberation Theology*. San Francisco: Harper & Row, 1988.

Isasi-Díaz, Ada María and Fernando F. Segovia, eds. *Hispanic Latino Theology: Challenge and Promise*. Maryknoll: Orbis Books, 1996.

Keller, Catherine, Michael Nausner, and Mayra Rivera, eds. *Postcolonial Theologies: Divinity and Empire*. St. Louis: Chalice Press, 2004.

Lozada, Francisco. *Toward a Latino/a Biblical Interpretation*. Resources for Biblical Studies 91. Atlanta: SBL Press, 2017.

Lozada, Francisco and Fernando F. Segovia, eds. *Latino/a Biblical Hermeneutics: Problematics, Objectives, Strategies*. Semeia Studies. Atlanta: Society of Biblical Literature, 2014.

Mize, Ronald L. *Latino Studies*. Short Introductions Series. Cambridge, UK-Medford, MA: Polity Press, 2019.

Parratt, John, ed. *An Introduction to Third World Theologies*. Cambridge: Cambridge University Press, 2004.

Petrella, Ivan. *Beyond Liberation Theology: A Polemic*. London: SCM Press, 2018.

———. *The Future of Liberation Theology: An Argument and Manifesto*. London: Ashgate Publishing, 2014.

Pinn, Anthony and Benjamín Valentín. *Creating Ourselves: African Americans and Hispanic Americans on Popular Culture and Religion*. Post-Contemporary Interventions. Durham: Duke University Press, 2009.

Recinos, Harold J. *Hear the Cry! A Latino Pastor Challenges the Church*. Louisville: Westminster/John Knox, 1989.

Rieger, Joerg. *No Rising Tide: Theology, Economics and the Future*. Minneapolis: Fortress Press, 2009.

Rivera, Mayra. *The Touch of Transcendence: A Postcolonial Theology of God*. Louisville: Westminster John Knox Press, 2007.

Rodríguez, José David and Loida Martell-Otero. *Teología en Conjunto: A Collaborative Hispanic Theology*. Louisville: Westminster John Knox, 1997.

Romero, C. Gilbert. *Hispanic Devotional Piety: Tracing the Biblical Roots*. Faith and Culture Series. Maryknoll: Orbis Books, 1991.

Ruiz, Jean-Pierre. "Beginning to Read the Bible in Spanish: An Initial Assessment." *Journal of Latino/Hispanic Theology* 1 (1994): 28–50.

Saldaña-Portillo, María Josefina. "From the Borderlands to the Transnational? Critiquing Empire in the Twenty-first Century." In *A Companion to Latino/a*

Studies, edited by Juan Flores and Renato Rosaldo, 502–512. Malden: Blackwell, 2007.

Segovia, Fernando F. "Approaching Latino/a Biblical Criticism: A Trajectory of Visions and Missions." In *Latino/a Biblical Hermeneutics: Problematics, Objectives, Strategies*, edited by Francisco Lozada and Fernando F. Segovia, 1–44. Semeia Studies. Atlanta: SBL, 2014.

———. "Mujerista Theology: Biblical Interpretation and Political Theology." *Feminist Theology* 20 (2011): 1–7.

———. "Toward a Hermeneutics of the Diaspora: A Hermeneutics of Otherness and Engagement." In *Reading from this Place*. Volume 1: *Social Location and Biblical Interpretation in the United States*, edited by Fernando F. Segovia and Mary Ann Tolbert, 57–74. Minneapolis: Fortress Press, 1995.

———. "Toward Intercultural Criticism: A Reading Strategy from the Diaspora." In *Reading from This Place: The Global Scene*, edited by Fernando F. Segovia and Mary Ann Tolbert, 303–330. Minneapolis: Fortress Press, 1995.

Taylor, Kate. "Denying a Professor Tenure, Harvard Sparks a Debate over Ethnic Studies." *The New York Times* 2 January 2020:A12.

Tombs, David. *Latin American Liberation Theology*. Religion in the Americas Series. Boston-Leiden: Brill Academic Publishers, 2002.

Valentín, Benjamín. *Mapping Public Theology: Beyond Culture, Identity, and Difference*. London: Bloomsbury T&T Clark, 2002.

Names Index

Afzal-Khan, Fawzia, 122
Agosto, Efrain, 94, 99–100, 113, 120–23
Aldama, Frederick Luis, 259, 280
Alfaro, Sammy, 29–47, 123, 212–14, 231
Alinsky, Saul, 199
Almaguer, Tomás, 239, 257–65, 278, 280–82
Amaladoss, Michael, 22–23
Anderson, Allan H., 42
Anderson, Benedict, 253, 279
Anderson, Victor, 85
Andrews, George R., 133–34, 144, 146
Aponte, Edwin, 85, 273
Applegate, Judith B., 117, 123
Aquinas, Thomas, 49, 52–54, 59–60, 62, 67–68, 184, 186, 211
Aquino, María Pilar, 99, 121–23, 193–94, 196, 202–3, 222, 273
Archer, Kenneth J., 30, 42
Aristotle, 55, 57, 60, 62, 67–68, 143
Arnez, Desi, 82
Arrington, French L., 43
Ashley, Wayne, 197–98, 203
Assemblies of God, 43
Ateek, Naim Stifan, 183, 185–86
Ayé, Babalú, 82–83, 86
Azadegan, Ebrahim, 184, 186

Bailey, Randall C., 86, 145, 271, 283
Bañuelas, Arturo, 65, 198
Barth, Karl, 11
Bell, Catherine, 202–3
Benavente, Toribio de, 57
Benz, Ernst, 131
Bethel Bible College, 30
Bevans, Stephen B., 185–86
Binenkorb, Aaron L., 253
Blowers, Paul, 68
Bonhoeffer, Dietrich, 12
Bonnet, Maximilus, 144
Brading, D. A., 165
Brenner, Athalya, 143
Brown, David H., 106, 245
Brueggemann, Walter, 184, 186
Buber, Martin, 184, 186
Bultmann, Rudolf, 11, 166
Burrell, David B., 184, 186
Bush, George H. W. Bush, 246
Byron, Gay L., 130, 132–33, 143–44

Campbell, Charles L., 69
Cárdenas Bunsen, José Alejandro, 67–68
Cargal, Timothy, 42
Carrasco, Davíd, 274–75
Carter, J. Kameron, 136, 138, 140, 145–46

Carter, Jimmy E., 241
Castro, Daniel, 66
Chan, Simon, 32, 43
Charleston, Steven, 122
Childs, Brevard S., 67
Chomsky, Avi, 144
Christian Latina Leadership Institute, 97
Church of God, 43
Cilliers, Johan H., 69
Clark, Brian, 42, 120
Clementina, Mamma, 22
Clinton, William Jefferson, 246
Clooney, Francis X., 184
Cohn, D'Vera, 279
Colón-Emeric, Edgardo, 47–72, 210–12, 231, 234
Comas, Juan., 66
Conde-Frazier, Elizabeth, 107, 113, 115, 120–23
Cone, James H., 145, 268, 282
Costas, Orlando E., 108, 121
Council of Scientific Affairs, 123
Cox, Harvey, 41–42
Crespo, Orlando, 95, 98, 100
Croatto, José Severino, 16–17, 23
Crow, Jim, 144
Cullmann, Oscar, 12

Dahm, Charles, 198–99, 203
Davalos, Karen Mary, 197, 202–3
de la Fuente, Alejandro, 144
de la Torre Villar, Ernesto, 165
De La Torre, Miguel, 75, 80, 82, 85–86, 98–100, 165, 175, 185, 273
Deloria, Vine, 145
Díaz, Miguel H., 17, 79–82, 85–86, 90–91, 98–100, 121, 165–66, 192–93, 196, 202–3, 215, 222, 269–70, 282–83
Diego, Juan, 154, 158, 162–63, 165
Dillenberger, John, 184
Dryness, William H., 283
Dube, Musa W., 94, 100, 122
Dyer, Jacob A., 143

Ebeling, Gerhard, 11
Eco, Umberto, 94
Elizondo, Virgilio, 15, 17, 23, 79–80, 86, 104, 120, 153, 157–60, 166, 193, 195, 198, 202, 220, 222, 269–70
Empereur, James, 76, 85, 198
Erickson, Millard J., 100
Espín, Orlando O., 65, 77, 85, 121, 153, 157, 159–60, 165–66, 174, 185, 192–93, 201–3, 220, 222, 273
Espinosa, Gaston, 75, 85
Ewart, Frank J., 30, 42

Fakhry, Majid, 184
Fanon, Franz, 128, 137, 143, 145, 279
Felder, Cain Hope, 269, 282
Fernández, Carlos A., 135, 145
Fernández, Eduardo S., 76, 85
Fernandez, Eleazar, 272, 283
Flores, Antonio, 279–80
Flores, Juan, 144, 239, 243–46, 249–53, 257–60, 274, 278–81
Fontaine, Carole R., 143
Ford, David F., 62, 69, 241
Ford, Gerald T., 241
Frades, Eduardo, 68–69
Fraga, Luis R., 279–80
Freire, Paolo, 190, 201
Fuchs, Ernst, 11

Galeano, Eduardo H., 144
Gálvez, Alyshia, 197, 202
García, Sixto, 65, 85, 92–93, 95, 98, 100, 216, 269–70, 281–83
García (García-Rivera), Alejandro, 66, 189, 191, 201
García-Johnson, Oscar, 283
García-Treto, Francisco O., 92–93, 95, 98, 100, 216, 269–70, 283
Gibellini, Rosino, 10–13, 15, 22–23, 271
Gogarten, Friedrich, 12
Goizueta, Roberto S., 23, 85, 185, 193–94, 201–3, 222, 269, 282

Gomez-Kelly, Sallie, 198
González, Christopher, 259, 280
González, Justo L., 15, 17, 23, 43, 65, 89–90, 98, 100, 108, 121–22, 128, 143, 145, 175, 185, 203, 222, 225, 231, 269–70
Gonzalez (Maldonado), Michelle A., 73–88, 127, 142, 202, 224
the Great, Gregory, 56, 63, 129–31, 137, 140, 143–44, 146, 254, 256
Groody, Dan G., 202, 222
Groome, Thomas, 198, 203
Guardiola-Sáenz, Leticia, 98–100, 109, 113, 121–22
Guerrero, Andrés, 269–70, 282
Gutiérrez, Gustavo, 23, 65, 67, 283
Gutiérrez, Ramón A., 239, 257–61, 263–65, 278, 280–83

Hall, Douglas John, 118, 121, 124
Hall, Stuart, 282
Healy, Nicholas, 68
Heim, Mark, 176, 186
Heschel, Abraham Joshua, 186
Hidalgo, Jacqueline, 120
Hughes, Krista E., 283
Hussein, Saddam, 256
Hyatt, Eddie, 42

Institute for Signifying the Scriptures, 120
Isasi-Díaz, Ada María, 79–82, 85–86, 90–91, 98, 100, 121, 192–93, 196, 202, 215, 222, 269–70, 282–83

Johns, A. H., 183, 186
Johnson, Lyndon B., 240
Jorge, Angela, 135, 144
Junior, Nyasha, 108, 121

Kärkkäinen, Veli-Matti, 31–33, 42–43
Kearney, Richard, 139, 146
Keller, Catherine, 283
Kelsey, David H., 234
Kendall, Daniel, 164

Kennedy, John F., 240–41, 247
Kilgallen, John J., 124
Kilgore, Louis A., 100
King, Joseph, 32, 42, 63, 66, 86, 129, 178, 181
Kitahara Kich, George, 135, 145
Knitter, Paul F., 185
Küng, Hans, 12
Kwok, Pui-Lan, 108–10, 112, 121–22

Las Casas, Bartolomé de, 47–69, 210–12, 234
Laso de la Vega, Luis, 153–54, 159–60, 165
Lavastide, José I., 123
Lee, Michael, 79, 86
Leon, Luis D., 203
Levine, Daniel H., 120
Liew, Tat-siong Benny, 86, 271, 283
Lillie, Charisse, 123
Lillie-Blanton, Marsha D., 123
Limburg, James, 186
Lipsius, Ricardus A., 144
Lockhart, James, 165
Long, Charles H., 32, 48, 50, 81, 94, 105–6, 112, 123, 137, 145, 159, 169, 175–76, 199, 233, 238, 242, 246–47, 250, 255, 263, 277, 279, 281
López Rodríguez, Darío, 36–37, 43
Lorde, Audre, 122
Lozada Jr., Francisco, 23, 78–80, 84, 86–87, 209–34, 272–73, 283
Lozano, Nora O., 89–102, 215–17, 231
Lyra, Nicholas, 130, 143

Machado, Daisy L., 99, 122–23, 273
Macy, Gary, 47–48, 65, 85, 165
Maldonado, David, 73–74, 76, 78, 80, 82, 84, 86, 89, 98, 121
Marinho de Azevedo, Celia Maria, 144
Marshall, Bruce, 68
Martell-Otero, Loida, 91, 98, 103–26, 215, 217–19, 231, 269, 282
Martin, Dhawn B., 66, 184, 186, 283
Masferrer, Alberto, 144

Matovina, Timothy, 99, 153–57, 164–66, 202–3, 220, 222
Maynard-Reid, Pedrito U., 43
McGee, Gary B., 42
McGinn, Bernard, 146
Medina, Lara, 100, 203
Mejido, Manuel J., 191, 201
Memmi, Albert, 144
Menocal, María Rosa, 184
Menzies, Robert P., 42
Metz, Johann Baptist, 10, 12, 22
Migne, J.P., 67
Míguez, Néstor, 62, 69
Mize, Ronald L., 239, 257–66, 278–82
Moltmann, Jürgen, 12
Montesinos, Antón de, 50, 63
Müller, Gerhard Ludwig, 283
Muñoz-Mas, Félix, 123

Nausner, Michael, 283
Navarro de Anda, Ramiro, 165
Nina Rodrigues, Raimundo, 134, 144
Nixon, Richard M., 240–41, 247
Norris, Richard A., 143
Nyssa, Gregory, 131–33, 137–40, 143–46, 227

Obama, Barack, 254
O'Collins, Gerard, 164
Origen, 129–32, 139, 143–44, 146, 227
Ortiz, Fernando, 86, 134

Padilla, Elaine, 127–50, 203, 225–28, 231, 283
Palés Matos, Luis, 138, 140, 146
Pannenberg, Wolfgang, 12
Parham, Sarah E., 30, 42
Parratt, John, 283
Pascal, Blaise, 171, 184
Pedraja, Luis G., 185
Peek, Monica E., 123
Pessoa Câmara, Dom Hélder, 23
Peterson, Anna L., 85
Petrella, Ivan, 191, 201, 283
Pew Research Center, 172, 185, 279

Pineda-Madrid, Nancy, 151–68, 219–21, 231
Pinn, Anthony, 85, 272–73
Poole, Stafford, 67, 165
Pope, Marvin H., 129, 131, 143, 165–66

Rahner, Karl, 11, 142
Ramírez de Arrellano, Annette B., 120
Raup Wagner, Henry, 66
Reagan, Ronald L., 246–47
Recinos, Harold J., 17, 86, 121, 269–70, 282
Reinhartz, Adele, 234
Renich Fraser, Elouise, 96, 100
Richard, Earl, 139, 143, 146, 160, 164, 166, 220, 240–41
Rieger, Joerg, 283
Rivera, Mayra, 50, 66, 145, 185, 189, 191, 201, 283
Rivera Pagán, Luis, 50, 66, 185
Rivera-Rodríguez, Luis R., 70
Rodríguez, Daniel A., 38–39, 44
Rodríguez, José David, 121, 269
Rodríguez Trias, Helen, 120
Rogers, Eugene F., 60–61, 68
Rosaldo, Renato, 239, 243, 245, 249, 274, 278–79, 281
Rosario Rodríguez, Rubén, 169–86, 228
Royce, Josiah, 164
Roy-Féquière, Magali, 146
Ruiz, Jean-Pierre, 69, 86, 153–54, 157, 165, 220, 269–70, 282

Saldaña-Portillo, María Josefino, 281
Sánchez, David, 153–57, 164–65, 220
Sánchez, Miguel, 153–57, 159–60, 166, 220
Sasson, Jack M., 186
Schillebeeckx., Edward, 12
Schreiter, Robert J., 185, 190–91, 201
Schroeder, Roger P., 185–86
Schüssler Fiorenza, Elisabeth, 94, 99
Segovia, Fernando F., 3–26, 80–81, 85–86, 92–94, 98–99, 108–9, 113, 121–22, 185, 200, 203, 216, 235–84

Seipp, Conrad, 120
Sepúlveda, Juan Ginés de, 57–62, 67, 212
Seshadri-Crooks, Kalpasa, 122
Shohat, Ella, 111, 122
Siker, Jeffrey S., 86
Simon, Uriel, 32, 43, 117, 186
Smith, Andrea, 112, 122
Soliván, Samuel, 34–35, 37–38, 43
Sousa, Lisa, 165
of St. Thierry, William, 133, 143–44, 146

Tamez, Elsa, 60, 68–69
Tannehill, Robert C., 160–61, 163–64, 166, 220
Tarango, Yolanda, 269, 282
Taylor, Kate, 281
Texas Baptist Convention, 98
Thomas, John Christopher, 33, 42–43, 52–53, 60–61, 67–68, 85, 132, 198, 203, 211
Tillich, Paul, 11, 151, 164
Tirres, Christopher D., 189–206, 221–23, 231
Tolbert, Mary Ann, 22–23, 98–99, 283

Tombs, David, 282
Torres, Jeremías, 99
Tracy, David, 184
Trump, Donald, 254–55, 266, 278–79

Valentín, Benjamín, 23, 74, 76, 85–86, 202, 273
Vásquez, Manuel A., 78, 85
Vicioso, Sherezada, 144
Villafañe, Eldin, 29, 41, 203

Ward, James M., 186
Warrior, Robert, 122
Weaver, Jace, 122
Weems, Renita J., 94, 99
Wheeler, Brannon M., 186
Williams, Delores, 145
Williams, Teresa Kay, 135
Wright, Winthrop R., 144

Yee, Gale A., 94, 99, 109–10, 112–13, 122–23
Yong, Amos, 42

Zamora, Laciel, 83, 86

Subjects Index

Abrahamic faiths: Islam, 169, 171–72, 177, 182, 228–29, 255–56; Judaism, 169, 171, 177, 181, 228–29
Academy of Catholic Hispanic Theologians of the U.S. (ACHTUS), 81, 200
Acompañamiento, 194
Act of alchemy, 257
African, 13, 22, 43, 49, 83, 85, 104, 110, 122–23, 134–35, 140, 143, 145–46, 174, 224, 236, 269, 272–73, 277, 282
agency, 7, 192, 195, 216, 222–23, 231–33
Amerindian, 49, 62, 64, 104, 110, 112
authority: authoritative, 31, 54, 90, 92, 105, 107, 114–15, 152, 170, 209, 211–19, 221, 223, 225, 228, 230–31, 233, 269; of scripture, 32–33, 91

biblical criticism: contemporary biblical criticism, 4, 22, 99; global-systemic criticism, 5–6; historical criticism, 5–7, 12, 16, 93, 267; ideological criticism, 5–8, 22, 109, 113, 267–68, 270; literary criticism, 5–6, 16, 93, 267–68, 270, 277; postcolonial criticism, 108–10, 217, 219, 268; religious-theological criticism, 270, 272, 274, 277; sociocultural criticism, 5–6, 267–68
biblical figures: Barnabas, 33; Jesus, 31, 41, 48, 51, 55–56, 64, 67, 79–83, 86, 104, 115, 117–18, 121, 130, 152, 157, 159–61, 163, 171, 173, 176, 179, 181–82, 185, 194, 197, 211, 218, 220, 223, 234; Jonah, 176–83, 185–86, 229–30; Moses, 56, 137, 145, 155, 171; Paul, 11, 33, 41, 59, 62, 68–69, 91, 131, 151, 160, 164–66, 185, 220; Peter, 22, 33, 132, 140, 142, 144, 163; Stephen, 40, 185–86

canon: canon from the canon, 91, 215–17
Catholicism, 11, 69, 73, 75–77, 81–85, 104, 108, 120–21, 123, 151, 158, 162, 164–66, 172, 174, 185, 192–93, 198, 200–203, 222, 224–25
church: ecclesial, 8–10, 12–13, 15–16, 18, 74, 84, 107, 156, 176, 217–18, 221, 229–32, 268, 273, 276; ecumenical, ecumenism, 10, 12, 42, 108, 173, 185, 229–30, 267–68, 271
colonial discourses: anticolonial, 111, 113, 118; colonialism, 48, 63, 69, 78, 103, 105, 108–11, 118, 120, 122, 133, 135, 141, 156, 159,

165–66, 217–18, 226, 242, 245, 251; imperialism, 58, 66, 69, 109–10, 156, 166, 177, 241–42, 245, 251; postcolonial, postcoloniality, 94, 100, 107–13, 118–19, 121–22, 146, 156, 200, 217, 219, 252, 268, 271, 273, 283
concientization, 6, 18, 81, 197, 238
conservative, 32, 75, 89, 198, 215, 218, 251
contextual, 7, 17, 60, 74, 77, 107–8, 128, 172, 185–86, 189–91, 200–201, 234, 262, 264–65
Corito, 35, 37
creation, 36, 42, 50–51, 76, 136, 140, 152, 158, 166, 171, 183, 246, 253
Culto, 34–35, 37, 39–40, 86, 213–14
cultural discourse: contextual, 7, 17, 60, 74, 77, 107–8, 128, 172, 185–86, 189–91, 200–201, 234, 262, 264–65; cultural analysis, 3–4, 18–19, 235–37, 239, 266, 274, 276; cultural resistance, 195–96; cultural studies, 4, 7, 22, 93, 108–9, 113, 216, 236, 276, 278, 280–81; diversity, 6, 58, 75, 86, 135, 158, 215, 226, 228, 252, 255, 258–59, 263, 265, 272, 276, 281; indigenous, 35, 49–50, 64, 66, 69, 105, 111, 113, 142, 154, 157–58, 162–63, 165, 174, 210–12, 264; intercultural, 48, 98–99, 121, 123, 200, 202–3, 234, 283; multilingual, 95–96, 216, 264; religious pluralism, 169–70, 176–77, 229; tradition, 3, 5, 8–10, 14, 16, 19, 21, 23, 37, 43, 47–48, 52, 59–60, 65, 76, 79–80, 85–86, 91, 103–4, 107, 121, 128, 133, 153–56, 159, 165–66, 169–78, 183–84, 192–93, 199, 202, 212, 215, 220–22, 227–32, 235, 268–69, 272–73

demon, demonic, demonization, 21, 106, 132
dialogical process, 116, 199, 201
dignity, 16, 54, 117, 152, 183, 195

Divine Wisdom, Las Casas, 51, 54, 56, 58, 60–62, 65
divinity: deity, 138; divine, 48, 51–54, 56, 58–62, 65–66, 90, 92–93, 106, 114, 127, 132, 136–42, 155, 158, 164, 170–71, 177, 179–80, 182–84, 186, 211–12, 218, 223, 229; *imago dei*, 80, 127–28, 132–33, 136–37, 140–43, 226–27; incarnation, incarnational, 13, 48, 52, 60, 82, 114, 170, 173; monotheistic, 82, 169–70; theistic, 176; Trinity, 56, 62; triune, 105, 113, 152, 218–19

elite, 109, 251, 255
empire, imperial: empire-building, 105
empowerment, 80, 89, 91–99, 105, 194, 215–17, 239, 254, 258, 260–63, 265, 273, 278
ethnography, 190–91, 197, 200, 203, 222, 260
Europeanization: Enlightenment, 19, 22, 136, 141
evangélica, 75, 98, 103–4, 106, 108, 112–14, 118–22, 217–19
evangelical, 38, 94, 97, 100, 103, 172, 218
evangelism: missionary, missionaries, 33, 37, 51, 56, 59, 64, 106, 120, 158, 171; non-violent, 51, 53–54, 211–12; violent, coercive, 51, 53–54, 57, 62, 66, 158, 211–12

field of studies, 5–6, 108, 239–40, 243, 249, 258, 263, 266, 274–75
flesh-and-blood reader: ethnic-racial studies, criticism, 209, 235, 250, 268–72, 277; hermeneutics of suspicion, 172; Latino/a criticism, 17, 19, 23, 78, 81, 84, 200, 212, 224, 232, 266, 269–72, 274, 283; peripheric reading, 104, 106, 113, 115; reader-response criticism, 93, 270; reading against the grain, 103–

Subjects Index

5, 107, 109, 111, 113–15, 117, 119, 121, 123, 217, 219
from below, 65, 261, 265

gender and sexuality studies: feminist, feminism, 12–13, 85–86, 94, 99–100, 109–10, 117, 121–23, 142–43, 145, 196, 202–3, 261, 267–69, 271–73, 282; kyriarchy, 152; masculinization, 132; patriarchy, 39, 94, 110, 118, 152, 196, 222; sexuality, 6, 196, 200, 222–23, 232, 252, 265
genocide, 111, 118–19, 135
gentiles, 33, 55, 178, 180, 182, 229
global studies: Afghanistan War, 256; Cold War, 241, 246–47; Cuban Revolution, 241, 245; Global North, 6, 19, 256, 268; Global South, 6, 14, 19, 241, 245, 247, 254–56, 268, 272; globalization, 86, 249–52, 261; Great Recession, 254, 256; Gulf War, 247, 255–56; Third World, 10, 12, 16–17, 23, 111, 251, 283; Vietnam War, 241, 245, 248; World War II, 247
Good News: Bible as good news/book, 90, 94–95
grassroots, 34, 81, 104, 107, 112–14, 119, 218, 261–65
Guadalupe, 151–66, 202, 219–21

Hispanic: Chicano Studies, 244–45, 250, 258, 280, 282; *Criollos*, 156, 162; Iberian, 47–48, 65, 104, 158, 174, 192–93, 211, 222; *latinamente*, 47, 75, 211–12, 224; *latinidad*, 75, 78, 227, 258–66, 274, 278; Latino/a American, 4, 14, 86, 236, 269, 272; Latino/a Studies, 4, 236–40, 242–43, 249, 257–59, 263, 266–68, 270, 273–81; nomenclature of, 158, 227, 233, 243, 250, 258; *peninsulares*, 156; Puerto Rican Studies, 244–45, 258, 280; transnationalism, 251, 260, 262

humanity: hermeneutic of humanity, 59–60; solidarity, 10, 84, 121, 135, 172–74, 194, 222, 250

identity: social location, 22–23, 77, 79–80, 86, 94, 98–99, 104–5, 113–14, 116, 190, 215, 217–19, 232, 283
ideology: hegemony, 103, 175; ideological, 5–8, 14, 18–20, 22, 91, 93, 95, 109, 112–13, 154, 156–57, 226, 231, 244, 250, 252–53, 258, 263, 267–68, 270, 273–75

justice: discrimination, 17, 105, 109–10, 134–35, 243, 265; equality, inequality, 91, 94, 100, 140, 255, 271; exploitation, 16, 66, 68, 109, 116, 176, 262; injustice, 10, 66, 119–20, 131, 176–77, 184, 241–42; liberation, liberationist, 10, 12, 15–17, 19–22, 73–77, 79–80, 84–85, 89, 91–99, 110, 116, 118, 120–21, 157–58, 169, 171–75, 177, 179, 181, 183–85, 189–97, 199–202, 215–17, 220–25, 228–30, 232–33, 241, 245, 248, 251, 261, 267–69, 271, 273, 278, 282–83; oppression, 10, 16, 68, 74, 80, 93, 107–10, 112, 118–19, 133, 141, 157, 172, 177, 196, 215, 241–42, 244, 251, 261, 265; resistance, 21, 39, 77, 110, 136, 140–41, 146, 156–57, 174, 194–96, 200, 217, 242, 262, 264, 266; violence, 54, 57, 59–60, 65, 78, 105, 107, 110, 117–19, 132, 169, 171, 177, 184, 212, 228–29, 248

kin-dom of God, 80
kinship, 105, 252

liturgy, 34, 82, 181–82, 198, 213
lo cotidiano, 105–6, 109, 114, 120, 189, 194, 217, 219

margins: marginality, 64, 79, 108, 115, 130, 145, 192, 222, 224–25; marginalization, 14, 17, 48, 63, 75–81, 84–85, 93, 103, 105–6, 110, 112–14, 116–19, 136, 172–76, 211–12, 216–18, 223–24, 229, 263; nativism, 255–56, 278; otherness, othering, 23, 64, 80, 98, 128, 130, 141, 203, 227, 278, 283; xenophobia, 92, 255–57, 278

Marian, 156, 159–60

Mestizo, Mestizaje, 23, 64–65, 78, 85–86, 104, 108, 157, 166, 193, 202

migration studies: border, 74, 79, 89, 94, 113, 116, 121–22, 202, 256; migration, immigration, 7, 106, 108, 121, 123, 134, 142, 144, 238, 248–51, 253, 255–57, 262, 271

ministry, 33, 36, 38–40, 79, 173, 202–3, 282

minority: ethnic-racial formation, identity, 236; minoritized, minoritization, 4, 11, 14–15, 18–19, 21, 236, 268–69, 271, 276–78

Mujerista, 17, 79–80, 86, 90, 98, 121, 143, 196, 282

mulataje, 135, 226

mulatto, 64, 66

Nahuatl, Nahua, 100, 153–54, 158, 163, 165

native, 105, 112, 118–19, 122, 134, 145, 158, 192, 195, 236, 277

Negritude: danza negra, majestad negra, 138, 140–41, 146

neoliberalism, 248

Nepantla, 97, 100, 123

Nican Mopohua, 153–55, 160–63, 165

non-innocent, 48, 108–9, 165

normatizing myths, 105, 117

objectivity *vs.* subjectivity: Eurocentric assumption, 175, 200

orthodoxy, 77, 130, 133, 177, 182, 192, 222

pedagogy, pedagogical, 189–91, 193, 195–97, 199–201, 203, 221–23

Pentecost, 42, 50, 151–53, 155, 157–66, 219–21

Pentecostal: Pentecostal hermeneutics, 31, 42, 213

poor: poverty, 16, 65, 83, 105–8; preferential option for the poor, 172, 174, 176, 282

popular: popular Catholicism, 85, 104, 166, 174, 185, 192–93, 202; popular Protestantism, 104; popular religion, religiosity, 73–74, 76–78, 82, 85–86, 121, 173–74, 189, 191–96, 199, 202–3, 222, 224, 229; popular theology, 224

Posadas, pastorelas, and *via cruces*: Definitions of, 76, 137, 192, 261

postmodern, postmodernity, 6–8, 31, 42, 201

praxis: liberative praxis, 198; praxis-centered reading, 114; social praxis, 109, 174–75, 229

progressive reality, 161, 164, 220

prophetic, 32, 35, 38, 49, 56, 62, 97, 113, 116, 160, 176–80, 182–83, 186, 198, 216, 282

race: blackness, 85, 129, 131–33, 136, 143–44, 226–27; darkness, darkened, 64, 127–29, 131–32, 136–42, 146, 225–28; luminosity, 132, 136, 138–41, 226; one drop rule, 226; racial, racialized, 3–5, 14, 17–18, 21, 86, 127–28, 133–36, 140, 145, 162, 175, 209, 219, 225–27, 232, 235–36, 250, 255, 258, 262, 265, 268–72, 276–77; racism, 123, 136, 226, 243, 255, 264, 278; White Supremacy, 255; whitening process, 128, 132–37, 140–41, 145–46, 225–27, 264

ressourcement, 47–49, 65, 155, 211–12

Samaritan: As stranger, 103, 217

Second Vatican Council, 155, 182

Subjects Index

sensus fidelium, 193, 202, 222
slave, slavery, 49, 66, 68, 82, 113, 146
Society of Biblical Literature, 5, 86, 143, 271
spirit: Holy Spirit, the Spirit, 29–34, 36–41, 43, 56, 58–60, 104, 106, 113, 116, 119–20, 140, 152, 157–64, 174, 212–14, 218–21; spiritual, spirituality, 29, 32, 35–39, 41–43, 53, 58–60, 65, 68, 95, 107, 123, 128, 132, 139, 145–46, 174, 177, 196, 213, 218, 221
symbol: metaphor, 38, 131, 137–38, 215

testimonios, 105, 113–14, 116, 165, 214, 218–19, 264
theology: Black Theology, 12, 14–15, 268–69, 282; Christian studies, 4–5, 8–10, 14–15, 18, 21; Christology, 79–80, 84, 86, 185; comparative theology, 169–72, 176–77, 184, 228–30; Dialectical Theology, 11, 13; Ecumenical Theology, 12, 185, 267–68, 271; eschatology, 76; Feminist Theology, 12–13, 86, 99, 121–22, 202–3, 268–69, 271, 273, 282; Latino/a Theology, 15, 17, 19–20, 73–74, 81, 172–75, 210, 219, 228, 233, 268, 270, 272–73, 276; Liberation Theology, 12, 15, 19–22, 74, 76, 172, 177, 185, 189, 191, 194, 199, 201–2, 222, 224, 267–69, 271, 273, 282–83; Planetary Theology, 13, 267–68; religious-theological, 236–37, 263, 270, 272, 274, 277; Scripture, Holy, 3, 16, 19, 29–37, 39–43, 50–53, 55, 57–62, 64–65, 67–69, 84, 91, 103–4, 107–9, 113–19, 152–53, 156, 160, 164–65, 171–72, 180, 193, 202, 209–19, 221, 223, 225–34, 269, 274; theological studies, 3–5, 7, 10, 14, 17–18, 89, 96, 155, 164–65, 235–36, 263, 266–68, 270, 272–74, 276; theological tradition, 9, 48, 128, 174; Theology of Religions, 12, 170, 185, 228; Word of God, 11, 19–20, 31, 65, 80, 90, 152, 173, 178, 180, 182, 218, 221, 230, 269, 274

United States, 4, 13–15, 17–18, 21–23, 38–39, 49, 74–75, 81–82, 84–85, 89–90, 98–99, 103, 105–6, 108, 111, 120–21, 123, 128, 134–35, 142, 144–45, 151–55, 165, 172–75, 189–95, 198–203, 211, 217, 222, 226, 228, 236–39, 241–42, 244–45, 247–48, 250–52, 254–57, 260–63, 265, 272, 276–81, 283

Western: Eurocentric, 106–7, 109, 175, 185, 200
women, woman: astute reader, 92–93, 95; in ministry, in church, 33; role of women, 89; struggle of, 47, 91, 95–96, 215; subjugation of, 110; women submission, 91, 196; women voice, 92, 109–10, 112, 114–15, 118–19, 126
worship, 31, 34, 37, 40, 43, 170, 177, 179, 202, 213, 219, 228

www.ingramcontent.com/pod-product-compliance
Lightning Source LLC
Chambersburg PA
CBHW021346300426
44114CB00012B/1106